D1213075

EUGÉNIE

EMPRESS OF THE FRENCH

Books by Octave Aubry

THE EMPRESS MIGHT-HAVE-BEEN

THE EMPEROR FALLS IN LOVE

THE PHANTOM EMPEROR

THE LOST KING

THE EMPRESS EUGÉNIE
From the Portrait by Edouard Dubufe

OCTAVE AUBRY

EUGÉNIE
EMPRESS OF THE FRENCH

TRANSLATED BY
F. M. ATKINSON

WITH 17 ILLUSTRATIONS

PHILADELPHIA & LONDON
J. B. LIPPINCOTT COMPANY
MCMXXXI

PRINTED IN THE
UNITED STATES
OF AMERICA

FIRST EDITION

TO THE MEMORY OF AN ADMIRABLE FRIEND

THE COMTESSE ROEDERER

PREFACE

Nous en bastirons un corps entier
Sans fournir du nostre que la liaison,
Comme la soudure d'un aultre métal.
Montaigne.

To try to show the Empress Eugénie in her true human aspect was an undertaking of such thorny delicacy that I hesitated a long time before I decided to venture upon it. In modern history there are few figures that have received more homage and more affronts. That life of hers, so full of contrasts, so varied, stretched out through a century, knew every turn and start of fortune. A *femme du monde* who had become a sovereign, a Spaniard become French, enamoured of power and wielding it, then flung into the abyss without losing one jot of her pride, she saw her son disappear in the most futile of adventures and waited fifty years for the turn of the wheel to avenge her dead and allow her to depart in peace.

I have been encouraged to write this book by finding assistance I could never have hoped for and an eager interest that was of incalculable value. It may contain gaps and possibly errors. But no one, I hope, will doubt my desire to be impartial. I have tried not so much to depict as to narrate. I have invented nothing. I put forward nothing that does not come from the Empress's confidences to her close friends, from the memoirs of her contemporaries, both friends and enemies, from the despatches of foreign ambassadors, from diplomatic, military, or police documents taken from our archives. Here will be found nothing but facts and authentic speeches. Every line can be verified by a definite reference. I did not, however, think well to burden my text with notes that would often have occupied half the pages. But I hold myself at the disposal of any one who may desire justification or explanation of any point whatever. I have not given, and could not give, anything in the shape of a verdict. That life is only just extinguished. And again, too many elements in a character will always remain too foreign to us to allow us to judge. And what right have we to decide upon the fundamental merit or demerit of a soul when every day we find so much in ourselves that is unknown? I have confined myself here to bringing together tested and proved material. It is for every individual to shape from this material his portrait of the Empress as he may. It will but be all the more living to him for taking colour from the lambent flames of the imagination.

Certain traits, certain details hitherto omitted or concealed may, I fear, give some displeasure. Will my good faith be allowed to excuse me? Meanwhile it is my belief that candour, when it is not insulting, is of greater service to historical personages than deliberately calculated toning down and manipulation. The Empress Eugénie was a woman, that is to say, a variable creature. Why should we be dumb about her mistakes, gloss over her shortcomings, so long as we do not forget on the other hand all the nobility and greatness of spirit she displayed? To give life to her portrait we must avoid investing her with a fixed and conventional appearance. She herself would not have wished for such a thing; she was too much a lover of truth, of movement, of life.

Next to the dear friend whose name I have set at the beginning of this book, who to her last days devoted herself to it, and with delicacy and patience obtained for it so many new sources of information among high personages of the Imperial family and the Imperial society, all of whom accorded me the most generous reception and made me free of their archives, their collections, their memories, searched their correspondence, often even undertaking lengthy researches to verify points on which I had doubts and to solve questions hitherto undetermined, I must in the first place address my most grateful homage to His Highness the Duke of Berwick and Alba, to the Princesse de la Moskowa, *née* Princesse Eugénie Bonaparte, to Comte and Comtesse Baciocchi, to the Duchesse d'Abrantès, to Mlle Pauline de Bassano, to the regretted Marquise de Loÿs-Thandieu, *née* Pourtalès, to Comtesse G. de Leusse, to Baronne de Noirmont, *née* Castelbajac, to Mlle H. Conneau, to Baron and Baronne de Beauverger, to Monsieur and

Madame G. Poignant, to the late Colonel Nitot, to the Duc de Montmorency, to Comte de Germiny, to Comte Serge Fleury, to M. Lucien Daudet, to Comte Allard du Chollet, to Baron Sautereau, to M. Maurice d'Ocagne, to M. G. Lenôtre, to Docteur Le Monier, to MM. de la Martinière, Edmond Pilon, Jean Bourguignon, and Sarradin.

It is thanks to their active goodwill that I have been able to carry my task to its conclusion. Few writers without party ties have been treated with greater confidence and liberality. I hope they will forgive my not making better use of them. There is no doubt a little touch of betrayal, but a pardonable one, in inadequacy of talent.

O. A.

CONTENTS

PART I

MADEMOISELLE DE MONTIJO

I Eugénie's Home. Madrid—1830 17

II Youth 24

III The Prince. 1850 48

IV The Great Adventure 56

V The Decision. January Twelfth 68

VI Marriage 77

PART II

EMPRESS

I The New Life 89

II The Child 107

III The Regent 118

IV Compiègne 132

V Power 146

VI Biarritz 165

VII The Difficult Times 176

PART III

DOWNFALL

I	WAR	203
II	DISASTERS	213
III	FLIGHT	234
IV	EDDIES	256

PART IV

EXILE

I	CHISLEHURST	271
II	MOTHER AND SON	291
III	WANDERINGS	309
IV	THE OTHER WAR	331
V	THE PALACIO DE LIRIA. SUNDAY, JULY 11, 1920	342
	PRINCIPAL WORKS CONSULTED	349
	INDEX	351

ILLUSTRATIONS

THE EMPRESS EUGÉNIE *Frontispiece*
From the Portrait by Edouard Dubufe

PROSPER MÉRIMÉE 18

PRINCESS MATHILDE 50
From the Portrait by Edouard Dubufe

THE EMPEROR NAPOLEON III 56
From the Portrait by Flandrin

THE TUILERIES 78

THE EMPRESS EUGÉNIE AND HER LADIES OF HONOUR 92
From the Painting by Winterhalter

QUEEN VICTORIA 102
From the Portrait by Winterhalter

PRINCE NAPOLEON 110
From the Portrait by Hebert

COUNTESS DE CASTIGLIONE 114

THE EMPRESS EUGÉNIE 126
From the Portrait by Winterhalter

PAULINE, PRINCESS METTERNICH 130

COMPIÈGNE. THE GARDEN FAÇADE 132

COMPIÈGNE. INTERIOR 132

THE EMPRESS EUGÉNIE WEARING THE FAMOUS "BIBI" HAT 134

THE SOVEREIGNS GOING TO THE EXPOSITION OF 1867 188

THE PRINCE IMPERIAL 288

COUNT PRIMOLI 316
From the Portrait by Spadini

PART I
MADEMOISELLE DE MONTIJO

CHAPTER I

Eugénie's Home. Madrid–1830

As Prosper Mérimée, following the Count de Teba, came to the drawing-room, he heard bursts of laughter and shrill children's voices. When the door was opened he saw in the middle of a huge room a sturdily built young brunette and two little girls of five or six who were running and jumping from chair to chair like kittens. Books and toys were scattered over the carpet. At the sight of the stranger the little girls ceased their gambols and took refuge under a table. Doña Manuela, however, straightening her hair and with her face on fire, not at all embarrassed but full of smiles, came forward to greet him.

The Count had met Mérimée in the stage-coach from Granada, and in the course of the long jolty ride they had made friends. Don Cypriano had invited the young writer to come to the Calle del Sordo during his stay in Madrid–the Countess, who thought highly of his works, for she read everything that appeared in France, would be delighted to see him.

Don Cypriano expressed himself with exquisite courtesy and punctilious gestures. He was already old and infirm. A black bandage covered his right eye, which he had lost in 1814 in the service of France when as Colonel Portocarrero he commanded the battalion of Polytechnic students at the Clichy barrier. Tall, bony, swarthy, almost bald, he limped and one arm hung in his sleeve. He used to say himself, smiling in a tired fashion, that he was not so unlike Don Quixote after his fight with the windmills.

The Countess fixed her intelligent eyes, with their warm black iris and strong lashes, on the young Frenchman. She was little over thirty, but her features were already coarsening under the dull skin over-dusted with powder. She showed a high forehead like a man's and her hair was not too carefully done. Her mouth was close shut, her chin firm. Her bosom was full in her cream silk dress all over tiny flowers, all frills and flounces.

She could not help laughing at Mérimée's first phrase. He spoke an old-fashioned Castilian that smelt of the school.

She replied to his compliment in good French with hardly any more accent than a native of Toulouse.

She had as a matter of fact read everything M. Mérimée had published: "La Guzla, la Jacquerie," and the "Chronique du règne de Charles IV," and the delightful "Carosse du Saint-Sacrement" which had appeared the previous year in the *Revue de Paris* to the scandal of the devout, so much so that the Duchesse de Berry had cancelled her subscription. Doña Manuela had it lying on her table. In her opinion M. Mérimée had never written anything better. But to tell the truth she had imagined that this author who was capturing the attention of the cultivated and liberal classes was a man of mature age. She was delighted to see that he was only beginning his career,—which would be a glorious one if it was to be judged by its dazzling early successes.

The tone of the Countess was gay, simple and full of the ease of an accomplished woman of the world. Mérimée, who hid his shyness under an air of imperturbability, felt himself blushing before his own praises. He was slightly annoyed and embarrassed. Doña Manuela made him sit by her, and began to talk about Paris, which she did not know, but which was nevertheless the place above all others where she would have wished to live, especially now that the overthrow of the Bourbons had prepared the place for a liberal monarchy. But it was not merely politics that attracted her to the French capital. It was the free, active life that one could lead there, the lettered, artistic society among which one might move, devoid of arrogance and prejudices alike. Here in Spain under the obscure tyranny of Calomarde, you lived in stupid ignorance and fear. She broke off as a servant came in to offer refreshments and asked the young man what salons he visited habitually. Did he go to see the Duchesse d'Abrantès, Madame Ancelot, Baron Gérard, Madame Récamier? Did he know M. le Vicomte de Chateaubriand?

He answered that he did, and that he would be happy to take her to the Abbaye-aux-Bois when she came to Paris. She would certainly be disappointed. M. de Chateaubriand, ensconced in his armchair by the fire, sat mumchance for hours together. And Madame Récamier often talked very poor stuff. She kept a certain grace, but her mind was altogether commonplace.

The Countess refused to be disillusioned. She had dreamed

Les Archives Photographiques d'Art et d'Histoire

PROSPER MÉRIMÉE

Museum of Versailles

so long of the divine Juliette! And of her friend Madame de Staël. A woman great enough to have disturbed Napoleon! It was from "Corinne" as much as from the "Génie du Christianisme," added Doña Manuela volubly, that she had learned French. And she had learned it almost by herself and very rapidly. That was natural enough: was she not one-fourth a Frenchwoman? Her grandmother was a Grivegnée, a scion of the old Walloon nobility. Her father was descended from the Barons Kirkpatrick of Closeburn. And so her arms were French and Scots as much as Spanish. On this theme she would have descanted inexhaustibly. Though she was modern in spirit she remained enamoured of blue blood and historic ancestors. She calmly told how she herself could trace her descent back to Finn MacCual, the king of the Fenians, who lived about 200 years before Christ.

"I am very much afraid," the Count said sometimes, "that Manuela may have contracted a misalliance in marrying me; for the Montijos barely go back to the fourteenth century, under Alfonso XI."

The Countess would laugh at that point. Her father, descended though he was from the kings of Scotland, had sold fruits and wines at Malaga, with sufficient success to provide her and her sisters with dowries. Indeed she made no secret of the fact. Had not a Bourbon prince of the blood been a schoolmaster during the Revolution, the same prince who had been on the throne of France for the last two months?

Settled down on a great sofa at the other end of the room, Don Cypriano listened absently to his wife's talk. Little Eugenia had placed herself between his knees, while Paca continued playing on the floor with her rag dolls and paid no heed to the visitor. Pleased and amused by the Countess's greeting, Mérimée nevertheless did not forget to look about him. As well as a traveller and a writer, and even more perhaps, he was an antiquarian and a connoisseur. Wide and lofty, and rather sombre, with its two windows shaded from the outside light by Venetian blinds, the room he was in was furnished in an incongruous fashion. On the walls, painted a pinky grey, there were nailed a few religious pictures and a Gobelin tapestry representing Hercules at the feet of Omphale. Heavy black and gilded armchairs, their backs crested with armorial carvings, were set on either side of a console table of carved wood with a superabundance of volutes and a purple marble top worthy of a cathedral altar. But other chairs were displaying their horsehair, the carpet was in holes, the curtains were old and faded, there was no mirror on the chimney piece, merely a miserable kind of clock between two brass candlesticks, the commonest imaginable.

Although it was October, it was hot.

"This salon gets the sun all afternoon," said Doña Manuela. "We are very badly housed here, dear Monsieur. Our home in Granada is much more agreeable. We were obliged to come to Madrid to protect the Count's interests. We have serious family worries. . . . I like Madrid, I have my own circle here. But I have long regretted our old house in the Calle de Gracia. I hope the Count took you over it?"

Mérimée replied that he did not know the Montijo house. He had only met Don Cypriano when they were both coming away from Granada.

"What a pity," cried the Countess. "You would have loved our garden! Eugenia was born in it, poor little angel. We had taken refuge in it to escape the earthquake that had knocked down half the houses. I was so terrified that I was confined in a tent there a fortnight before my time. Perhaps it was that terror of mine that has made her so timid. Eugenia, say *bonjour* in French to Monsieur. For she knows French already."

Eugenia said never a word. She raised her big blue eyes, somewhat close together, to Mérimée and shut her lips tight.

"Bah," said Doña Manuela, "we may leave it at that; it's impossible to get anything out of her if she doesn't want to. That child is as obstinate as a mule. Her father spoils her terribly; she's his favourite."

"She has been delicate for a long time," said Don Cypriano. "We have had to indulge her a little. But she always obeys me. Eugenia, my rosebud, say *boujour* to the Señor."

"Bonjour, Señor," repeated the child. Her voice was strong and very full for her years.

The Count kissed her.

"She will do anything for me," he said, smiling with his faded lips.

The little girl held his hand and looked at him with a secret gentle look, full of admiration. She was like him. Her delicate face was white as milk. Her bright hair twined in curls on her slender neck. Her elder sister, Paca, was like a little blackamoor beside her. Don Cypriano slowly stroked the little head and whispered in her ear affectionate words that made her flush with pleasure.

The Count loved his children passionately. For this man broken in the wars, disappointed in ambition, who had not found in the overvivacious, overgay Doña Manuela, too much enamoured of movement and society, in a word, too young, the companion suited to his tastes, paternal affection was the last joy left to him.

Often in the evening when he was alone with them, and the Countess had fluttered off to some fête or had been carried away by her friends, he would repeat to them stories of the good or the bad moments of his life. He told them of the interminable guerrilla war that had devoured Napoleon's armies, of the battle of Salamanca where a bursting cannon had covered him with wounds, of the day when the great Emperor himself had pinned the cross on his breast, as he lay half dead in hospital.

He had spoken to him:

"Commandant Portocarrero, you are brave and loyal. If all Spaniards were like you, this war would soon be over."

And Napoleon, who hardly ever gave his hand, even to the members of his family, had with that small white hand, which was the envy of women, and which had overturned Europe, clasped the hand of Don Cypriano.

No doubt the two little girls were unable to understand the whole of a theme and a language so little suited to them, but they listened as to a kind of chant lulling their own dreams; their young minds retained from it many proud and brilliant images . . . especially Eugenia's. When her father fell into silence, tired with talking, she would lay her cool little cheek softly against his, so hollowed and wrinkled, and they would remain like that for a long time together, while the night deepened.

Now Doña Manuela was asking Mérimée about his travels. It was his first visit to Spain and the Countess would initiate him in Spanish ways and manners.

He thanked her. At the very first moment he had seen in her

a woman pleasant to meet, somewhat breezy and talkative. He now felt in Doña Manuela a great deal of intelligence and culture, a mind nourished and filled with ideas and images. He would be happy, he told her, to become her pupil, since she was so kind as to offer to cure his ignorance.

As they talked she found nothing bitter in Prosper Mérimée's tone, but a smiling irony, somewhat dry, not usually met with in a man of twenty-seven whose first ventures into the world have been successful. Perhaps he thought that enthusiasm was in bad taste. He was so well bred; this slender *bourgeois,* the son of an artist, had perfect manners. He was elegant, even something of a dandy. His fine cornflower-blue coat with gold buttons, and his grey strapped trousers came from a good English tailor. At the first look he was ugly with that bristling hair, that retroussé nose which made the nostrils too prominent, that sharp chin cleaving like a ship's prow the flowing black satin cravat round his neck. But the piercing bright eye, like that of certain birds, and the thin, delicate mouth surprised and pleased by a witty charm that could not but make women wish to take possession of him less as a lover than as a friend.

Eugenia, curious and tamed at last, had left her refuge and come to the foreign Señor. Paca, nimble as a kid, leaped from armchair to armchair.

The Countess, yielding to her feelings, in spite of a discreet sign from Don Cypriano, went on to complain of Count Eugenio, who as owner by right of primogeniture of all the Montijo possessions, was treating his younger brother badly and nibbling away his already meagre portion. He had great estates whose revenues might have been abundant if he had administered them properly and if he had left litigation alone. Doña Manuela's children were his heirs. But in recent years he had fallen into the clutches of an ambitious *cigarrera* who was doing all she could to get him to turn his fortune from its natural destination. Shut away for months in his palace in the Plaza del Angel he refused now to see his sister-in-law and his nieces. Out of favour at Court, thrust aside by their family, the Tebas were therefore reduced for a time to a straitened way of living. But God be thanked they had kept their friends, and neither Ferdinand VII nor Count Eugenio would last for ever!

The Countess for her part would lightly have risked her ease and more to play a part in affairs of State. Her husband had to restrain her a little. Once he was out of sight she forgot all prudence. She delighted in intrigue.

"Ah, if I was a man!" she exclaimed. "But women have to be content with talking instead of acting!"

Nevertheless she acted, and to the best of her ability, helping the harried liberals with her influence and out of her slender purse, becoming the soul of a fairly powerful group, which already, since it had ramifications touching the administration and the army, was giving grounds for the suspicions of the Court. To such an Amazon Prosper Mérimée seemed a trifle lukewarm in tone. But there, he was a Frenchman, an unrepentant son of Voltaire, believing neither in God nor in the devil, in the courage of men nor the virtue of women, and was very likeable in spite of it. He kept all the indefinable attraction that resides in the word *gentillesse*. She had already experienced this through her liaison with a young diplomat in the French Embassy, Louis de Viel-Castel, who had now left Madrid. Mérimée decidedly pleased her. He had talent, and he was spoken of in the world. He was intelligent, refined, ingenious, full of good sense. He would be an amusing and useful acquaintance for the future, an adroit friend. More than a friend? Who could say, who knew? The Countess was first and foremost a woman of her head, neither very sensual, nor very sentimental. But very curious. And curiosity had on occasion taken her a long way. . . . She would see.

CHAPTER II
Youth

THE relations between Doña Manuela and Mérimée if they did not pause upon the heights of the *Pays du Tendre* never quite strayed outside the border of that country, but fairly speedily fixed themselves on the frontier under the ensign of friendship, thus becoming capable of lasting throughout their whole lives, without weariness or discord.

Back again in Paris, Mérimée wrote to his dear Countess. He told her all the news she was so eager to hear; the whispers of the Court, echoes of the town and the theatre, gossip about art and letters. He was an animated gazette, in a position to see everything, and with the right turn of mind for telling everything.

Doña Manuela eagerly answered all his letters. She paid him subtle compliments, caressed his vanity, sent him advice, playing the wise and sensible lady from a distance (while she was having a gay time with the Duke of Osuña), approved him for not having persevered with his momentary affair with Georges Sand, but scolded him for going and drinking a sacrilegious orangeade with certain wild artists on the towers of Notre Dame at midnight. She too described her days, still eager for stir and bustle, always in the middle of some activity, of intrigues that came to nothing, but which slaked her thirst for action. She said little about the Count, retired and anxious, much about her daughters who were growing up, prettier than ever, and who did not forget Don Prospero.

In 1834 she informed him of a great event, the death of her brother-in-law, Eugenio de Montijo. That fortune was coming to her at last, a fortune that was, however, greatly impaired and massive rather than liquid in resources. Doña Manuela was about to leave the Calle del Sordo and take up her abode in the old barracks in the Plaza del Angel, a mixture of a palace and a fort, deserted by the wicked *cigarrera*. Don Cypriano, now became Count de Montijo, Duke of Peñaranda, loaded with titles enough to fill a muniment room, inherited as well a seat in the senate. It was a tempestuous moment. Ferdinand VII was no more; the little

Queen Isabel, under the regency of her mother Maria Christina, was entering upon one of the most troubled reigns in history. The Carlists were inflaming half of the provinces. In Madrid the various agitations, as constant as the ebbing and flowing tides, were bringing up to power the most widely opposite parties and casting them away again. The Countess swam strongly amid all this turmoil, bemoaned her country, was indignant, burned to play a conspicuous part, and did actually play a part now and then, in the wings of the stage.

In the July of this same year, she announced to her friend that she was starting for Paris with her daughters. Cholera was spreading in Spain; it was causing as many deaths as it had two years previously in France. Count de Montijo, who was kept in Spain by the session of the Cortes, would join Doña Manuela later. She was delighted over this journey. Mérimée knew her vagabond humour. He gathered also that her rash nature must have brought her into some political or other disfavour, and that it was convenient that she should be out of Madrid for a while. She covered the ground by short stages, sometimes in a post-chaise, mostly by coach. In the coach that took her to Barcelona she met with the famous picador Sevilla, whose polite attentions enchanted her. At Barcelona the board of health wanted to impose a quarantine upon the travellers, with the exception of Sevilla whom the whole town was eagerly expecting for a bull-fight, and who no doubt was above all sanitary laws. The picador refused to take advantage of this.

"If Madame and her companions are not allowed to pass free," he said, "I shall not perform."

The board gave way, so that Sevilla might be seen in the ring. And they were wise. The people, who laughed at infection, would have stoned the board or pulled down the quarantine building. The Countess de Montijo entered proudly into Barcelona by the side of the torero. She attended the bull-fight, which was magnificent.

Crossing the frontier she halted at Perpignan where General de Castellane, who was in command of the garrison, received her with every attention. He caressed Paca and Eugenia, and finding the Countess full of decision and intelligence, he gave her letters for his parents at Toulouse. Doña Manuela broke her journey there for a little, then took the public coach for Paris.

Mérimée welcomed her as a faithful friend and took pains to find her furnished lodgings, for it was necessary to count the pennies. The Count had given her little money. His properties, ruined by requisitions and by robbery, were bringing in nothing, and he was obliged even to help his tenant farmers. And so, uneasy as to the future, and thinking that his children might perhaps be in want, he wished to accustom them to Spartan ways of living. He asked Doña Manuela to make Paca and Eugenia wear linen dresses on all occasions; he gave instructions not to buy umbrellas for them or take them out except walking.

"It's most inconvenient," the Countess told Mérimée, "but here, as he is far away, I shall do as I please."

All the same she lived on a simple scale. A salon, and three modestly furnished rooms. But the Bohemian-minded Countess was quite contented as long as she could bring a few intimate friends around her and go into society.

Don Prospero introduced her to his friends, and especially to Henri Beyle, who became very intimate with them.

Stendhal was wearing out his last years. He was broad, thick, high-coloured. He wore a youthful *toupet;* his whiskers and his fringe beard were dyed a ruddy brown. He was a dandy in his clothes, with tight-fitting nankeen trousers, a coloured coat and flowered waistcoat, from which hung down jingling fobs that greatly amused Eugenia.

He had already published without much success, "Le Rouge et le Noir"; he was working on "La Chartreuse." Mérimée and he had met at Stapfer's. They saw one another a great deal, and appraised one another with the eyes of intelligent amateurs, always alert, afraid of being taken in. They did not love one another, perhaps, but liked each other enormously. They often spent their evenings together at the Countess's. Paca and Eugenia sat up a little later on those evenings. Tea was served. The two little girls, sitting each on one of Stendhal's knees, listened enchanted to hear the fat man with the bright eyes talking about Napoleon. France was still haunted by that importunate ghost. He told them of Napoleon's glory, his distress, his brilliant victories.

Paca clapped her hands. Eugenia wiped her eyes. This Stendhal who among trusty friends in a little group would let his high spirits boil and bubble along, often let himself go and dropped into unrestrained talk, maintained perfect propriety before the children. Instinctively he acted on the noble verse of Juvenal, and would have been careful not to shock them even in seeming. These two pretty, refined little girls had both touched a pure chord in him. Perhaps he liked Eugenia best. He gave her a print of the battle of Austerlitz, which she put away with great care and was very proud of. And one day he said to her with a somewhat strange burlesque gravity:

"When you grow up, you will marry M. le Marquis de Santa-Cruz. Then you'll forget me, and I won't bother about you any more."

The Marquis de Santa-Cruz, a name of whimsy, smoke without substance, promise of a future he would never see, that he did not even wish to see, for under his cloak of gaiety he was desperately said to be no longer young.

Stendhal—or rather M. Beyle, for they never called him anything else—was their great friend, their favourite. But Mérimée remained their friend of every day. As the Countess concerned herself especially with Paca, he devoted himself to the younger, gave her lessons in writing, corrected her French or English exercises, then if she had been good and done well he would take her to the confectioner's. A boulevard dandy meeting him one afternoon in the Rue de la Paix began to laugh seeing Mérimée holding this little girl's hand, and asked him rather maliciously if she was a close connection.

Mérimée said in an offhand way:

"She is a little Spaniard, the daughter of a friend of mine; I am taking her to eat pastries."

There was a little scandal in Paris that was still quite provincial. The Countess troubled about it no more than Don Prospero. Now and then when Eugenia had committed some misdemeanour Mérimée carried her off from a scolding and took her to the Tuileries or the Champs-Elysées. He would treat her to light sermons that she hardly listened to, all her attention being turned to admiring the shop windows or the dresses of the ladies driving by in the roadway. He often told Doña Manuela that he was a strong believer in an education for children founded on frankness and indulgence.

The Countess, who often argued against him, was in agreement with him on this point. If the two little girls were brought up pretty much anyhow, it was at any rate without constraint or coldness. Doña Manuela had a hasty hand. But she was as generous as she was hasty. She loved her children, cosseted them when she felt like it, and when she neglected them it was because before she was a mother she was a woman, and exuberance itself, and still too young to renounce pleasure. . . .

In the autumn of 1835, while Don Prospero, appointed inspector of historic monuments after the fall of Count d'Argout, was travelling in Languedoc and Provence to save old stones from destruction, the Countess de Montijo went to Pau, and then to Toulouse, where she remained for several months installed in the house of the Marquis de Campaigne, in the Rue Croix-Baragnon. The children had been taken as boarders in the school kept by the Berryer ladies in the Rue Espinasse. On Thursdays they were sent to the Arnichan riding school. Paca and especially Eugenia already rode splendidly. Jean de Campaigne, their host's son, took lessons with them. The riding-school rang with their shouts and their laughter.

On their return to Paris Doña Manuela and her daughters were joined by the Count de Montijo. He only stayed a short time. In his youth he had loved France, but because he himself had changed he now hardly recognised it. Grave and formal Spain alone was home to this knight of the sorrowful countenance astray in the turmoil of the age. The Countess, who enjoyed that turmoil so much, frightened him with her verve, her loud voice, and all those people, strangers to him, of such different kinds, who came and went in her house. As soon as he could Don Cypriano went back to Granada, and lived in the old house in the Calle de Gracia, an invalid disgusted with a life that held no more promise for him. His daughters remained in France; that had to be, he thought, for their education. And for their safety, for the throes that shook Spain, the civil war, the struggles between parties, or cities, or generals, had not come to an end. But at certain hours, while he sat in the garden where Eugenia was born and thought of her, his favourite, this disillusioned old man must have almost died of loneliness.

The Countess had given her daughters masters for drawing and for music. Water-colours by Eugenia, of no particular merit, decorated one wall in the drawing-room. She had little liking for music; her guttural voice discouraged her from singing. Paca and she played the piano a little. Above all they danced, like true daughters of Spain. Meanwhile the more essential elements of their education were neglected. Mérimée said so, with enough adroitness to arouse his friend's attention without offending her —if she liked to rule others, she did not much like advice herself. She decided to send them to the convent of the Sacré Cœur in the Rue de Varenne. There Eugenia and Paca made their first communion . . . Eugenia with a faith and with a scrupulous ardour that for a moment perturbed her mother.

"But I would not at all like her to become a nun," she said to Don Prospero. But Don Prospero, who knew the world better than she did, replied:

"Wait till she is sixteen and lovers come flocking. Eugenia is not a girl to turn into a nun."

To change the trend of her ideas the Countess on her days of exeat took her to pay visits and to theatres.

Mérimée had brought to see her one day Rachel, who was receiving high applause at her early appearances. The two women became friends, and Rachel often sent her box to the Countess. In "Camille," in "Hermione," in "Athalie," she simply transported Eugenia. Mérimée happened to hazard an objection to such and such a play somewhat overpassionate. "Was 'Phèdre' suitable for these children?"

"Bah!" replied the Countess, "is it not a classic? And then they're so young! They won't understand anything they shouldn't."

It was the rash mother that triumphed over the cautious friend. The children noticed nothing untoward in these evenings. Paca, already more of a woman, was interested in the audience. Eugenia saw nothing but the play. Sitting in the front row with eyes dilated, pale with emotion, holding her breath, the child watched the heroine, as she moved about the stage, declaimed, struggled. She imagined herself on the boards with her, escaped into that romantic universe where she was more at home than in the common round of her days. Real men seemed dull and little in her eyes, she preferred the clear-cut, noble, gallant characters that were born of her dreams.

Among all these new friends of the Countess, the most intimate were the Delesserts. M. Gabriel Delessert, prefect of police and already past middle age, had a wife much younger than himself, pretty, gay, witty, of infinite variety, easy-going, full of vivacity and taste, a delightful creature made rather to live in the seventeenth century in the company of Madame d'Epinay or Madame Helvétius than in the stiff and scandalmongering salons of the July monarchy. The Countess de Montijo from the very day she met her at Madame de Laborde's, her mother's, became close friends with Valentine Delessert. She was as gentle as Manuela was self-willed, as pliant as the other was determined. They liked one another for this contrast in character. They spent their days together, could not do without each other. Through Valentine the Countess came to know the whole of the Orléanist society. When Mérimée who had long been Valentine's *cicisbeo,* slipped into a more concretely defined position, she was their confidante and chaperon.

Cécile, the Delessert's daughter, became the favourite companion of Paca and Eugenia. And it was from the dining-room at the prefecture of police that on November 12, 1836, Eugenia saw through a glazed fanlight Prince Louis-Napoleon Bonaparte, who had been taken prisoner after his attempted coup d'état at Strasbourg. He was sitting on a chair with a plate of biscuits and a glass of champagne on a table before him, waiting for the post-chaise that was to take him to Lorient where he would set out for his American exile.

The little girl had found him ugly, with his eyes downcast, his pallid complexion, his black coat all creased with two days and a night of travel. But he retained an incomparable prestige for his unfailing aspiration towards the heroic from his birth. He was the heir of the Emperor, his name was Bonaparte, he conspired. Eugenia had lived in the atmosphere of conspiracy as the merest child, she was steeped in it through and through. How often had she not heard her mother weave plans for overthrowing the absolutists who were in power? She had helped her to hide a refugee in a huge Indian vase, and to mislead the civil guards who came to search the house. Born and brought up among political agitations, she found plots and plotting altogether natural, just like the sudden ups and downs of fortune. Perched up on a tall stool, she looked long at the prince. When Cécile Delessert wanted to make her come down, so that she could have a look in her turn, she said, "Wait a moment, wait." Did she hope to see the shadow of Napoleon rise up above that young man sitting numbly there?

Sometimes, to please Mérimée, the Countess went with her daughters to visit Mérimée's mother.

Exquisitely dainty, with a Charlotte Corday cap on her head, wearing a crossed fichu and mittens, Madame Mérimée sat enthroned in her *bergère,* surrounded by cats and birds.

She gave Paca and Eugenia the tips of her fingers to kiss, presented each of them with a pastille, and then dreading restlessness and noise she would send them off to the farther end of the room to turn over an album of sketches. She said of Eugenia, "It's a pity that little girl is red-haired; she will be pretty."

She received the Countess de Montijo with polite courtesy, but never pressed her to prolong her visit. Did she think, with a touch of jealousy, that he saw too much of this Spanish lady of the great name who lived like this in detachment from her own hearth and home?

For Doña Manuela had become the most invaluable of friends to Mérimée. Far more than Valentine, the pretty do-nothing, she took thought for his work, and found fault with his laziness. She gave him themes for novels and stories. She encouraged him by her enthusiasm and her confidence, she did him a thousand good offices, spread his name and his praises in all the houses she visited.

With that trio, in their furnished lodging, full of the mother's hearty voice, the babble and games of the girls who often pummelled one another like boys, he found himself happy. When they left Paris, for the Countess de Montijo could never stay in one place, and when she had received money from Spain she would suddenly start off for Toulouse, or Pau, or Baden, or

London (where her old friend Clarendon was now leader of the House of Lords), Mérimée left solitary, his occupation gone, bored beyond endurance in spite of Valentine, would decide to travel too. And filled with administrative zeal, he would go off inspecting châteaux or abbeys in Touraine, or Saintonge, or Brittany, and send the minister minutely detailed reports on them.

The little girls had left the Sacré-Cœur, whose over-stringent discipline did not allow of all these comings and goings. The Countess had brought back a governess from England, Miss Flower, a good creature with the face of a sheep whose patience Paca and Eugenia tried severely. When their mother was away they often took French leave and ran round the town alone, which in those days was a scandalous thing to do, although they were in reality very innocent escapades. They would go along the boulevard staring at the shop windows. One day they took the boat on the Seine and voyaged in ecstasy as far as Meudon. A memorable spree that was; they were sent to bed that night well scolded and with no supper. Another time, seeing a poor hearse jogging on its way to the cemetery without a friend, without a wreath, they followed it to Père-Lachaise out of the generous pity of youth, praying for the poor unknown left unattended and unremembered on his last journey.

The Count's health had long been a cause of anxiety. M. de Montijo never complained, wrapped up in his stoicism, but a friend warned Doña Manuela that he was not well. She set off hastily for Madrid in the beginning of March 1839. The girls and Miss Flower were to follow presently. She put them in Mérimée's charge. He took his duties seriously, and hardly ever left them. Then in the morning of March 17 he took them to the Messageries, and sceptic though he was he saw them go with a heavy heart. Paca and Eugenia were now fourteen and thirteen; they were little girls no longer; they were not yet young women. Uncertain, unprepossessing, and delicious period of adolescence. Their pigtails hung down their backs, the eldest's black, the younger girl's tawny red; their embroidered white drawers still came down below their skirts, but those skirts were already lengthening, and they saw to it that they did. They were starting for Spain, their father was dying, was perhaps dead. The Countess would have to establish herself or at least make a stay in Madrid.

Would they come back, and when? He almost had a mind to go with them. Suddenly he felt, not old, but worn and sad. He took himself to task, "I am full of nerves!" But it was not a matter of nerves, and well he knew it.

Miss Flower and the girls duly installed in the stagecoach, he made them promise to write to him. He gave them sweets, and little flasks of perfume for the journey. Then he bade them adieu in his most measured tones, his hand tightened a little on the gold knob of his cane. The postilions cracked their whips, the heavy vehicle got under way, left the courtyard of the Messageries, turned out of the street. Eugenia at the window fluttered her handkerchief. Mérimée did not see, he had gone already, walking briskly, his head high under the tall grey beaver, his figure tightly buttoned up in his puce frockcoat. He went to see Valentine, and then to the Théâtre des Italiens at night. A week later he packed up and went to Italy. From Oloron, when the snow had held up the travellers, he had received from his little friend, Eugenia, a short letter on ruled paper, of faulty spelling but full of grace.

The Count de Montijo had died before their departure. As Mérimée had foreseen, Doña Manuela was obliged to remain in Madrid. Her affairs were greatly entangled. She had to raise money, to put an end to lawsuits, to liquidate debts. Her presence was no longer offensive to the Court. Her liberal friends were coming into the highest offices. Narváez was Captain-General of Old Castile. Installed in the Montijo palace, in the Plaza del Angel, she began to receive as soon as it appeared seemly and proper. Mistress of her actions, her activities had free rein. Age was approaching. No longer was she merely a woman of the world, merry of temper, keeping open house till far into the night. She aimed at becoming a factor in politics, and she succeeded. Edging her way in between the parties, she pushed on her protégés and found places for her satellites. She was much talked about; she had many enemies, but she also enjoyed esteem, had a host of partisans, troops of persons indebted to her for good offices. She was seen everywhere.

In this whirl her daughters were neglected. Miss Flower luckily kept watch over their education. But she had more good-will than intelligence. The two señoritas read hardly anything except a few English novels.

"Pooh," said the Countess, "life is the true school!" She thought that for their marriage (the great matter that was already occupying her mind) their beauty and grace would serve them better than education. In the Spain of that period she was not far wrong in her reasoning.

Paca and Eugenia regretted their life in Paris so free and simple, and their comrades Cécile and Edouard Delessert. They found Madrid society provincial, and the girls of their own station stupid, thinking only of clothes and gossip. The calls they were obliged to make seemed like school tasks to them.

Their delight was to go often with their governess to a country house the Countess had at Carabanchel, two leagues out of Madrid. This was a great block of a building set down in the fold of a hill in an arid piece of land where flowers died away and trees remained dwarf and scrubby. The Countess de Montijo's uncle, François Cabarrus, Finance Minister to Charles IV, and the father of Madame Tallien, had in some passing whim made himself this desert retreat in the days of his prosperity, and been sick of it almost at once.

Just as the fair Terezia had done some sixty years before, the little girls ran about the rocky paths under the fir trees, hid among the bushes or the grotto shaded by starveling willows, scattered the sheep and the goats, rode on donkeys or on horses, tomboys delighting in unrestricted movement, their cheeks stung by the rough wind of the hills.

Living in this way in closest companionship the sisters loved each other dearly, in spite of their different dispositions. Paca, originally the livelier of the two, had grown gentle, was becoming almost shy. She was bored by the *tertulias* and the evening parties at which she was beginning to appear. Eugenia ruled her, overflowing with unexpected turbulent ideas. She talked a great deal, with a sort of eloquence inherited from her mother. She was afraid of nothing.

Falling one day from the balustrade of the stair astride which she had perched herself rather too foolhardily she had been picked up by an old gitana who was passing in front of the open door of the house. As she thanked her and was giving her money the gitana took her hand and scrutinised the palm for a considerable time.

"Good mother," asked Eugenia, ill at ease, for she was superstitious, "can you tell me what my future will be?"

The old woman answered gravely:

"You will be a queen, and you will live a hundred years."

The Countess de Montijo and Paca laughed heartily. So did Eugenia too, though a little less heartily, and with an *arrière pensée* that did not prevent her going on with her boyish games.

One night, when they were alone at Carabanchel with Miss Flower, they heard a noise. Thieves had got into the house. A not uncommon affair; the troubled times were responsible for swarms of bandits. The room in which the three women were had a high wide chimney. The Englishwoman and Paca trembled and wanted to hide inside it.

"No," exclaimed Eugenia, "a Montijo does not hide. Come, Paca!"

And holding her sister by the hand she opened the door, stamped her foot and called down the dark corridor in her strong deep voice.

"Who's there? What do you want?"

The intruders took fright and made off.

Back in the Madrid house, Paca and Eugenia resumed their jerky and disjointed studies somehow or other. They corresponded frequently with Mérimée and also with Beyle, whose stories they had not forgotten. In December 1839 Eugenia wrote to him.

Monsieur, I received your letter with great pleasure. I am impatiently waiting for the year 1840, since you gave us the hope that we should see you again. You ask me what I am doing now. I am learning to paint a little in oils, laughing and working as in the old days. Mamma still finds time to give us a few lessons, and we try not to forget all we learned in Paris.

At present Spain is in a great turmoil. Everybody longs for peace, and Maroto the Carlist general has gone over to the camp of Christina for a very large sum of money, which is not pretty behaviour, and all the other little officers have followed his example. Navarre, Alava, Guipuzcoa, Biscaye have recognised the queen as legitimate. It is said that Don Carlos and the Duchess of Bura have gone to France; Cabrera has made for Jaramon and twenty horsemen have gone out to observe the enemy's movements. In Madrid there were great rejoicings in honour of the proclamation of peace, but it has been proclaimed so many times that I don't believe any longer. All the same everybody wants peace. Mamora, my sister and Miss Flower present their respects to you, and I, monsieur, am devotedly your affectionate friend

E. GUZMAN Y PALAFOX.

Poor Beyle, tucked away in his consulate at Civita Vecchia, must have smiled as he read this curious letter from a child so early concerned with politics and war. He did not come to Spain as Eugenia hoped, and as he himself had wished. His days of travel were over. Already he was declining. Two years more and he would have left his consulate, which he loathed, and life, which he loved so much.

But Mérimée came, and with great delight. To reward himself for having written "Colomba," the proofs of which he was correcting for the *Revue des Deux Mondes,* after ten years he revisited Madrid, and found his friends there once more. He was present at a revolution, to which he attached no great importance. Spain remained volcanic. The Montijo House, solid and well built, was in the heart of the city, an important strategic position, coveted both by the rebels and by the government. Mérimée even claimed that his room, which overlooked the Plaza del Angel, was the key of Madrid. He was quite proud of it.

Between two bouts of pistol shooting when they were tired of seeing the pavements torn up and hearing bullets whistling past their ears, and eating bread a week old, the Countess and her friends withdrew to Carabanchel, where they enjoyed themselves immensely. Every evening they danced or had private theatricals on a stage built in the old days by Cabarrus, which Mérimée, promoted by Doña Manuela to be stage carpenter and producer, had transformed. He had painted the scenes, arranged the props, devised a magnificent lighting with Carcel lamps. When the plays were acted he was the prompter. With this powerful aid the Countess did not shrink from giving operas. Thus they played Bellini's "Norma," a sombre piece, in the midst of the most charming gaiety.

As Eugenia did not sing, she had been given the part of a woman with a child in her arms. To the strains of the orchestra, consisting of several violins and guitars, she appeared wrapped in a great black shawl carrying a bratling from the neighbouring farm lent for the occasion. The poor little thing cried without stopping. Intent above everything on her entrance, Eugenia held it head down and heels in air. Audience, orchestra, actors, the prompter in his den broke into inextinguishable laughter. Eugenia all out of countenance marked down a chair, planted the child on it and escaped into the wings. And never again would she face the footlights.

In this society given over to pleasure light intrigues were constantly flowering and fading. Mérimée would tease the Countess about this. He assured her that he used to hear sighs from every corner and that her gardens, though rather bare for lack of water, evoked for him the groves of Paphos and Idalia! Doña Manuela laughed, and then, always the arrant matchmaker, she would praise up the charms of this or that señorita of the lovely eyes, her friend or relation, who was at Carabanchel at the moment, and who would ask nothing better than to become "Madame Mérimée."

Don Prospero made no answer. But he showed the Countess the bezel of his ring, which bore the engraved motto in Greek *μέμνησο ἀπιστεῖν*—remember to mistrust.

Then, still light and slender, the sire of "Colomba" took to flight. Doña Manuela, now very heavy of build and not fond of running, called out laughing from afar:

"I shall never make anything of you."

When his visit came to an end Paca and Eugenia, like their mother attentive to every echo of France, would fain have tacked themselves on to Don Prospero's coat tails to go with him to Paris and see the Return of the Ashes. All Europe waited in expectation for that heroic spectacle. By it Louis-Philippe thought he planted his throne firmly and gave it a touch of colour with the Imperial gilt. He could not foresee that the wave rising at St. Helena and reaching the shores of France under the network of meridians and parallels of latitude would little by little spread over the whole country and drown out his inglorious Monarchy. Alive the Emperor had been conquered. Dead he was invincible; his mortal remains would reconquer a nation naked and defenceless before the tyranny that comes from a great memory. Their imaginations all afire, like two French girls, the little Spaniards, daughters of a soldier of Napoleon, saluted from

Madrid this unprecedented procession that through the wintry mist bore the Corsican to the Invalides amid a silence brimmed full of the anguish of all hearts and the flapping noise of the flags.

Many members of the Spanish aristocracy at this period were touched with a desire for going abroad, consequent upon the insecurity of the country in these years of civil war, and the comfortlessness of their magnificent houses, peopled with servants, but in which they froze in winter and roasted in summer, without conveniences of any kind. They lived at home for six months, in the city or on their estates, then went off to Paris, London, Germany or Italy. Doña Manuela, given to activity and change, carried this tendency to the point of mania. Her daughters, Eugenia especially, shared her cosmopolitanism, though in a less degree. Comparing their travels to the periodical migrations of the sheep from their lands at Cacèrès she said jokingly, "We're changing pasture too." After a season in Madrid interrupted with the visits to Carabanchel, she crossed the Pyrenees, stopping at Pau or at Saint-Sauveur, or at Bagnères de Luchon, or Cauterets or Eaux-Bonnes. Almost everywhere she met old friends, made new ones, thanks to the easy familiarity of hotel life. She made friends quickly; her daughters scolded her for it. "You can never have too many contacts with people," she replied. Eugenia, whose chest was always delicate, took the waters. When they lived at Pau they were often received by the Marquise de Castelbajac, the mother of a handsome and courteous diplomatic secretary, who accompanied the girls in their mountain promenades. In her drawing-room one evening they heard an artist of already mature years, who went from town to town giving concerts, a Madame Gordon. She sang with some talent the fashionable operatic songs and drawing-room ballads. Paca and Eugenia knew nothing about her except that she had played an important part some years before in that Strasbourg conspiracy of which the Orleanists spoke with contempt, but which had very nearly placed Prince Louis-Bonaparte on the throne, that nephew of the Emperor whom they had seen at the Delesserts before his departure for America. Later on, having returned to be at the deathbed of his mother Queen Hortense, and being subsequently an exile in England, he had engaged in a truly mad affair, an attempt at a *pronunciamento* in the Spanish fashion, which came to grief at Boulogne and brought him before the Cour des Pairs, and to the fortress of Ham. Madame Gordon talked of *her prince* (to whom indeed she was attached by tender recollections) with untiring complacency. Eugenia plied her with questions. What was the prisoner doing? Was he unhappy? Could he escape? Madame Gordon was delighted to answer interminably. She had it in mind to go and visit him soon, for he was allowed to see his friends. He read, wrote, published articles, in a word, enjoyed very lenient treatment. Eugenia became excited, dreamed of making a pilgrimage herself to the prison of Ham. She spoke of it to her mother, who could easily be carried away by odd ideas if they had an air of generosity about them, and it was agreed that the Countess and her daughters should accompany Madame Gordon on her visit. The plan came to nothing. Fresh troubles took the Montijos back to Madrid and Madame Gordon went to the Picardy marshes by herself.

Paca had passed her eighteenth birthday. She was of middle height, with a warm complexion, with grave eyes; she showed fine teeth when she laughed. But Eugenia dazzled. Tall, beautifully made, with long legs, slender waist and her shoulders already ravishingly rounded, she carried on a supple neck a rare and unusual face in which the blue eyes might seem too close together under their shell-like lids, the aquiline nose a trifle austere, though delicate, but on which the tiny mouth, the colour of pink coral, marked its exquisite Cupid's bow. Her hair was no longer fiery, but of a tawny fairness like that which gleams from the heads of Titian.

That hair had long been the despair of Eugenia.

"What can be uglier than red hair?" she would say, and fall to tears, in spite of Paca's and Miss Flower's efforts to console her. She used to comb them secretly with a leaden comb bought from a pedlar at Carabanchel. Perhaps it had some effect. When she was about fifteen her hair toned down to harmonise with her complexion. And that complexion was the miracle that drew every eye. Transparent, as though lighted from within, it no doubt came to her from her mother's Scots ancestors. But from her father Eugenia derived the inborn distinction, the remote and subtle charm of the ancient races. She had the Count's hands, fine, delicately veined, her feet were very small and very slender. Her walk was marvellous, free, spirited, as though she trod on air: neither a step nor a glide; she moved with swift and seemingly unconscious grace.

Doña Manuela, who loved fine feathers, spent money freely on the adornment of her girls. Their elegance would sometimes have been improved by greater simplicity. All too soon Eugenia and her sister were clad in silk, and wearing jewels. But the Spanish fashion was always heavier laden than the French. When the whole trio came into a drawing-room all the various conversations languished and little by little there might be seen the men of Madrid society or foreigners gravitating towards them as quickly as propriety allowed. The mother, famous for her verve, her intelligence, her culture, the daughters, already practised in all the ways of society, and gracefully accepting every homage, on every occasion kept an eager circle round them. The women were very jealous of them, and slanders and petty perfidies ran all about Madrid from behind one fan to another.

The Countess knew it and cared very little. For her it was the price and the sign of success. Spain was at last coming to a period of political stability. After seven years the Carlist flame was quenched. Narváez triumphed over Espartero. Fêtes sprang up again at the court of the young queen Isabel, and in society. Madrid in the spring of 1843 was gayer than Paris. Carnival had an immense success. For disguises the three ladies had recourse to Don Prospero. Mérimée, who on the banks of the Seine was now playing the grave and reverend seignior, the historian engrossed in studies upon ancient Rome, in order to lull the mistrust of the academic spheres and to slip into the Institut, Mérimée haunted tailors, embroiderers and milliners on the quiet. For the sake of the Countess and her daughters that egoist would have compromised his election. He sent them costumes, for a rococo shepherdess, a Cracow girl, a Scottish girl, head-dresses, shoes, powder, down to Chinese lanterns and paper umbrellas to decorate the gallery and the winter garden of the Montijo House. And all of it travelled, as was right and proper, by diplomatic pouch. Louis de Viel-Castel, a friend of Doña Manuela ever since his time in the Madrid embassy, was now a director at the Ministry in Paris.

Mérimée very boldly tried to send the Countess a calash by the same method. But the minister, that sullen fellow Guizot, raised obstacles, and the calash journeyed to Castile by less uncostly ways. The Countess de Montijo repaid these manifold attentions by supplying Mérimée with *fosforos,* for he hated the Paris matches. She sent him also mantillas for Valentine Delessert and Cécile. Between two chapters of Catiline he tried the mantillas on those French heads. They would never carry them like the far-away heads of which he thought so often, and profiles of which he used to draw in excellent likeness, on the margin of his letters, when he was alone with his lamp in the evenings.

The Countess had for a long time aspired to great marriages for her daughters. They might aim at the very highest, she often said. They belonged to the very first society. As her friends were in power, their mother's influence was strong. And their fortune, though not well administered, included wide domains in Castile and Estremadura. Especially for Paca's portion, as she inherited, by right of the eldest born, two-thirds of the Montijo patrimony.

Suitors had come forward already, whatever the ill-willed might say. The most brilliant of them, indeed a magnificent match, was the Duke of Alba. Of royal lineage, a Stuart through his ancestor Berwick, twelve times over a grandee of Spain, master of an unmeasurable fortune, palaces in every town, estates vast as provinces, he might have married an infanta. He was not particularly handsome, and rather small; he had been weak in health originally. But underneath this chilly and frail exterior was a subtle mind, a soul. Everywhere the two sisters appeared the young duke was seen to arrive. Madrid looked on with amusement. He seemed to make no choice between Paca and Eugenia. Perhaps he loved them both. He wavered for a long time. Then he made up his mind, and paid open court to Eugenia. To be Duchess of Alba, Her Highness, to have the foremost rank in her own country, that was something to dazzle and intoxicate a girl who was tempted and swayed by the glory of this world. For some days Eugenia made no secret of her joy. Eyelids downcast over her blue eyes, she smiled at the bitter annoyance of her friends.

But Paca was wandering pale and sad from room to room through the house. She no longer cared to dress, to go out. More than once Eugenia surprised a fixed, dull look, more touching than tears. She perceived that her sister loved Alba. Paca was infinitely dear to her. Without consulting either the Countess or Miss Flower, without even very much reflection, having prayed and communicated, she sacrificed herself and told Alba, who came to broach the matter of betrothal, that she would not marry him, and that it was Paca to whom he ought to offer his ring. She praised her elder sister, confided to him the secret inclination she had discovered, flattered him. . . . A strange conversation for these young people sitting in the winter garden under the palm trees by the whispering fountain. Paca in distress was watching them from behind a door. At certain moments Eugenia clenched her beautiful teeth and lost her smile. Then once more she urgently repeated her words. Alba let himself be persuaded. He was only in the dawn of love, still full of uncertainty. Paca still pleased him so much! He had no trouble in transferring his homage to her. The Countess approved the change . . . she had always preferred her eldest daughter. Eugenia too often stood out against her. Fearing the possibility of a *volte face,* she hurried on the wedding, which took place with great splendour on February 14, 1844. Paca was resplendent with joy. For this one day of her life she was more beautiful than her sister. But she remained simple in all her triumph. When one of her friends in the diplomatic corps saluted her by her new title, she cried out very gaily, "A fig for the Duchess! I'm Paca all the same."

Eugenia endured the looks of everybody gallantly. The wildest tales were flying round about her. Was it not spread abroad that she had tried to poison herself in despair at Alba's desertion? Deep down, for all her courage, she could not help feeling some regret. No doubt she felt nothing but sincere friendship for her brother-in-law. But to be Duchess of Alba! . . . Pious though she was, she harboured a violent pride. It would always be her besetting sin.

That regret was to make a certain mark upon her. Later in life, in moments of disillusion or displeasure, there would escape from her, "I should have done better to become Duchess of Alba!"

Mérimée was invited to the wedding, but sent his excuses. He could not leave Paris. A candidate for the Académie, he was in the thick of his canvassing. Since November he had been in the Institut. But what was the Inscriptions after all? A stool to help in mounting to the true armchair. Nervous and anxious, he consulted fate by opening Homer at random. The first words on the page served as his oracle. What will passion bring men of intelligence to! He congratulated the *duquesita,* sent her his present, a very beautiful old missal, which for an atheist was a work of merit.

A month to the day after the wedding he was elected. Doña Manuela and Eugenia were very proud of his success. They resumed their peregrinations, and went to Paris again, where Eugenia rode every morning in the Bois, and every night went to a ball with her mother or Don Prospero, or to the play, or the opera. They were seen at Bordeaux hunting with the Marquis de Dampierre or the Count de Bryas, then in London, at Bath, at Schwalbach, at Homburg. Society there was cosmopolitan, but without any ragtag, it was still select; great numbers of people of high name, who all knew one another. These watering-places were still society. But European society. Life was gayer than elsewhere. There were excursions, concerts to listen to, picnics were got up. You took the waters, you played—sometimes very high—but the tone was always elegant.

Everywhere Eugenia was a centre of attraction. She danced a great deal, laughed, ate sorbets, talked animatedly, quick in repartee, especially with men, whom she treated with the best form of camaraderie. She cared very little for women's conversation; they froze her by their artificial reserve which was frequently hostile. Her mother's spirit lived in her again, at least in one part, turning towards history and politics, indifferent to matters of art, very cut and dried, very realistic, almost virile. Doña Manuela was a superior woman of profound culture. Eugenia was merely intelligent, with a rudimentary education. But she showed more balance than her mother, less taste for pleasure, higher breeding. Always wearing dresses by the best makers, from which emerged her sloping well-rounded shoulders, sometimes winking her eyes, outlined with the lightest touch of the pencil, without rouge, only a bloom of powder, in rising, in sitting, in crossing a drawing-room, in making a curtsey, in the turn of her head, in replying to a compliment, in opening or closing her fan, she had an unerringness, a grace, a pride of gesture that dazzled in a girl so young. Many were the suitors for her hand. Eugenia wanted to marry, but she meant either to marry where her heart bade her, when that still silent heart should come to beat, or if it continued to be silent, to make only an alliance of the highest rank, which would ensure her a place equal to her sister's in European society. In that she shared the Countess de Montijo's ideas, even if on other matters they did not agree.

Doña Manuela aimed still higher perhaps than her daughter. At the entertainments that in the autumn of 1846 celebrated in Madrid those famous *Spanish marriages* which had so greatly busied Louis-Philippe and so greatly perturbed the courts of Europe, Queen Isabella marrying her cousin Francisco d'Assisi and the Infanta Louise marrying the Duc de Montpensier, the son of the French King, the attentions of the Duc d'Aumale to the young Countess de Teba were very noticeable.

At the French ambassador's, the Comte de Bresson's, they chatted together throughout one whole evening. The Countess de Montijo allowed their betrothal to be talked of. Nevertheless, smitten as he was by a beauty that he was not soon to forget, the Duc d'Aumale did not declare himself, no doubt from fear of his father.

Not long after Eugenia refused the Duke of Osuña, the ambassador in Paris, a man of ripe age who she feared might have been too friendly with Doña Manuela. In the friendliest way she discouraged Edouard Delessert who had been in love with her since boyhood, and also the Vicomte Aguado, whose father, a highly successful financier, had handed down an enormous fortune to him, and who appeared as an intimate friend of the family at the receptions and the *medianoches* of the Montijo home.

The Countess was at the height of her political activities. Narváez' friendship had raised her to the post of Camarera Mayor, after a palace revolution that had driven out the Queen Mother and isolated the King-Consort at Pardo. As mistress of Isabella's household the Countess de Montijo took a real share in the government. But she could not refrain from overstepping. She wanted to lead every one, the young men, the ministers, the generals. Narváez, who was very jealous of power, stopped her in full career. He put forward the pretext that she gave the Court too gay an air. Disdaining an authority so impaired that it reduced her to a position of mere subordinate acquiescence, the Countess de Montijo resigned her post and set out for Paris. She was extremely annoyed. But like a good gambler she held little resentment and very soon was home again with Narváez.

The fall of Louis-Philippe found her in Madrid. She had foreseen it. But what neither she nor Eugenia foresaw, what in France even the most experienced men of affairs, such as Thiers, could not imagine, was that the prisoner of Ham, the slightly comic conspirator and subsequently the obscure deputy in the Constituent Assembly, would rise without striking a blow to become President of the new Republic by an enthusiastic vote.

This power, which he had twice tried to seize by surprise and violence, had dropped into his hands. He was the nephew of the Emperor, and France had for ten years been brooding and pondering and chewing the cud in the cult of the Great Shade. The Return of the Ashes had set the seal on this subterranean advent of Napoleon. The Emperor, in whom the upper classes no longer saw anything more than a historical figure, lived again with a secret, dominating life for the soldiers, the workers, the peasants of France. They forgot the spilt blood, the country laid open and harried, tyranny and distress; they saw nothing now but the sun of Austerlitz and the little pale-faced officer who, with a hand under his coat-tails, took kings to task. His legend elevated them with a sad and noble love; they gave themselves up to his mere name, and since universal suffrage made them masters, they gave France as well.

Not long after, in February 1849, there arrived as ambassador in Madrid in place of the amiable Ferdinand de Lesseps—at first to the grief of his relatives the Montijos—the President's own cousin, the son of the former King Jérôme of Westphalia, the Prince Napoleon. Head of the French faction in Madrid, and Bonapartist always, the Countess could not be unfriendly to this other nephew of the Emperor. A frequent visitor, the Prince paid very pressing court to Eugenia. Rugged and headlong in disposition, and, though the son of a German mother, a real Corsican by his black hair and olive complexion, of all his family he was the most like Napoleon. His vivid, picturesque speech interested Eugenia. They often talked of politics. More concerned with events in France than with Spanish affairs, which were too commonplace to maintain any prestige, the Señorita thought, and did not fear to say, that the Prince President would not wait long before he declared himself Emperor. The Napoleonic curve would be repeated in him; the Consulate brought on the Empire. The Prince appeared astonished; he declared energetically that any such enterprise would be doomed to failure. And in any case both his cousin and himself were sincere republicans.

"Republicans," said Eugenia, "but that's nothing but a word. A Republic cannot last in France. For my part I would be delighted to see the President exalted to the Empire, if the Bourbons are not to come back. For at bottom I am a legitimist myself."

The Prince would have liked to bring this Spaniard, who spoke so well in French, to gayer speeches. She refused to be caught. Marry this Bonaparte, bold enough, but a beggar, whose ambition manifested itself in . . . No. She had other views. The young Marquis of Alcanizes, son of the Duke of Sesto, had just been playing Musset's "Caprice" with her before the élite of Madrid, at the Montijo house. Eugenia did not know her part very well, but clad in white, with a mauve silk sash, she had annoyed all the women and enraptured all the men. It was her birthday, and the house was overflowing with Parma violets, her favourite flowers. He fell in love with Eugenia, and told her so. She did not resist. Her friendship for him had easily glided into affection. They became engaged. Eugenia was happy. She would not be a princess, but a grandee in her own country. In her heart of hearts that was what she preferred. In spite of the gipsy's prediction, which indeed was all but forgotten, she did not aim so high as her mother.

However, this plan, which had even been hinted at by certain newspapers, soon met with obstacles. The Sestos were not favourable. The Montijo fortunes were impaired, the mother a nuisance, the daughter a coquette and too much accustomed to homage. And then Alcanizes, somewhat fickle by nature, had paid court to Paca. Eugenia learned this by chance. She was jealous, and took umbrage, dismissed the handsome Pepe, and to make sure of not seeing him again, she went off with her mother to Paris.

They stayed as usual in the Place Vendôme, at that Hôtel du Rhin which a year earlier had been Prince Louis' headquarters when he was a candidate for the Presidency, and then, as they decided to make a longer stay, they rented a handsome furnished suite in the house of M. de Montgermont, number twelve in the same Place Vendôme, and thither speedily came their old Paris friends, the Delesserts, the Labordes, the Castellanes, and Viel Castel, Cousin, and Viollet-le-Duc, and, with hardly an added touch of grey, the devoted, the subtle, the indispensable Mérimée.

CHAPTER III

The Prince. 1850

PRINCE LOUIS-NAPOLEON leaned over to his cousin Mathilde, who had invited him to a dinner party, and discreetly indicated a young woman with a radiant complexion under her reddish gold hair, wearing a pale blue frock, generously décolleté, who were talking with the marine painter Gudin, Mérimée, and the Delesserts at the other end of the drawing-room.

"And who is she?" he whispered.

Mathilde replied carelessly.

"A new-comer here, belonging to an Andalusian family, Mademoiselle Eugénie de Montijo."

"Ah! But you must present her to me . . ."

Smilingly Mathilde went to bring up Eugénie and her mother, and presented them to the Prince-President. She did better still. By a word in the ear of the *maître d'hôtel* she had the girl's place at table altered. She was anxious to please her cousin. She knew how much he liked pretty women. In her eyes Eugénie de Montijo, who at that moment was bending her white neck and sinking down in an exquisitely perfect curtsey, was nothing but a beautiful foreigner, who had already been somewhat talked about and who might be a pleasant diversion for the Prince. She looked upon her as frivolous and light, following in this the opinion of certain houses of the Faubourg Saint-Germain whose doors the Montijo ladies found only half-opened to them. Their free ways, their elegant cosmopolitanism were not to the taste of the old society—especially of its women. They were invited to the rural luncheons and dinners the Vicomte Sosthènes de la Rochefoucauld gave in the pretty estate of La Vallée aux Loups, which had belonged to Chateaubriand, but they never were asked when the Vicomtesse invited her women friends. Doña Manuela and her daughter mostly frequented the Orleanist drawing-rooms to which they had been introduced by their relative de Lesseps, and by Mérimée.

The Prince took Eugénie in to dinner, and she began to talk without embarrassment but with an air of discreet admiration, which was not merely assumed. With eyes half closed, and twisting his moustache, Louis-Napoleon as he listened looked at that marvellous face, so mobile, so finely bred, those faultless shoulders, those slender pale hands that came down upon things like birds alighting. Sensitive even to excess to women's beauty, Mlle de Montijo's attracted and charmed him. But he was also struck by her frank grace, so far removed from the petty tricks of society, the clear prompt mind that might perhaps be lacking in depth but which displayed varied knowledge not usually expected in a girl, which she owed to her intercourse with distinguished men, to her travels, and her reading. Louis-Napoleon told her he thought he had already met her, but he could not tell where. She assisted his memory. They had seen each other in September, at the Satory review. The Montijo ladies had taken a *pied-à-terre* for the summer at Versailles, in the Rue de l'Orangerie. The Prince-President had come from Paris on horseback, in the uniform of a general, increasing his stature by a lofty white plume. Surrounded by a magnificent staff he had passed by under their window. The sky was heavy with clouds. Eugénie and a number of the Versailles ladies had followed the President on horseback to the parade. The guns thundered without ceasing, and the air smelt of powder and storm. The troops marched by in front of the President in splendid array, with weapons gleaming. Some ranks as they passed raised the shout *"Vive l'Empereur!"* The crowd massed on the surrounding terraces took up these cries, which joined to the military noises made the horses rear. Some of the amazons were frightened. But Eugénie de Montijo sat upright in her saddle, smiling, radiant in her long green dress, on her head a felt hat with a long drooping feather. She looked like a heroine of the Fronde. The Prince had noticed this intrepid horsewoman, but no one in his entourage could tell him her name. She too, he thought, had cried *"Vive l'Empereur!"* Then the rain fell in waterspouts, in niagaras, and a wild stampede ensued to the carriages and to the houses of Satory. Eugénie alone made no attempt to take shelter with her mother. With the rain coursing down her shoulders, she rode back at a sedate pace to Versailles.

"I remember," said Louis-Napoleon. "You had a fine dappled Arab, rather spirity. You ride to perfection, Mademoiselle, and I know something about riding."

She might have told him, but did not, that she had seen him another time, long before, in a darker hour, after the Strasbourg attempt, when he was awaiting the decree of Louis-Philippe. She did not think of it: he was now utterly unlike that too ancient picture she had long kept in mind. His face was now long and yellow, with a high forehead from which the hair was receding, a big nose, a chestnut moustache the points of which he had a trick of twisting. His grey-blue eyes, slightly closed, gave him an expression both astute and dreamy. But he had a tender smile, a gentleness of gesture that no doubt came to him from the Beauharnais and the Western Islands, and with all that, from having lived so long alone among dreams of glory, a sovereign aspect.

The Princess Mathilde, seated by her cousin, did not hear everything he said to Mlle de Montijo, for Louis-Napoleon spoke with a rather low voice and an accent that betrayed his German schooling. But the loud tone and the rapid speech of Eugénie, and sometimes her laugh, reached her and kept her in a state of slight irritation. Louis seemed to have eyes only for this Spaniard and her gold hair and her satiny shoulders on which the light gleamed slidingly. Mathilde's instinct warned her of danger.

Once upon a time, in the days of Arenenberg and Queen Hortense, she had been betrothed to her cousin. After the Strasbourg affair her father, the frivolous selfish King Jérôme, had made her give up the idea. Louis-Napoleon, he insisted, was compromising by his mad tricks the Bonaparte future fortunes. Some years later he gave his daughter to a wealthy Russian, Count Anatole Demidoff. A splendid debt-paying marriage that very quickly went to the bad. The Cossack was not content with keeping the Duchesse de Dino under his wife's very eyes, but he even ill-treated the daughter of the Napoleons. She threw herself at the feet of the Czar and obtained a separation on most luxurious terms. Thenceforth she lived with the utmost freedom, a friend of artists still more than of the arts, serving as a link between society and the President, who was cold-shouldered by the aristocracy. At the Elysée she received at his side, handsome and massive, with imperial mien. She imagined that since she had not been able to be Louis-Napoleon's wife, he at least would not marry, and that beside him she would thus keep the first feminine place in France. For why should he enchain himself, now already ageing, when he

Les Archives Photographiques d'Art et d'Histoire

PRINCESS MATHILDE

From the Portrait by Edouard Dubufe in the Museum of Versailles

was a great woman-pursuer, seeking diversity, adventure? As for the continuance of the Bonaparte family, that was ensured by Mathilde's brother Napoleon.

After dinner, in the drawing-room, it was still Mlle de Montijo with whom the Prince conversed most. He of course courteously went the round of the other guests, talked with his uncle King Jérôme who showed under the candelabra the touching mask of a mummified Napoleon, with Lady Douglas Hamilton, his cousin, his childhood friend and even something more, with Alfred d'Orsay, a dandy on the decline, to whom Louis-Napoleon's friendship had given by way of pension the post of superintendent of the Beaux-Arts, with Drouyn de Lhuys, a cool and solid head on whom he relied greatly, with Morny, and Persigny, still more in his confidence, the former his natural brother, a man of affairs and pleasure too, a high politician capable equally of the most elegant acts and of crimes, the latter, a henchman with the manners of a non-commissioned officer, sure, brutal, indiscreet.

Calling on the President as witness Persigny recalled in front of the ladies an incident of their youth. The Prince and he had been walking in the country near Arenenberg. At night, being extremely tired, they were very glad to hire a wretched cart to bring them back to Queen Hortense's. Lying in the straw Persigny (who was still only Fialin) laughed at their miserable turn-out, and asked the Prince:

"What would the Emperor say if he could see his nephew in such a plight?"

And Louis-Napoleon had replied unmoved:

"What would he say? He would say, 'The wheel goes round. . . .'" And puffing out his bulldog face Persigny wound up with:

"The wheel has gone round indeed."

And for the benefit of the people just at hand, he added:

"This is only the beginning, it will go round further."

The President, somewhat vexed, shrugged his shoulders, then resuming his round of affability he asked Mérimée about the "Carrosse du Saint Sacrement" which had just been put on at the Théâtre Français. The last two performances had been uncertain. A little hissing had even been heard. The Prince said he would go and applaud.

"It will only be given twice more, Monseigneur," said Mérimée, bowing.

He was quite aware that this was mere politeness. Louis-Napoleon was but a poor amateur in the arts. He only appreciated the sciences and history. He fancied himself a journalist, and had written a great deal in a dull and flabby style. Rich in ideas, his taste was poor.

When he found his way back to Eugénie, they talked of England, which they both loved, and where they had friends in common: Lord Clarendon, the Malmesburys, that agreeable Marchioness of Ely who in London the year before had done Eugénie the honours of the "season."

Then seeming to become confidential and friendly, he said a few words about the cares of the moment. He desired to restore France to the first place in Europe. But many distinguished minds, in Parliament, in the press, in society did not understand him yet. He counted on time to win them, as also to improve the lot of the populace, which had for a long time been much on his mind. Eugénie in reply displayed a generous heart; she, too, felt that authority ought to take thought for the poor. She had read Fourier and admired him without following him in everything. He was, she said, full of strong views, but of clouds as well. Her mind was too realistic not to distinguish the part played by dreams in his plans for the cities of the future.

Passing from one subject to another without much reflection, as she often did, Eugénie suddenly said to the Prince:

"Monseigneur, we have often talked of you with a lady who is greatly devoted to you."

"And who is that?"

"Madame Gordon."

Louis-Napoleon gave Mademoiselle de Montijo a strange look. Did the lovely Spaniard know what Madame Gordon had been to him? What relations had she had with that kind and gallant, though slightly tarnished lady?

Hesitatingly he said:

"Yes, I know Madame Gordon."

Then he changed the conversation. Eugénie felt that she might have committed a *faux pas*.

Meanwhile Doña Manuela, very brilliant and very gay, as usual leaving her daughter to look after herself, was entertaining Drouyn de Lhuys, whom she had known as ambassador in Madrid, teasing Nieuwerkerke, the pasha with the fair beard, upon whom the Princesse Mathilde every now and then cast a heavy glance. Their liaison was accepted by everybody and the Princess's influence was beginning to move this bad sculptor in the direction of official posts.

At eleven the Prince, after a sign to Morny, took his leave of his cousin. He had to work. As a matter of fact his carriage was not bound for the Elysée but for the Rue du Cirque, where Miss Howard was expecting him, his official mistress, who had lent him millions during his presidential campaign, and who without obtaining fidelity from him had little by little attained great influence through her free and easy companionship, and through the power of habit also, which so often enslaves men.

In their carriage Eugénie spoke of the Prince to her mother and to Mérimée, who was escorting them home.

She had liked him infinitely; she had found him simple and noble.

"Is that to be wondered at?" said Mérimée. "He took notice of nobody but you."

Then regretting his causticity, for he was always quick to relent, and to pacify Eugénie who was already becoming annoyed, he explained. He confessed that at bottom he had little love for Louis-Napoleon.

Not that for his own part he shared the forebodings of certain Orleanists. The Prince was not the "idiot who will be led by the nose" announced by the sour voice of Thiers. The man had no genius, but he was intelligent, amiable, and had charm.

"All the same," added Mérimée, "he would have to have a hundred times more charm to make me turn Bonapartist. His Presidentship is nothing but an adventure. It has given a kind of order to the country. The result remains to be seen; but how will it all end?"

"In Empire!" cried Eugénie.

She thought of it constantly. To her mind a Bonaparte must wake up as Emperor sooner or later. From the first day her opinion had not varied a jot. When she had an idea she clung to it.

"Empire?" said Mérimée. "But it is the victorious generals who make Emperors. Louis-Napoleon is only a show soldier. He has the civilian mind; I approve him for that. He will have more sense than his entourage, among whom you can find nothing but headlong fellows."

Huddled up in her cloak, Eugénie made no answer.

The Montijo ladies were soon after invited to the Elysée receptions. The President showed them particular attention. They now often saw his factotum the Comte Baciocchi arriving at the Place Vendôme to bring them boxes for the Opera, reserved seats at official ceremonies and reviews. Later on they received an invitation to dinner at St. Cloud, where the Prince had taken up residence for the summer. When they reached the palace they found a carriage waiting to bring them to Combleval, a pleasure pavilion ensconced in the park on the Villeneuve l'Etang road. The Montijo ladies, in full dress, expected to find a large company. They were greatly astonished on their arrival to see only the Prince and Baciocchi. Still they put a good face on it. After dinner, while it was still broad daylight, Louis-Napoleon proposed to walk round the park, and offered his arm to Eugénie, while his friend offered his to the Countess. At that Eugénie with flaming cheeks said to the Prince in a very marked voice:

"Monseigneur, my mother is with us . . ."

She fell back. Louis-Napoleon had to take Madame de Montijo, while Eugénie followed with Baciocchi. It was a short and silent walk. The President twisted at his moustache. Baciocchi, who was generally full of high spirits, stammered constrained phrases. The Countess quickly said she was tired and asked for her carriage.

The Duchess of Alba was then in Paris. Eugénie next day told her about this awkward affair. Paca scolded her very seriously, and the Countess as well, for their impudence. What were they thinking of? For women of their rank a trick like that was an insult. Prince Louis-Napoleon took them for adventuresses. It would be said all round that Madame de Montijo was aiming at establishing her daughter as the President's mistress.

Eugénie protested loftily. The Countess reflected. Paca was certainly right; they had blundered. Their free behaviour and their modest establishment might have led Louis-Napoleon to believe that Eugénie would be an easy prey. But he was wrong, and they would let him see it clearly.

Did she begin at that moment to think of the possibility of marriage between him and her daughter? The position of the President, heavily assailed by the monarchist parties, looked upon with mistrust by the Assembly, still seemed so ill-assured that the match offered no inducements. And then he was said to be chained to Miss Howard. In any case, Eugénie did not think of it for a moment. She was confused and irritated. She persuaded her mother to leave Paris almost at once and to visit the banks of the Rhine.

On their return they kept the Prince at a greater distance, still appeared at the Elysée, but in a less conspicuous fashion, which discouraged the scandalous talk that had been provoked for a moment. Besides, Louis-Napoleon himself had other diversions. He continued attentive when he met Mademoiselle de Montijo, but he seemed to have given up any thought of conquest.

CHAPTER IV

The Great Adventure

THE political situation in France had become obscure. The National Assembly and the President were entering upon an avowed struggle. On the one side the Legitimist and Orleanists, on the other the social Republicans were the two sides of the pincers squeezing the breath out of Louis-Napoleon's government. He wished to obtain an extension of his magistrature now about to come to an end. A coup d'état was certain. Would it be carried out by the Assembly throwing the Prince into the dungeon of Vincennes or by Louis-Napoleon dissolving the Chamber? France would belong to whichever was boldest, promptest. Eugénie did not doubt that this would be the Prince. In his speeches he denied that he aspired to a dictatorship, but his conspiratorial past, the handful of risk-loving gamblers who surrounded him, and above all his name, that name of Bonaparte, so weighted with glory, constrained him. In the closing days of November 1851, without consulting any one, in one of those bursts of friendliness that sometimes carried her away, Eugénie wrote to Baciocchi that she placed everything she possessed at the disposal of the Prince, if he were to fail in an enterprise she supposed to be imminent. Everything she possessed . . . Words without substance. She had a very scanty purse and estates she could not alienate. But for her it was a fashion of throwing herself into action. She was a true cavalier, and like a Longueville or a Chevreuse, she would willingly have fired a shot for a principle, for a friend, even for less, for the pleasure of the fight. Baciocchi no doubt so judged her. He was clever beneath his butterfly exterior. He kept the letter in his pocket. But after the second of December when the danger was over—and for a few hours it had been serious—when the Assembly had been dissolved, the republican resistance crushed, and the Prince-President was invested with unlimited power, Mlle de Montijo's letter was handed to him. He kept it for a moment in his hand, surprised and touched. He was infinitely sensitive to devotion, to friendship, to the sweetness of human intercourse. Then he went to the fire-

Les Archives Photographiques d'Art et d'Histoire

THE EMPEROR NAPOLEON III

From the Portrait by Flandrin in the Museum of Versailles

place and burned it. While the paper was being consumed his eyes were filled with the vision of Eugénie.

After a stay in Madrid, the Countess de Montijo and her daughter spent the summer of 1852 in the Pyrenees, at Eaux Bonnes, where Eugénie, whose chest was always delicate, followed the treatment. There they found many Spanish and French friends. Eugénie displayed an activity that nothing could tire. Every day she went off on some excursion on horseback or on foot, every evening she danced with an ardour, a thrill of life, that made the Countess sigh.

"I was just like that at her age. But *I* was married by then!"

That was her one preoccupation. Having established her eldest daughter and to such high advantage, Doña Manuela was tormented by this fixed idea, to marry her youngest equally well. But Eugénie had reached the age of twenty-six and continued to rebuff would-be bridegrooms. Several more wooers had declared themselves, young Huddleston, the Comte d'Oultremont whom she had met at Brussels, charming Camerata, a grandson of Elisa Bonaparte. Eugénie had dismissed them all. She had discouraged a Rothschild too. No doubt all she wanted was a great name coupled with a fortune such as would rescue her from the continually arising difficulties into which, in spite of their substantial revenues, her mother's prodigality threw them. But in their careerings through Europe, the Montijo ladies had never found the French or English duke, the German prince, who might have tempted Eugénie.

In Spain she had aroused many jealousies which were actively antagonistic to her. A woman with a head on her shoulders, Doña Manuela had a very exact appreciation of the position of her daughter, upon whom her bohemian ways had brought a certain amount of detraction. She felt that with increasing years, after so many refusals, the chances of a great match for Eugénie were diminishing. She took her to task accordingly, or rather she endeavoured to argue with her. But Eugénie immediately rebelled.

"You will be left an old maid!"

"We shall see!"

She had *"coiffé Sainte Catherine,"* come to five and twenty with apparent calmness. At bottom she perhaps occasionally felt some uneasiness. She had moments of nerves, in which she would suddenly be harsh to her maid Pepa. The Countess sometimes came upon her in her room in the hotel sitting in front of her window with a book on her knees. She was not reading, but gazing in front of her with a grave, almost melancholy air. That did not last long. She quickly resumed her marvellous smile, her light step like a reddish-haired Diana. Never had she been more beautiful. Her full flowering had come. She was less like a girl than a woman. Her toilette, costly and exquisite, helped to produce this effect. She hated "schoolgirl clothes." And although her French friends, like Cécile Delessert, might have let her know her mistake, she sometimes wore diamonds.

At Eaux-Bonnes she had met with a young Jew, Bernard Bauer, the brother of a Madrid banker who was received by the Montijos. He sometimes went with her in her excursions. Bauër was entering upon a period of mysticism to which he saw no end but the cloister. He was subtle and handsome, and talked well. Eugénie encouraged him to become converted, and since he felt himself called by God, to enter into orders. In this fashion, she said, he would have the highest life of all; if her mother had not accustomed her so much to the world, she would herself have chosen to be a nun.

In the meanwhile she enjoyed herself greatly with no false modesty, happy to be the cynosure of all eyes and to be fêted everywhere.

The proclaiming of the Empire was drawing nearer. The Prince-President would willingly have waited still longer before putting on the crown. Morny and Persigny urged him forward, eager and impatient for titles and places. Nothing in the public order would be stable and secure, they repeated, so long as the Empire was not re-established. For France as for Europe there was no stability save in monarchy. And in any case it was merely a question of a word. For a year the Republic had been as dead in men's minds as it was in outward manners.

Not long before this investiture, and as though to display the unruffled posture of affairs, Louis-Napoleon gave a great hunt at Fontainebleau, to which he invited the Montijos. Slender and elegant in her dark riding habit, with a laced three-cornered hat,

Eugénie rode by the Prince with a boldness and grace that, as a consummate horseman himself, he greatly admired. In these few days of life in common, during which tête-à-têtes were easy, Louis-Napoleon was smitten, with a violence he had never felt before, by desire for this rare beauty, for that agile body, so full of energy under its delicate limbs, for that transparent face, crowned above with gold, smiling, so proud. Everything in her enchanted him, the little feet, the long legs of the huntress, the slender waist, the round pure bosom, the dazzling shoulders. When he held her hand in his, he tightened his lips to control the thrill of pleasure that ran through him. Women were his delight, his rest, his deepest pleasure. Brought up in their society by his mother, he was never happy except with them. But he was quite as sensual as he was sentimental. Without good looks, he had had many successes, in Italy, in Switzerland, in England, in France, from Madame Gordon down to Eléonore Vergeot, the servant girl of Ham, from the Duchess of Hamilton down to the grisettes and prostitutes of Paris. But no woman had ever troubled him to this degree. At the first he had only felt a caprice, and Eugénie's reserve had seemed to quench it. But seeing her again in a new setting that made a royal frame for her beauty, finding her before his eyes, exercising a disdainful coquetry towards others and softening towards him, he fell into a fever. He wanted this woman, he had made up his mind to win her. Yet his thoughts did not go so far as to envisage clearly the means of achieving such a conquest. As he did in his political activities, he was pursuing a result, leaving the consequences to chance. A fatalist, he left it to destiny which had already fulfilled so many of his dreams.

Adopting with Eugénie de Montijo the tone of respectful gallantry with which he usually covered his methods of attack, he told her she had made an impression upon him against which he was defenceless, and that he thought of her among the most important affairs. Eugénie looked at him smiling as though it was a gay jest. Her bright and candid eyes made it almost impossible to go further.

He did her the honours of the palace, went with her up and down the galleries through which there had passed in old days François I, Catherine de Médicis, Mary Stuart. A place filled with history, and amorous history, where the initials of Henri II and

Diana de Poitiers were still entwined. When he had shown her the chapel in which he had been baptized, in the culminating time of the First Empire, she wanted to visit Marie-Antoinette's apartments. She had read many works on her life, her court, her admirable, heart-rending end, stripped of everything save her common humanity. She honoured with a special devotion the memory of that poor queen, so covered with adulation, whom only death had never betrayed. On the Prince's arm she entered her music room, her boudoir whose mahogany floor still displayed her cipher, her bedchamber . . . Eugénie was greatly moved. Louis-Napoleon took her hand and pressed a long kiss on it. She drew it away, but not harshly.

The Prince sighed. He would have liked to speak but did not dare. They rejoined the guests of the château. Next day, taking advantage of an excursion in the park during which they found themselves alone for a moment, he burned his boats. Leaning towards her he told her he loved her, that he believed she had a feeling for him, but that it was not enough, that he hoped one day to inspire her with affection.

She took the declaration jestingly, replied that he had the reputation of being a dangerous man, that he talked flatteringly to women but was no very true or very faithful knight, and that in any case everybody knew that his vows were paid to a beautiful foreigner. She was alluding to the English tie: Miss Howard. He at once warmly protested. The person she had in mind was nothing but a very true and devoted friend. He would never see her again, if that was Eugénie's desire.

She said she had no such desire, and that in any case she had no rights over him.

"You shall have every right, if you wish, and you will make me very happy."

She shook her head and hastened on to return to the château. Louis-Napoleon asked permission to write to her when she returned to Paris.

"With pleasure," she said, "but I warn you that my mother sees all my letters."

The Prince declared that nothing he should write to Eugénie could meet with Madame de Montijo's disapproval.

In this way she kept him in suspense, promising nothing, yet not discouraging him. She knew how loud was the voice of desire once it was aroused in him. She was flattered by his homage, very much aware of his attentions, but completely determined not to allow herself to be carried away. A Montijo could not become a mistress. But would the Prince leap the marriage ditch? The Countess assured her he would, provided that Eugénie followed her advice and consented to be adroit. In the eyes of Doña Manuela, the wooing of Louis-Napoleon, the head of the State and to-morrow's Emperor, offered an unhoped-for and magnificent opportunity of an establishment for her daughter. It must not be let slip. Smitten as he was, a subtle manœuvre that would make him still more so would throw him at Eugénie's feet. At the idea, the Countess, hardened matchmaker that she was, could not contain herself for joy. What would they say at Madrid? Her daughter an empress! She did not tell her everything that was in her thoughts on this aspect. Eugénie's straightforwardness and pride might have rebelled. At the same time she made her understand that it depended solely on herself, by a skilful and supple defence, whether she should one day wear a crown, not a duchess's crown like her sister's, but a sovereign's, and become the first woman in France and thereby in the world. Eugénie at first shrugged her shoulders.

"Pooh, that's just *tonteria,* nonsense."

Then on Doña Manuela returning to the charge she bit her lips, cast down her blue eyes, and put on a sulky air. But when she was alone she reflected . . .

The evenings in the great gallery of Henri II under the gilded coffers and the Primaticcio frescoes were cordial and pleasant.

General de Saint-Arnaud improvised a charade, there was dancing. The Prince, a good waltzer, told Eugénie of his earliest attempts at this art at Arenenberg and Augsburg. He talked a great deal, with the frankness that made him so winning. On the eve of Saint Eugénie, November 14, he presented a bouquet to Mlle de Montijo and gave her the bay she had ridden in the hunt, which she had praised for its cleverness and gentleness. It seemed a quite special attention, but it gave rise to very little talk. The visit came to an end. Political preoccupations dominated all minds. The plebiscite upon the re-establishing of the Empire was about to open. The result was not in doubt, but some further trouble might be feared in Paris, where the harsh repression of the year before had left bitterness. Meanwhile the messages from the republicans in exile in Jersey, in London, in Brussels, the Count de Chambord's manifesto, had no perceptible echo in a nation thirsting for order, in which the middle classes held the primacy. The plebiscite surpassed all the wishes of Louis-Napoleon—7,824,189 ayes to 253,145 noes. France was cheerfully putting her neck under the yoke.

On December 2, 1852, Napoleon III, surrounded by Saint-Arnaud, Magnan, and Castellane, marshals of that morning's making, left Saint-Cloud on horseback, and passed under the Arc de Triomphe to enter Paris. He followed the avenue of glory down which twelve years before, while he was a prisoner in Ham, the coffin of the first Bonaparte had taken its way. He crossed the Place de la Concorde, the Tuileries garden, and on the Place du Carrousel he held a review of troops who acclaimed him with enthusiasm. From the windows of the château the Princesse Mathilde, the Duchess of Hamilton, Eugénie and her mother, old Flahaut, Morny's father, Abd-el-Kader, set free at last, clapped and applauded. In the evening the skies were red with the illuminations in the city, which came out of its long fit of sullenness and smiled too upon the master.

The Emperor did not forget the Prince-President's promise. He wrote to Mlle de Montijo in a tone of respect through which affection made itself manifest. He set out the loneliness of his mind, complained of the anxieties of power, expressed the longing to find a tranquil happiness in which he might take refuge from the strife of politics. Eugénie replied under cover of Bacciocchi; with letters the rough drafts of which were revised by her mother and often written by Mérimée. With perfect propriety she spoke of her reading, gave news of their common friends, expatiated upon Spanish affairs, which she knew better than Napoleon and with regard to which he had asked to be informed. This correspondence gave the Emperor a high opinion of Eugénie's intelligence. He was filled with admiration to find in a young society lady penetrating views and reflections of a superior intelligence, which in very truth her conversation did not suggest.

He had decided to make a short stay at Compiègne soon after he was proclaimed. He put this off so that Mlle de Montijo might be cured of a cold and join the party. The guests were most select. Eugénie and Doña Manuela, escorted by the Count de Galve, a brother of the Duke of Alba, found Prince Napoleon, Princesse Mathilde, Prince Murat and his daughter, the English ambassador and Lady Cowley, the Maréchal de Saint-Arnaud, Minister for War, Drouyn de Lhuys, Minister for Foreign Affairs and Madame Drouyn de Lhuys, Persigny, the Minister of the Interior and his young wife, the Duc de Mouchy, the Marquise de Contades.

Upon Eugénie's entering the drawing-room where they were awaiting the Emperor, the women were very chilly to her. Her success at Fontainebleau roused their jealousy. Only the kind-hearted young Anna Murat greeted her graciously, and also the Marquise de Contades, daughter of Castellane, who had long been friendly with the Montijo ladies.

Following their example, the other women one after another, and keeping watch on one another, abandoned their deliberately set attitudes. When the Emperor arrived the Court was all smiles. He seemed relieved. Subtle beneath his sleepy exterior, he felt the hostility of his relatives and many of his friends hovering round the lovely Spaniard. But possibly the obstacle spurred him on the more. After all, he thought, he was the master, and he would show it if he saw the necessity.

Again there was hunting. Eugénie followed on horseback, beside the Emperor who now never left her. Carrying a little whip with which she often tapped her japanned riding boots with gold spurs, like a Louis XV amazon, she displayed a radiant face: lips half apart over the fine teeth, pink cheeks enlivened by the air, eyes like jewels. At every moment Napoleon turned his head towards her, never tired of looking. At the *hallali* he marked her for the honours of the foot. In the château, in the Galerie des Cartes where the guests assembled before and after dinner, scandal was going at full blast. The Emperor's assiduity towards Mlle de Montijo was plain to every eye, as well as the discreetness of the mother who was never by any chance in their way. The women were indignant at a favour they declared to be simply scandalous. The idea of a marriage never entered their heads. They thought that Eugénie de Montijo was aiming at becoming the Pompadour of the new reign. Perhaps in virtue of her distinguished birth, and seeing that her mother was the soul of cunning, she might obtain from the Emperor, by holding the lollipop up out of his reach, a morganatic union. Nothing more. But it was enough to envenom their speech, to whet their hate. When Napoleon was beside her, eager and smiling, a veritable court surrounded them; then when, in the desire to avoid looks that were becoming irksome to him, he left her to seem busy about the hunt, an ebb was seen. Every one followed the Emperor. On one occasion, being deserted in this way, Eugénie lost herself in the forest. The hunt had been over a long time, and it was almost night. The Emperor, very uneasy, walked up and down the guard-hall, the windows of which opened on the court of the Château. He had sent Toulongeon and Maupas to search for Eugénie. They found her in the great black rides, coming back on foot, leading her tired horse, which had gone lame. When he saw her appear in the court Napoleon restrained himself from hurrying out to meet her. But he could not hide from her how anxious he had been.

The animosity of the wives of ministers and generals made Eugénie's position more difficult day by day. On several occasions she was distressed by deliberate slights. The words "foreigner," "adventure," "intrigue," were too often uttered in her presence. Past patience, she complained to the Emperor one evening in the gardens. His reply was to take a trail of ivy, bend it into the shape of a crown and set it on her brow.

"En attendant l'autre," he said.

Was that a promise? Eugénie believed it was. In these days at Compiègne in which he was escaping from the trouble of affairs, Napoleon felt himself without defence against love. His desire for Eugénie was too strong. She had long resisted it, and now he could resist no longer. On the terrace of the Château, arm-in-arm with Fleury, a tried friend, succumbing to his need to speak, for all that he was so secretive, he praised her grace and her charm. And suddenly, easing his heart, he exclaimed:

"Ah, I am terribly in love with her!"

"I know, Sire," said Fleury, "and I can see that it is not a matter of to-day. But then there is only one thing to do: marry her."

"I am seriously thinking of it," said the Emperor. And they continued to walk up and down, still talking of Eugénie.

There was a review, a ball, finally a play in the theatre built by Louis-Philippe. The company from the Gymnase came and staged "Un fils de famille," a poor vaudeville, excellently played by Bressant, Lafontaine and Rose Chéri. The Emperor had placed the Montijo ladies in the front row of his own box. Eugénie was wearing in her bodice an emerald trefoil, covered with diamond dew, which Napoleon had just given her as a Christmas present. Mocquard, the Emperor's *chef de cabinet* and his confidential friend, Baciocchi, and Fleury, taking sides for beauty, were dancing attendance on them.

Back again in Paris, the Countess confided her hopes to Mérimée. Still sad and grieving for the death of his mother, he spent an hour every day at the Place Vendôme. He gave his friend little encouragement. Although he placed his pen at Eugénie's disposal (it was a game that amused him), he judged it a dangerous venture. That was due to the fact that sticking as he did to his Orléanist ideas, he never managed to acquire a liking for Napoleon III. The Second of December, the Empire, had definitely forced Mérimée to take him seriously. But he judged him to be wavering and uncertain. He would never make up his mind, he thought, to marry Mlle de Montijo. He would have to overcome too much hostility in his immediate circle. The longer the intrigue continued, the more would Eugénie's future life be compromised by it. One fine morning the Emperor's marriage with some princess would be announced, and there would be nothing left for the Montijo ladies to do but to take the first train back to Spain. And even if by some capricious turn of chance the *dynast,* as he called him, were to raise Eugénie to his side, Don Prospero had grave doubts as to his young friend's happiness. A splendid, an unheard-of position, but on the other hand, what anxieties, what risks! The Empire was not solid, and never would be; it would always be at the mercy of a political reverse, of the bullet or the dagger of an assassin.

"I can see," he said to Eugénie, "you still love precipices. I will not try to hold you back. But when you fall I shall hang on to your crinoline."

For the reign of the crinoline was beginning. Without indulging in the excess it was soon to display, it was rounding out the skirt and recalling the old *paniers*. The dancing walk of Eugénie drew from it an added grace.

Sage and prudent and middle-class as was Mérimée's advice, it fell without effect upon obstinate ears. The two Spaniards would not listen to him. He might be an excellent antiquarian, a clever historian, a subtle word-spinner, but what did he know about life?

Chin in hand, Eugénie repeated her usual phrase.

"We shall see."

"You put the worst face on everything," said the Countess. "People don't sit and wait for their happiness, they make it."

To which the writer replied gloomily:

"If they make it, I've never known it."

What is called happiness may assume many shapes, thinks Eugénie. She has known a time of hesitancy, but now she is resolved. If he asks for her hand she will marry the Emperor. He loves her. She does not love him at all, but she does not dislike him. He is delicate and kind, she finds an engaging charm in his smile and his blue eyes. Much older he is than she, but old husbands are the most attentive. And then finally, he is the Emperor. Since she has not been able to choose according to her heart, since, having no settled fortune, and surrounded by perils in which her reputation is crumbling away, she must still marry if she wants to arrive at a normal life; well then, she will marry. But at any rate her marriage will be a fairy-tale marriage, such as no one has ever seen except in the olden time when shepherdesses became queens, a marriage that will be the talk of the whole wide world. Eugénie de Montijo will become an Empress. Not having love—which she would perhaps have preferred—she will put satisfied pride in its place. She will try to be useful to the country over which she is to reign. To a proud and active nature that may bear a distant resemblance to a sort of happiness.

On December 31, she went to an evening at the Tuileries wearing a white satin dress the skirt of which was sprinkled with silver knots. When she entered the supper-room on the arm of Colonel de Toulongeon, Mme de Fortoul, the wife of the Minister of Education, who had already at Compiègne contemptuously taken precedence of her, loudly expressed her astonishment that an "adventuress" should dare to go before her. Eugénie turned very white, drew back and said:

"Passez, madame."

The Salle des Maréchaux was set out with small tables. Eugénie took her place at the Emperor's, where her mother was already seated. She could not eat. The public affront she had received made her look like a corpse. Napoleon saw her agitation, got up and came to her.

"What is the matter?"

Mlle de Montijo murmured:

"Sire, I beg of you; everybody is looking at us."

And indeed all eyes, friendly and malevolent, were fixed upon them.

The Emperor went back to his seat, out of countenance. After supper he offered Eugénie his arm and took her apart, insisting on being told the reason for her emotion.

"I want to know it," he repeated anxiously. "What is it?"

Eugénie, looking into his eyes, replied:

"This, Sire, that I have been insulted under your roof this evening, and that I shall not be insulted a second time."

She shivered as she spoke. Her white bosom heaved and panted in her white dress.

"To-morrow," said the Emperor, in tones of firmest promise, "no one shall insult you ever again."

CHAPTER V

The Decision. January Twelfth

THE next day the Montijos awaited a visit or a letter from Napoleon to ask for Eugénie's hand. Nothing. The days followed in the same silence. Alarmed, the two women asked each other what incident or what influence could have altered Napoleon's intentions. They had always foreseen the opposition of the Imperial family. But they could not imagine that it would beat so violently against the projected marriage. King Jérôme had seemed indifferent enough to the first overtures made by the Emperor. He was old, and too fond of his last pleasures to disoblige a nephew whose coffers paid for them. But Prince Napoleon had said to his cousin:

"The rumour goes that you are thinking of marrying Mlle de Montijo. I know her and her mother. I saw a great deal of them in Madrid. Listen to me, Sire, don't commit this folly! One may make love to, but one does not marry Mlle de Montijo."

With this piece of impertinence he took himself off and sent his sister to the Tuileries.

The Emperor retained a lively friendship for Mathilde. The tender memories of Arenenberg still for him hovered around her heavy beauty. He admired her energy and good sense. In spite of her foolish marriage he had been delighted to adorn her with the title of Altesse Imperiale. On her side she received in his palaces with massive grace, full of pride. When she was with him, and he confessed his intention to her, she did not conceal her disapproval, telling him plainly that he had fallen into the net long skilfully spread for him by the two Spaniards. He shook his head in silence. He knew that Mme de Montijo was exceedingly capable of weaving such a snare. He had little liking for her. But Eugénie, he thought, would have turned her back on such calculations.

However, Mathilde ruthlessly reminded him of the nomad existence of the Countess and her daughter. There had been far too much talk about them. This marriage was unworthy of him, of his race, of his throne. A mere society woman, Eugénie de Montijo would never know how, would never be able to assemble round her the Court the new Emperor needed. Undoubtedly he must marry, to ensure direct successors. But he must make a princely marriage and no other.

Napoleon replied, less perhaps to convince her than to strengthen himself in his resolution. He was a parvenu. Europe was at that very moment making him sufficiently aware of the fact. All his efforts for the past year to obtain the hand of a foreign princess had failed. Was he to humble himself to worm his way into the family circle of kings? No. For by this he would be humiliating France, from which he held his title. Were the sovereign houses turning a cold shoulder to him? As they pleased; he would bid them a polite good-day. He would remain in his own proper rôle, would preserve his character as the people's choice. Free from all dynastic prejudices, he would make his marriage an entirely private matter. He loved Mlle de Montijo. She was of distinguished birth, half French by education; her father had shed his blood for the Emperor. He believed her to be proud and generous. He would follow his inclination and marry her. In this he would merely be once more following in the footsteps of his uncle, in whose prints he had always endeavoured to set his own feet. Eugénie de Montijo, raised to the place of Joséphine de Beauharnais would know like her how to win the hearts of a nation that applauded courage, delighted in romance, and adored beauty.

These arguments failed to pacify Mathilde. At bottom she was never consoled for having by her own fault lost that title of Empress which she would have borne so well. She might admit, for reasons of dignity or national advantage, that it should be given to a princess. But this Spanish woman who had nothing to recommend her but her complexion, her walk, and her eyes! Never would she accept that.

The Emperor allowed her to go away, not discouraged, but melancholy. His family was not alone in attacking him. Among his ministers, Drouyn de Lhuys and Fortoul threatened to send him their resignations. Persigny, that surly mastiff, made a furious scene. Morny, who could smell the wind a long way off, made ready to give way when the Emperor should declare his will.

In any case, external difficulties arise to distract his mind at this moment. The Powers have greeted the Empire grudgingly. England alone, in spite of Queen Victoria's friendship for the Orléans princes, has recognised the new régime. Berlin and Vienna are holding back. The Czar affects an insulting attitude. Napoleon, so intent always on the opinion of Europe, is very much agitated by this diplomatic crisis, as serious for his prestige as for the renown of France. Discussions with Drouyn de Lhuys, with Morny, with Hübner, the Austrian ambassador. . . . Napoleon forgets Eugénie for a moment.

The days go by. The Emperor does not write to the Place Vendôme. The Countess de Montijo, raging, inveighs against Napoleon's duplicity.

"The man is a rogue; he's been a cheat all his life!"

Eugénie, outwardly calm, busies her hands with a piece of embroidery. Mérimée tries to quiet Doña Manuela. Perhaps all is not lost. But he is gravely afraid he was right when at an earlier moment he had counselled more distrust. Cousin Lesseps, who seems always between one dream and the next, but who is at the same time the most practical and realistic of men, has squared himself into an armchair, humming a tune. He has never approved the unbounded views of the Countess. She stops short before him and lays her hand on his shoulder.

"What do you think we ought to do?"

"Go away," replies Lesseps calmly.

"Go away! . . . That's what Paca has been advising us for a long time. But I wouldn't. To go away means giving everything up."

"Who knows?" says Mérimée. "Didn't *the Other* say, 'In love, flight is often victory'?"

Then Eugénie breaks her silence. She too thinks they must go. That is the only proper course for a woman of her rank and station who has been badly treated. Let their trunks be packed. She does not know Italy, and has always had a great desire to see Rome, to kneel before the Holy Father. She will send back the Emperor's emerald trefoil and his letters. She will not write to him; he shall hear of her departure from the gazettes.

She sets a good face to adverse fortune. She has gambled, she has lost. But her heart was never on the table. Nothing in her but her pride is wounded. But that wound is a deep one.

The Countess seems to be resigned at length. She consents to go, and to go to Italy, since Eugénie wishes it. Still, she has received the usual invitation for the Tuileries ball on the twelfth of January. Three days away. Why not appear at this ball? Eugénie would then announce her departure to the Emperor. Perhape a change of front would ensue? A slight hope, a last chance. . . .

"No," says Eugénie, "let us go to-morrow, without a word."

Mérimée backs up the Countess. Lesseps, a diplomat in spirit as well as by profession, says that at any rate, if one goes away, one must never seem to be running away. For Eugénie's reputation, for the sake of the future, it is better to make the proper adieux to the Emperor. Eugénie acquiesces. Lesseps' argument touched her to the quick. Run away . . . she! With such a word she could be brought to face a wilderness of dangers.

It was the first great Imperial reception, in the restored Tuileries. At nine o'clock the guests, ascending the great stair, entered the Galerie des Travées, the Galerie de la Paix, the Salle des Maréchaux, made new by the architect, Visconti. At the four corners of this hall, on huge trophies surmounted by eagles, gleamed the names of victories. Portraits and busts of the Marshals of the Empire peopled the walls. An imposing setting; the women in their spreading dresses brought the brightest colours to it; the men wore uniform or court dress. A brand new and still rigid etiquette prescribed all attitudes. In the salon of the First Consul, Napoleon III, surrounded by his household, received in the first place his family, the ministers, the great dignitaries, the diplomatic corps. Then while the orchestra played Queen Hortense's air "Partant pour la Syrie," he proceeded to the Salle des Maréchaux, followed by that whole cortège. He wore his full dress costume: a general's tunic, white kerseymere breeches and silk stockings. After bowing in all directions, he took his seat in the great chair that had been set for him on a little dais. Coming out from the crowd, Mlle de Montijo, on the arm of Baron James de Rothschild, and her mother behind her escorted by the Baron's son, moved towards the bench on the Emperor's left hand occupied by the ministers' wives. As they drew near Mme de Lhuys drew herself up. Passionately hostile to Eugénie, hard and unbending, she informed her in a loud voice that the places by them were reserved. Napoleon then perceived the Countess and her daughter retiring in the face of this fresh affront. He hastened to them and after some words of welcome, brought them to the velvet stools on which the members of the Imperial family were sitting. Eugénie bowed to the Princesse Mathilde. The daughter of the Napoleons made a slight inclination of the head and did not offer her a hand. She showed still greater impertinence to the Countess, whom she pretended not to see. All around the two women rose unfriendly whispers. The Duchess of Hamilton, the Emperor's cousin, stared them up and down and laughed. Under so many eyes Eugénie slowly waved the feathers of her fan, her features rigidly fixed. She had managed to compose a smile, but she could scarcely breathe, and if any one had spoken to her at that moment, she might well have burst out sobbing.

She was to have time to calm down. The chamberlains in scarlet evening-coats cleared a space for dancing. The quadrille of honour opened the ball. The Emperor danced it with Lady Cowley, the wife of the English ambassador. A little later a master of ceremonies came to fetch Eugénie on behalf of Napoleon, who offered her his arm for the second quadrille. At his side, following mechanically the to and fro of the dance, she answered his cordial phrases with briefest speeches. He looked at her in astonishment. She seemed colourless, her eyes pale with emotion, but never had he seen her more beautiful. At the touch of her hand a wave of blood swelled up in his heart. When the quadrille came to an end, he was about to lead her back to her place. Plucking up all her courage, she told him she wished to speak to him alone.

"Come to-morrow," he answered.

"No, to-night, I want to bid you adieu."

"Adieu?"

"Yes, I am going away."

A brief colloquy, observed by no one. Eugénie, behind her fan kept her head high, her eye proud. But the Emperor grew pale in his turn, he felt his legs give way.

"Come," he said.

And while the orchestra played the prelude to a waltz, he drew her to the salon of Louis XIV, which served as an official bureau.

There, under the portrait of the Roi-Soleil, he made her sit, and bending over her, he questioned her in hurrying words.

"What is it? What do you mean? Why are you going away?"

"I believed your promises and you never kept them."

As he made no reply, and only showed a facial contraction, a kind of rictus that made his cheeks come out, she added:

"You have deceived me or I have deceived myself. I have no wish to embarrass your destiny, nor to compromise myself further. There has been enough talk about us. I have no ill-feeling towards you, but I shall not see you again."

He got up and took a few steps without replying. The music penetrated to them, gay and noisy. Eugénie was glad of it; without this orchestra would not Napoleon hear the beating of her heart?

He thought, pondered. To let her go, never to see her more, well he knew it to be beyond his strength. She was right. He had not treated her as she deserved. . . . All those interests, all those animosities banded together against her . . . And that mother too, who was such a handicap to her . . . By her rebelling Eugénie had recaptured his esteem. He felt guilty towards her. He wished to pacify her, soothe her, to win her again. But how? This time he must lose her or crown her. With slow, deliberate step he came back to her, with features that had resumed their repose, and said:

"You shall not go."

"I cannot stay here longer except on one condition, and you know this is so."

"This very evening I shall ask Madame de Montijo for your hand."

She closed her eyes, dazed.

At last, he surrendered! Because he could not endure never to see her again, he was this time definitely offering to share his throne with her. He had not come to this point without struggles, without sacrifices. This victory, so ardently desired, now that it had taken shape, she seemed to set less store by it. The marvellous marriage did not bring a humble and tender joy, but power, glory, proud shapes that moved among the high places of her soul. At this moment when she was winning so long and hard a game, a game she had thought was lost, she threw all back into the hazard by a noble revulsion. She repeated to the Emperor the objections his family had brought to bear upon him. No doubt it was her desire that not the Emperor's passion alone should raise her to his side, but a more complete consent in which reason should have its due share.

"Reflect again, Sire. I bring you nothing. You ought to marry a princess. . . . Willingly I restore you your word, if you feel the least regret."

"What a ninny!" the Countess would say if he took her at her word.

But too great eagerness to accept would no doubt have displeased the Emperor. This uncertainty convinced him of Eugénie's straightforwardness and sincerity. In his turn he says that he understands her hesitation. The Empire is as yet only a façade behind which a durable régime must be built up. The army is but half won over. A great part of the bourgeoisie turns a cold shoulder on him. Europe is reluctant to admit him into the association of Sovereigns. The French populace seems to love him, but how long will their confidence, their enthusiasm, continue? He might make war and be beaten, or be assassinated. The place he offers her so close to himself, is brilliant but dangerous . . .

She replies that the splendours of the throne alarm her more than its dangers. If she shares good fortune, she will know how to endure bad fortune. And she adds:

"It is not the crown that affects me. What I wish for first and foremost is a constant and faithful affection . . ."

"Yes, faithful . . ."

Faithful . . . Does he not know himself? However, from the perfidious stab lately delivered by the Prince Napoleon he has sustained as it might be a troublesome scratch. He says, with a touch of embarrassment:

"I am about to put a question to you the boldness of which you will please excuse. Answer me honestly. Can you love me? Is your heart quite free?"

Without pausing to reflect, she replies in plain terms:

"Sire, I am perfectly aware that I have been calumniated. My heart has beaten already, and I saw afterwards that it had made a mistake. What is certain is that I have remained Mademoiselle de Montijo."

He kisses her hand, his jealousy completely quenched. He could not doubt her. He has often observed Eugénie, he has found in her exaggerations, caprices, errors of judgment, he has never come upon a lie.

She has remained Mademoiselle de Montijo. And in fact it is much to her credit. So much courted, so flattered, in a society that was sometimes easy and light in morals, poorly protected by a mother who has got her talked about, she might have had excuses for letting herself be carried away. She has been saved by the straightforward nature she inherited from her father. Not very emotional, sensual still less, she has managed to remain pure among tainted surroundings.

Napoleon repeats:

"I shall speak to Madame de Montijo without delay. . . ."

"Speak to her?" says Eugénie. "It would be better to write to her. She must reflect. In her respect for you and her affection for me, seeing the distance that separates us, she may at first be tempted to refuse. She is quick and headstrong. It is never easy to make her change her mind when she has made it up."

Has she cogitated upon this request? Or has it been inspired by her mother? In any event it is very clever. A letter from the Emperor, intended to overcome the Countess's apprehensions, pledges him and will also silence those who would like to pretend that his hand has been forced by some manœuvre.

Napoleon never thinks of that. He sits down at his table, and writes. Eugénie has gone to the window and raising the damask curtain, she lays her hot brow on the glass. Outside the sky and the gardens are pitch black. She hears the scratching of the quill on the paper. Seconds when her life hangs in the balance.

He has risen, she turns round; he comes up to her and holds out his letter.

"Is that right? Are you satisfied?"

His eyes caress her shoulder, he breathes in her perfume. She reads, and droops her head; her eyes fill with tears.

"I told you that you would not go away."

She gives him her two hands with a swift gesture.

"This proof of your attachment is enough. I leave it with you. Think well once again, and if you have a single regret or scruple, do not send it. I shall go, but with no bitterness, only a very sweet memory."

This was said again in a *caballero* spirit. But this time, she is quite certain she runs no risk.

He shakes his head, beaming, and laughs with an astonishingly youthful laugh. Going to the door of his *chef de cabinet,* who to-night has been working late, he calls out:

"Monsieur Mocquard!"

Enter the one-time friend of Queen Hortense, a chilly old dandy whose face is all seamed with wrinkles. His eyes glisten at sight of Eugénie. He knows his master's inclination; he was among the first to approve it. A man of pleasure, he could not hold out against love.

"Monsieur Mocquard," says the Emperor, handing him the letter open, "be so good as to seal this and take it to-morrow personally to Mme la Comtesse de Montijo in the Place Vendôme."

Mocquard makes a long bow, without answering. But the salute of this exceedingly experienced, subtle, knowing servant is the first homage paid to the Empress.

They return to the drawing-rooms, through the Throne-room. On the Emperor's arm Eugénie passes before the high baldaquin of crimson velvet surmounted by an eagle with outspread wings. In its shadow stands the throne, the throne of Napoleon the First's coronation.

The Emperor says in a gay voice:

"There will soon be two of them; I am going to order yours."

They reach the Salon d'Apollon, in which most of those who do not dance are assembled. All eyes are fixed on the radiant Emperor, on Eugénie who displays her smile, and her little head held very high with a slight fluttering of the eyelids.

No one doubts that a decisive step has just been taken. The Spaniard has conquered. At once attentions begin to hover round. As soon as the Emperor has left her, with a tender look, to join the ambassadors, a deferential circle is formed about Eugénie. Morny, the Walewskis, Fould, are exceedingly gracious. Mathilde, who has remained near the dais, leans to her cousin, the Duchess of Hamilton:

"Look: the Montijo triumphs!"

Persigny is biting his nails in fury. Prince Napoleon, shrugging his shoulders, moves through the drawing-rooms and goes away.

CHAPTER VI
Marriage

"THE most difficult thing to do with the Emperor," Morny used to say, "is to get a fixed notion out of his head and to give him a firm determination."

This time his resolution never flinched. The Stock Exchange might fall, the Faubourg Saint-Germain might pull scandalised faces, M. Thiers display vulgar wit—"Napoleon is a man of foresight; by his marriage he is making sure of a Spanish grandeeship for himself, in case he has a fall"—the intimates of the Tuileries might venture a last objection, he simply smiled, with waxen countenance, eyelids dropped, a cigarette in his hand, blinking dreamily at the smoke.

To the Council of Ministers he said simply:

"There are no observations to make, no discussion to open, this marriage is a settled affair. It is my wish."

There was nothing left to do but to be silent in public and to talk noisily at home.

In Paris the opinion of the masses was not hostile. Many of the women were captivated by the romantic nature of the choice. The men talked like connoisseurs about Eugénie's beauty. Since the Emperor had not found a princess who was willing to accept him, he had done right not to wait any longer and to marry to his liking. But in the provinces the bourgeoisie, always great sticklers for forms, regretted that he should have given up the idea of a great alliance. Among the diplomatic corps and the courts the effect was unfavourable. As Hübner, the Austrian ambassador, said, a man who at five and forty, to satisfy a caprice, turns his flame into an empress is calculated to give rise to apprehensions. The Emperor had foreseen this displeasure. It did not displease him to seem to brave a Europe that had wounded his self-esteem.

As soon as Fould, the Minister of State, had gone to the Place Vendôme to make the official request for the hand of Eugénie in the Emperor's name, the Montijo ladies, surrounded by friends and by new flatterers, toured the shops, went the round of the jewellers, the costumiers, and Palmyre and Madame Vignon. So few days to collect the sumptuous trousseau! . . . Parts of it were presently adorning the windows of the Rue de la Paix, before which pressed a continually changing crowd. Napoleon had opened an unlimited credit for his betrothed, an attention appreciated by the Countess, who was deep in financial worries. With uncertain revenues, she had no sense of order or economy, spent too much in order to make a figure, borrowed from her son-in-law the Duke of Alba, from her wealthy friends, exhausted the patience of her tradespeople. The day before Eugénie's betrothal a *huissier* had brought her her dressmaker Barène's bill.

Towards noon on January 22, the Tuileries were buzzing like a hive in the sun. Military escorts, lines of carriages from which came dignitaries in full dress, very busy, glittering with crosses; ministers, *conseillers d'Etat,* senators, deputies, were bowing to one another on the steps of the stairway. In strict order of precedence they went up to the Throne-room, which was speedily filled by their commotion.

A chamberlain announces in a very loud voice:

"The Emperor."

Everybody is silent, everybody turns his head. A heavy little man with bandy legs, in a general's uniform, enters and slowly ascends the steps of the dais, bows, sits down under the crimson canopy without looking at any one. He holds a paper in his hand. Beside him, standing to right and left, are King Jérôme and his son the Prince Napoleon.

Throwing back his great head, Napoleon shows his pallid face, to which the "imperial" gives length. Nervously he twists his heavy moustache. Then rising to his feet he reads gravely and sedately, with a touch of an accent that still smacks of Augsburg, the declaration of his marriage.

I yield to the prayer so often expressed by the country . . . The union I am contracting is not in accordance with the traditions of old-time policy. . . . The lady who is the object of my choice is of high birth. A Frenchwoman at heart, as a Spaniard she has the advantage of not having in France a family to which honours and dignity must be given. Catholic and pious, she will offer to heaven the same prayers as myself for the happiness of France. I have chosen a woman whom I love and respect rather than an unknown whose alliance

Les Archives Photographiques d'Art et d'Histoire

THE TUILERIES

would have had advantages mingled with sacrifices. Without disparagement for any, I yield to my own inclination, but only after taking counsel with my reason and my inmost convictions. And indeed, in setting independence, qualities of heart, and my domestic happiness above dynastic prejudices, I shall not be less strong, since I shall have greater freedom. . . . Before long I shall go to Notre-Dame and present the Empress to the nation and to the army . . .

A commonplace rigmarole that has a bourgeois ring about it. The audience applauds, with acclamation. It is altogether dependent on the Emperor; its enthusiasm could be counted upon. Even so, it brings a little blood into his cheeks. His eyes gleam. Another Rubicon has been crossed.

When the ceremony was over he showed himself very polite and attentive to his uncle Jérôme and his cousin Napoleon, to gild the pill they could not contrive to avoid—a formal visit to the Montijo ladies.

The one-time King of Westphalia, slightly shaking his wrinkled tortoise head, and Prince Napoleon, Plonplon, whose Roman mask was now beginning to grow heavy, climbed the Place Vendôme stairs. They found Eugénie sitting on a stool in the middle of the drawing-room. At first she seemed altogether confused and taken aback. Her hair all loosened, clad in a very simple indoor frock, she looked more youthful than in her sumptuous evening toilettes. The conversation dragged. Luckily the Countess was an inexhaustible fountain. She piled anecdote on anecdote about the court at Madrid, about her travels, made Jérôme laugh. If he had been alone he would have stayed on and on. As they went away, he said to the Prince:

"After all I don't blame my nephew now. He is right to do as he likes."

Homage of an old connoisseur. But he could not get his son to smile.

A little later Eugénie and her mother received another visit, from the Minister for Foreign Affairs, Drouyn de Lhuys. An important man, and essential to the Emperor, he had stood out very stoutly against Eugénie. And yet he had in the old days been received as a friend at the Caseron Montijo when he was at the embassy in Madrid. Eugénie said to him with a good grace, but without beating about the bush:

"I thank you, Monsieur, for the advice you have given the Emperor with regard to his marriage. It was just what I gave him myself."

Disconcerted, the minister tried to find a way out. The Emperor, he could see, had betrayed him . . .

"It was not betraying at all," replied Eugénie, "it was letting me know the opinion of a sincere and devoted friend. I told the Emperor myself that he ought to consider the interests of his throne before everything. But it is not for me to judge if he was wrong or right to believe that those interests can be reconciled with his feelings."

The last phrase accompanied by a smile. M. Drouyn de Lhuys did not resist, he acquiesced in his defeat. There was no longer any question of surrendering his portfolio. He even proposed to the Emperor to place the Elysée Palace at the disposal of the ladies for the period until the religious marriage, fixed for January 30.

In the meantime Mérimée was employed in drawing up the Contract. Going through reams of parchments he wrote down the whole schedule of Eugénie's names, of her place in court, baronies and marquisates, and grandeeships. The Countess laid great stress on this, so did the Emperor, and Eugénie was pleased to see that they filled two pages in a fair round clerkly hand.

Napoleon had himself installed the Montijo ladies in the palace he had occupied for four years as President. He showed great attention on all occasions to Doña Manuela. But he was resolved to keep her at a distance in the sequel. He feared her trouble-making temperament. Mme de Montijo would be nothing of an empress-mother, without influence in politics, without personal rank at Court; she would be nothing in France beyond a foreigner of quality.

Eugénie had a dream of being married by the Pope. An unofficial despatch was sent to Rome. But Pius IX, in spite of all his obligations to the Emperor, did not forget the tribulations that had rewarded the complaisance of Pius VII. He declined the request, putting forward the pretext of his "great age and his infirmities," although he was still young and vigorous.

The Conseil Municipal of Paris had voted a credit of six hundred thousand francs for the purchase of a diamond *parure* for the Empress. Eugénie of her own accord refused to accept the gift.

She wrote a letter requesting that the sum might be devoted to charities. "It is my desire," she said, "that my marriage shall not be the occasion of any fresh burden for the country to which I shall henceforth belong, and my own ambition is to share with the Emperor the love and esteem of the French nation."

She did not refuse the dowry that Napoleon assigned to her, but earmarked it for the *Œuvres Maternelles* and the *Incurables.* This disinterestedness touched a number of still mistrustful minds, especially among the lower orders.

Among his wedding gifts her fiancé had included what he called *Charlemagne's talisman,* a pearl and sapphire pendant enshrining a fragment of the True Cross, which had been sent to the Emperor of the West by Harun-al-Rashid with the keys of the Holy Sepulchre. Charlemagne had turned it into a clasp for his cloak and wore it practically always. On his death, it was left with him when he was laid in the vault of Aix-la-Chapelle. But in the twelfth century his tomb was opened and the reliquary taken out for the worship of the devout. In 1804 the Chapter of Aix had presented it to Joséphine, who wore it at her Coronation. Hortense had inherited it and had bequeathed it to her son. To Napoleon III the sanctity of the jewel meant little. But Eugénie, seeing the fragment of the True Cross, ordered a little reliquary from Froment Meurice. She paid it a kind of superstitious respect, and promised herself never to part from it.

The fever of the hurried preparations animated Eugénie. She received all the time, talked a great deal, made merry. But to her most intimate friends, such as the Delesserts, the Count de Galve, the Bedmars, Mérimée, she appeared strung up rather than gay. The day before the civil marriage, being alone with the Marquise de Bedmar, whom she had known since childhood, and who in Madrid had been the confidante of her inclination for Alcanizes, she suddenly said to her, turning upon her finger a ring that she had kept in memory of him:

"If Pepe was here and asked me to go away with him, I should go."

Then she shrugged her shoulders, and laughed a jerky laugh. Alcanizes, yes, she had loved him. But she had refused him. And now he no longer thought of her, he was far away. When he saw her again, he would perhaps regret . . . But she would be Empress, for ever severed from him by the inequality of their destinies.

From the Emperor she was also separated by age, by birth, by so many ideas and habits. But to unite them there would come, she hoped, ideas, habits, new interests. That he had overthrown all obstacles to raise her to the highest rank, that to her was the behaviour of a paladin, for which she was penetrated with deep gratitude to him. Perhaps she would one day love him? She had seen friends of her own, ice-cold brides, who fell in love with their husbands. But then too, their husbands were not reigning sovereigns. On these heights love, like the air, becomes rarefied and rare. At least she would give Napoleon all the affection her impulsive nature could provide. She would be loyal and devoted to him. She was most grateful to him for his having wished to please her in what lay nearest her heart; matters of religion. For love of her he had drawn nearer to God, had brought him into his speeches, had promised to take communion with her at the Elysée on the actual morning of the religious marriage ceremony. Thinking of this victory, she who so loved to be victorious, she believed she felt for Napoleon a warmth of heart superior to mere friendship.

On Saturday, January 29, at eight in the evening, the Duc de Cambacérès, the Grand Master of Ceremonies, went to the Elysée with two court carriages escorted by a picquet of mounted carabineers. Eugénie mounted the first with her mother, the Duc, and the Spanish Minister, Valdegamas.

At the Pavillon de Flore she was received by the Grand Chamberlain, the Duc de Bassano, Saint-Arnaud, and Fleury. At the top of the great staircase she found the Prince Napoleon, in a bad temper, and Princesse Mathilde, who having decided to come to terms, did it with good grace. Between them, after a ceremonious bow, she walked towards the Salon de Famille where the Emperor was.

Her dress was pink satin and lace. She wore about her neck a string of pearls, the gift of her bridegroom. She had put on a little rouge. But she seemed fatigued and troubled.

The Emperor, in a general's uniform, surrounded by all the

Bonapartes, greeted her, radiant with joy. He kissed Eugénie's hand and giving her his arm brought her to the Salle des Maréchaux. The ambassadors' wives and the ladies of the court rose at their entrance with a long silken rustle.

The ceremony of the civil marriage began at once. The bride and groom were seated at the end of the brilliantly lighted hall. Before a little table M. Fould, the Minister of State, took the place of the functionary. The register in which the marriage was to be inscribed was the same Napoleon I had caused to be prepared for the Imperial House. It opened with the adoption of Prince Eugène, it ended with the birth certificate of the King of Rome. Napoleon III had examined it the previous day. He had looked at the last page, murmuring:

"The King of Rome . . ." and had remained in long contemplation.

Leaning over his table, M. Fould read the formulas prescribed by law.

"Sire, does your Majesty declare that you take in marriage Her Excellency Mademoiselle Eugénie de Montijo, Countess de Teba, here present?"

The Emperor, no doubt touched with emotion, answered in a voice so low that no one heard it.

"Mademoiselle Eugénie de Montijo, Countess de Teba, does your Excellency declare that you take in marriage His Majesty, the Emperor Napoleon III here present?"

Eugénie, forgetting not to roll her *rs,* said:

"I declare that I take in marriage His Majesty, the Emperor."

Whereupon the Prince Napoleon obligingly breathed into his sister's ear.

"Now we know which of the two will lead the other."

M. Fould pronounced the union of the bride and groom. They signed, on the table which had been lifted up to a level with them. Then M. Baroche, President du Conseil d'Etat, handed the pen in turn to the Countess de Montijo, the Prince and the Princesses, the Spanish Minister, who came and signed their names.

The company then passed into the Salle de Spectacle, where a concert was given, the chief merit of which, in every one's opinion, was that it ended almost as soon as it began. A cantata by the ancient Auber, who had been conducting ever since the days of Louis XVI and had seen six régimes flourish and vanish. And with the same pomp and circumstance as before, Eugénie now a sovereign, was taken back to the Elysée to await the ceremony of the morrow.

In the sunshine, preceded by the bands of the dragoons and the lancers, and a long line of carriages and soldiers, the Coronation coach, all plate-glass and gilding, flanked by marshals and high officers of the Crown, makes its way at the sedate pace of its eight black horses in front of the hastily erected stands from the Palais Royal by the quite new Rue de Rivoli and the Place de l'Hôtel de Ville to the precincts of Notre-Dame. All the bells in Paris are pealing their loudest. Minute by minute the guns of the Invalides rend and shatter the air. The cheering rises in gusts, dies down, springs up again. Behind the gleaming windows of the coach the pale face of Eugénie in her veils and the profile of the Emperor, bare-headed, with his great nose sitting on his waxed moustache, bow to the crowd. He smiles with a tender light in his blue eyes. Never, even on the day of his election to the Presidency, has he felt his cup so full. She, dazed by the clamour, the slow piaffing of the horses, the dazzle of light on cuirasses and muskets, the shouts of the people, shuts her lips tight, rallies up her strength, thinks of nothing definite, of no one, not even of the gitana who long, long ago foretold a crown for her, not even of the dreams of her youth, so different from to-day, not even of the future, glorious or terrible, not even of the man of mystery, who to win her has laid France at her feet. She seems to be floating out of space, out of time, out of reality.

For a moment Napoleon touches her hand, holds it in his. She withdraws it softly. That blue eye turned towards her shows a gleam of desire that she finds embarrassing.

It takes an hour to get to the Parvis, with its wooden houses giving the atmosphere of the middle ages. Viollet-le-Duc has decorated it in pompous bad taste. He has not thought the cathedral beautiful enough in its grey hallowed stone, and has hidden it away behind a porch of loud colours, loaded with plaster statues and cardboard shields. Luckily a wealth of flags, great oriflammes, banners embroidered with heraldic figures flap and fly in the

January breezes, as mild in this sunshine as the winds of Spring.

Descending from the coach before Notre-Dame, Eugénie does not take the hand Napoleon offers her. She turns to the square and, as though in a drawing-room, she makes her great Court curtsey to the vast crowd, so supple, so low bending that it always looks as if she would never be able to recover. A storm of acclamations is the answer. An eloquent gesture, which wins thousands of hearts.

The Imperial pair enter the church, where they are received by Monseigneur Sibour, swimming in a scarlet sea of cardinals and bishops. The nave is ablaze with fifteen thousand wax candles. Five hundred musical instruments, backed by the grand organ, play a solemn march. Between the gilded mitres Eugénie glides with footsteps light as air over the white carpet. The women gaze at her in amaze. Her dress is white velvet, with a little coat bodice, sown with brilliants and an endless train of English point lace. Upon her wavy bandeaux, half hidden by the veil, sits the diadem of sapphires and diamonds that Joséphine wore at her Coronation. Her waist is girdled by the sapphire belt given by Napoleon to Marie-Louise.

She is very pale. She kneels down so limply on her prie-dieu sown over with bees that the Emperor at her side imagines that she is going to faint. But she straightens up her little pale head, reassures him with a gentle, almost timid, smile, and dropping her forehead into her hands she begins to pray.

Now she feels herself face to face with the Presence she has adored with profound faith ever since she was born, and will always adore. God is there; she is before Him, trembling and disarmed. It is He who has led her through so many snares and ambushes to this altar where the Crown awaits her. Bending her long white neck in its fairy adornment she prays with all her might, humbles herself within her soul. "I am not worthy, Lord, I have not deserved such gifts. But the power to which I now ascend, I promise to lay before Thee, to employ it to Thy ends and to Thy glory. Eugénie the Empress remains Thy handmaid."

She rises to her feet, appeased, lighter of spirit. The Archbishop, advancing with upraised hands, pronounces the sacramental words and hands to the Emperor the ring, which he places on Eugénie's finger. The organ blares under the lofty vaults lit up by the lights from the great windows. The Mass begins, with the chants once heard by Napoleon and Joséphine on their Coronation day. The candles of the offering are presented to the Emperor by the Prince Napoleon, an imposing figure in his gala uniform, to the Empress by the Princesse Mathilde swathed up in a tunic of gold-embroidered red velvet that looks as though it had been cut out of a curtain.

Forty years before, a brand new glory, a greater one, sought to find the purple in this same shrine. Then also clanged the great bourdon, pealed the organ, pressed to the altar-steps a gathering of princes, captains, lovely and jealous women. And all that greatness of men, as though before the breath of the Eternal, had crumbled and dispersed to be nothing but dust. Who at this moment recalls the *Sacre?* A few old men like Jérôme, the mummified old King in his marshal's coat. His nephew, the fortunate conspirator of December, haunted by generous ideas, bold but secret, with neither splendour nor genius, will destiny treat him better than the soldier of Marengo? Will the new Empire one day crumble away like the first? Or will France, tired of so many storms, allow the fourth dynasty to take root in the very depth of her soil? . . .

Open doors bringing back the skies. Cataracts of sound from the organ. A clamour that sends a shiver down the spine. Along the quays bathed in honeyed light the procession once more, returning to the Tuileries; the Emperor and the Empress show themselves on the balcony. Then having doffed the bridal lace, Eugénie reappears, clad in ruby velvet and sables. She talks gaily and with simplicity, takes leave of the princes and princesses and the dignitaries. She sets off with Napoleon for the little Château of Villeneuve l'Etang, hidden away in the park of St. Cloud, where the honeymoon will be spent. The Emperor's eyes never leave her; he does not try to conceal either his impatience or his joy. Eugénie embraces her mother, all stiff with pride, bids her write this very evening to Paca, who has not been able to come as she was expecting a baby. She takes the Emperor's arm. The night now drawing near makes her seem tired, even sad.

PART II
EMPRESS

CHAPTER I

The New Life

EUGENIE DE MONTIJO was Empress of the French. In this dazzling position, which she had long aimed at, and attained, not without stress and trouble, was she happy?

Happy no one is completely save for brief moments, and marriage did not bring her, and never would bring her these moments of absolute self-abandonment. She never felt more for Napoleon than friendship, gratitude and respect. No love. She was neither particularly sensual, nor emotional: she doubtless never felt the need of love.

In the early days she seemed a little shy before Napoleon. Although he surrounded her with attentions, he rather overawed her. He was not just a husband in her eyes, but the Emperor first and foremost. Middle-class in his ways, in spite of his high breeding, he might *tutoyer* her in public, call her *Ugenie*. Before other people she always addressed him "you," and never called him Louis beyond the fireside. Every time he entered her apartments, even if she was alone she rose and went to meet him. Her deference was not courtesy; it was addressed less to the man than to the sovereign. Upon his auburn hair, which was already falling and would have been greying without a little artificial aid, she always in fancy saw the crown.

Not for a moment did Napoleon regret the adventurous part he chose in marrying her. In any case his mind always cast forward, hardly ever pausing on the past. His violent desire was appeased. He continued to love her, but this love had rapidly turned to affection. In spite of his ardour for pleasure, he revered the domestic hearth, and saw in it a warm and tranquil haven. Eugénie was his wife, and if it so pleased God, would be the mother of his children. A high and sufficient title. He surrounded her with delicate attentions, dreamed of training her gently to her new duties. He found her too careless of forms, she remained too vivacious, too unreflecting for a position that in the very first place calls for calm and moderation. But the habit of reigning, he thought, would mould her. She had a consummate knowledge of the world and its social ways. Once her beauty and her grace had attained something of maturity, when experience had made her more sedate, she would make an incomparable Empress.

He was very different from her. Composite of nature, underneath his kindness moved a certain astuteness and ruse. She was open and direct. He was indulgent; she could keep a grudge. He was patient; she could be angry. But both were proud, both were romantic, and both had the cosmopolitan mind. Napoleon loved France to such a point that he would unquestionably have sacrificed himself for her advantage, her greatness. Yet his education had made him a European first of all. His soul knew no frontiers. Eugénie, Andalusian by birth, with strong English connexions, had lived in every western country. She too, was a European. She spoke English and Italian easily, with Spanish and French. Little by little her duties, her responsibilities, the prospects of the future were to make her really and truly French. But she would never know the narrow nationalism that curbs the judgment.

The Austrian ambassador, who saw a great deal of Eugénie, and in a way that was almost of the family, wrote to his court: "The Empress appears sombre." Sombre? No. Baron von Hübner failed to grasp the exact shade. She was a little *exiled,* only by an effort did she instal herself in a life that was so full of things new, so empty of things old.

The Countess de Montijo left for Madrid two months after the wedding. The Emperor would have liked her to go immediately. He generously gave her, or paid out for her, very large sums of money. She might come back to France when she pleased, a little later, even make a stay, but without being too conspicuous. Eugénie obtained a little delay for her departure . . . for the sake of appearances. At heart she was of the same mind as Napoleon. She had never, even as a child, altogether been in sympathy with her mother. She realised that her mother's freaks, which had already been prejudicial to her before her marriage, would be seriously out of place now that she was Empress. Doña Manuela, disappointed and offended, stormed to Mérimée against the Emperor, whom she comically dubbed *Monsieur Isidore.* Then she resigned herself and started for Madrid, escorted as far as Poitiers by her faithful *cicisbeo.* He consoled her as well as he could.

"It is a terrible thing to have daughters and to marry them. Still, there it is. The Scriptures say that the wife must leave her parents to follow her husband. Now that your duties as a mother have been fulfilled, and indeed no one will deny that you have married your daughters exceedingly well, you must think of living and giving yourself a good time. Try to become a little selfish."

Selfish was what Mérimée was more and more professing to be, and what in the end he undoubtedly did genuinely become.

"I wish to enjoy life and the world without giving anything of myself."

Saying so, he gives lavishly of himself. The *ataraxy* to which he fancies he has attained he wraps about with so much grace that he makes it agreeable. Nevertheless, Napoleon had begun by distrusting him. Before the wedding, speaking at the Tuileries with Panizzi about the political situation, Mérimée had said one day:

"We have just shaved a reef and we are sailing towards the unknown."

The Emperor heard him and whispered to Eugénie:

"This Monsieur Mérimée is not one of the right-minded."

"Sire," replied the girl so earnestly that she reddened, "you do not know Monsieur Mérimée. I have known him ever since I was a child. And in France he has always been our best and surest friend."

Napoleon looked at her affectionately and smiled.

"Then I see that he must become mine too."

He offered him through Eugénie the post of *secrétaire des commandements* to the Empress. Don Prospero declined the honour. At first Eugénie was annoyed with him, then she declared:

"I understand, you would not be sufficiently free, but we will give you something else, and if you don't accept it, it will be a sign that you don't wish to see me any more."

Shortly after he received his nomination to the Senate. This made trouble for him with the Faubourg St. Germain. But he thought he looked well in his blue and gold coat, "more favourable to the complexion," he said, "than the tail-coat of the Académie, with its tarragon embroideries." With scrupulous delicacy he refused to take his new emoluments as an addition to those of his post as inspector of historic monuments, in which he wished to continue. He would never be more than a senator for show, never touch politics with more than the tips of his fingers. However, being far more intimate in the palace than any one else, he will go there at any time he pleases and in any costume; he will jest, scatter the droplets of his wit, amuse the women, turn play-producer, as he did at Carabanchel, author, scene-painter and prompter; he will say pretty nearly everything that comes into his head. No courtier, but an intimate, the "secretary for secrets," with perfect independence, so much that he boasts of never having been baptised, he pokes fun at the clergy and slanders the Pope in front of Eugénie. She takes everything from him for the sake of the old days, and in his turn, the Emperor, who outside the necessary essential parade likes nothing so much as ease and even bohemian ease, will grow accustomed to him and end by liking him.

The Emperor's household was made up in rather makeshift fashion. Napoleon would have liked to surround Eugénie, like himself, with the historic names of the royalty, or failing these, with those dazzling names his uncle had taken from his victories to adorn his marshals. He had very little success . . . refusals, hesitations, reluctancies. He had to be satisfied with a few fine patronymics that threw a gleam of armorial bearings over more modest names: the Duchesse de Bassano as dame d'honneur, the Princesse d'Essling for Grand Mistress, and for ladies of the palace the Marquise de la Tour Maubourg, the Comtesse de Montebello, the Vicomtesse de Lezay-Marnesia, the Baronne de Pierres, the Marquise de las Marismas, delicious under her flaxen English curls.

The Princesse d'Essling, Masséna's daughter-in-law, small, fine, pretty, kind but a little stiff in bearing, applied herself, in conjunction with Count Tascher de la Pagerie, the Grand Master of the Empress's household, to establish the restored etiquette of the old régime in which the Emperor saw the necessary enhancement of a throne that was too brand new.

For the Empress's audiences, when the wives of generals, prefects, high officials were to be presented to her, the Princess used to give Eugénie a short note about each of them, so that the Empress might know what subject of conversation she could broach.

THE EMPRESS ENGÉNIE AND HER LADIES OF HONOUR

From the Painting by Winterhalter in the Louvre

The ladies were introduced into her blue drawing-room in an order arranged beforehand, corresponding with the order of the notes setting out their position, the town they lived in, the number of their children, and so forth. Conscientiously Eugénie would learn her task by heart. When the moment of the reception came, sure of her memory, wearing her most attractive smile, she complimented each lady, spoke to her with an air of personal friendliness. Often they went away enchanted. But occasionally some mistake or some delay caused a change in the order of the presentations, and the result was a terrific muddle. By her visitor's confusion, Eugénie would see that she was on the wrong track. Then she would curtail the conversation, still amiable, but really at heart annoyed. She did not dare to complain too much to the Princess who had brought her into the mess, and who for that matter could not foresee every possible *contretemps.*

Anxious to please everybody, the Emperor, his entourage, the public, Eugénie studied to acquire the tone and the attitudes proper to her new rank. For though she was accustomed to the best society, she was not a princess; she lacked that indefinable prestige possessed by women born close to a throne, which simultaneously attracts and keeps at a distance, gives value to the smallest favour, to the shadow of a smile, to a few hollow words, to a glance.

Returning one night from the Comédie Française where they had seen Rachel, Napoleon praised the nobility of her gestures. Eugénie started. Rachel—why had she not thought of her before! She had known her so long. She was almost a girlhood friend. She sent for her to come to the Tuileries and asked her to give her a few lessons in deportment. Before the long mirror of her dressing-room, she practised the whole series of bows in accordance with the actress's directions—the bow for an official audience, the bow for the grand circle at Court, the bow for a private visit, curtsies, inclinations of the head, the wave of the hand in a familiar farewell. . . . Very rapidly she became past mistress of an art to which her natural elegance disposed her. She brought to it, especially in the curtsey, a correctness, a measured grace of which Rachel might well have been jealous. And when the lessons were no longer necessary, Eugénie continued them; in memory of the first bohemian days in Paris, and for the pleasure she took in hearing Rachel recounting in the palace the rumours of the city, the gossip of the wings, that little light equivocal wind from outside, which fluttered and stirred the dust of the Tuileries. The Empress invited a few ladies of the palace, the youngest ones, and her friend Cécile Delessert, who having married the Count de Madaillac, an ardent Legitimist, never appeared at official parties, but came frequently to the Tuileries to see Eugénie whom she always addressed as *tu*. Mérimée was often there. There was easy talk, easy laughter. Tascher, a comical fellow, afflicted by a heavy Germanic accent, went through his imitations. He gobbled like a turkey-cock: he made himself like the sun, blowing out his cheeks till they were ready to burst. And the moon, too. Innocent games, but a little too familiar. They were found fault with at Court, ridiculed in Paris. One day the Emperor, hearing laughter in Eugénie's private apartment, made his appearance, displeased and freezing. The statue of the Commander. The gay company dispersed. Alone with his wife, Napoleon made a few pointed remarks; she replied with some heat. Then she calmed down and the next day Madame Rachel was invited to bring her lessons to an end. But the Empress, unable to receive her any more, now went to Rachel's in secret.

She goes there in the morning, when she finds a moment's leisure, after her tasks as a wife and a sovereign have been done. Rising early, she dresses very rapidly with the help of Pepa, the swarthy chambermaid she has brought from Madrid, devoted to her but a prey to nerves, jealous, timid, indiscreet, who takes bribes on every hand in return for the influence she has *not* got. Eugénie barely listens to her, but talks to her much too confidentially and Pepa sometimes abuses her confidence. Then Eugénie receives her coiffeur, Leroy, her dressmakers or tailors, Virot and Lebel, Laferrière or Palmyre. She attacks the daily task of the official post-bag with her grave secretary, Damas-Hinard: petitions, complaints, requests for assistance. After this, with one of the ladies of the palace she mounts into her little landau—wall-coloured, as she calls it—and often slightly disguised, for she loves dressing up and going about incognito, with a false fringe, spectacles, a hat that makes her look old, a mantle that shrouds her up, she perambulates Paris here and there. Not always to see her friends or do her shopping. She goes, too, on her charitable errands. She wants to see for herself, not to be deceived, unlike the Emperor who gives immediately, without counting, without knowing. "Don Quixote charity" Eugénie calls it. In this way she relieves genuine distress. Sometimes she visits hospitals, asylums, crèches, workrooms, without warning and on the spur of the moment, delighted to take the doctors by surprise, to flurry the lady patronesses, and to send the big caps of the Sisters bobbing in agitation.

She comes back to the Château, lunches alone with the Emperor, in the Louis XIV salon where the pair seem lost at that little table under the great lustre. After a chat in her *cabinet de travail,* Napoleon smokes a few cigarettes, she lies down on her *chaise longue,* skims through the newspapers, reads the books that have been picked out for her; on occasion, if it is history or science, makes a brief summary of them in a school exercise-book, to help her to remember them. She knows the gaps in her education and steadily tries to fill them little by little.

She reads with her own eyes; her reader, Mme de Wagner, need not give herself all those airs under her blond wig, decked at night with leaves and flowers: her post is nothing but a sinecure. Eugénie would never have the patience to listen to her ceremonious delivery. She also writes her letters, quantities of letters and often very long ones, to her mother, to Paca, to her intimate friends. She writes anyhow, on her table or on her knee, naturally and vivaciously, just as she talks, in a large, firm, almost virile handwriting. She hardly reads over what she writes and her spelling is not too certain, but she is the first person to poke fun at herself over it.

This working-room, which she had arranged to suit her own ideas, was the only one in which she felt at home "in this big furnished house, which is what the Tuileries is." ("But," she adds, laughing, "I have known worse ones.") The panelling and woodwork were mahogany, the walls stretched with green striped grogram. On either side of the red marble fireplace, upon which was a rather poor statue, were the portraits of the Duchess of Alba and Anna Murat, who had become very dear to Eugénie since the day she had so bravely declared herself for her. On another panel was Napoleon III, by Cabanel, a careful portrait and an excellent likeness. Thick crimson hangings, furniture in the Empire style, satin-covered thickly-wadded chairs, great quantities of knick-knacks on the tables and what-nots, dwarf palm trees, artificial flowers, photographs of every size. The whole effect was heavy and stuffy, but homely and cosy. The Empress had made a nook for herself behind a glass screen adorned with live plants. There she used to sit in a low armchair, with her feet on a stool, protected from the fire by a green silk screen. On a little table at her left was her blotting-pad, her inkstand, her goose-quill pens, a few bindings with Marie-Antoinette's arms (found for her by her old friend, Louis de Viel-Castel, an ancient flame of Doña Manuela's), an "Imitation" that had belonged to Queen Hortense, the miniature of Count de Montijo, blond, pale, a little sad, with one eye bandaged. All these in a set order. Eugénie was very particular, and when any article or any piece of furniture was out of its place she was cross and scolded her servants in a hoarse voice in which her Spanish accent reappeared.

Now we have come to the hour for the daily drive. Another task, but a necessary one, for she would like to win Paris, which, the excitement and wonder of the marriage once over, lends an ear to evil tongues and looks askance. She climbs to the Champs Elysées in her big barouche with four horses and postilions followed by a squadron of lancers. Her golden hair shines under the hat surrounded by a filmy veil. A few cries of *"Vive l'Impératrice"* go up. She bows her head with a graceful movement, shows her distant smile. The carriage reaches the Avenue de l'Impératrice, swings round the lakes, then comes back to the Tuileries in the setting sun that transforms the Arc de Triomphe to a gate of ivory opening on heaven.

Then a little relaxation, a little intimacy, a few visitors who are friends. But sometimes there are still belated audiences to be given. "What a deadly trade it is!" thinks Eugénie. But she applies herself to it conscientiously. And often when the first moment of sheer boredom is past, her part carries her away and she finds pleasure in it. Especially when she is receiving some foreigner of quality or a diplomat accredited to Paris. She puts them at their ease, adopts a tone of equality, displays a familiar graciousness that surprises some, but which enchants the majority.

Now she must dress for dinner, and quickly, for Eugénie always waits till the very last minute, so plunging her ladies, who are slower, into despair.

The table is laid in the Louis XIV salon, gleaming with lights and gold. Twelve or fifteen places as a rule, never more than forty, round Napoleon and Eugénie. The circle is held afterwards in the Salon d'Apollon, where coffee is served. The Emperor plays a game of patience or talks with his guests, very amiable and often very gay. The Empress talks rather disjointedly. If a word strikes a spark, she answers it flowingly, jumps without reflecting from one subject to another, evokes incidents of her former life, her travels, discusses a fact or an idea with interest and animation, even a trifle overkeenly. Then may be seen Eugénie de Montijo as she was yesterday, under less illustrious panelling among a group of less deferential friends. And just as she used to then she calls for dancing now. The perfection of bodily pleasure, she loves dancing like a true daughter of Andalusia. When she was a girl she never left a ball till she was tired out and ready to drop. The mechanical piano rolls out a Strauss waltz. Or Mademoiselle de Tascher arranges the figures of the lancers quadrille, just imported from England, and all the rage. The finale is a farandole through the suite of drawing-rooms. At eleven there is tea. The Emperor slips away, and before her bowing guests Eugénie sinks into a delicious curtsey addressed to all in which each one can fancy he finds a private particular share.

So it goes on ordinary evenings. But twice a week at least the palace is thrown open for a gala assembly.

"Your Court must be brilliant," Jérôme has told his nephew. The former King of Westphalia, frivolous to the very grave, is not wrong. For Europe as for France a new régime can take root only in splendour.

And the Château that saw the quiet receptions of Louis-Philippe, the modest vigils of Marie-Amélie bending over her embroidery between two wives of officers of the National Guard, while princes and princesses, stiff with boredom, were pinching themselves in the shadows of the drawing-room to keep awake, the Château blazes up with a vast array of candles. Dinners, concerts, plays, balls keep the diplomatic corps, the high administrative and military society on the stretch. The Paris shopkeepers sell gold lace, feathers and silk in masses and vie with one another in putting up the imperial arms on their windows.

Luxurious as the fêtes are, the Court still remains in a state of improvisation. It presents quite striking contrasts. The Archduke Maximilian of Austria, who had come to Paris as a kind of scout, writes as much to his brother, Francis-Joseph. "Everywhere one has the impression of something momentary." And Mérimée, although a dignitary, has no confidence. He murmurs, "It will last as long as it can. But the end is a trifle alarming. . . ."

The most enticing baits have not tempted the greater part of the Faubourg Saint-Germain. It keeps aloof from the official world. The uncle would have devoured it in the long run, the nephew barely manages to nibble at it. Around them the sovereigns have, and will have throughout their reign, nothing but the Bonaparte family, eaten up with jealousies and hatreds, the members of their Household, the nobles of the First Empire, a few converted Orléanists, the State officials—ministers, senators, prefects—many officers, a great number of foreigners also, ambassadors and distinguished residents or travellers, especially English and Spanish. Never was a court so motley and so cosmopolitan. In the evenings Eugénie appears in dresses of faille, satin moiré, lace, all cut very low, which show off her magnificent shoulders, her low bosom, laden with the crown jewels. The eighteenth-century fashions are her favourites and she would like to see them revived. Thanks to her, the crinoline becomes shorter and less stiff. But bodices, skirts and trains will long continue to be burdened with ribbands, with knots, flowers, artificial pearls and so forth. Eugénie makes very frequent changes of dress. She is coquettishly well aware of her beauty, and the Emperor takes pleasure to see her in fine feathers. At the same time, though there are envious folk who inveigh against her extravagance, her evening frocks very seldom run to more than a thousand francs. Many of them are "freshened up" at home, and worn again without any one recognising them. As for her white satin shoes, so tiny that no ordinary grown woman could get her feet into them, Eugénie wears them once only. Then she sends them to the orphans of the convents of which she is patroness, for the first communion.

Accustomed to society life from her earliest youth, these Court gatherings are not burdensome to her. In any case she receives less like a sovereign than a great lady, going from one to another, just as she pleases, joining groups without ceremony, with the evident desire to please everybody. An instinctive aristocrat, she certainly prefers women of birth to the dowdy, over-dressed wives of certain parvenu ministers or generals. Nevertheless, she tries not to let it be seen. Well served by her acquaintance with European circles, she displays a special amiability to the diplomatic corps. She has a particular liking for Hübner, the ambassador of Francis-Joseph, a subtle person with hard eyes and perfect manners. Eugénie talks to him freely, not concealing her leanings towards Austria. She takes no interest in affairs, but in politics she already has her preferences. The Hapsburg monarchy attracts her by its proud maintaining of traditions, its old-world distinction. She often has Hübner placed on her right at dinner so that she can talk to him. She makes bold one evening to take him to task for having too large an acquaintance among the royalists.

"You spend a great deal of time," she says smilingly, "in the society of our enemies."

"Do, please," returns the diplomat, "say the society of my old friends who are in any case too well bred to play at politics in an ambassador's drawing-rooms. But," he added slyly, "I am anyhow assured that the Empress sometimes honours Madame Delessert with her visits. And yet it is no imperialist atmosphere she will find there."

"That's quite true," says Eugénie frankly, "and I am rather proud of it. The Delesserts were very kind to me when I was still going into society: I never turn my back on my friends."

"Will the Empress allow me to follow her example?"

"That's settled," said she, laughing.

In spite of all this good-will, even of deliberate effort when she is tired or depressed, she does not please everybody. The men, captivated by her beauty, are generally favourable. But many of the women criticise her caprices, her failings, her indiscretions. They find fault with her elegance, which they call ruinous, take her reserve for arrogance, her warmth for hypocrisy, her gaiety for brazenness. Under formal deference and the flattery of attitudes Eugénie divines the spite and animosity and at moments she is discouraged.

"It is hard," she tells Anna Murat, "to make a success in this country."

So then, and occasionally after a word from the Emperor who finds the Court too "lax," in order to afford less grounds for criticism, she resolves to confine herself within a stricter observance of etiquette. She has little love for it, but comes to find it useful, except among a little circle of trusty friends. The life of the palace thus swings between two poles: caprice and strictness, which is rather complicated for the habitués, who have to pass too quickly from unconstraint to stiffness. And vice versa, for constraint never lasts very long.

When she is at Fontainebleau or Saint-Cloud in the early days of summer, there are picnic luncheons, rustic entertainments in flounced frocks and top-hats, when Mérimée "*officier de bouche* for the nonce" insists on horrible cookery recipes, poisons the dishes with garlic and raw onions to get the ladies of the palace crying out in protest. The Empress laughs heartily, the Emperor walks up and down saying nothing. Don Prospero is not at heart particularly proud of his buffooneries.

"I do believe," he says, "that there has never been a time when the world was more stupid than now."

Yet in spite of these pleasures, and though she did retain a few old friendships, and made some new ones, the position to which Eugénie had risen made her lonely and lonely without remedy. The Emperor could never become a companion for her; he was too much her tutor and her sovereign. Certainly they had their conjugal privacies, hours of intimacy and unconstraint. But the claims of duty curtailed or repressed them. Like Napoleon III, or even more, being a woman, Eugénie had turned her back on a normal life. Her first intoxication had now passed. Now she saw before her a long road lined with chamberlains and pitfalls. She had chosen it, and would have chosen it again. Empress! She had not, perhaps, the head or the heart of one. . . . She would strive, little by little, to acquire them.

She accompanied the Emperor on the visit he paid in April 1855 to Queen Victoria.

In the Crimean War, undertaken under the pretext of protecting the Holy Places, Napoleon had sought an occasion for strengthening his position in France by playing a great part, and if possible the foremost part, abroad. He saw in it also a means of drawing closer to England, even to the point of an alliance, a solid pivot for his policy. Eugénie was broadly aware of these plans. Abandoning its first aloofness, the Court of St. James's, being extremely interested in barring Russia's path to the East, had become cordial. Victoria had sent the Emperor the will of Napoleon I, which had been brought back from St. Helena. The first successes in the Crimea, Alma, and Inkermann, then the hardships and difficulties that followed, the terrible winter endured in the trenches before Sevastopol, had tightened the link between the two powers. Napoleon wanted more: he wished to establish personal relations with the royal family. An object-lesson to Europe—the French Empire raised to the same plane as the ancient monarchies. Persigny, his ambassador in London, disclosed his wish to meet the Queen and Prince Albert in order to consult with them as to the conduct of the war. Victoria, hard-set in cant and dynastic traditions, was not at all eager in the matter. But, as her hand was forced, she invited the Emperor and the Empress to Windsor.

For the first time Eugénie was about to be treated as a sovereign in a foreign country. She knew that the English pair were distrustful and puritanical. They had to be won over. The importance of the stake troubled her. In the sea mist, on the deck of the *Pelican,* which was carrying her to Dover, she walked up and down, wrapped in a dark plaid, nervy, only answering yes and no to the Emperor, who was delighted at the idea of once more seeing England, which he loved and where the memories of his youth awaited him.

At Windsor the Queen, common and sure of herself, embraced Eugénie, who blushed as she repeated the stereotyped phrases of courtesy. The children saved her. She admired Edward, a fresh fair lad, caressed shy little Victoria, who fell as she made her curtsies. These attentions touched the Queen. For the evening gala, Eugénie's suite was for an hour in a turmoil of the most cruel embarrassment. Félix, the coiffeur, had been so seasick that he could not attend her. Colonel Fleury came to make his excuses to the Empress who laughed and said:

"I hope he won't kill himself in despair. Look, my women have pretty well taken his place."

Her trunks—another *contretemps*—had not arrived. She borrowed a very modest white and blue dress from one of her ladies and when, by the help of innumerable pins, it had been fitted on to her, with no other ornament than forget-me-nots in her hair and bodice, she came into the drawing-room where Victoria sate enthroned, adorned like a shrine with the Koh-i-noor in the middle of her forehead. Such simplicity pleased every one. The air perceptibly thawed. The Emperor by his good grace, the quiet unobtrusive sympathy that emanated from him in private talk, made the Prince Consort forget his misgivings. Eugénie took courage, became animated. Her friend of old days, the Marchioness of Ely, one of the Queen's ladies, made her path smooth, told her the right people to show attention to. Her beauty, her charm, softened by an air of restraint, her good English, tinged with a slight foreign accent, made the conquest of the Court.

"She is a Scotswoman," they said. "Look at that hair. And what a complexion, how dazzling! . . ."

Throughout the days that followed the cordiality of relations continued to increase. While Napoleon, Albert, and the ministers conferred upon the situation of the troops in the Crimea, Victoria and Eugénie, freed from ceremony, proceeded like a pair of real friends to exchange confidences. Victoria gave matronly counsels to Eugénie, who had already had two miscarriages, had been slow in recovery, and was afraid she would never have a child. She ought, the Queen advised her, to avoid very hot baths in future. Eugénie promised. Then the round little Englishwoman broached politics. Her love for Albert, her affection for her children never made her forget to reign. The Empress admired her experience in affairs, her active authority. This hereditary Queen who desired to see to everything herself, and who in fact exercised a quiet yet vigorous control over the gentlemen of her government, seemed to her a superior being. She, by comparison, was only an ignorant young woman, who presided over the entertainments at her court, but had no share at all in power. She knew the essential substance of events when once decisions had been reached, like the majority of her subjects. Victoria impressed upon her to take greater interest in them for the future.

Les Archives Photographiques d'Art et d'Histoire

QUEEN VICTORIA

From the Portrait by Winterhalter in the Museum of Versailles

She believed, from the example of her own household, that two united and confiding minds can govern better than a single head.

Eugénie would undoubtedly need to apply herself seriously. But by mastering the facts of history, by collecting the opinions of eminent men, she would form herself by degrees, would insensibly acquire a wise influence over the Emperor, would enlighten him on side issues, on consequences that by himself he would not perceive. For instance, Napoleon was proposing to go to the Crimea and take command of the Anglo-French forces. Now that was an imprudence that Eugénie ought not to allow him to commit. If he met with a check, his prestige would be ruined. Paris was by no means certain. A revolution might always break out there. . . .

Inclining her beautiful head, Eugénie listened with deference to these confident phrases that were slowly to make and leave a profound impression on her mind.

It was late. The Marchioness of Ely came to inform the Queen that luncheon was waiting. But the Council had not come to an end. Eugénie pressed Victoria to break in on it, "to go and fetch their husbands."

"I should not dare to disturb them," she added, "but Your Majesty can."

The Queen rose and, followed by Eugénie, went to the room where Napoleon, Albert, and the Secretaries of State were in full discussion. She knocked at the door, opened it and asked "if they had to wait any longer." All the men stood up. The Prince Consort said they were "on the point of coming." However, as they delayed overlong, the ladies finally lunched without them.

A review in Windsor Park, a Chapter of the Garter held by the Queen, in which Napoleon in full costume was invested as a Knight, a procession through London, a ball at Buckingham Palace, a gala performance at Covent Garden, a banquet in the Guildhall, hours of splendour, full hours, sometimes a little heavy. Eugénie pleased everybody by her nicely discriminating attitude. The English were quick to note that she was less a sovereign than Victoria. While the dumpy Queen sat down with majestic unconcern at the theatre or at the ball, beside her the Empress, lovely and noble as a fay, instinctively looked behind her to make sure of her chair. She had not had chamberlains all her life.

The royal couple never tired of praising their guest. Their ministers were not displeased to see the tightening of the alliance. Napoleon was enchanted by the hearty hurrahs that broke out along his route through this London where seven years before he lived in exile, almost unknown. (As they passed by King Street he pointed out to the Empress the house where he had lodged after his escape from Ham.) Eugénie was proud to have succeeded in a difficult Court, to be able now to call herself the friend of the most powerful queen in Europe. At the departure from London, after many embraces, Victoria, Eugénie, the children, the ladies-in-waiting, all wept as they promised to see each other again soon.

Every day between four and five, Napoleon rode in the Champs Elysées, with one of his favourite aides, Edgar Ney or Fleury. A week after his return from England an Italian republican, Pianori by name, fired two pistol shots at him, but missed. The fellow was knocked over and disarmed. The Emperor cried out:

"Don't kill him!"

Then saluting the crowd that had hurried up, he started at a gallop for the Tuileries to prevent Eugénie's hearing of the outrage from any one but himself. He ran up the great stair and dropped into a chair in the Empress's room, wiping his forehead. Gaily he told her of the abortive attempt.

"A strange country," he said, with his friendly laugh, "where they shoot at people like sparrows!"

His indifference was natural and unassumed: he did not believe in danger. He had already escaped the plots of the White Queen and the plain of the Virtues. Believing himself a man under care of Providence, raised up to re-establish order and happiness in France, he constantly repeated that he ran no risk as long as he had not ended his mission. And unquestionably it was far from being fulfilled.

He embraced the Empress and went to his own apartments humming an air.

All the rest of that afternoon Eugénie remained by her fire, pensive and shivering. Brave though she was, she was afraid. The splendour that surrounded her could not deceive her as to the real want of solidity of the régime. Little more than founded as yet, and still unstable, it depended solely on the existence of the Emperor. And that existence, whatever he might pretend, remained hanging on a thread. If Napoleon were killed, the Empire would fall into dust. Once again it would be riot, pillage, the Tuileries invaded and overrun, as in the days of the Revolution. Eugénie thought that she would perhaps end like Marie-Antoinette. A few days later she could not refrain from confiding to Hübner that she was haunted by that memory. She told him that at the moment of her marriage some one had come to offer her a lace veil that had been worn by that unhappy Queen. Eugénie was tempted, but had not enough money to buy it. What a surprise for her, a surprise delightful and melancholy at the same time, when the first thing she found on opening the *corbeille* presented by her betrothed was this very veil. Was that not a sign of destiny? The ambassador reassured her to the best of his ability. She did not listen to him. And presently she murmured:

"To die on the scaffold. . . . I would rather be assassinated in the street! . . ."

She insisted vehemently with the Emperor that he should not go to the Crimea; in this she followed the advice she had in England. She also spoke of her own fears. Without too much resisting Napoleon gave way to her entreaties. He had some peccadilloes to atone for. And other ties, tender and fleeting, kept him in Paris at that moment.

By nature he was unfaithful. Any and every petticoat stirred him. In the Court itself he had allowed himself a few "distractions." He was often the cause of great trouble to Hyrvoix, the chief of his private police, through his escapades in Paris. Eugénie knew nothing of these. But she had been informed that barely six months after his marriage Napoleon had seen Miss Howard again. Eugénie treasured a sentimental idea of love. The momentary hunt after pleasure disgusted her.

"What is the matter with all these men?" she would say. "I can't understand them."

Already on more than one occasion her voice had rung out in tones made guttural by anger, when, alone with the Emperor, she had overwhelmed him with reproaches that he well deserved, and certainly deserved even better than she imagined. Then she denied her door to him. Napoleon sought to return to favour by the aid of presents, of little delicate attentions. In the end she allowed herself to give way. The customary way of life began again. But these trials made her more abrupt at first. Sometimes she had moments of bitter regrets. One evening she said to Pepa, who was helping her to dress for a dinner:

"Ah, Pepa, I should have been happier if I had been Duchess of Alba!"

And without a doubt she sometimes had a thought of Alcanizes.

CHAPTER II
The Child

THE Crimean War, long, difficult, murderous, and as near as possible ending in a deadlock, had come to a fortunate end by the taking of Sevastopol. The Peace Congress had assembled in Paris. Baroche, the President of the Conseil d'Etat, was giving a dinner to the delegates of the sovereigns, and was still at table when one of the Emperor's orderly officers was announced. The Empress was about to be confined, and by the terms of the Constitution the President must be present as a witness.

For three days the birth had been expected at any moment. The whole entourage of the sovereigns were buzzing about the long dark corridors, the ante-chambers, the drawing-room. The Emperor did not go to bed, did no work. He hardly even left the Empress's apartments, talking to one person and another, eaten up with anxiety.

The pains had begun. Between the spasms, Eugénie took a few steps, bending double in accordance with the advice of the doctors. In her room all gorgeous with gilding, and the ceiling covered with amorini, every candle was lit. From without it looked almost as though it was on fire. After two or three painful, torturing steps, Eugénie would halt, lean on a piece of furniture, on an arm, utter a moan. They held her up, laid her on the horrible state bed with its heavy curtains, and once more with teeth clenched and eyes closed she resumed her torment.

She had a presentiment that she would not survive the ordeal, that she would die in her confinement. Her mother, come in haste from Spain, encouraged her with voluble phrases. The Emperor took her hand and caressed it gently, his blue eyes full of tears. She pushed both of them away, held her breath, and then suddenly uttered a strident cry from a rigid breast. . . .

The doctors were anxious. There had been serious imprudence. To prevent the birth from taking place before March 20, a solemn date in the annals of the Empire, Doctor Dubois had during the last few weeks made Eugénie take a dose of laudanum every morning. And besides, the child was badly placed. Conneau, the Emperor's old friend, had warned him that it would be necessary to use the forceps. It would endanger the child's life, but the Empress was becoming exhausted. Incapable of further effort she was losing breath and her pulse was failing moment by moment.

The third doctor, Jobert, being laid up with an attack of indigestion, Dubois and Conneau, terrified of the responsibility falling upon them, brought Doctor Darralde into consultation. After a brief colloquy in a window recess the last named went to the Emperor.

"If the instruments are not used at once," he said without ceremony, "your wife will be gone in half an hour."

"Do so," said Napoleon, sobbing: "above everything save her."

The great chamber, through which there hovered the smell of ether, was full of people. Besides the doctors, the Countess de Montijo, the Princesse d'Essling, the wife of Admiral Bruat, who had been appointed Governess to the future Child of France, the Marchioness of Ely, sent by Queen Victoria, Pepa making a nuisance of herself with her lamentations, other women of the household staff. Behind a screen Prince Napoleon, gnawed by anxiety over a birth that according to the sex of the infant would give him or cost him the succession to the Empire, Prince Louis Murat, Fould, Abatucci, and Baroche were exchanging a few words in low tones and often looking at their watches. In the dressing-room close by, between the lavabo and the bath, Princesse Mathilde and Princesse Murat, livid with fatigue, were asleep in armchairs.

At three in the morning the child was born. Conneau dashed to the blue drawing-room where the Emperor was tramping up and down.

"Sire, it is a son. Come!"

Madame Bruat presented the child to Napoleon. He hardly looked at it, ran to the bed, surrounded by princes and officials of the Crown. After a short period of unconsciousness Eugénie was opening her eyes. Kneeling on the steps of the bed, close beside her, she saw the Emperor who was smiling with wet cheeks, strangely aged by his fears, his tufted beard quivering.

"Is it a girl?" she asked in a weak little voice.

"No," said the Emperor.

Delighted, she almost shouted:

"It's a boy!"

Napoleon, no doubt fearing the effect of too strong an emotion for her, shook his head.

"Then what is it?" murmured poor Eugénie.

But the Emperor's gratitude and tenderness as he covered her with kisses assured her better than any words that she was the mother of a son. And she was alive! She closed her eyelids to shut out the sight of Prince Napoleon's furious monocle, and seemed to fall asleep, weary but at ease, as though bathed in the waves of a happiness such as she had never imagined.

The Emperor had gone out of the bedchamber, radiant with delight. He dashed through the drawing-rooms, going up to the dignitaries and court officials who crowded them, crying in a loud voice:

"A boy! It's a boy! I am so happy!"

In the expansion of his heart he embraced the first five or six persons he encountered, both men and women. He recognised nobody. At that moment he was no longer the Emperor, but a man who after all that agony was intoxicated with his joy. At length recovering himself, he said very loudly:

"I cannot embrace you all, but I thank you for your sympathy and interest."

Meanwhile Prince Napoleon, overturned from his position of heir presumptive, and not attempting to conceal his anger, was making a strange scene. In the Empress's cabinet into which Fould and Baroche had pursued him, pen in hand, he refused to sign, in his quality of first prince of the blood, the birth certificate of Louis-Eugène-Napoleon, Prince Imperial. Prince Murat intervened, was repelled, then Morny tried. At the end, in exasperation his sister Princesse Mathilde threw at him:

"I've been here for twenty-seven hours. How much longer must I stay? What does this freak of yours mean? The evidence is there. Your bad temper isn't going to alter it!"

She held out the pen to him threateningly. . . .

Day was breaking. The cannon were beginning their thunder to announce to Paris the birth of the heir to the Empire. The Prince shrugged his shoulders and signed, so roughly that he made a smudge on the document. After him the members of the family and the high officials signed. The guns continued to make the windows shake. From the gardens of the Tuileries where the crowds were packed there rose a long murmur of joy.

Eugénie was not to learn till afterwards of the insolent behaviour of her "cousin." She was highly indignant at it, but not astonished. All the efforts she had forced herself to make to overcome his ill will had so far brought her nothing but affronts. He remained the open enemy of the "Spaniard," the "adventuress," as he dared to call her even in her own court. He absolutely hated her. Still more now perhaps than before the marriage, for now his fears had taken on flesh, and Eugènie's child had robbed him of that crown on which he had reckoned, and for which he was waiting as a belated compensation from destiny. For him Napoleon III was merely a bastard of Hortense's. It was he, the son of Jérôme, and, in spite of his German mother, so like the Emperor by his *mat* complexion and Roman countenance, who ought to have been occupying the throne. He was always willing to forget that without the cold daring, the visionary calm of his cousin, the perils of Strasbourg and Boulogne, the six years of the fortress prison, the risky coup d'état which might well have brought him to the scaffold, the Empire would not have been restored and he himself, a jealous kinsman, would never have been in a position to grumble and pocket gifts and apanages. He had no mind to reflect, to relax his attitude, to recognise the kindnesses done to him. His dark obstinate nature fought against it. He never resigned himself. He knew his own worth. It was that of a chief—he had not alone the mask of a Cæsar, but the brain and the hand. He could have done great things, but fate persisted in refusing him the means. An Emperor aborted, Prince Napoleon was always to remain in the background, never rising to the first rank, which alone could show what was in him, never acting except in a subordinate position, and therefore not acting well. His last hope gone with the birth of the Prince Imperial, there was nothing left for him except to torment his relatives and eat out his heart.

His sister Mathilde shows more wisdom; as a woman direct ambition is forbidden to her. But she has no love for Eugénie, and

Les Archives Photographiques d'Art et d'Histoire

PRINCE NAPOLEON

From the Portrait by Hebert in the Museum of Versailles

if she maintains decent outward behaviour towards her she can never forget that in her young days she herself was betrothed to Hortense's son, and that with more patience—or more love—she would be Empress to-day. She still twists round her finger the little ring Napoleon gave her long ago at Arenenberg. . . . Eugénie in her eyes remains an intruder. She never speaks of her without constraint, avoids naming her, always says *She* in a tone that betrays her spite. Proud of her descent, through her mother, from Saint Louis and from Mary Stuart, of claiming cousinship with all the Kings of Europe, above all else, of being the niece of the Emperor, whose very footsteps she adores, she looks down on this Castilian countess, who as the result of a caprice has been run up to the very top of the mast. Eugénie has tried to win her, like her brother, by her attentions, a gentleness that is not really in her habits, and which comes hard to her. She admires her frankness, her imposing mien. Rebuffs have tired her out in the end. And at bottom everything holds them aloof from one another; mind, beliefs, manners. Let them then live apart, the one in her Tuileries, her great châteaux peopled with officials; the other in her chosen court in the Rue de Courcelles or the Rue de Saint-Gratien, where artists and writers give free play to slanderous gossip and light, loose, gay talk. Mathilde will keep the Emperor's friendship, to which she holds above everything else. Eugénie respects this feeling and will make no attempt to assail it. She will remain generous, since she has the upper hand.

Her recovery was long and troublesome. The doctors had warned her that another confinement would certainly kill her. She stayed for several weeks lying at full length on a *chaise longue,* receiving no one but a few intimate friends of the old days, to whom she showed her baby pet asleep in the sumptuous cradle presented by the City of Paris.

"Isn't he pretty?" she repeated naïvely. It was quite true. A fine child, strong and good-humoured. He was like his mother, had her eyes, but his complexion was darker already, and his ash-blond hair came from the Emperor. An imposing household had been appointed for him. Two governesses, under Madame Bruat, two nurses who suckled him by turns. Too weak to nurse him, Eugénie did everything for her baby herself, like any common mother, dressed him, rocked his cradle, sang him the little tunes of her native Spain. When she was able to leave her bed she went with him to St. Cloud. By degrees she regained her strength under the cool shades of the park, and only came back to Paris when it was time for the baptism of the child whom the whole country called *the little prince*—a pet name that had never before been bestowed upon a son of France.

The baptism was magnificent. The Pope for godfather, the Queen of Sweden for godmother, and a pomp and ceremony still more splendid and dazzling than for the imperial wedding. Wrapped in an ermine cloak and carried by Madame Bruat, the child rode through Paris in a coach, amid the most enthusiastic acclamations. The Emperor, in the carriage that followed next behind, continually saluted the people now wholly won over. By his side the Empress bowed her head at intervals. Lovelier than ever, she was wearing blue; her brow, her neck, her arms shimmered and sparkled with the Crown diamonds. She was silent, overcome by a joy that sent the blood from her lips and left her no strength for speech. But she was thinking. She was thinking that this son, who had caused her such suffering, was about to root the Bonaparte dynasty within the soil of France, for a future loftier still than that of the Capets. The task of social and political regeneration begun by Napoleon III would be fulfilled and completed by her son.

When Cardinal Patrizzi, the legate of Pius IX, had sprinkled the water on the forehead of the prince, and when amid the pealing thunder of the organ the Emperor lifted him up in his arms for a long moment to show him to the crowd, Eugénie was obliged to sit down, twisting her hands to keep herself from crying out.

On the way back to the Tuileries the Emperor said to her:

"Such a baptism is as good as a coronation."

The Coronation the Pope had denied him. . . . Napoleon was perfectly right. A baby in its lace robes was doing more to rally France to the régime than the victories of the Crimea and the success of the Congress of Paris. This new happiness was the crown of the young fullness of the Empire. Europe that lately was uneasy or mocking was now cordial towards him. Vanquished Russia smiled on him. Austria and Prussia made haste to pay their attentions, sent him their princes and their statesmen. England remained a steadfast friend. Pius IX sent the Empress the Golden Rose and sang the praises of the new Constantine. Napoleon III was becoming great with the twofold prestige of power and ideas. He appeared as the sovereign of progress. The Exposition Universelle, the first of them all, had displayed the wealth of the country, wealth that had been prepared, but repressed by a miserly reign, and was now expanding and blossoming. Now began those great public works that were to transform Paris and the principal cities of France. Everything succeeded with Napoleon. "What luck he has!" said the people always ready to burn incense before successes. And in the royalist drawing-rooms or the republican garrets, bewildered before this torrent of fortune, those who did not become adherents at any rate held their tongues.

The Court had never shone with such lustre. Neither had Paris, where Society, roused to life once more, was dancing, supping, flinging hoarded crowns about in a frenzy of elegance and pleasure. In the Tuileries, at Saint-Cloud, at Fontainebleau, in honour of the foreign princes who had come in battalions, Frederick William of Prussia, the Grand Duke Constantine, the King of Bavaria, the Queen of Holland, the Queen dowager Maria Christina of Spain, the Duke of Brunswick, fête followed fête without a pause. The first costume balls ventured on by Eugénie had originally almost created a scandal; soon the whole city was giving them.

The idea had been Napoleon's. He loved disguise just as in politics he loved secrecy. Then too, dressing up sometimes gives an opportunity for a fleeting adventure . . . To the sound of the Viennese waltzes, under the illustrious panelling of the Salle des Maréchaux or the Galerie de Diane, there were stealthy amorous tête-à-têtes. The Empress knew it and was jealous enough (from pride if not from love) to try to keep an eye on him. But she was defeated by a maze of pretences and complicities in which her suspicion lost its way.

Spring evenings at the Tuileries . . . A triumph of everything resplendent—beauty, money, happiness. Under the crinoline, that distant daughter of the Renaissance farthingale, the prettiest women of Europe, the most elegant, the lightest and gayest, are all there, dancing, chattering, laughing, all striving to intrigue, to climb, to please or simply to appear. Countess Walewska, a pale gleaming blonde, with a high forehead under a crescent of sapphires. The son of the Corsican and the Pole had married her in Florence, after his long liaison with Rachel (now consoled by Prince Napoleon). An insinuating and exquisite creature, who conquers all too many hearts, the Emperor's like other men's, and cannot bear to see them unhappy. Eugénie has taken a liking to her for her distinction, her supple grace. For a long time she will refuse to believe that she has granted her favours to Napoleon. Countess de Persigny, not beautiful but ravishing, and very eccentric, whose naïve impoliteness has driven her husband to give up the embassy in London. The freedom of her language, which no circumstances can ever check, is no ill match for the freedom of her pleasures. Persigny, morose and prone to anger, a bulldog immersed in politics, is her excuse; she ends by deceiving him.

The Marquise de Contades, daughter of the Maréchal de Castellane, is an old acquaintance of the Montijo ladies, who once upon a time in Paris had opened the gates of her own world to them. Long brown eyes, and the slenderest of waists, she is adroit, easy, astute and kind. Her tastes are those of a horsewoman; she rides up the stone stairway of her Château. The Duchesse de Malakoff, a poor cousin of Eugénie's, pleasant but not gay, who has allowed herself to be married to Maréchal Pélissier, the conqueror of Sevastapol. She often sulks at the Empress, who endures her ill-humours. Is she not a relative? And her husband is so old! Countess de Solms, fantastic in body and in mind, a far-off cousin of the Emperor against whom she inveighs and frets. Napoleon smiles at it all till the moment when, having exhausted all his patience, he gets angry and packs her off out of France for a change of cabals and love affairs. Countess Le Hon, the wife of the Belgian minister. Another blonde (the coming of Eugénie was the dawn of the era of the blondes), with a fading complexion. Long has she held Morny in her thrall, Morny who to see her more easily had built a pavilion in the Champs Elysées adjoining his house. Paris called it the *niche à Fidèle*. This dreamy beauty—a daughter of the banker Mosselmann—is a formidable business woman. When Morny married the young Princess Trubetzkoi, in Russia, she was only pacified after a particularly severe settlement of accounts in which the Emperor was obliged to intervene to prevent a scandalous explosion. Eugénie feels very little drawn to her. None the less she keeps on terms with her, for the sake of the

Les Archives Photographiques d'Art et d'Histoire

COUNTESS DE CASTIGLIONE

diplomatic proprieties, and because she receives all the politicians of the day. The Duchess of Hamilton, a cousin of Napoleon III and one of his earliest flames, the only woman, along with Miss Howard, to whom he confided the hour of the coup d'état. Hostile at first to Eugénie, she has gradually settled down to good relations with her. The Empress is sorry for her. The Duke is a drunken fellow who every night goes alone or with loose women to drink in the cabarets. Unhappy, but proud, she throws herself into the whirl of society. The Countess de Castiglione, the Florentine patrician, the princely courtesan sent by Cavour to ensnare the Emperor and incite him to war against Austria. The Walewskis presented her at Court and Napoleon had her at the first glance.

When Easter was past, every Monday, after the family dinner that brought together at the imperial table all the Bonapartes then in Paris, Prince Napoleon, Princesse Mathilde, Prince and Princesse Charles Bonaparte; Princesse Baciocchi, the Gabriellis, Roccagiovine, Primoli, a little ball began at the Tuileries in the Salon du Premier Consul, for persons in direct relations with the sovereigns. This is what was known as the "Empress's little Mondays"—*les petits lundis de l'Impératrice*. To be invited was a favour greatly coveted among the converts of society and in the official world. The men appeared in evening coat, knee breeches and black silk stockings. The Emperor and the officers of his household wore dark blue tail-coats with velvet collar and gold buttons stamped with an eagle. The women gave free rein to sumptuousness. Besides the ladies of the palace, all the inner circle gathered about Eugénie: Princesse Anna Murat, the Duchesse de Malakoff, Mesdames Walewska, Bartholoni, de Morny, de Persigny, de Galliffet, de Pourtalès. When the dancing began, the Empress sometimes let herself be tempted by a waltz, but usually she installed herself in the next drawing-room in the midst of her usual group: the Austrian ambassador Hübner, the handsome Prince Reuss, the Prussian minister, the English ambassador Lord Cowley, the Aguados, Mérimée, Edouard Delessert. They talked without constraint on the events of the day, the news from abroad. Often the Empress left her chair. If she became warmly interested in a subject, she spoke excitedly, forgetting the place and the hour, giving vent to her impressions, her sympathies or her prejudices with no further thought of her position. A glance from Napoleon, who was never far away talking in a low voice with a minister or a diplomat sometimes warned her to give another turn to the discussion. Questions of pure politics seemed more and more to interest Eugénie. She brought to them what for her might still pass for reserve. Yet since she became a mother she had put on an assurance, a weight that she had previously lacked. Every one admired her memory and the easy flow of speech that when she had a cause at heart rose to eloquence . . . The announcement of the cotillion brought her back at length to the Salon du Premier Consul. The accessories were simple enough, paper flowers or paper ribbands . . . Anna Murat and the Marquis de Caux nearly always directed the game. The Emperor did not disdain to take part in it. He had retained very youthful tastes; under his outward air of mystery he adored gaiety, games, practical jokes, when he felt himself among friends. About one o'clock there was a stand-up supper at a well-laden buffet, and the imperial pair retired almost immediately after. These "Mondays" Eugénie preferred to all the Court receptions. She recaptured in them something of her atmosphere of former days.

Spring suspended the life of the palace. St. Cloud, for which the Empress had little liking, which she found too close to Paris to feel really in the country, St. Cloud nevertheless brought her some relaxation. Under the chestnuts of the park she held out her hands to help the first footsteps of her little boy. He was chubby and gay. As soon as he was firm on his legs, he would have a little grenadier's uniform. For him the charming house of Villeneuve l'Etang where his parents had spent their honeymoon, in memory of which Napoleon had given it to the Empress, reserved a flowery garden where Tascher's children came to play with him, under the watchful eye of his English nurse, fat Miss Shaw. In an outhouse near at hand, Eugénie had set up a dairy, but a more modest one than Marie-Antoinette's at Trianon.

In the middle days of summer, when the long evenings linger on, she used to drive out with the Princesse d'Essling or the Marquise de las Marismas, in an open vis-à-vis, a *würst,* along the banks of the Seine, towards Meudon. She would even go as far as Versailles. Eugénie walked around the hamlet, on her friend's arm, under the stars. She dreamed of the poor Queen whose luxury and whose misfortunes dwelt in her memory. And then through the great empty gardens where the fountains in her honour flung up their murmuring plumes and aigrettes lost in the blue of night, she would make her way back towards St. Cloud. As though suddenly eager to arrive, she urged the horses on; the Emperor did not like these escapades. He said as much. Eugénie disobeyed him two or three times, to assert her independence; then she gave them up.

CHAPTER III

The Regent

A LANDAU rolling through the black streets, between lances swaying to the full trot of the horses, towards the lighted peristyle of the Opéra. Two indistinct silhouettes, the Empress in white, the Emperor in black evening coat and tall hat. In front of the theatre a pretty large congregation of sightseers greets them with acclamations. Then three explosions, as loud as cannon shots. All the lights go out simultaneously. Dreadful cries, hoarse death-rattles, the tramplings of terrified horses . . . At length torches give their red light. The street is strewn with bodies. A secret police agent, Alessandri by name, helps Eugénie to climb down from the imperial carriage lying on its side. Her dress is splashed with blood, but she is untouched. As Alessandri is bleeding, she bids him go and have his hurts dressed immediately. People press round her in anxious solicitude; she shrugs her shoulders, she is actually more incensed than frightened. Anger keeps her up. The Emperor has slight grazes on nose and cheek, his hat is pierced by a number of splinters from the bomb. Cool and calm, he takes measures for the wounded. Instead of going back to the Tuileries they appear at the Opéra to the accompaniment of a tremendous ovation. Eugénie bows, manages to smile, and conceals under her scarf the spots of blood now turning black on her dress, the starchy stiffness of which sends a shiver through her when she composes her hands on her knees.

Orsini has just reminded Napoleon III of his Carbonaro past. Once upon a time he swore to set Italy free. If he does not make up his mind at length to keep his oath, he will never escape the vengeance of the Italian patriots.

In spite of his cool courage the Emperor is stricken. He knows how unavailing is the best police against a handful of resolute men. This is the fourth plot. It came within a trifle of succeeding. Now that he has a son—a son so tenderly beloved—Napoleon owes it to him to live. The Empire, in short, what is it but a military dictatorship? A three-year-old Emperor, under the tutelage of a foreign mother, could never reign. Once his father is gone, he will be driven out, killed, at the very least dethroned (perhaps to the advantage of Prince Napoleon, highly capable of playing the part of Philippe-Egalité). A magnificent unstable stage effect, which maintains its illusion only in fêtes, the man who erected it well knows how artificial it is. He cannot find in it the false but amazing security a principle bestows. Born of a brutal success, one well-placed shot will bring it down in ruin.

In vain does Eugénie strive to recapture her poise of mind. She feels herself delivered over to chance. None the less she faces it like a caballero. To Mérimée who insistently urges her to take precautions when she goes out she replies:

"Pooh, if we thought of that we should never sleep again. We must just disregard it and trust in Providence!"

But she does think of it, unceasingly. She loses her appetite, becomes thin, her cheeks are pale. Her imagination runs wild. Romantic by nature, she believes that clemency would have power to disarm hatred. She entreats the Emperor to pardon Orsini. She has been struck by the dramatic aspect of his life, the self-denial of his principles; she cannot, with so many other women, refrain from admiring his lofty defence before the Assize Court. Napoleon hesitates, balancing between his natural generosity and reasons of state. For a moment Eugénie prevails. But the reasons of state return to the attack. The Conseil des Ministres, the Conseil Privé are against a pardon. Such a piece of weakness would outrage public opinion. The outrage had left so many dead on the street! The future of the dynasty—the same words always serve—would be in jeopardy. Easy though he is, Fould ventures to say:

"Do not forget, Sire, that it was French blood that was spilt in the Rue le Peletier!"

The Emperor droops his shoulders; he gives in. However, since he leaves Orsini to his death, he knows he will have to make another and a heavier sacrifice to Italian liberty, which cries out against him from the depths of its tomb.

He set about it conspirator-fashion, according to his usual habit. "Scratch the Emperor," Guizot used to say, "and you will find the political refugee." All his plans were wrapped in secrecy. Unknown to Walewski, to Fould, to his friend Conneau, the envoy to Turin, he invites Cavour to come and see him in the summer at Plombières, and comes to an agreement with him to set a war on foot against Austria, which if it does not free the whole of Italy, is at any rate to make of Piedmont a great State carried all the way down to the Adriatic. Napoleon will be paid for his soldiers' labours by the cession of Nice and Savoy. Thus the treaties of 1815 will be torn to shreds and the Empire "will give France her dowry." A family alliance will join the two crowns by the marriage of Prince Napoleon to the Princesse Clotilde, the daughter of Victor-Emmanuel.

The next thing is to obtain the assent or the neutrality of the powers. England is less friendly since the Orsini outrage. Persigny has annoyed her by his truculent airs. An interview at Cherbourg with Victoria gives poor results. Prince Albert, German in his very marrow, no longer sees in Napoleon anything but an adventurer. Engénie in her white and lilac silk dress takes the utmost pains. She asks the Queen if English feeling "has really become hostile to France."

"No, no," replies Victoria, "these are only clouds; another wind will clear them away."

Nevertheless, she seems ill at ease. The good days of the Entente are past.

Next the Emperor sounds the Czar. He sends his cousin Napoleon to Petersburg to exploit the ill-feeling aroused in Russia by the menacing attitude of Austria during the Crimean War. The Czar rejects the idea of an alliance, but will remain neutral. As for Prussia, that helmeted enigma, it is impossible to know what she wants or what she will do. No doubt as usual she will sit on the fence, ready to bleed the vanquished and to carry the train of the conqueror.

No more than to his ministers did the Emperor disclose his intentions to Eugénie.

"Not a word to any one," he reiterates to Napoleon when he sends him to the Czar. "And in particular be careful of the Empress who suspects nothing."

Suspects nothing? That does not last long. Put on the alert by Walewski, who is opposed to a fresh war, she penetrates the Italian project. And just as Prince Napoleon and Mathilde, out of ambition and a desire for glory, press on its fulfilment, so she strains every nerve to thwart it, to discourage the Emperor.

Her sympathy for Austria, a devout monarchy, covered with a

lichen of prejudices and ritual, has not decreased. She still has a specially privileged welcome for Hübner. But above all, oh, above all! she fears that if Northern Italy unites around Piedmont a national movement may develop in the rest of the peninsula. And in it the temporal power of the Pope would be swallowed up. Pius IX, her son's godfather, from whom she had received the Golden Rose! She sees her honour and the honour of Napoleon involved in ensuring that no possible harm shall come to him. She has always thought and acted as a fervent Catholic, and in these last few years her devoutness has increased still more, perhaps by reason of her troubles as a wife. Devoutness, too, not bigotry. She speaks very little about religious questions. If she honours the clergy, she gathers very few black robes around her. Her feeling for the Pope proceeds more from a chivalrous care than from any uncompromising faith. She explains herself to the Emperor, walking up and down her room with long strides, her jaw clenched, her hands behind her back, her blue eyes turning black at the thought of St. Peter's patrimony destroyed, the pontiff despoiled, perhaps an exiled wanderer . . .

Napoleon evades her questions, tries to cajole her fears.

"You will be overwhelmed," she cries. "The Italian liberals will not be satisfied with incomplete results. They will want Rome!"

"We shall know how to bring them to reason," says the Emperor. Not only would the Pope keep his states, but he would become the president of the new Italian confederacy . . .

She shrugs her shoulders. Napoleon, she reflects, is recaptured by his 1830 chimæras, he is once more becoming the "slave of Mazzini."

Her attachment to the Emperor no longer prevents her from judging him, and, in private, opposing her own opinion to his. Since her talks with the Queen of England, and especially since the birth of her son, she takes a keen interest in foreign policy. She reads history assiduously. Foreign envoys and French ministers now are surprised to hear her broach serious subjects on which her clean-cut though somewhat circumscribed views, her logical realism, and her impeccable memory sometimes leave them at a loss. Henceforward it not seldom happens that she influences a decision of the Emperor's. He finds in her, despite her prejudices, good sense and intellectual rectitude, he believes—what an example he had in his mother!—in the intuitions of women.

After lunch, when he comes to her room to smoke his cigarette, he sometimes asks her advice, or rather he pours out before her the overflow of his dreams. She is all attention, happy at last to be of use and to count for something. Often he goes away, with a word of apology, before she has said all she wishes.

"I have an appointment," he murmurs, and leaves the room with his heavy tread.

With regard to what she calls "the Italian venture" she is not listened to. In vain she reiterates to Napoleon that he is going to play "a mug's game," that France would remain all the stronger by keeping weak States for neighbours. He smiles without answering, or if pressed too hard replies:

"Nothing is settled; we shall see. . . ."

He moved towards his objectives, as though dominated by a force that nothing could have overcome. At the diplomatic reception on the first of January 1859, he made a calculated outburst.

"I regret," he said to Hübner, dropping his eyes, "that our relations are not so good as I should wish, but pray write to Vienna that my feelings towards the Emperor are unchanged."

Prince Napoleon left Paris a few days later to marry Princesse Clotilde of Savoy. Piedmont was arming. England proposed a congress. Turning aside from his chosen path so as to avoid a quarrel with Victoria, Napoleon assented. But blinded Austria refused and by a headstrong stroke that put her in the wrong before all Europe she sent her troops across the Ticino.

The French army set out for the Alps. One morning a number of regiments filed by in front of the Tuileries, their bands in front, cheering the Emperor. He saluted them with a hand, grave, pallid, sometimes biting his lips to overcome his emotion. Beside him Eugénie, holding the Prince Imperial in her arms, displayed the child to those young men many of whom were going to their death, who gaily waved their képis at him. She wept. Her tears fell, too heavy for her to hold them back. Yet a little while and the Emperor too would leave her to take the supreme command. He was absolutely determined upon it. It was, he assured her, a matter of his prestige. He imagined that he had military talent.

He also, like his uncle, would have his campaign of Italy. He was haunted by a thirst, a need for glory.

At the Tuileries, on May 10, a farewell Mass was celebrated in the Chapel by the Archbishop of Paris. Eugénie, kneeling on her prie-dieu, her head buried in her hands, summoned up all her courage.

She went with the Emperor in his train as far as Montereau. At every station a crowd acclaimed them. The war was popular, especially among the working-classes. The old dreams of 1848 were still working in men's souls. Dinner was served. The Empress distributed religious medals among the officers who were going with the Emperor and shook hands with them all. Then without showing any signs of weakness, although for six years she had never been separated from him, she embraced Napoleon.

She went back to Paris, the country's Regent.

Letters-patent communicated to the Senate gave her the exercise of sovereignty during the Emperor's absence. She had not asked for it. She even at one time thought that these functions should be conferred upon King Jérôme. But Napoleon thought it a good opportunity for Eugénie to undergo her real apprenticeship as a sovereign. The country would grow accustomed to seeing her govern; she would in this way win additional authority and renown, invaluable in case, if he should perish, it should be necessary for her to take the power into her hands during her son's minority.

She was happy in so high a token of esteem. Nothing could touch her more. Her pride forgot in this the misconduct of Napoleon in falling once more into the arms of the Castiglione, which in recent months had disturbed their harmony. She now thought only of fulfilling her task well, of plying her trade, as she said in all seriousness to Mérimée, who coming one morning to St. Cloud, found her committing the Constitution to memory. He was on his way back from Carabanchel where the Countess de Montijo had made in his honour fêtes that recalled those of the good days. But he had very soon crossed the Pyrenees again when he discovered that Doña Manuela, the incorrigible, was once more plotting to marry him. Eugénie laughed, and then asked him in Spanish for news of her sister, her relations and her friends in Madrid. Almost at once she looked at her watch, tucked away in the belt of her dress.

"You shall lunch with me, Monsieur Mérimée. We shall be able to talk better then. I must go to the Council now."

She presided every alternate day (sometimes at St. Cloud, sometimes at the Tuileries) over a Council of Ministers at which occasionally there were also King Jérôme and certain members of the Conseil Privé. Attentively she listened to the reports and took part in the discussions. Her questions and her rejoinders showed the growing interest she took in affairs. After the session she made one or other of the ministers give her a detailed explanation of the questions she did not understand. Rouher adroitly consulted her apart from his colleagues. Hence she had taken him into great favour.

"When peace comes," she would say, "I am going to miss all this!"

At home everything remained tranquil. The wheels of the administration went round normally. The public had accepted the Regency with a good grace. The official newspapers overflowed with eulogies upon the precocious wisdom of the Empress, the ripeness of her judgment. Eugénie took it all in. She displayed decision on the occasion of a cabmen's strike, which she put down by giving orders to replace them by soldiers from the transport service. Her energy was lauded to the skies.

The news from the war was good. Although the army lacked provisions and munitions, although the high command showed divisions under the ignorant and slack direction of the Emperor, the vigour and dash of the troops brought success. On June 4, the guns of the Invalides had saluted Magenta. Dawn was breaking at St. Cloud when there came the telegram from Solferino.

Great battle—Great victory.
NAPOLEON.

With such an awakening, Eugénie could not remain in her bed. It seemed she would stifle, she must needs move about, talk, display her joy. She rose, dressed by herself in a moment, and went down into the park, where she announced the news to the sentries and the guard.

The National Guard presented her with a golden wreath of laurel. When she went with the Prince Imperial to Notre-Dame for the *Te Deum,* her carriage, already filled with bouquets by the troops, was smothered with flowers. The little prince laughed, very red and excited. He threw the flowers back at the crowd, flinging them kisses too. His mother could not make him sit in his place. She kept repeating:

"You will behave nicely in the church, Loulou, won't you?"

The child replied jauntily:

"I shall behave just like a man."

He was three. He kept his promise and never budged throughout the service.

On the way back to St. Cloud, he said to Miss Shaw:

"I would love to have another *Te Deum."*

He was never to have another. Never again.

Two days before, the peace preliminaries had already been signed at Villafranca.

These proud moments had been interspersed with times of strain. The Czar Alexander had sent his aide-de-camp Schuvalov to Eugénie to inform her that Prussia, jealous of the French successes, was mobilising. Her movement of troops towards the Rhine provinces had actually begun. The danger was extreme, with the frontier left bare, and the country empty of trained soldiers. In the Council meeting that followed, when Walewski disclosed the Prussian menace, the ministers seemed overwhelmed. Eugénie preserved a firm countenance. King Jérôme proposed to mobilise 300,000 National Guards instanter. The majority of the Council approved this. Eugénie would have none of the decree.

"I shall not sign such a confession of our military weakness!" she declared.

The old king rose up, heavy and sententious.

"My niece," said he, "you are exposing France to invasion."

The Empress rose in turn and replied to the last of Napoleon's brothers.

"In any case, uncle, I shall not behave like Marie-Louise. Even if you were to advise me to it, no one would ever see me running away before the enemy!"

When the Council broke up she kept Walewski. They talked for a long time together and agreed that it was necessary to treat with Austria without delay. For all her courage Eugénie was in a hurry to see this rash war at an end, and the Emperor no longer exposed to danger. Walewski for his part had never ceased to pray for mediation. Prussia's attitude did not allow further hesitation. That very night Eugénie wrote to the Emperor. Napoleon too was eager to get out of a campaign the perils of which he had appreciated too late. The slaughter of the battles had cast him into a vertigo of distress.

He felt himself diminished in the eyes of the army. Without tactical knowledge, an armchair general, he had several times lost his head. Eugénie's information decided him. In spite of Prince Napoleon (who presently gave way to his reasons) he sent Fleury at once to the Emperor Francis-Joseph to propose an armistice. Francis-Joseph clearly saw the awkward position of the French. But he was afraid of a rising in Hungary, where the ashes of 1848 were still smouldering. He treated.

When amid the general joy that masked the haste and unaccomplishment of the peace, Napoleon had come home, Eugénie gave him an account of matters in hand. She showed him the very full notes she had taken, which formed as it were the Diary, clear and vivid, of her Regency. She laid stress on foreign questions, her relations with the ambassadors, the difficulties she foresaw where England was concerned, with regard to the annexation of Nice and Savoy . . .

Her attitude, her every tone had changed. Napoleon, who was a very quick and clever person, felt it from the first few minutes of his return. This participation of Eugénie in power, short as it was, but in which she had engaged all her intelligence and energy, had raised her to the status of an immediate co-worker, an equal. The gay or shy young woman, who was looked on as frivolous, engrossed above all things in elegancies, had turned into an Empress.

He was by no means annoyed at this. For he was less jealous of power than he had been at the beginning of his reign. Age was beginning to sit heavy on his shoulders. That Eugénie should develop such a taste for affairs did not displease him. In that he saw a safeguard for the future. He saw in it too a lightning-con-

Les Archives Photographiques d'Art et d'Histoire

THE EMPRESS EUGÉNIE
From the Portrait by Winterhalter in the Louvre

ductor for conjugal storms. Absorbed in politics Eugénie would be less intent on reproaching him for his infidelities, which were always many and varied.

Henceforth she appeared at the Council on every occasion when an important question was under discussion. For her this was the reward of her Regency, the work of which was magnified by her lively imagination. She could have no doubts, after all that newspaper flattery and the homage of the ministers, of her rare aptitude for government. As she had been advised by Queen Victoria, who was enamoured of joint husband-and-wife reign, she meant, in close association with Napoleon henceforth, to tame the flight of his chimæras, to incline him to measures of conservative authority on which she felt the welfare of the country and the future of the Prince Imperial depended. She would bring a woman's address to influence foreign policy, which had always interested her and which now was a passion with her. In this matter she had quite simple ideas. She linked the national interests with her own personal feelings, her aversions and sympathies; she distrusted Russia, feared Prussia, hated the new Italy. She wished to nurse the entente with England, which had now become decrepit, and to draw Paris and Vienna together, because of her tendency to absolutism and the better to defend the Pope against the enterprises of Victor-Emmanuel, who now, strengthened by the possession of the Milanese, was setting out to eat the whole Italian artichoke leaf by leaf.

Eugénie's participation in affairs, which was considerable and which was to become still greater, was certainly not to the taste of the Emperor's relatives, nor of his old advisers. Princesse Mathilde gave vent to her disapproval at her dinners in the Rue de Courcelles, among her poets and painters. Prince Napoleon, whom Eugénie openly thwarted in his Italian interests, displayed vituperative anger. He attributed to the Empress's influence all the high-handed measures, all the administrative and police restrictions of a régime that did not as yet dare to trust freedom. He accused her of clericalism, showed her as bringing France into subjection to the plans of Rome. If any mistake was made in home or foreign policy, he and his friends immediately set her down as responsible. Eugénie was to suffer terribly from this enmity that all her attempts at conciliation only served to aggravate. Prince Napoleon was unquestionably the one man of whom she was afraid. He impressed her by his violent language, the intelligence that emanated from his sallow mask, and the strange ascendency that through so many squabbles and quarrels he maintained over the Emperor. Unable either to pacify him or to be rid of him, she endured and hated him. But with a hatred that could never match his hate for her, bitter, deadly, the hatred of a dispossessed Corsican who took the Court for his island *maquis.*

Morny, much too clever, did not quarrel openly with her. He had long since taken Eugénie's measure, knew that she had the mind and the tendencies of a man, found it natural that she should wish to play a part in affairs. He would flatter her without seeming to, with his supple arrogance befitting a grandson of Talleyrand, but would know how to oppose her projects when they ran counter to his appetites, his intrigues, his bargainings, and yet without incurring her ill-will.

Persigny had always loved the Emperor jealously, teeth clenched, headstrong, surly, faithful. He detested Eugénie since her marriage. That she should have any share in power exasperated him. In the *Conseil des Ministres,* when he had become Minister of the Interior once more, he was never afraid to interrupt and contradict her, with the rudeness of an imperfect upbringing. If for a mutual understanding to have the same ideas is enough, then those two ought to have agreed. They both upheld the same principles of strict order, national pride, authority. But Eugénie, annoyed by Persigny's rude outbursts, thought he had no lucky hand in exercising power.

"Nothing," she used to say to the Emperor, "nothing ever goes right with Persigny."

And in fact she was not altogether wrong. He was only made for strong measures. He governed like a convict-warder, reserving what little weakness there was in him for his own home, where his wife reigned like a fairy queen of unruliness.

Eugénie had very little liking for Fleury, who was too liberal for her, and too much of a sceptic, and in the end she packed him off to an embassy. On the other hand, Fould, always sedulous to please her, and the solemn, courteous Walewski, were regarded by her as allies on whom she could reckon. Rouher, who had long ago nosed out his path, very speedily became her chief adviser. This astute, massive Auvergnat, a worker and very ambitious, and completely honest, had at first only been taken half-way into the confidence of the Emperor, whose mildness indeed covered a very considerable contempt for his fellowmen. Keeping the Empress informed upon internal affairs, constituting himself the agent of her intentions, the interpreter of her views, watered by her continual favours, he grew like a great cabbage, stifling under his leathery leaves colleagues slighter or more discreet. In a few years, pushed on by that elegant hand, he attained the heights, with a finger in everything, distributing money, places, votes, the efficient concrete master of France so much that he was dubbed Vice-Emperor by the public, who without seeing very clearly are very good at feeling things.

More than ever Eugénie, aware of the gaps in her knowledge, eager to understand and to form herself, plunged into books. Not the books of novelists or poets, which never interested her. But history, memoirs, the reviews, the foreign papers, the important articles which she pointed out to Napoleon or even made summaries of them for him. In this way she spent a good part of her mornings. Reading, with pen or pencil in hand, was always her favourite diversion. She was no artist, had no taste except in decoration, and that was poor. Without ear or voice, she neither liked nor knew anything of music. She mixed up tunes in her head to the extent of not even recognising "Partant pour la Syrie," which was nevertheless so dreadfully hackneyed that Napoleon, patient as he was, at last said:

"Really, my mother had no idea what an ordeal she was preparing for me when she composed that ditty!"

But to read, and fill her mind with the stories of the past, to gather facts either to discuss them or to draw examples from them, to furnish her docile memory, which never failed her, that has always been her humour. And to-day she thinks of finding in it means for performing her task as a sovereign with great confidence and usefulness. Conscientious as she is, she even takes lessons with Fustel de Coulanges. Napoleon approves her choice of such diversions. Rumours about them spread through Paris. Some find them a matter for jest, but the officials put fragrant little anecdotes into circulation.

Immediate witnesses of her ascent, the diplomats showed Eugénie a greater deference. She had long interviews with them, talking as she always did, rather disjointedly, but perhaps with more reserve than formerly, when she knew nothing of the responsibilities of government. She listened better, was a little more mistrustful. Her friend Hübner had been replaced at the Austrian embassy by Prince Richard Metternich, a tall young man with fair whiskers and soft features, much spoiled by women. His exquisite manners, and that air of the grand seigneur which had always captivated Eugénie made her welcome him with the greatest favour. When as a bridegroom he was invited with his young bride to spend a few days at Biarritz, the Empress went in person to find the Princess at the Hôtel d'Angleterre, where she was staying, surrounded her with attentions, and very rapidly made of her, if not her bosom friend, at any rate her most intimate and constant companion in all fêtes and pleasures. And yet they were very little alike. Pauline Sandor, Princess Metternich, was ten years her junior, and very ugly. She made up her little pug face to excess. But under the thick black brows her eyes sparkled with intelligence and wit. She was very elegant, adored horses like a true Hungarian, as well as luxury, art, flowers. She brought her wild fantastic verve into the life of the Court, and transformed it. Everywhere she went she left a whirl. While never forgetting and never allowing it to be forgotten that she is a great lady, Eugénie attached herself to her for the gaiety she created; she thought she would make an impression on the Princess, would mould this young impetuous spirit. And it was she herself who on the contrary underwent the influence of that gallant creature, so far from simple under her childish exterior. Having full access to the Empress both formally and informally, Pauline Metternich in one season became the arbiter of fashions, the confidante of her conjugal troubles, her political leanings. She often came in the mornings to the Tuileries to talk clothes, lunched with the sovereigns, caressed the little prince, whom she loaded with playthings, accompanied Eugénie on her drive to the Bois, chattered with her, and especially let her talk, if necessary asked her questions. . . .

She enlivened the heavy imperial evenings with her repartees, shook up this somewhat bourgeois Court (which in her heart of

Les Archives Photographiques d'Art et d'Histoire

PAULINE, PRINCESS METTERNICH

Cabinet des Estampes, Bibliothèque Nationale

hearts she despised) with her bursts of gaiety. Meanwhile she was serving her husband and her own Court, and doing more and more to incline Eugénie towards a close entente with Austria, which should set up a wall against the Italian floods. Napoleon, less captivated than the Empress, was quite aware of these manœuvrings. But he too was amused by the Princess's high spirits. And he liked Richard Metternich for preserving a certain Viennese *Gemütlichkeit*. Besides, he considered that he was strong enough to direct his diplomatic action without yielding to pressure, and for the best interests of France, the only ones that really counted with him. He was wearing himself out; his ardour in pleasure fatigued him, already his bladder was giving him trouble, the exercise of unlimited power was leading him towards a growing scepticism. He now practically believed in nothing except fate. Trusting to the miraculous luck that had brought him out of Ham to raise him to the topmost peak of Europe, so long as Eugénie did not show too much irritation at his gallantries he left her to deal with ministers, nominate bishops, bestow decorations on her friends, even on occasion, when Persigny was not on the lookout, promote prefects, and especially and above all, talk high politics with ambassadors, with touches of temper, a frankness that disturbed them, an eloquence that captivated them, and a keen desire to be feared and admired by Europe.

CHAPTER IV

Compiègne

THE Court was in the habit of spending the first weeks of autumn at Biarritz, where Eugénie had built a large villa, adorned with her own name, which was something between a railway station and a hydro. October saw the return to Fontainebleau or to St. Cloud. But with the early days of November the imperial household was transported to Compiègne. Napoleon enjoyed himself there. He could keep up that diminished, merely seigniorial style, which suited him better than the pomps of state. Eugénie too liked Compiègne for its greater freedom, for the shooting and hunting, the long excursions in the forest. She was less sensitive than the Emperor to the voices of earth and sky, the varied songs in the thickets, the fleecy drift of the clouds. But she loved nature for its gift of bodily relaxation, the joy of movement, of breathing, of change of scene, the fundamental craving that lived within her since her childhood, and which she would never lose. No doubt too the memory of her first visits to Compiègne, in the days when as an ordinary guest she had seen the Emperor's inclination declare itself, brought her, now that she occupied the throne, a keen sense of pleasurable pride. Furthermore, like Napoleon, she appreciated the country-house life, more varied and gayer than the life of the palace. Besides the royal or princely guests she must receive there she had conceived the plan of inviting parties of all the most outstanding persons in the Empire, foreign aristocrats, personal friends, and also the savants, writers and artists whom her own shrewdness rather than her inclination advised her to attach to the régime by a few favours. To make up these parties was no easy matter. Eugénie drew up the lists herself. Over these sheets she sometimes sat pensively nibbling at her pencil. The Emperor laughed at her about them, and even took a delight in throwing at her names of incompatibles.

It was the old problem, she said, of the goat, the wolf and the cabbage. To keep note of all the precedences, the friendships, the jealousies, to play up to the vain, reassure the shy, bring together

Les Archives Photographiques d'Art et d'Histoire

COMPIÈGNE. THE GARDEN FAÇADE

Les Archives Photographiques d'Art et d'Histoire

COMPIÈGNE. INTERIOR

The Furniture is of the Second Empire

the intelligent, counterbalance and neutralise the sober-sided and the stupid . . .

"I give it up," she cried, throwing her papers away. "They can manage for themselves!"

Then, seized once more by a sense of duty, she set to work afresh, marking off names.

Usually in the first batch she worked off "serious people," ministers, generals, high officials and their wives, who were usually old and prim, whom the Emperor wished to honour, but from whom it was impossible to hope for much in the way of easiness or fun.

Besides ambassadors there were invited numbers of distinguished foreigners. Having only succeeded in getting an insignificant proportion of the old society to recognise them, Napoleon and Eugénie had fallen back on cosmopolitan connections. Every year Compiègne saw the return of Lady Catherine Egerton, the Marchioness of Ely, Prince Czartoryski, many Spaniards belonging to the circle of the Montijos and Albas, the Count de Galve, Alcanizes, now Duke of Sesto, handsome José Hidalgo, an old habitué of the *tertulias* of Carabanchel, now a secretary in the Mexican Legation in Paris. The Empress looked on him with special favour. Ardent, pleasant and gay, he had in mind great projects in which he flattered himself he might interest Eugénie. He would have liked Napoleon to intervene in Mexico, sadly torn by factions, and help to found a huge military and Catholic Empire there.

Eugénie, all athrill with the thought of Cortez and Pizarro, gradually entered into his plans.

The ladies, even more than at the Tuileries, vied in magnificent dresses. The special train that brought the smart party had six waggons added for luggage. Princess Metternich and the Countess de Pourtalès filled one whole van with nothing but their evening dresses packed upright in huge deal cases. The Empress might rank among the most simple. During the day she often wore above a black cloth skirt one of those red flannel blouses known as Garibaldis. In the evening she was enchanting in full dress, blue or white or mauve satin, her favourite colours, adorned with her magnificent pearls. In the lights her complexion recovered the transparency it was beginning to lose by day. The Emperor often looked at her with affectionate satisfaction. The passion he had entertained for her was dead; he sought distraction elsewhere, only paying his wife a visit at long intervals (which Eugénie found all too short, fearing another pregnancy). But he was proud and happy to see her so full of grace and dazzling beauty. He would compliment her.

"You really are very lovely, Ugénie!"

She would answer, not without some impatience:

"I have to be!"

Princess Metternich, who had just "discovered" Worth, persuaded her to make him her chief dressmaker. Laferrière gave her less elaborate dresses for travelling or visits to watering-places. The Princess was waging war on the crinoline, which she considered ungraceful, and which at all events was not becoming to herself, making her look heavy and awkward. The Empress always remained rather attached to it, on account of its resemblance to the eighteenth-century fashions she loved. However, the sceptre of elegance, which she had wielded when she was not taking part in affairs, was to-day slipping away from her hands to pass into those of Pauline Metternich and Mélanie de Pourtalès.

It was to her beauty that Madame de Pourtalès owed her entry into the inner circle about the Empress. One of the Court familiars having asked for an invitation for her to a ball at the Tuileries, Eugénie who was not in the best of moods at the time had replied stiffly:

"No. The lists are closed. It's too late."

Two days after, as she was driving in the Bois with the Princesse d'Essling, her Grand Mistress, she saw in a brougham a charming fair young lady, with a Greuze face, sweet blue eyes, a delicate mouth, the loveliest of complexions and an air of supreme distinction.

She put up her *face-à-main.*

"Now who is that?"

"Countess Edmond de Pourtalès, *née* Bussière," replied the Princess.

"Really? How beautiful she is! My dear, when we get home, send her an invitation at once for the ball."

She adored pretty faces. Sure of herself, she had none of those fears and mean jealousies that are sometimes displayed by the

THE EMPRESS EUGÉNIE WEARING THE FAMOUS "BIBI" HAT

most beautiful women. She loved to surround herself with brilliant young women. Some whose light conduct was the subject of censure still found favour in her eyes for their charm or their beauty. It was so with regard to Madame Le Hon, Madame de Persigny, even with regard to the Countess de Castiglione at the beginning.

One of the women at the Court was exceedingly poor in intelligence.

"How stupid she is! How can any one endure her?" said Pauline Metternich, who never erred by being over-indulgent.

"Oh, well," replied Eugénie, "she's so pretty!"

She thought that a Court, and especially a French Court, owed it to itself to bring together all the beauties of the time. That was the way to attract men and to keep them there, and so to make it the active, live centre of society. And besides she knew it pleased Napoleon, who bloomed under the influence of feminine graces.

"The poor Emperor, who has so many worries," she used to say, "he must have a little fun."

She might have to regret her liberal view, to curse her confidence, when she perceived that the poor Emperor was having too much fun.

In the mornings everybody was free to do as he liked. They might go out, meet in each other's rooms, even dash up to Paris between two trains to scold a defaulting dressmaker or give an order to a stockbroker.

Quite early, when she had not too much writing to do, Eugénie would take a turn in the great avenue of the park. There she often encountered Mérimée. In frock-coat, white waistcoat, and grey trousers, he must have watched from his window to see her go out, and run after her as well as his asthma would let him. Coming up to her, he would slow down and pretend to be surprised. He was happy to find himself alone with her. Pleased too, she would welcome him with a smile.

"Bonjour, Monsieur Mérimée; have you slept well?"

Eugénie was perhaps the woman this sceptic had loved best in all his life. In any case in her he saw the friend he had known as a child, who had lifted her beautiful frank eyes to him when he told her a story, who had squeezed his hand with her impatient little fingers when he was taking her to the pastry-cook's, or to have a ride in a goat-carriage.

Beneath the now slightly heavier features of the Sovereign he could, with that sense of drawing he always possessed, find the delicate lines of the face of other days. To serve her, to defend her, to save her from storms and rocks he would have done a great deal; he would have come out of his egoism. What little warmth remained in him, what little indulgence, was all for Eugénie. He was troubled for her troubles. He knew them, either because she had confided them to him, or, more often, because he had guessed them. He was not blinded by the brilliant externals of the Empire. He knew its weaknesses. He liked the Emperor very well now, he had been won by his affability. But he distrusted what he called *"ses brumes"*—his *fogs*—those great projects for the reconstruction of Europe. He discovered in him vast desires and restricted powers. Napoleon's imagination, his taste for the extraordinary made him uneasy.

"He's a German," Mérimée would say to himself, thinking of his early education, the years at Augsburg. "A Frenchman would have more sense of proportion."

There was some truth in that. But Napoleon III was above everything a European. And Mérimée, who was rather crampingly national, would ask himself:

"What will be the end of it all?"

At noon the Salon des Cartes brought together the eighty or a hundred guests belonging to the party. Luncheon was without ceremony, every one sitting as he pleased. Only the places to right and left of the sovereigns were assigned to persons they wished specially to honour, different ones each day. Eugénie settled the programme for the afternoon, which in principle was not supposed to bind any one. In actual fact it was very seldom that any one escaped. Drives in chars-à-bancs through the forest, where Mérimée and Octave Feuillet almost always caught a chill, in spite of the wraps Eugénie made them wear; visits to Pierrefonds, the ruins of which Viollet-le-Duc was restoring at the expense of the privy purse, archæological excursions to the Gallo-Roman cemetery of the Croix Saint-Ouen or to Mont Berny where there were the remains of a Gaulish villa. Once a week there was a stag hunt. Following the cries of the huntsmen, the baying of the hounds, the fanfares of the horns, the imperial brakes swung along under the blackened boughs, filled with women huddled up in their furs. The Emperor and the Empress rode at the head of the hunt in Louis XV costume. When it was cold, the general rendezvous was fixed near a hut erected under a great oak in a clearing. The ladies coming down from the carriages stamped their little patent leather boots on the ground covered with russety leaves, and by twos and threes beat each other's hands to warm themselves. Plenty of noisy bright laughter was heard. Napoleon, grave under his three-cornered hat, made punch in a silver bowl set on a tripod. He set it on fire; that bluish flame dying in the twilight, amid the trees, had a weird look. Then the hunt began again to end often in the dark, and they made their way back by torchlight to Compiègne.

On other occasions, when she had nothing else to propose, the Empress would invite the ladies to a long walk. Most of them would a thousand times rather have remained indoors, making music, or doing fancy-work, or gossiping. But Eugénie, a hardy walker in all weathers, dragged them off regardless of their long faces. Princess Metternich trotted valiantly along by her side, amusing her by her repartees, her sometimes odd whimsies. Meeting in one of the alleys in the park a chimney-sweep all black with soot, she bet that she would go and kiss him. Everybody set up an outcry. Tucking up her skirts, she ran up to him and threw her arms about his neck. The Savoyard gave one frightened yelp and ran away at top speed, while the Princess came back to the others, laughing, her face all smutted. One day she inspired Eugénie with the wish to cut down a tree. Throwing aside mantles and gloves, the improvised woodswomen wielded their hatchets in so clumsy a fashion that the Empress for fear of an accident speedily had to put an end to the game. She got up paper-chases in the park. A young officer or a page took the part of the hare. Twenty, thirty, elegant women ran on his track through the bushes. When they came back their dresses lacked many a frill and flounce. Eugénie with her quite plain skirt was triumphant.

Back again at the Château, the Empress was taking tea with a select group in the music-room, when the Emperor appeared in the door and said:

"Eugénie, here is a kennel man asking for you."

The Empress gathered her brows a little in surprise. Standing aside, Napoleon made way for the entrance of a little figure in huntsman's costume, red waistcoat, short breeches, white stockings, laced hat, a horn slung round his shoulders, and holding the leash of two great white hounds that were pulling him along. It was the Prince Imperial, whom his father had dressed up with his own hands to give the ladies a surprise. Every one applauded. Eugénie laughed and shrugged her shoulders. The Emperor kissed his son, with moist eyes, and went out with him, helping to hold on to the dogs.

These teas of the Empress were for the guests of Compiègne a compensation for many fatigues. The music-room, where every day she invited only six or eight persons by a note specially delivered to them in the morning, seemed the pleasantest room in the palace. Great chests of Coromandel wood adorned it, and Gobelin tapestries fadingly setting forth the story of Esther. Eugénie, reclining on her *chaise longue,* placed beside her Mérimée always, often Feuillet, Viollet-le-Duc, the Metternichs, the Walewskis, the Mornys, Madame de Pourtalès, Chevalier Nigra, the young Prince Reuss, sometimes a savant, a writer or a famous artist invited to Compiègne for the week: Pasteur, Le Verrier, Chevreul, Carpeaux, Gounod, Arsène Houssaye, the younger Dumas. The Empress guided the conversation, an inexhaustible talker, putting question after question to the man of the day, as though eager to know and to understand. She would interrogate Le Verrier on the plurality of worlds, shudder to think of the insignificance of the earth as a part of the universe; she would like Pasteur to explain his discoveries about the diseases of wine, the diseases of silkworms. One evening at her request he gave a kind of lecture. Eugénie made herself his assistant and officiated at the microscope under his directions.

Sometimes the Emperor would come in for an hour. He would say as he entered:

"May I come in?"

He took very little part in the discussion, which was too animated for him, but as he smoked his cigarette in a corner he would talk in a low voice with one or another about inventions or on history.

If Gounod was present, he would take his seat at the piano

and sing very softly, ballads or Spanish songs. Though not very sensitive to music, Eugénie would listen without interrupting, her head resting on her hand. Everything that reminded her of her youth and her own country always moved her.

Her health, which was somewhat delicate in the early years of her marriage, had become robust again. Rising early, going late to bed, walking for hours at a time, always animated and athrill, she astonished her entourage by her powers of endurance.

"That," she used to say, "is because I wasn't brought up in cotton-wool."

She was grieved, and as though offended, that her son had not inherited her energy. He was quick and lively, a pretty face, with a charming disposition, sprightly, self-willed, but affectionate. He remained delicate, and was slow in growing. In spite of the advice of Conneau and Corvisart, Eugénie used to give him strange nostrums on the quiet, the recipes for which the Countess de Montijo had sent her to strengthen the boy.

Ill-natured people declared that she had no love for him. That was a very coarse way of looking at it. Perhaps she was not altogether a *maman* in the true French style. All the same she was a mother—in her own fashion, without effusive demonstrations of affection, yet profoundly. She was not given to caressing her son, and did not allow him to be petted and coddled. And so she rebelled against the weakness of the Emperor, who for his part would have spoiled him excessively, have gratified every whim. She wished to make a man of him. She saw in him not merely her "little lad" as she used to call him with unexpected softness, but also the political heir, the future sovereign. She had, she thought, a double task to perform: to help the Emperor in the government and to form their son to succeed them. This duty governed her feelings and her actions.

When her circle was still smaller, Eugénie would propose table-turning. For a while she was quite devoted to spiritism. A medium who was very well known in Paris, Douglas Hume, a Scotsman who had become naturalised in America, and who said he was a distant relative of the Hamiltons, had been presented at the Tuileries and had struck her imagination by certain experiments at which sceptics like Prince Napoleon or Mocquard poked fun, but which made the Emperor, who was always reverent towards the mysterious, repeat Hamlet's phrase, "There are more things in heaven and earth, Horatio, than are dreamt of in your philosophy." By help of tables Hume had called up various spirits, and by no means of low degree: Queen Hortense, Napoleon, Louis XVI. The widow of General de Lourmel, one of the Empress's ladies, and something of a ninny, one evening asked the medium to call up her husband, who had been killed in the Crimea. This was at the Tuileries, in the blue drawing-room. The lustres had been extinguished, and the lamps turned low. Patiently Napoleon, Eugénie, Madame de Lourmel, Madame Kaledji, Hume, Baciocchi, spread out their hands chainwise round a small table. They heard knocks, then a gilt chair placed against the wall came forward by itself, tripped on a seam in the carpet, and recovering itself glided up to the table. It rose up and sank down again. Madame de Lourmel, greatly agitated, recollected that when her husband was sitting he used to sway exactly in the same way. Hume then said he saw the General sitting plump on the chair and described him exactly, though he had never seen him. He described the two wounds from which he died, in the head and in the chest. At that moment Madame de Lourmel felt a breath on her face. She uttered a cry and fainted.

Another day, at the request of the Empress, Hume mesmerised Baciocchi, the first chamberlain. He appeared distressed, and uttered moans.

"Are you in pain?" asked Hume.

"Yes, terribly!"

"Where is it?"

"In my heart . . ."

"You are not sleeping well here?"

"No."

"Where would you like to be?"

The Empress did not let him answer this. She knew Baciocchi was given to the spiciest of jests.

"Doctor," she said to Hume, "do not ask him that. He sometimes says stupid things."

Whereupon Baciocchi decided to wake up.

The Scotsman then caused a hand to appear, seemingly gloved

in silk. No one dared to touch it. Eugénie, although she shuddered, bravely touched it.

"It is my father's hand," she murmured and she fell back in her chair.

The Emperor then touched it in turn and said:

"How cold it is!"

Next day the unbelievers pretended that the phantom hand was nothing else than Hume's foot, adroitly slipped out of the patent leather shoe. But the Empress would not listen to any talk of cheating. She protested vehemently. For several weeks she was quite cool to Walewski because he declared that Hume was an impostor, and a spy from the Court of Berlin into the bargain. He calculated that by making his way like this familiarly into the Tuileries he was getting hold of important information and furthermore gaining a regrettable influence over the mind of the Empress. Hume had predicted that the Prince Imperial would never reign. Eugénie was so disturbed at this that Walewski took advantage of her agitation to have Hume forbidden the Court, after a long interview with the Emperor in which he threatened to resign his office if Hume did not leave Paris.

The Empress was never persuaded. For a long time she thought wistfully of the Scotsman. She tried to repeat the experiments that had fascinated her. But she found no medium within her reach and arrived only at uncertain results. She did not, however, turn her back on them altogether, and her attention would always be caught if some one spoke in her presence of Allan Kardec, of Crookes, and their emulators. Morny, who in direct contrast to his enemy Persigny, retained under the external forms of elegance complete freedom for his ironical wit, asked her how she could reconcile spiritism with her religion. Eugénie took fire, maintaining that religion does not prevent belief in spirits, in their existence alongside of mankind, in their intervention in our actions. Morny smilingly bowed his bald forehead and confessed himself vanquished.

At Compiègne strict decorum was often forgotten. Certain people were rather shocked at it. Lord Malmesbury, the English Ambassador and an old friend of Napoleon's, returning to Paris in the Imperial carriage, a great omnibus drawn by six horses, in company with the Mornys, the Walewskis, and Madame de Pierres, a dame d'honneur, was astonished to see that the last named, an American by birth, and Madame de Morny, a Russian, smoked into the face of the Empress throughout the whole of the journey. And then he did not know that Princess Metternich occasionally flaunted a cigar or a pipe. The Englishman found them all very bad form and thought that Eugénie showed too much indulgence. It is true that when you were one of her friends she allowed anything, or very nearly anything. She had even gone so far as to accept a kind of lesson from the same Princess Metternich, who at an official evening party, because the Empress, forgetting herself while talking with some one else, had not come to find her in her ambassadorial place, actually left the drawing-room.

"I have no *amour-propre* where my friends are concerned," said Eugénie. "And when I am in the wrong I acknowledge it."

Pauline Metternich, though covered by the Empress with evidences of her friendship, nevertheless had nothing but a mere surface regard for her. Perhaps she was vexed that "Richard" should find her so beautiful. She took care never to forget that Eugénie had not been born near a throne. One day at Fontainebleau, when, always on the search for some rather showy idea in dress, she had suggested to the Empress to go to the races in short skirts (an audacious novelty for that period), the latter, not seeing the underlying malice, at once adopted the idea. Madame de Pourtalès, who was very intimate with the Princess, protested when they were alone together at the eccentricity of the notion.

"That dress is good for you, not for the Empress, whose frivolity is already being criticised. Now would you advise your own Sovereign in Vienna to get herself up like that?"

The Princess gave vent to her insolent laugh.

"Oh, that's a very different thing. No, decidedly, I would never suggest to the Empress Elizabeth to go out in short skirts. But *my* Empress is a princess, a real Empress, while yours, my dear, is only Mademoiselle de Montijo."

Eugénie had no suspicion of this disdain; her confidence in the Princess was complete and entire. The Emperor, not so easy to hoodwink, often warned her to be less confiding.

"We are surrounded by spies," he told her.

She lifted her shoulders.

"Oh, no! Oh, no! . . ."

All the same he saw clearer than she in this case.

In spite of the self-interested homage of Europe, Eugénie had never been able altogether to achieve the position of a sovereign. Even at home she seemed only the first lady in her own court. And even then she had to wage a struggle against the commanding looks of Mathilde, the too obvious coolness of Clotilde of Savoy, Prince Napoleon's young wife, who was pious and modest, but proud of belonging to the oldest house in Europe, and who from her first arrival had repulsed Eugénie's friendly attentions. Above all she had to protect herself against the affronts that from time to time Prince Napoleon dared to put upon her. After dinner at Compiègne, one Saint-Eugénie's day, the Emperor had unfortunately taken it into his head to ask him to propose the health of the Empress, on whose right he was sitting. The Prince pulled a face. Eugénie said jokingly to him:

"I don't insist on a harangue. You are eloquent, but your speeches sometimes alarm me."

He remained silent. The Emperor persisted, and he replied in a surly tone:

"I can't speak in public."

The Empress rose, and all the guests too, astounded and aghast at this brutal discourtesy.

The Emperor went to his cousin and took him by the arm.

"You won't propose the health of the Empress?"

"If your Majesty will permit me, I shall forgo it."

"Very well, very well," murmured the Emperor, gloomily.

Eugénie in the centre of a group in the family drawing-room seemed to pay no heed to the incident.

But that night she had a painful discussion with the Emperor, whom she asked to send his cousin from the Court. Napoleon III temporised, tried to excuse the Prince. He remained attached to him by memories of their youth; in spite of his delinquencies he still had an affection for him. Eugénie flared up.

"He is your fireside enemy," she exclaimed. "He is your Lucien! He plays at being a liberal and a republican from hatred of you, without whom he would be nothing at all. What he is waiting for is a revolution or some set-back that would bring him to the throne. If you were not longer there, he would never let Loulou reign, he would take the crown from him!"

The Emperor tried to soothe her. The Prince was hot-headed, but not disloyal. He promised to make him apologise. To send him away was impossible. He was the King of Italy's son-in-law; the scandal would have made too much noise. It would have decreased the Emperor's authority in France and in Europe. Eugénie understood, and gave way, but never had any apology. Often she thought:

"As long as he is there, I shall never be really Empress."

Fortunately other thoughts soon came to distract her mind. Her adorers made her forget her adversaries. Certain men turned up their eyes ecstatically when they spoke of her, and seemed determined to die for this inaccessible beauty. So it was with the philosopher Caro, who spent himself in sighs, Count Beust, who sent her little verses, von der Goltz, who made play of jealousy, even Richard Metternich and the Chevalier Nigra, the last two for political reasons. Eugénie laughed at these assiduities; none the less she was flattered by them. Romantic at bottom, she would never forget how young Camerata killed himself because she had married the Emperor. Prince Reuss, the Russian charge d'affaires, had a sincere admiration for her. She had discovered this, and by degrees, touched by his silent devotion, she had come to show him special friendship. Since Alcanizes, who had become Duke of Sesto, and whom she now saw at the Tuileries unmoved, Prince Reuss was the only man who had touched her heart. It was suspected, it was whispered about, the Emperor even was aware of it. But he paid no heed to any insinuations. "Who is master of his feelings?" he thought. He knew that in her own mind, as well as by temperament, Eugénie was destined to remain beyond reproach.

At the end of an amateur play at Compiègne there appeared, in a grenadier's uniform, his chubby face buried under the huge bearskin, the Prince Imperial, who represented the Future. Addressing himself to General Mellinet, who, clad as a disabled soldier from the Invalides, with the Saint-Helena medal, represented the Past, the child sang in a quavering little voice:

En contemplant le si noble visage
Du vieux soldat et son front sillonné,
J'aime à penser qu' à mon jeune courage
Pareil honneur, un jour sera donné.

He was so agitated, so charming, that the General, forgetting his part, the play, the audience, took him in his arms and covered his cheeks with kisses.

A storm of applause broke out. Completely abashed, the General put the child down on the stage. The Emperor was biting at his moustache to keep the tears back. Eugénie, radiant with delight, was triumphant. A wave of tenderness and confidence elevated every mind. Cares and uneasinesses were for a moment forgotten. This little eight-year-old prince, frail and vivacious, seemed to every one, but especially to his mother, marked out for a long and happy destiny, the harvest of what the Emperor and she had sown.

CHAPTER V

Power

SHE was sitting in her *cabinet de travail* at the Tuileries. A single lamp and the shimmer of the fire were the only lights. The thick curtains shut out every sound. There was a book in her hands, but she was not reading. Every now and then her activity relaxed like this; she felt herself suddenly at the end of her strength. She let herself go for an hour or two; and then her State duties or some sudden idea took hold of her and set her going again. She came and went once more, plunging back into the fever of living. Interests, aversions, angers re-animated her spirit and her eyes.

She was still very beautiful. But her fortieth year was approaching, her complexion was becoming duller; encouraged by Princess Metternich she was now taking to rouge. And she was also dyeing a few white strands of her hair. Her bust had thickened, while her waist, fashionably pinched, remained slender. The effect was not too happy in the dresses for day wear, which were made tight to the figure. In the evening, under the lamps, with her full skirts of light-coloured velvet and satin, with very low neck, and gorgeous jewels sparkling on her dazzling white skin, she remained incomparable for grace and majesty.

Nevertheless, a heavy grief had saddened her for a long time. Her sister Paca had died in Paris, at the Hôtel Bristol, when Eugénie was with the Emperor finishing a triumphal visit to Algeria. After the grand fantasia at which she had so enthusiastically clapped her hands, intoxicated by the light, the smell of gunpowder, the colours, the warlike din, Napoleon, who had received the news some hours earlier, told her with the most tender precautions that the Duchess of Alba was ill and that they must go back to France without delay. Eugénie looked at him, stricken. He tried to reassure her, but she did not listen. She foresaw the worst. Choked with tears, she let herself be taken to the steamer, and threw herself down in her cabin during the whole crossing, a long and bad one. To make the journey as short as possible, they landed at Port-Vendres and from there the Emperor and Empress and their suite got to the Perpignan railway, the women crammed into four carrioles, the men in an old stage-coach. Eugénie never ceased repeating:

"Shall we arrive in time? Shall I see her again?"

She did not see her again. When she reached Paris, the last prayers had already been said over Paca's coffin. Eugénie fell into sullen sorrow. She loved her sister very closely. She had in old days made heavy sacrifice for her. Her three children, especially the two girls, were as though they had been her own. Her memory never left her, the memory of the girl, the brown young woman, pale and gay, who had not at all the same tastes, but who nevertheless was in touch with the most secret fibres of her being, and whom she would have given her own blood to save.

From these really critical hours Eugénie was never again to show the same high spirits, the same exuberance, the same desire to please. She would always speak with animation, would still laugh, and often, but in a harder, more nervous fashion. Her character changed, or rather it discovered facets long kept in the shade, which suddenly came into a high light while others were darkened. She had adored personal adornment, now she took less interest in it; the pleasures of society now seemed hollow and bitter. She had spent lavishly like her mother; she became thrifty, cast up her accounts every day. Out of the considerable sums—more than two millions a year—the Emperor gave her, of which she saved at least half, she built up, assisted by the advice of the Pareiras, the Aguados, and the Rothschilds, a private fortune in house property and in shares, which might perhaps later on become a necessary stand-by for her husband and her son.

Harried by this grief, she saw in it as it were the herald of a change of fortune. Fate had erected about her a marvellous setting, such as takes shape in dreams, but it might crumble, sink and vanish all in a moment. She never had had complete confidence in the solidity of the Empire. Since she had been reading and pondering on history she had a better understanding of the brittleness of a power that arose from the will of a people. She reflected that to give a dynasty root, even in France, glory is less than time. Her youthful liberalism had fled with the years. She now envied the strength, the stability of the old absolute lineages.

Napoleon III accused her jokingly of being a Legitimist. She flared up:

"Legitimist . . . me? I am not such a fool! Of course I have always felt a respect for the Bourbons. I don't like the Orléans. They represent no principle. I believe that it is impossible to reign unless by an immemorial tradition or by the overwhelming desire of the country."

At bottom, if she had had the choice, she would by far have preferred her son to derive his vocation from Saint Louis rather than from General Bonaparte. Turning her back on frivolities she threw herself more and more into affairs. Her taste for power, encouraged by the example of Victoria, developed by her regency during the war of Italy, strengthened by the Metternichs' flatteries, the acquiescences of Rouher, the opposition of Persigny, became her chief preoccupation, her deepest pleasure, the real passion of a soul that had never known the softer ones. Perhaps it was the only one her virile nature could feel.

The Emperor allowed her to go forward. He recognised that, in default of coolness, she had decision, good sense, the instinct for command, a loftiness of view that women rarely possess. By relinquishing to her a greater and greater share in the government, he obtained, as well as peace in his home, freedom in his pleasures. He continued to abuse those pleasures, in spite of the sage counsel of his age. In the years that came after the war of Italy, he had grown old very rapidly. On several occasions Eugénie had been alarmed. She saw the wrinkles pleating up the corners of his eyes, the complexion that had never been clear becoming earthy, the cheeks turning puffy under the waxed and dyed moustaches, the whole face assuming the dull flaccid aspect of a chrysalis. His swaying horseman's walk became hesitating and wavering. He often fell into somnolence. He spoke less and less. However, he frequently woke up, showed returns to energy, astonishing spells of vivacity, and in his blue eyes, when by chance he opened them wide, a still luminous youthfulness. Then he would fall into his torpor again. Eugénie attributed it to his amorous excesses. She had spoken of it to Corvisart and to Conneau. They always replied—gout, gravel, bladder trouble. She always snubbed them, did not believe them. For her these were mild complaints. If the Emperor would only be prudent he would recover his former health. But he strenuously tried to "play the young man," while he had passed his fiftieth year.

Although Napoleon III was very fickle by nature, Eugénie forgot that she herself had a certain amount of responsibility for his errors of conduct. Their conjugal relations had gradually become less and less frequent after the birth of the Prince Imperial. Not wishing to run the risk—undoubtedly fatal—of becoming a mother a second time, her coldnesses, her refusals, had little by little tired the Emperor out. They were now little more than friends, partners, united by their child, their common life, the interest of the throne, which was enough to maintain confidence between them and, to a certain extent, affection. In this aloofness Eugénie might have shown herself more lenient to the Emperor's escapades. But she was very faintly sensual and in that vivid imagination of hers the flesh had no part. She could not admit that Napoleon should not at length tire of all that "bed-work," often so vulgar. At his age he ought to have "kept quiet!" What was in all these men to keep them hunting after petticoats?

"Do they never think of anything but that?" she asked disgustedly of Princess Metternich.

"Parbleu!" replied that witty little creature, "we feed them too well!"

She refrained from adding what she told others.

"To quiet Richard I have to take him down a peg every morning!"

In the autumn of 1860, while she was still shaken by the death of the Duchess of Alba, Eugénie, going unexpectedly down the little staircase of the Tuileries, in the close-shut super-heated rooms where the Emperor mooned away his time, had surprised him in the company of a pretty girl whose déshabille should have meant a bolted door. She had thrown the intruder out, and then after a scene, had declared that she would not go to Compiègne that year, that she wished to leave the Court and have a quiet holiday in Spain with her family. She would take her son with her. During her absence Napoleon could "amuse himself" as he thought fit. The Emperor, borne down by her violence, realised that if he tried to impose his authority, to "take the stick" as Prince Napoleon advised, he would bring on a terrific explosion. He tried gentle methods, got Pauline Metternich to talk to

Eugènie, Mérimée too, got the Countess de Montijo to write to her. The Empress calmed down a little. All the same she did not abandon her intention to go away.

"I feel an urgent need," she said, "for change and solitude."

The Emperor submitted, and the newspapers announced that she was going to spend a few weeks in Scotland. On November 14, he accompanied her to the Gare du Nord. Their farewells were chilly.

"The season was not well chosen for such a journey" was the whisper at the Court and in Paris. Nevertheless, accompanied by the Princess d'Essling, Madame de Saulcy, and the Marquis de Lagrange, Eugénie toured in mist and rain from Carlisle to Holyrood, from Dalkeith to Glasgow, visited the Trossachs, Loch Lomond and Loch Katrine, was entertained by the Duke of Atholl and by the Duchess of Hamilton. This circuit, which exhausted her entourage, soothed her nerves. She returned to London much calmer, paid a short visit to the Queen, saw good Panizzi at the British Museum, was charming to everybody. When she returned to the Tuileries Napoleon thought he was forgiven.

But there were other alarums. Numbers of women, at Court, did not wait until the Emperor tossed them the handkerchief. They used to pluck it out of his pocket. He said to Princess Baciocchi:

"As a rule the man makes the attack; but I defend myself and sometimes I surrender."

He surrendered very often, too often for his physical health and for his mental vigour.

Among these sultanas some had but a very brief reign, whether it was that Napoleon, as forgetful as he was weak where women were concerned, quickly tired of them, or that Eugénie interfered to bar them from the imperial palaces. Thus she kept out the Countess de Castiglione, who ventured to struggle for a moment, and speedily had to confess herself vanquished. When she appeared at a ball in the Tuileries without an invitation, the Empress gave orders for her to be shown back to her carriage.

The Emperor's liaison with Countess Walewska, variable and intermittent as it was, had long remained hidden from Eugénie. Scandalous gossip opened her eyes at last. She was forced to restrain her anger, as Count Walewski's position in the government obliged her to a certain amount of reserve. But after bitterly reproaching Napoleon she extorted from him a promise that he would break with the lady immediately. It appears that he kept his word, with no great credit to himself. He was embarking on another affair that was to continue for a long time. Arriving almost in *sabots* from Saumur to lead the wildest life in Paris, Marguerite Bellanger had captivated him by her gutter-snipe grace. He installed her in a house in the Rue des Vignes, where nearly every day he drove in a discreet coupé to spend an hour or two. When he could not come he sent a note, and Marguerite in male attire slipped into the Tuileries by a door on the quay.

Marguerite had a son. The Empress heard of this. It was not the first child Napoleon had had out of wedlock. Already a pretty needle-woman at the Tuileries had had to be married off in hot haste to one of the Emperor's valets. This fresh paternity annoyed Eugénie excessively. She was afraid it might be a future embarrassment for the Prince Imperial. She foresaw blackmail. A thousand ideas jangled in her head.

"I want to keep control over my mask and show a laughing face," she wrote to an intimate friend. "But my power ceases there; agitation, insomnia, almost madness, that is all that is left to me."

Excessive fears. Marguerite Bellanger, satisfied with being the mistress of Napoleon, who loaded her with money and jewels, and whom in any case she deceived quite cheerfully, had very little idea of provoking a scandal. But a last incident drove the Empress, whose complaints had been utterly unavailing, completely beside herself.

One evening, while the Court was at St. Cloud, she was told that the Emperor had just come back to the palace very ill. He had had a fainting-fit with Mademoiselle Bellanger, who occupied a very well situated villa in Montretout: the whole of St. Cloud could see her windows. The Empress hurried to his room. Helping Corvisart she bathed his head with cold water, made him drink a draught. She uttered no single word of reproach. But early next day she ordered a carriage and got into it unaccompanied. Mocquard at that moment was returning to the Château. He bowed and came up, and heard Eugénie calling to the coachman:

"To Montretout, to Mademoiselle Bellanger's!"

"What, Madame," stammered Mocquard in terror, "Your Majesty can't be thinking of it! What will the Emperor say!"

"He can say whatever he likes," retorted the Empress, eyeing Mocquard, whom she liked well enough, but whom she accused of abetting the master's amusements. "That can't go on any longer! Off you go," she bade the coachman.

The carriage started off, bowling along through the lovely sunshiny morning, and climbed the slope of Montretout. At the villa Eugénie got out, rang without hesitating and said to a maid who at first did not understand and then seemed ready to disappear behind her apron:

"I wish to see Mademoiselle Bellanger at once. I am the Empress."

She went into a little drawing-room. Marguerite was lying at full length in her dressing-gown on a divan. She jumped up. Eugénie standing in front of her looked at her, blinking her eyes, her mouth shut in a thin line.

"Mademoiselle," she said, "you are killing the Emperor."

The pretty young woman could only burst into tears. Which she did; falling at the Empress's feet she begged her to forgive her.

"You must be out of this house by to-morrow."

She turned her back on her, went down the steps, took her seat in her carriage with an extraordinary swift precision in all her movements. At every window round there were people gaping in astonishment. . . .

Marguerite Bellanger would have obeyed. But Napoleon did not allow her. This extraordinary behaviour had offended him deeply. Besides, he was more attached to Marguerite than to any other of his mistresses. Seeing herself defied, Eugénie exclaimed:

"Since she is not going, I will!"

Almost immediately it was announced that the Empress was suffering from nervous spasms in the stomach, and was going to try a cure at the Schwalbach waters, in the Duchy of Nassau. She left St. Cloud in the handsome imperial train in which Napoleon had had a regular apartment fitted up for her, hung with light-coloured silks and filled with sumptuous furniture.

With a small suite she travelled under the name of the *Countess de Pierrefond,* and at no moment consented to abandon this semi-incognito. At Schwalbach she had the house where the Czarina usually stayed. There she received a visit from Queen Sophia of Holland, an excellent woman, devoted to the interests of France, and with whom she was very friendly. Then King William of Prussia came to pay his respects to her on his way to Baden. Already contemplating his future war against Austria, he thought it a good opportunity for winning over Eugénie. A few days later the Empress Elizabeth, whose simplicity was full of pride, and who had not up till that time wished to accept "Mademoiselle de Montijo's" hospitality in France, arrived in Schwalbach. She saw Eugénie, had a long talk with her and abandoned her former prejudices.

The cure was coming to an end. However, Eugénie liked Schwalbach; she felt a kind of secret repugnance to returning to St. Cloud. Very uneasy, Napoleon, who was making his usual visit to Plombières, in vain addressed telegram after telegram to her. She would hardly answer, and kept continually putting off her return. At last she decided to leave. At the invitation of the Grand Duke she spent a day in Baden. There she found the Duchess of Hamilton and William of Prussia, this time accompanied by Queen Augusta, very curious in her turn to meet Eugénie. She greeted them in her travelling dress, a black silk skirt and a red woollen bodice, over which, finding herself at the last glance too unstudied and informal, she had donned in spite of the heat a cloak of otter-skin, in which she was very nearly stifled.

Back again with the Emperor, she found him anxious to return to her favour. But she had reflected a great deal in those days of separation; she had decided upon the attitude she maintained ever after. Since Napoleon was incorrigible, and was incapable of giving up his love affairs, there were to be no more conjugal relations between them, henceforward they would be merely a good pair of sovereigns. She would remain the Empress, but as she told him in a private interview, "there would be no Eugénie any more." Napoleon with drooping head and a contrite air counted on time to smooth things over. Eugénie remained firm.

Politics were her refuge. Seated beside Napoleon at the Council, she listened, usually in silence, to the ministers' report. But if the subject interested her, she intervened at once and without beating about the bush. There was no shyness now. She spoke at first quietly, then presently, carried away by her ardour, her voice rose, vivid, full of images, exuberant. Napoleon went on drawing little men on the great sheet of paper placed in front of him. When he thought the Empress was going too far he would murmur: "Ugénie, Ugénie . . ." or pluck her sleeve.

In actual fact she now shared the power with him. She even exercised it with greater efficiency, for direct and tenacious that she was, she never, like him, allowed herself to be discouraged by the dilatoriness or deceived by the pretexts of the ministers. Several of these ministers were in any case devoted to her. Rouher was both a warning and an example to them. Eugénie, who liked Fould, had insisted on his return to the Ministry of Finance. He was her very eager servant. Maréchal Vaillant was at her feet. And she had in the long run succeeded in getting rid of Persigny. Over a long period he had defended his position against Eugénie in the mind of Napoleon, whose oldest remaining friend he was. His arrogant partisan zeal dominated the Emperor's hesitations. But he could only maintain himself in success. At the elections in 1863, which he meant to "run with a riding-crop," the Empress had interposed to procure modifications in certain directives communicated through the official press. There was a kind of wavering as a result. The elections were middling in the provinces, bad in Paris. Closeted with the Emperor, Persigny threw the blame on Eugénie. She attacked him vehemently, blamed his clumsiness, "his brutalities that multiplied the enemies of the régime," procured his dismissal by her insistence. Napoleon to console him gave him the title of duke and endowed it. He still appeared at Court and remained a member of the *Conseil privé*. But debarred from any active business he lost all influence, though he never resigned himself to this.

The Empress had her *party,* her adherents, her views. These views sometimes ran counter to the Emperor's intentions. Napoleon dreamed of rebuilding a harmonious Europe, in which nationalities would be at their ease and in which, with prosperity enthroned, wars would be more and more rare. Devoted to the idea of material progress, he foresaw the increasing importance of the economic factors in the life of States. Eugénie, attaching herself to a traditional line of policy, the lessons of which she found in the ancient monarchy, preferred that Europe should be maintained in its condition as it was. She took fire when Italy was under discussion. To the Minister for Foreign Affairs, Thouvenel, who had in open council spoken for giving up Rome, she addressed such bitter reproaches that he showed himself deeply hurt.

"Madame," he declared, "if the Emperor had said half of what Your Majesty has made me listen to, my resignation would have been on its way already."

A few days later his place was taken by Drouyn de Lhuys, with whom Eugénie was on better terms.

"Now at last we are dis-Italianised!" she exclaimed.

The Republicans, the dynastic opposition, with Prince Napoleon at its head, pretended that the Empress's constant interposition on behalf of the Holy See was the result of her fanatical piety. That was going a little too far. While Eugénie remained devoted to the interests of the Pope she never thought them opposed to those of France.

She believed that the Imperial Government could not dispense with the support of the French Catholics, who were then very active and exacting, and that if Napoleon allowed himself to uphold a policy hostile or too indifferent to the Pontiff, he would encounter the worst kind of difficulties at home.

"We must not," she said, "drive our friends to despair!"

She was greatly affected by the defeat of the Papal troops at Castelfidardo. She wept at the phrases of Monsieur Dupanloup saluting "the martyrs fallen in defence of the faith."

The Metternichs encouraged her in this attitude. Several times they discussed the Roman question at St. Cloud. Twice over Napoleon promised them that the possession of Rome would remain secured to the Papacy, if necessary by force of arms. Writing to Vienna, Richard Metternich could affirm: "The Emperor will not give way on this. The Empress is a guarantee of that, she who in the eyes of the Catholics, represents the dignity and the loyalty of France."

Eugénie's animosity against Italy led her into rash speeches that were sufficiently serious. Talking at Fontainebleau with

Nigra, Victor-Emmanuel's new ambassador, whom for that matter she liked and personally treated with friendship, she went so far as to say:

"It is you who pillage and rob on others' ground; and who want to turn us into your accomplices. But wait, the day of vengeance will come. You will see your Mazzinis and your Garibaldis grow under your very hands, and on the day when you are ruined I promise you I shall not come to your help!"

Her sentiments towards disloyal and greedy Prussia were very similar. She wanted to defend Austria and the little powers of Germany against her encroachments. For her the Austrian alliance was to become the pivot of the whole imperial diplomacy.

She did not dislike the Czar. His absolute power impressed her enormously. But he was Orthodox in religion and he was trampling upon enslaved Poland. For that the chivalrous Eugénie always blamed him. A close understanding with England (and here she was in full agreement with the Emperor) seemed to her indispensable for the security of the régime and for the peace of Europe. The coolness that had come between the two cabinets since the war of Italy and the annexation of Savoy was a real grief to her. She took every opportunity of paying attentions to Queen Victoria whose friend she was proud to be and determined to remain, and also to her ambassadors.

In internal politics the Empress's action had less continuity. And home affairs, too, had less attraction for her; they were a matter of *dossiers*. But here again her ideas, even if they might be found shortsighted, were very definite. The Empire, she thought, had no meaning unless it remained autocratic. Napoleon, whom Morny was urging towards liberalism, was tending to become a constitutional sovereign. Eugénie was opposed to this. To do everything for the good of the people, their moral and material needs, is the first duty of governments. But to give them a share in the guidance of the country is simply rushing upon destruction. Her realism rejected ideology. An aristocrat by birth and habits, democracy revolted her. At bottom, though she might never confess it, France always frightened her a little. This turbulent nation that had within sixty years three times dethroned its kings and killed a queen she never quite understood, and she mistrusted it.

Her passionate good-will did not prevent her from often being unfortunate in ideas or actions. But her adversaries imputed to her every mistake in diplomacy, all the blunders of the government. Newspapers and pamphlets attacked what they called her rash and roughshod interference, represented her as the Emperor's evil genius. Public opinion, wrought on in this way, was decidedly hostile to her.

"I am not popular," she said to Pauline Metternich, "and yet I do all I can. But they don't like me. I am a foreigner. The French never forgive their queens for that. Look what it cost Marie-Antoinette. Who knows what it will cost me?"

To win the heart of this nation, fundamentally generous but fickle as a weathercock, was a hope she never gave up. She showed herself everywhere, often with her son, was prodigal of herself at exhibitions, at galas, at reviews. She redoubled attentions, smiles, audiences. She accompanied the Emperor on all his visits to the departments. Her charities were regular and well thought out. Accompanied by her Alba nieces, who now were continual guests at the Tuileries, she used to visit slums in distant quarters. In the cholera epidemic she went through every ward in the Beaujon, Lariboisière and Saint-Antoine hospitals. A dying man called her "my sister." She clasped his hand. She went to Amiens, spoke to all the sick. To the bishop accompanying her she said:

"Take good care of your health, monseigneur." For herself she had no fears.

"Monsieur le Maréchal," she said to Vaillant, "this is our woman's way of going into battle."

She was not at all puffed up by the praises of the Court and the dithyrambs of the official newspapers. She wrote at this time:

"Don't let us speak of heroism. I have not saved a single life. Let us keep great words for great things, for example, for the devotion of the nuns, who not content with visiting the sick for an hour, tend them until they are cured or die."

Modesty and good sense. This behaviour touched many people. On her return from Amiens, Paris cheered her. A fire of straw, but it made her pantingly hopeful.

"If they knew," she said, "what I would give to be really loved! There is nothing but a people's affection that can repay sovereigns. For theirs is an arid life. If only they would not call me the

Spaniard any longer! The Austrian, the Spaniard, it is with words like these that dynasties are killed!"

She envied the Emperor; *he* was loved, especially among the labouring classes, the poor, the peasants, the workers. But in spite of all her efforts, public feeling remained unfriendly to Eugénie. She was never resigned to it. Insinuations of journalists, or calumnies wandering about society, made her furious. Every opportunity was snatched at to belittle her, to besmirch her. A scandal was trumped up because she went skating in the Bois. Clad in furs, with a woollen skirt, she had leaned on the arm of the Marquis de Massa, not being very expert at the sport. The Emperor was there, and hundreds of people who had seen nothing wrong in her attitude. But the Faubourg Saint-Germain veiled its face and the "reds" cried out on depravity because the Empress had been seen having a skate fixed by one of her own chamberlains.

People talked gloomily about the "orgies" of Compiègne and Fontainebleau. The scenes, charades and proverbs of sufficient insipidity that were acted there were depicted in the crudest colours for the credulous. Besides, certain habitués of the Imperial evenings exaggerated the freedom of those parties in their tales. From this sort of gossip the Empire took on an air of gilded Bohemianism that sapped at its prestige and even its solidity. Eugénie felt it: it distressed her. But what defence was there? Letting her pen run, as she always did, somewhat overfreely, she confided to a friend:

I am very weak against malevolence *that has no hatred for its motive;* when by chance I find in my way persons looking for evil where it is not and tearing their neighbours to pieces *for the love of it,* without object and without cause, I am seized with terrible depression because I say to myself: one needs to be very cruel to find a pleasure in wringing the hearts of those who are holding out a hand in good will; for not only do the stabs pierce home, but distrust takes the place of every other feeling, and as the anonymous takes the mask of friendship, one distrusts without knowing whom. . . .

My enemies will always find me strong against them. I cannot say as much for my friends. . . . I add, for those who by idle words are fain to deprive us of the little time we enjoy air and freedom: if they knew how precious is this time for those who are condemned to the preoccupations of the present and the anxieties of the future, they would leave us this oasis where we try to forget that we must always walk and speak with the passions of some . . . and the fears of others! . . .

This evening then, thinking by her fireside, Eugénie indulged herself in a brief spell of melancholy leisure—alone for a whole hour. Afterwards she must needs pull herself together, smile, *appear*. From time to time, as a tiny click of a chain made her raise her eyes, she gave an absentminded caress to the little pet monkey her cousin de Lesseps had brought her from Egypt. She called it Ferdinand, by way of a little teasing joke at the giver, whom she had never ceased to like and to protect. Then she sank into herself once more, caught up in the endless procession of her own thoughts. Sometimes a muted sound made its way to her: the Porte-Saint-Martin—Grenelle omnibus passing in front of the Tuileries. This big vehicle, drawn by its three great percherons, full of people all swaddled up against the wintry cold, for her represented Paris. Unjust, formidable Paris, which she both adored and detested.

The clock struck something, but she paid it no heed. Yet presently she gave a nervous start to see Madame de Saulcy slipping through the half-darkness, coming from the blue drawing-room.

"What is it?" asked Eugénie impatiently. "I said I would not see anybody."

The lady of the palace bowed and murmured:

"The Mexican minister has just come. He assures me that he has an audience with Your Majesty for six o'clock."

Eugénie made a movement of vexation:

"M. Hidalgo? Ah, yes, that's true, I had forgotten!"

As if she could not immediately bring herself to relinquish her solitude, or to give herself a little longer respite, she said:

"Ask him to wait a moment, will you?"

Hidalgo . . . Mexico . . . Would to God that she could have left at her door, with the man, the cares, the anxieties, the regrets that now beset her every time she heard that name which only the other day filled her with such pride and hope. Mexico, her master idea, her great work, the symbol of her will, of her power. Mexico, which was to preserve her name from oblivion. . . .

Three years had sufficed to destroy her illusion. Henceforth she was at a point where a visit from Hidalgo, coming to talk of affairs, perhaps to ask once more for troops, for credits, or simply for delays, fell upon her like an entangling network of dismay and fear.

José Hidalgo, a friend of her youth, again become an intimate friend to such an extent that Eugénie had entrusted to him the task of accompanying her sister's coffin all the way to Madrid, had little by little won her over to his dream of rescuing Mexico from distress and poverty, and making it a great modern State, a moral extension of the French Empire. Eugénie was all feverishly intent on this plan, the romantic and magnificent sides of which Hidalgo set before her in dazzling fashion. When it was a question of persuading Napoleon, she had found an unexpected and tenacious ally in Morny, who was secretly interested in the repayment of the Jecker notes. In spite of Persigny's opposition, and Fleury's too, the Emperor allowed himself to be brought round. Easily. The idea linked up with old echoes within himself. While a prisoner at Ham, he was already thinking of the creation of an inter-oceanic canal by cutting the isthmus of Nicaragua. In 1846, he was writing that "the establishment of a considerable State in Central America, capable of preventing any fresh encroachments on the part of the United States" was devoutly to be wished for.

After dinner one evening, at Biarritz, the Empress had gone into his cabinet with Hidalgo, who had set out his plan before them in detail. Everything seemed favourable. The half-breed Juarez had by his brutalities irritated both England and Spain. Revolt against his corrupt despotism was hatching in the country. The United States, absorbed in the War of Secession, could not rise up against intervention from Europe. France would reap valuable commercial privileges and new glory. . . .

"What sovereign can we propose to the Mexicans?" asked Eugénie.

"Have you a candidate in your mind's eye?" said Napoleon. "For my part I have none."

The Empress fanned herself.

They spoke of German princes. A Hohenzollern, a Saxe-Coburg. . . . None of them seemed to suit. The Duc d'Aumale? Very sympathetic, but to give a throne to the Orléans house was dangerous.

Hidalgo then remarked:

"The Archduke Maximilian wouldn't accept? . . ."

"No, certainly not," said Napoleon.

Eugénie, after some reflection, shut up her fan, and struck it on her breast, and said crisply:

"My impression is that he would accept."

Hidalgo became eager.

"We could have him sounded; it would be an excellent choice."

"I shall speak of it to-morrow to Prince Metternich," said Eugénie.

"Yes," said the Emperor, "but without laying any stress on it, so that we can easily withdraw."

The Empress talked about it first with the Princess, then with the ambassador. At first they hesitated. Then, thinking of the Archduke's position, kept aloof from any active employment by the mistrust of his brother Francis-Joseph, of the ambition of the Archduchess Charlotte, who was intriguing to find a throne in the Balkans, they became eager in their turn.

The expedition had begun with the somewhat lukewarm support of England and Spain. Napoleon III had sent to Vera Cruz only 500 zouaves and one battery of artillery. But as Hidalgo kept urging, and Eugénie continually backing him up, he decided to despatch 7,000 men. Badly led by General de Lorencez, they failed before Puebla. At this moment Juarez made his peace at London and at Madrid, which promptly deserted France and recalled their ships. Eugénie wrote to the Archduchess Charlotte, with whom she had entered upon direct relations.

"Thank God, now we have no allies!"

She thought her hands would be all the freer. At the same time she made an attempt to regain the co-operation of Spain. She set out for Madrid. She had never been back there since her marriage. Staying at the Alba palace, her sister's memory saddened her at first, then life, politics, and pride got the upper hand. She was returning to her original compatriots, many of whom in old days had treated her lightly, with the retinue and the stir of a crowned Empress. She showed herself simple, amiable, conquered many old enemies. The Countess de Montijo was ready to burst for joy.

At Court she had a marvellous success. The United States ambassador, who was alarmed at her action, wrote to his government:

"She has put Queen Isabella in the shade."

It was a personal success, but a political check. Eugénie did not obtain what she had come for. Spain, with her black eyes fixed on England, imitated England in her reserve, almost in her hostility.

France remained alone, with her honour engaged to win a triumph over a savage country, and an unstable and feverish people, devoured by a passion for independence. Urged on by Eugénie, Napoleon laid the foundation of a real war of subjugation. The Corps Législatif voted credits, after a speech by Rouher, who declared, adopting a sentence of Eugénie's that "the Mexican expedition would be the great thought of the reign." General Forey, with 28,000 men, 56 guns and great numbers of Mexican volunteers, carried Puebla after a siege of sixty-two days.

The Court was at Fontainebleau when the news arrived. An aide-de-camp brought the Emperor a telegram. He asked his neighbours Princess Metternich and Madame de Pourtalis for permission to open it. He read and said aloud:

"Puebla is taken."

The noise of delight ran round the table. Hidalgo was bursting with pride. The Emperor handed the telegram to a footman who carried it on a silver salver to the Empress. She unfolded it in her turn and exclaimed:

"But you didn't read the whole of it!"

"Well, read it to us," said Napoleon.

"Galliffet seriously wounded."

Eugénie appeared greatly moved. Around her every one commiserated Galliffet, a general favourite at Court for his gaiety and escapades. Eugénie stared into her plate. It was she who had forced the young captain of the Guides to go to Mexico, because his pressing attentions were compromising a lady of high position. . . . At this moment the servants were offering sorbets at table. The Empress, like a real daughter of Spain, adored them. She refused, saying to Nigra, her neighbour at table:

"I shall never take another until Galliffet is quite well again."

Later it was known how, his belly torn open, left for dead, he had crawled to the ambulance, carrying, as he put it, "his tripes" in his képi. He was destined to recover, and live to ripe old age, with the help of a silver cuirass. Until he got back to France, Eugénie kept her superstitious vow.

The French then entered Mexico City. A junta of notables had proclaimed the Empire, appointed a Regency, and offered the crown to Maximilian. Eugénie was triumphant. Almost every day she held council with Hidalgo at the Metternichs', who had settled at La Jonchère for the summer. With her friend Madame d'Arcos she used to go over there from St. Cloud, covering her face with a veil. These conspiratorial meetings were her delight.

Negotiations had been set on foot with Vienna; they were slow and difficult. Francis-Joseph, before allowing his brother to lay hold of that foreign crown, demanded that he should abandon his rights as a Hapsburg. Maximilian resisted. He wanted to break off all parleyings: Napoleon was disconcerted, Eugénie was furious. Telegrams composed in the Empress's cabinet bombarded the nervous, flaccid, unstable Archduke. His wife, very eager to reign, at length made him consent. He accepted the title of Emperor in melancholy mood, left Trieste and his beautiful palace of Miramar in tears. As soon as he was in Mexico, and had made his entry into his capital, troubles and difficulties piled up against him. Divisions among his supporters. A conflict with the Pope. The war of secession coming to an end, the United States were every day assuming a more truculent air and arming Juarez, who had taken refuge in their territory. The scattered rebels were plucking up heart. A guerilla war, hot and ruthless and exhausting, was beginning.

Eugénie was now in grievous distress. She saw in Mexico a furnace gathering strength, in which the best regiments of France were melting away and millions in gold turning into thin air. The loans, coming too close together, were not being well taken up. Pereira and Rothschild, who the other day, licking their lips at the thought of the mines of Sonora, had guaranteed their success to the Empress, were now looking at them with a tired and disdainful eye. The French press was hostile. In Europe, the position of the Empire, which had for a moment been eminent, seemed to be crumbling away. It remained isolated, without alliances, under the eye of a Prussia on the watch, of a sulky Italy, of a distrustful England. And Maximilian, a booby, taken up with wine and women, never wrote, never made Charlotte write, except to give vent to recriminations, to beg for troops, to beg for money. Bazaine, who commanded the army, sent alarming reports about the rebellion. Hidalgo nevertheless kept on declaring that all would be well, that they must not believe Bazaine, who had his own private views and plans.

"A little further effort," he reiterated, "and the country will be pacified."

But every effort was heavy and costly. France was murmuring. The Emperor and his ministers were unwilling to give another man or another sou.

Eugénie still supported Hidalgo out of loyalty and obstinacy. She had long placed her trust in him, because he was an old friend, a compatriot, and also because she liked him. Now she was doubtful about him, scented a whiff of adventure about his tracks. Suppose she had been mistaken! If Maximilian could not establish himself! If in the end they would have to recall the troops and leave Juarez master of the country, what a disaster for the Empire, what a humiliation for herself! And on the other hand, by dint of throwing herself into this Sisyphean labour, France was on the way to exhausting herself. She would offer herself a prey to the covetousness, the jealousies of Europe. . . . Between the two abysses Eugénie trembled to take a step.

She looked at her watch. Half-past six. No doubt Hidalgo was becoming impatient; she must receive him, dispel his mirages, discuss his requests, feed him with half promises. What a dreadful trade! But she had chosen it. Power must be paid for. She did not repudiate responsibilities. Proud and over-proud, she had rather wrapped them about her closely like a cloak. After all nothing was lost. Politics, like war, have their lucky turns. Perhaps Hidalgo was bringing good news, true news . . . Come then . . .

She rose, settled her hair in front of the mirror, called Madame de Saulcy, and said to her, the smile back upon her lips again:

"Bring the Mexican minister in."

CHAPTER VI

Biarritz

MERIMEE is walking on the terrace of the Villa Eugénie with a tall stout man with round prominent eyes, and a moustache sheltering a jowl like a mastiff's; Count Bismarck, the Chancellor of the King of Prussia. For two hours now they have been talking like this without a break. Mérimée, after a certain time of reserve, has opened up, and talked about his travels, his archæological researches, and tactfully, although an author, about his books. Bismarck knows them, seems to appreciate them. He has verve and cordiality, and is very courteous, and suddenly breaks out into whimsicalities that open up abysses in one's thought.

They touched on music, and Mérimée asked if that strange fellow Wagner who fled from Paris four years ago after the ignominious failure of Tannhäuser "was still composing grotesque operas." The Chancellor raised his massive shoulders without replying. It displeases him that a light *welche* should make fun of a German. Nevertheless, he has little taste for Wagner; he really only loves Beethoven. Mérimée is just back from London, where he was the guest of Palmerston and Gladstone. He speaks of them freely, tracing somewhat acid portraits of them, which must be fairly accurate.

Lord Palmerston, he tells Bismarck, is a strange mixture of statesman and urchin. He has the aplomb of an old minister and the taste for adventure of a schoolboy. He would turn the world upside down to have a little triumph of eloquence in Parliament.

It was his old friend Panizzi who had presented Mérimée to Gladstone. He appreciates him less as a politician than as a commentator on Homer. He fears lest with him England may be sliding too much in the direction of democracy, and that her individualistic genius may be spoiled thereby.

In all countries, to tell the truth, the people please the sire of "Carmen" very little; he judges them harshly. Similarly the movement of the Empire towards liberalism frightens him. He has tried to turn Napoleon away from it, but the Emperor did not listen. He talked to him about Roman history. Disappointed, Mérimée thinks "all that might very well end by a first-class toss upside down."

With Bismarck, of course, he affects complete confidence. The man interests him greatly; he approves Napoleon for wanting to come to agreement with him. The Brandenburg squire, who since the Convention of Gastein had become one of the masters of Europe, has been invited to Biarritz by the Emperor, who has already conferred with him as to the arrangements necessary to satisfy Prussia's ambitions in Germany and to grant France legitimate compensation on the Rhine. However, nothing has been concluded. Napoleon, for fear of showing his hand, compromises, mixes the various questions together, surrounds himself with clouds. And Bismarck, who is resolutely following out his plan of bringing Austria down and uniting the whole of Germany around Prussia, Bismarck, who at first had in mind to buy the neutrality of France, feels that the Emperor is hesitating, that absorbed by the anxieties of Mexico, he will not interfere in Europe, that promises in the air will be enough to hold him. He has known how to flatter Eugénie, who finds him "more talkative than a Parisian," and who, although she is against Prussia, is of the opinion that it is possible to come to an understanding with this clever man who sees clearly.

If she was allowed to join in these conversations, she would undoubtedly change their tone. She would seek for positive foundations, would ask for clear definitions. But Napoleon has not desired her to be present. And when she questions him, he is elusive, says that there must be no hustling, that everything is going well. . . .

To Mérimée Bismarck sets out his admiration for the Empress. He considers her "still more beautiful than her portraits, gracious, intelligent, exceptional." Mérimée is enchanted. When any one praises his dear Eugénie he simply purrs. This afternoon, when he has retired to his own room he will write to the Countess de Montijo, and to that Scapin of a Panizzi, that "Bismarck is a great German, not at all simple, who seems absolutely devoid of *Gemüt,* but full of intelligence." "He has made a conquest of me," he will add.

Leaning on his black walking-stick with the gold head, a gift from the Duchesse de Cambacérès, the Emperor interrupts their tête-à-tête. He is slightly lame. His health has been uncertain this year. He had gone for a few weeks' rest in Algeria, leaving the Empress a second time as Regent, and she was by no means displeased to resume the reins and to preside over the Council, as though she was reigning alone. Now, after his cure at Vichy, he seems to be better. His colour is improved; the brisk sea air is putting pink in his cheeks. He smiles familiarly at Mérimée, gives his hand to Bismarck. All three walk together on the terrace for a moment, enjoying the bright sky and the long rolling waves melting softly upon the sand. Then Napoleon takes the Prussian minister's arm. Don Prospero slips away, thanked by the Emperor with a side glance, and goes to the drawing-room to join Eugénie, who has just come down, and whose laughter rings out loudly among her ladies, a few friends, and the little prince, very smart in his sailor's blouse.

Of all her holiday resorts Biarritz was Eugénie's favourite. When she used to come to France she had noticed this village, isolated in a vast and desert situation. As Morny created Deauville, so she created Biarritz. Mérimée, passionately attached to Cannes, where he spent his winters, had wanted her to build a residence there. She paid no attention to him. The Basque coast attracted her. She was quite close to Spain, could imagine she was breathing its air. Many Spaniards in society followed her example and settled there for the autumn. Any one who wanted to please her built a villa. Proud of the progress of the hamlet, she had vehemently opposed the setting up of an establishment for scrofulous children.

"My poor Biarritz would be deserted. Who would ever want to come to it after that?"

Life goes simply there, with more real gaiety than at Compiègne. No dressing for dinner. No "series" of guests. Ministers are rarely invited. A cabinet courier brings the Emperor important papers every week. Napoleon has with him only his secretary, Franceschini Pietri. He takes a rest from administrative affairs so as to give more attention to foreign politics. Madame de Montijo often comes from Madrid. Eugénie one season invited

Queen Isabella. She came, enormous, *enceinte,* thinking of nothing but eating and laughing. When she departed every one breathed a sigh of relief.

Emancipated from the trammels of etiquette, in a countryside that pleases her and owes everything to her, Eugénie is really herself. It seems as though she grows younger, that her taste for independence and for adventure becomes more pronounced. And politics absorb less of her attention here.

In the morning she goes here and there in the streets, alert, picking up her skirt, leaning on a tall stick with yellow tassels; she visits the shops, talks with the shopkeepers, hears all about local events, stops to look at new buildings, takes an interest in the progress of the jetty intended to shelter the little harbour. She asks the sailors if the fishing is good, if it will be fine tomorrow. In these comings and goings she is often accompanied by her chaplain, Monseigneur Bauer. This is the Bernard Bauer, the one-time dancer of the Caseron Montijo who at Eaux Bonnes, between one excursion and another, used to talk of leaving the world and giving himself to Christ. An equivocal creature, hovering between mysticism and pleasure, who has never found his balance, and perhaps at bottom has no desire to. He entered the Carmelite order and, accustomed to a life of comfort, he scandalised their austerities. For several years he preached in the Breton villages. He returned to Madrid; went to Vienna, to Rome, where the Pope made him a prelate. He next installed himself in Paris, in the Rue Saint-Florentin, near the Hôtel Rothschild. His subtle, ardent eloquence, the exquisite elegance of his soutanes, and his good looks, brought him great numbers of penitents. Fashionable women would have nobody but Monseigneur Bauer for their spiritual director. Recalling himself to the memory of Eugénie, who was always ready to help and advance the friends of earlier days, he appeared at the Tuileries, and made himself at home there. He loves intrigue, and seeks to play a part. But the Empress, although she has a lively liking for him, does not fall in with this. He may be a confidant, but she does not mean to fall under his influence. If he ever makes any attempt in that direction, she increases the distance between them. The Emperor has little liking for him. However, he is touched by his zeal for the poor. And he silences Princesse Mathilde, who hates the prelate and calls him out loud and when he is by "the Rabbi from Buda-Pesth."

Sometimes before lunch Eugénie rides with the little prince who, already well schooled, follows her boldly on his pony, Bouton d'Or. His health is her constant care; she often feels his hands, his neck, continually consults the doctors, even quacks. He was a very fine child, but as he grew he became delicate. He was like his mother, without her colour or her delicacy of feature. Now and then it seems as though he might grow up ugly. That makes the Empress very unhappy.

"It is *so* important," she says, "for the people that the sovereign should be good-looking!"

She thinks of him above all else as the heir to the throne, the future Emperor. The boy is headstrong and proud, but affectionate, fastidious, sensitive, and with a real artistic gift. He draws with astonishing spirit and sureness of touch. While Carpeaux was doing his bust, he modelled a head of the Emperor. The likeness was very striking.

"Really, Loulou," said Napoleon, laughing, "I had no idea I was so ugly!"

Then he did a little group representing a combat between a horse-soldier and an infantry-man, full of mistakes, but with a very true free sense of movement. The Emperor admires this dexterity, a legacy from his mother Hortense. He himself draws well. The Empress, who knows very little about art, is opposed to any encouragement of the child in this direction.

"One who is destined to reign," she keeps saying, "cannot think of being an artist. He will have too much thinking to do about his country. Such fancies are not for him!"

On the boy's behalf she fears his father's weakness and the adulation of the Court. One evening, at the Tuileries, before a small group, as Le Verrier, boasting of his discoveries, was drawing a sort of great chart of the sky, the little prince put to him very infantile questions, to which the savant, somewhat over-deferential to rank, gave obsequious replies.

The Empress, coming up to them, asked:

"But what are you talking about?"

"Madame," replied the astronomer, "His Imperial Highness

is so obliging as to put before me his ideas on astronomy: they are very remarkable."

The boy reddened with pleasure. Eugénie frowned.

"Ah, Monsieur," she exclaimed, "do not flatter this child who unfortunately never hears the truth. His ideas on astronomy! I can imagine what they must be!"

She took hold of her son by the hand and took him over to Madame Bruat, his governess.

"Monsieur Le Verrier is very kind to listen to you, Loulou. You are only a little boy like the others, and as far as astronomy goes the best lesson you can have at this hour is that it is time for you to go to bed."

Eugénie wants to make a man of this urchin. That, she says, is her first and most imperative duty to France. She allows no one, not even the Emperor, to trifle with that.

Her idea of her responsibility is a very lofty one. Most frequently she works upon the boy through his *amour-propre*. When he is naughty, she deprives him of his epaulettes, which is a bitter punishment to him.

He is brave like her. When he was barely able to walk, cannon did not frighten him. He has military tastes, loves the sound of drums and trumpets, to see the troops. He adores danger. One day at Saint-Jean-de-Luz the skiff in which he was with his mother, being badly handled, struck a rock and sank. A sailor swam with him on his shoulders to the shore. The sea was very rough, and the waves now and then went over his head. The Empress, who was borne along by two sailors, called out:

"Don't be afraid, Louis!"

Filling out his little voice, the child replied:

"A man is not afraid when his name is Napoleon."

Very hot-tempered, he often rebelled against his mother. After a scolding from Eugénie, his nurse, Miss Shaw, found him hacking into the palm of his hand with a penknife. The wound was dressed and tied up. He struggled with them, crying out:

"I don't want to have Spanish blood in me, I don't want anything but French blood any more!"

When he was seven he was given a governor, General Frossard, the Emperor's aide-de-camp. The general, a strict and very upright person, was appointed to this post in unexpected fashion.

He was talking with Napoleon when the little prince slipped into the cabinet, where he had the entry at any hour, and running to his father asked that he might ride Bouton d'Or in the Bois that afternoon. The Empress had forbidden it for disobedience. Napoleon, for once severe, bade him go away. The child became obstinate and persisted. Forced to be firm by the presence of the General, the Emperor tried to make him leave the room. The boy clamped himself to his father's legs and prevented him from moving. Napoleon was just about to laugh and give way when Frossard said in a serious tone:

"What, Monseigneur, you refuse to obey His Majesty!"

He opened the door and showed it to the boy, who promptly disappeared, covered with confusion.

Napoleon recounted the incident to Eugénie, who at once declared that there was no need to look for any one else to be Loulou's governor but Frossard. The Emperor offered him the post the very next day. The General accepted on condition that he was to be given complete authority over the child.

The Prince Imperial's tutor was Monsieur Monnier. An excellent person, cultivated, a little boneless, who feared the dryness of study for his pupil and endeavoured to teach him without effort on his part, by talks rather than by tasks. Loulou was a bad listener. He liked natural sciences, and history, especially military history; mathematics, Greek and Latin were repugnant to him. He worked side by side with Louis Conneau, son of the Emperor's physician and close friend, who was his own age and shared his life at every point. Napoleon very often paid them a visit. Finding his son once yawning over a passage of Quintus Curtius, he said gently:

"It is a very tiresome thing, a construe. I never could do one."

Monsieur Monnier thought it was up to him to reply like a good courtier:

"And yet, Your Majesty has translated Cæsar's *Commentaires* excellently."

"Oh," said Napoleon, "it wasn't I!"

Eugénie, if she had been there, would not approve of this imprudent kindliness. She constantly repeats that Loulou must apply himself, must take pains. His character will never be formed otherwise.

"He will have to take decisions for thousands of human beings, he will bear immense responsibilities in the eyes of his own country and of Europe; his judgment must be independent and firm, he must have the courage of thinking that goes before the courage to act."

She does not mean him, young as he is, to be ignorant of the sad things in life, of social inequalities, of squalid want.

"He probably believes that poor people are those who have no carriage. He must be brought to understand, to realise, he must listen to the stories of these unhappy people, in which there are many lies, but still more truths. He must know the dreadful houses without air and without bread, in which no happiness is possible. He cannot reign without having seen all that."

At Biarritz he does no work. These are holidays. He plays mostly in the gardens of the villa or on the sea-shore with Louis Conneau, his little cousins the Alba girls, and some boys of his own age, the little Murats, La Bédoyères, Corvisarts. The Emperor does not disdain to join in their games. Not the Empress. At heart does she really care very much for the society of children?

In the great drawing-room of the Villa Eugénie, which was originally stretched with a flower-patterned chintz, and was later on adorned with a handsome set of Gobelin tapestry setting out the adventures of Don Quixote, the evenings are spent in the most bourgeois fashion possible. In a quite simple frock, "hundred and fifty franc frocks," the Empress takes her place with a few women friends about a round table. Bending her gold head under the lamplight, she embroiders or knits, talking loudly and a great deal. Napoleon, sitting at a card-table with the little prince on his knee, sketches pencil plans for beautifying the villa and the gardens, or shows the maps of Gaul he has had made for his *Life of Cæsar*. If some wild sentence by the Empress reaches him he looks up and teases her. Thus before Baron Haussmann, bowing and smiling deferentially, she boasts that she is a descendant of Saint Teresa. The Emperor, with his cigarette held between his fingertips, asks:

"In the direct line?"

"Certainly!"

Every one laughs under cover. Napoleon assumes a sententious air:

"How history deceives us! So Saint Teresa did not die a virgin then?"

Eugénie blushes as if she were twenty, stamps her slender foot in its satin shoe on the carpet, exclaiming:

"Now then, you're trying to make me say stupid things!"

Or again, of the bull-fights, of which she is a passionate devotee, she enquires about the matadors who are to come from Spain for the display at Bayonne, organised at her wish. Certain names are given her.

"But I don't know them. I've never heard of them! Where were they when I was in Spain?"

Then the Emperor looks up from the book he is brushing with his *barbiche* to say with his cordial low voice:

"They weren't weaned. . . ."

Eugénie does not take it in all at once. She turns to Napoleon, sees his eyes gleaming with fun. Shrugging her shoulders with vexation, she flings at him:

"The impertinence!" Then she frankly laughs with her deep-throated laugh that sounds like a cackle.

The men in various corners are reading newspapers, or reviews, or leisurely sipping their coffee. Sometimes General Edgar Ney takes his seat at the piano. A few couples dance quadrilles, waltzes, the *"boulangère,"* the *carillon de Dunkerque* which amused Eugénie so much only the other day. Now she seldom dances it since her sister's death.

When he is in the mood, the Emperor, accompanied by Madame de La Bédoyère, with apologies for his low and untrue voice, sings in French or in German.

"Dis-moi, soldat, dis-moi, t'en souviens-tu?" or the *Two Grenadiers.* Princess Metternich follows him, and taking on a guttersnipe accent, rolling her eyes under her staring eyebrows in her snub-nosed, painted pug-face, she sings like a consummate artist *Rien n'est sacré pour un sapeur.* The Princesse d'Essling and Madame de Montebello seem a trifled shocked. The rest are heartily amused.

Some evenings the Emperor begins to read aloud. Usually he chooses an utterly dull and boring book. Yawning sets in.

Madame de La Bédoyère sleeps. The Empress, who loathes being read to, impatiently counts the stitches of her knitting. At last Napoleon looks up, sees all those long faces, and to bring back their smiles shuts his book and proposes a game, *"à la serviette."* Everybody perks up, delighted at the diversion. The men go off into the smoking-room. The women, left alone in the drawing-room, equip themselves with rolled-up napkins, holding the two ends tightly clutched in their hand. Each of them chooses a cavalier. Then the men are brought in one by one. Each goes to the lady who he thinks has chosen him. If he is right he is allowed to remain with the ladies. If he is wrong he is hunted out with blows of the napkins. The Emperor is always wrong. Pursued, he re-captures a most youthful agility, jumps over chairs and escapes to come back again next moment. The women laugh themselves out of breath. The Empress is one of the wildest; she runs about, shouts, gesticulates like a schoolgirl. At last she comes to a standstill. The chairs are taken away. The drawing-room resumes its normal aspect. Footmen hand refreshments round. Very soon everybody goes off to bed.

During Bismarck's short stay at Biarritz there is a truce to these noisy games. However, Mérimée, who in spite of age and poor health, keeps a mind always inclined to undergraduate practical jokes, takes advantage of the marked attention paid by the Prussian Chancellor to Madame de La Bédoyère to warn her gravely that if she seemed to encourage them her virtue would be in peril.

"Monsieur de Bismarck is notorious for his audacity, even cynicism where women are concerned."

As Madame de La Bédoyère seems incredulous:

"Yes, yes," says the Empress, backing him up, and preserving complete seriousness, "he is right, my dear, you must be careful!"

The night before Bismarck's departure, Mérimée cuts out a cardboard head of the minister and colours it, a perfect likeness. Telling Napoleon and Eugénie, he slips along with them on tiptoe after dinner to Madame de La Bédoyère's bedroom. They arrange her bolster under the bedclothes to look like a person, and on the pillow they placed the head, on which the Empress fitted a handkerchief knotted into a peaked nightcap. In the dim light of the candles the illusion was surprising. So much so that when a valet went in a little later to turn down the bed, he saw the simulacrum and withdrew with profound apologies.

In the drawing-room the evening drags along. Bismarck goes to bed rather early. About eleven o'clock Eugénie gets up, makes her beautiful curtsy to the company, and goes off with Napoleon.

They station themselves at the end of the long corridor on the first floor. Very soon all the guests come up to their bedrooms. Candlestick in hand, Madame de La Bédoyère goes into hers. Next moment she rushes out wildly and hammers at the door of her neighbour, Madame de Lourmel, crying:

"There's a man in my bed!"

Madame de Lourmel opens, exploding. In the darkness of the corridor the Empress breaks into laughter. Madame de La Bédoyère, simple though she is, now catches on to the truth, and begins to laugh with the others.

Many were the excursions, many the trips by sea. Sometimes they resulted in very miserable home-comings.

One afternoon, this time when the sea was calm, Napoleon, Eugénie and their guests set out on the *Pélican* for San Sebastian. The Empress wanted to see the village of Loyola where Saint Ignatius was born. For the journey they only found two wretched stage-coaches and a carriole. Everybody piled into them. The Emperor himself drove the carriole, gallantly cracking his whip. After two hours of crowding, hot sun and dust, behind the jog-trot of the wretched jades, the company arrived at Loyola. Fore-warned in some mysterious fashion, a troop of soldiers had assembled to do the honours. It followed the carriole of the Emperor of the French, who with his hat on one side drove his nags with an inconceivable air of dignity. A picturesque sight at which the little newspapers of Paris were scandalised. After a visit to the seminary of Saint Ignatius, which everybody found terribly boring, they returned to the coast in the same guise as they came.

Days of ease, of repose, when the body is relaxed, the mind is at rest and unbends. They are the best that Eugénie will ever know in her whole reign. She knows it well. When she must leave Biarritz to go up to Compiègne, to Paris, to the harness of the Court, to the uncertainties of power, she sighs:

"We must go back: farewell to the good days!"

CHAPTER VII

The Difficult Times

DIFFICULT days returned, after so many splendid years of prosperity. Unexampled luck had favoured Napoleon ever since 1848. For fifteen years everything succeeded with him. The two wars, of the Crimea and of Italy, though they were badly conducted and very costly, restored France to a pre-eminent place in Europe, and augmented her to the extent of two provinces that rounded out and covered her territory. The flourishing country was reinvigorated by vast public works. Money was abundant. Business was easy and profitable. Subdued and brought low, all opposition was dumb. And then by degrees, without the change being noticed at first, the lights grew dim on this splendid drama. No more successes, but disappointments, surrenders. Luck was wavering. And now it turned. The expedition to Mexico, a small thing in its beginning, became a cancer that drained the treasury, devoured the troops and depleted the arsenals. An economic crisis arose. The Emperor's prestige was becoming corroded. Now that he was less fortunate he appeared less intelligent. Europe accused him of being guided by the smoke of his own cigarettes, France of yielding to his wife's least whim in order to preserve his domestic peace and to be able to continue his night-raking.

There was a great deal of exaggeration; all the same there was a certain amount of truth.

Napoleon's tortuous diplomacy had led him to commit a heavy blunder. He trusted Bismarck. He believed that by favouring Prussia's designs upon Germany he would obtain territorial compensation on the Rhine for France, and for Italy, Venetia. Thus he would finish the work of the Capets and deliver Italy from the Teutons. A crowned *carbonaro,* as usual, he moved by underground paths, and turned himself into a broker for Prussia, ensuring her the co-operation of Victor Emmanuel. Eugénie was opposed to this policy, the progress of which she knew nothing of, but of which she had a secret presentiment. She had always been afraid of Prussia. When in the Corps Législatif Thiers showed the danger of German unification as Bismarck intended it, she read his speech to Napoleon, commenting on it strongly.

"I have no love for Monsieur Thiers," she concluded, "but I think he is right a thousand times over."

Drouyn de Lhuys, the Minister for Foreign Affairs, behind whose back the Emperor had arranged the Italo-Prussian alliance, thought with Eugénie. Napoleon was shaken by their vehement remonstrances. What was to be done? Convoke a Congress? An attempt was made. All the States made excuses. And Bismarck hurled his thunderbolt. On July 3, the Austrians were beaten at Sadowa by the Prussian needle-gun. Paris took fright, was indignant, all agitated: the Emperor, suffering from a severe recurrence of his bladder complaint, which he obstinately concealed, seemed stupefied. Eugénie, in the Council meeting at St. Cloud on July 5, courageously proposed, supported by Drouyn de Lhuys, to mass a few divisions in Alsace to make Prussia uneasy and oblige her to make concessions.

"Can we do it?" she asked the Minister for War, Maréchal Randon.

He replied:

"Yes, Madame; we can concentrate 80,000 men on the Rhine immediately, and 250,000 inside twenty days."

The Emperor said nothing.

Then Eugénie declared that "the fate of France was at stake." She did not venture to say "the fate of the dynasty." But that was her real thought. The country would never, she believed, forgive the régime for having brought it into a position so unstable and so diminished. La Valette, too self-confident, declared that by threatening Prussia the Emperor would inevitably come to an alliance with Austria, an embroilment with Italy, and so to a complete overturning of his policy. He added that Bismarck, if he was invited to do so by courteous negotiation, would not refuse to give such satisfactions as we might demand in the Rhineland.

The Emperor remained inert. Eugénie straightened up in her chair.

"When the Prussian armies are no longer engaged in the depths of Bohemia, and when they can be turned against us, Bismarck will snap his fingers at your demands!"

Then addressing herself to Napoleon, who with eyes downcast

and drooping shoulders was clasping and unclasping his hands, she exclaimed:

"Prussia had no scruple about stopping you after Solferino. Why should you hesitate to stop her after Sadowa? In 1859 we had to give way because we would not have had 50,000 men to block the road to Paris. To-day it is the road to Berlin that is lying open. And we would refuse to take advantage of it!"

Prince Napoleon, inimical to Austria and watchful for the interests of his Italian father-in-law, made answer that it was "essential to know what we wanted, and seeing that we had resolved on neutrality, to stick to it. Otherwise Europe would despise such an unstable policy."

"But if we have been wrong all the time!" replies Eugénie.

Rouher also is for waiting and seeing. He is afraid that a demonstration on the Rhine may lead direct to war. For that war we are wholly unprepared. Mexico still detains our best soldiers. The right thing is to wait and see what happens.

Eugénie shrugs her shoulders. She is *sure* that the mere prospect of French intervention would make Prussia amenable. She insists, and Maréchal Randon and Drouyn de Lhuys take the same view.

Exhausted, and utterly shorn of will-power, Napoleon at last gives way. Then the Council within ten minutes decides to convoke the Chambers to vote the necessary credits for mobilisation. Fifty thousand men will be thrown at once on the frontier. A note will be addressed to Prussia to warn her that we will not tolerate any territorial modifications in Europe that have not had our assent beforehand. And these decisions will be published in to-morrow's *Moniteur Officiel.*

Eugénie is exultant. At last France will recover her prestige. Success abroad will make it possible to curb the opposition grown over-bold, to reinforce authority, which has been assailed by the liberals.

But in the evening Prince Napoleon sees the Emperor. He shows him the danger into which he is throwing himself, insufficiently armed. Is the Mexican disaster not enough? Is he going to stake the country's destiny on a throw of the dice? Will he submit to the Empress's fatal influence until a catastrophe results? She has made such heavy mistakes already! If war breaks out the Empire is lost. . . .

The Emperor, dejected, weary, harassed, swaying from one side to the other, follows the advice of his apprehensions. He no longer trusts to Eugénie's intuition. He sends for Conti, since Mocquard's death his *chef du cabinet,* and revokes the orders already given. The *Moniteur* of the sixth of July is silent.

When Eugénie has read it she hastens to the Emperor, and questions him. He is so distressed and weak that in her heart of hearts she pities him. But it is a question of France, of the Empire, of their son. They do not belong to themselves. They are reigning sovereigns. He answers her patiently. The army is really too weak. He does not dare to run such a risk. She becomes incensed, predicts the violent attack of popular opinion, in which hostile elements already exist in increasing numbers. He leaves her, without any more words, and goes to bury himself in the dark of his bedroom where, tortured by his disease, he will be alone with his groans.

If Morny were there, thinks Eugénie, she would lean on him. With him she herself would govern, since Napoleon is giving up. But the best brain in the Empire, the most supple intelligence, the coolest will, have disappeared a year ago. Rouher is only an eloquent administrator. He can only act as a second in command. He will never be a statesman. During these stormy days whose agony she feels in all its poignancy, she reflects, ponders, concentrates herself in a way that perhaps she has never done before. She sees the Emperor so broken that an audacious idea takes possession of her. What if he were to abdicate! . . . She would assume the power in his stead. She is still young, vigorous, energetic. Responsibilities do not daunt her; she has a passion for governing. She would save the Empire, would preserve the throne for her son . . . She confides in the Metternichs, both the prince and princess, who, without being willing to compromise themselves, do not discourage her.

One evening, having driven alone with Napoleon in a buggy to the Château of Villeneuve l'Etang, in that park which had sheltered them in the first days of their marriage, she ventures to propose to the Emperor that he should relinquish his power. He opens his eyes, and looks at her. Reproachfully he seems to say:

"What, the woman who owes everything to me, whom I have crowned, wants to take my crown from me!"

Though she felt the strangeness, the almost odiousness of this step on her part, she nevertheless persisted because she believed in its necessity. The régime was declining. To sustain it changes of ministers were no longer sufficient. A change of sovereign might recapture the affection of France. A young Emperor, that little prince whom Paris loved so dearly, would rally round his minority all the healthy forces of the nation. Let Napoleon efface himself, at least for a time. Let him make this sacrifice, poignant as it seemed, and he would ensure the future of his race, and would save the country a second time from the disorder into which a revolution would cast it. He shook his head. No, there would be no revolution. Nothing was desperate. Calm was what was needed, calm . . . Sadowa? A diplomatic check. It could still be repaired. The great cities were no longer for the Empire? Had they ever been for it? It still had the enormous mass of the peasants, many workers, industry, part of the bourgeoisie, the whole administrative and judicial organism, the clergy, the army. To abdicate would be such a confession of impotence that the régime would perish of it. In France the minority of a sovereign had always provoked disturbances. For a few months they were touched and sentimental over the childhood, the weakness, of the prince, then they thought of how to take advantage of them. Peoples had no lasting moods of chivalry. Napoleon IV would practically not reign at all, especially with a foreigner as regent, a new Anne of Austria. . . .

"Yes, a new Anne of Austria! And the reign for which she paved the way was that of Louis XIV!"

"She found Mazarin. Whom would you find? It might have been possible, perhaps, if there had been no Mexico. But then there has been Mexico . . ."

She made no further reply. She let her arms fall to her sides and walked in silence, staring at the ground.

That rejoinder was calculated to overwhelm her.

Mexico, alas, which should have been the "great thought of the reign," had become the inexpiable crime. In vain had Eugénie prayed fervently, madly, in her oratory in the Tuileries, burned hundreds of candles to Our Lady of Victories, taken communion on behalf of the unlucky Maximilian: the disaster had run its course. In vain had she wept, and implored the Emperor. It had been necessary to recall Bazaine and the French troops. Without Mexico, Eugénie would not have attained this pitch of unpopularity, such as no queen had ever known except Marie Antoinette. For all the reproaches were levelled at her. The newspapers might be curbed, tongues could not. Most people, especially in Paris, repeated parrot-fashion: "It's the fault of the Spaniard!"

Hyrvoix, the head of the secret police, avowed this to the Emperor one morning. Eugénie overheard him as she entered. Hyrvoix excused himself in vain.

"The Spaniard!" cried the Empress, clenching her fists. "I have become French, but I shall let my enemies see that I can be a Spaniard on occasion!"

She let Hyrvoix see it.

"You have obeyed your conscience," Napoleon told him, shaking him by the hand.

But two weeks later he left his post to become *receveur général* in the Jura.

"Let him have any post, no matter what," Eugénie had said, "I don't wish to see him again."

To do away with a policeman was simple. Public opinion remained. And it was not in a moment when public opinion was running wild that a regency could be established and proceed to govern. Besides, ill as he was, broken as he was, the Emperor had kept the sense of his dignity. He was no coward. To reign has its obligations.

"First of all," he said, "mistakes must be repaired. This is not the moment to abdicate, but to act."

And he did take action. At Vichy, whither he went for his annual cure, he conferred with Drouyn de Lhuys, despite the horrible pain he suffered from his bladder, and determined on the instructions to be given to Benedetti, his ambassador at Berlin. He was to ask for Mayence and the Rhineland. But those few days' delay had ruined everything. The Nikolsburg preliminaries had already been signed. Benedetti pressed Bismarck to no purpose. The Chancellor at first was evasive, then bluntly refused. His regiments were now free. They could march against France next morning. He for his part had the army his policy demanded; Napoleon had not. Eugénie wanted to stand fast, and Drouyn upheld her to the end. But the Emperor was all too well aware of his inferiority in strength. He drew back. Then Bismarck hastened to inform the Southern German States of our demands and of our retreat. They all made alliance with him, ready for a war that only a blind man could fail to see was imminent at the first pretext Prussia could find.

At this moment the Empress Charlotte of Mexico arrived in Paris. Thwarted in her ambition, she came to beg Napoleon not to recall his troops and to agree to new credits. The Emperor, who had come back from Vichy exhausted, endeavoured to avoid this most trying meeting. Eugénie went to visit Charlotte at the Grand-Hôtel. She made excuses on Napoleon's behalf, displayed the utmost graciousness. Charlotte would not allow herself to be put off. She wished to see the Emperor, and see him she would at all costs. Already her tone was becoming stiffer. Behind the polite phrases, Eugénie divined the hideous reproaches. Weakening, she consented: Napoleon would receive her the next day at St. Cloud.

We know how dreadful a scene it was; Charlotte, tired of begging, turning to threats; the madness that hovered about her suddenly laying hold of her . . . She cried out to Napoleon that they were adventurers and murderers. Then she collapsed. Napoleon fled in terror, his hands thrust out in front of him like a blind man. He had not given way; he could not give way. It was no longer a question of prestige, of interests, of pledges, even of honour. The destiny of his people was at stake. Deprived of his experienced soldiers, in the midst of a diplomatic impasse, he knew he was at Bismarck's mercy.

Eugénie, utterly harrowed, tended Charlotte and said no word. "Your great idea is the kind that cost an Empire!" Prince Napoleon had flung in her face. She trembled as she thought that these words found by hatred perhaps contained a prophecy. And she felt guilty as she kissed her son.

Political distresses, and during the same days private distresses as well. The little prince had been endangered by a serious accident. At ten years of age he had had measles, and having caught cold during his convalescence he remained delicate. He practised gymnastics a great deal to become strong. He loved all physical exercises and went at them with too great a disregard for danger. One afternoon in the stifling summer, under the shady trees of the park of St. Cloud, by the pool of the Goulottes, as he was swinging on his trapeze, he caught sight of the Empress coming towards him in the little pony-carriage she drove herself.

"Mamma," he called to her, "mamma, see what I can do on the trapeze!"

Letting go the ropes, his feet caught on the bar, he swung head downwards. Eugénie, pleased with his skill, clapped her hands. Suddenly the boy's feet slipped; he fell down on to the ground, a hard fall, and remained unconscious. The Empress ran to him, picked him up and, helped by Monsieur Monnier, carried him to the Château and sent for Corvisart as soon as they got him laid on a bed. The child quickly revived. "It won't amount to anything," said the doctor. In less than a week, however, a large abscess formed in the hip. Every effort was made to avoid an operation, but in the end it was necessary. Nélaton performed it in the Spring. The boy did not want chloroform, but they paid no attention to him. The Emperor, who lost his head directly his son was concerned, remained in the room, drumming on the window-panes. Eugénie in the next room was on her knees, praying. The operation was successful. But convalescence was slow and protracted. Napoleon sat by the child's bedside and drew with him or did card tricks to amuse him. It was long before the little prince could ride again. Eugénie anxiously watched his hollow cheeks and his listless movements. He was lame. The enemies of the régime took advantage of this to spread the report that he was afflicted with an inherited scrofula and that he would not live. The Empress was indignant at these vile attacks. How many years of her life would she not have given to show him strong and vigorous to the country over which he was to reign!

He became strong again little by little, though constantly giving cause for anxiety. In November 1867, he was to appear with his parents at the opening of the Chambers. His appearance would demolish the calumnies that were current. When almost about to set out for the session, in his black velvet suit, with the ribbon of the Legion of Honour across it, he turned pale, was on the point of fainting. Corvisart was summoned immediately, and sounded him. Miss Shaw, the English nurse, who was allowed to say what she pleased, and was inclined to overdo it, reported that the day before the prince had received a violent blow from one of his comrades.

"It's M. Corvisart," she added, "who eggs them on."

"Is that true?" the Empress asked of the tutor, Augustin Filon, who had recently taken the place of Monsieur Monnier, considered inefficient.

Filon, shy, but frank, replied that he did not believe it; that the games the prince was in the habit of playing with his friends (the young Fleurys, Conneau, Espinasse, Lambert, Primoli) were not dangerous in the least.

"The Prince," said Filon, "has indigestion, no more and no less."

The Empress agreed. But the Emperor had not heard. So calm as a rule, he uttered sharp reproaches to Corvisart. Then Eugénie forgot herself.

"You are stupid," she threw at him. "You should know the facts before getting angry. Miss Shaw doesn't know what she is talking about."

Luckily the child managed to vomit and, thus relieved, the disorder of his clothes repaired by his mother and his nurse, he took his seat in the wheeled chair, which bore him, pushed by his tutor through the unfinished galleries of the Louvre, to the Salle des Etats where the session was about to begin.

More and more Eugénie's son grew into her life. When he was younger he was not so interesting to her. Now that he was taking shape, that he could reason, that she rediscovered herself in his bold likes and dislikes, his liveliness, she became much more closely attached to him. More than the Emperor he was her reason to fight, to be enterprising, for he is the future. She was not given to effusiveness. And yet when at Fontainebleau from her carriage she saw him go by on his pony, chest up, his white linen hat pulled down over his nose, she cried out delightedly:

"How handsome he is, my little boy!"

The boy, like a soldier presenting arms, faced his mother, saluted and then galloped along beside the char-à-bancs.

Sometimes in the evening, before appearing at dinner or going out to an embassy, in full dress, her bare shoulders glistening with jewels, she slips along to the room where her son is writing or reading with Louis Conneau. Augustin Filon is with them. He is a young man with wavy brown hair. A little moustache emphasises his delicate features. His manners are perfect. He is full of all kinds of knowledge. The little prince respects him as an elder friend who devotes his years to him. The room is dim. The shade of the big Carcel lamp lights only the boy's table. The frou-frou of silky skirts makes them leave their books. They are about to stand up.

"Go on working," said Eugénie, "don't disturb yourselves."

She strokes Louis Conneau's head, gives her son a kiss, then going to the window and standing with her back against the great plush curtains, she talks with Filon. Is he satisfied with the prince? His studies have been greatly neglected up till now. His illness has kept him back still more. The tutor does not flatter him. His pupil is often inattentive, he is too fond of games. But his honest and sensitive disposition gives a certain scope. He understands, and he has a good memory. If he will work harder everything will be well.

This "little prince," so lovable, France loved him, and yet Paris, Paris where he was born, was becoming more and more critical and hostile. But his mother's unpopularity fell to some degree upon him, compromised him in his turn. In spite of his tender age, Eugénie was too eager to bring him forward, to push him into the limelight. He did not always meet with acclamations.

Thus he was made to preside over the distribution of prizes for the Concours général. The son of General Cavaignac was among the first. When his name was called, he refused to rise and go up on the platform to take his prize from the hands of the prince. At a sign from his handsome, severe mother, who had never ceased to remember the Second of December, he folded his arms, and with head erect seemed to defy the son of his father's fortunate rival. His comrades from the Lycée Bonapart applauded him. With the cries of "Vive Cavaignac!" there even mingled a few cries of "Vive la République!"

The prince did not say a word. General Frossard, sitting directly behind him, thought he had noticed nothing. But going back with him to Fontainebleau, where the Court was assembled, in the railway carriage they occupied alone, he saw the boy suddenly burst into sobs.

On their arrival at the palace the general told the sovereigns of the incident. Eugénie clasped her son in her arms, her eyes filled with tears, repeating in a broken voice:

"My poor little boy!"

The Emperor raised his shoulders sadly.

"What can you expect? Sooner or later, Louis will have to face opposition."

The Empress was choking with grief and anger mingled. She said over and over:

"Now we are not spared anything."

The prince would not appear at the dinner table.

"If I could," said Eugénie, "I should do the same thing!"

Nevertheless, she showed an unmoved face, but in spite of all her efforts to make conversation her preoccupation was visible. Napoleon kept silence. Coffee was taken as usual in the salon de Saint-Louis, then the majority of the diners went down into the gardens to enjoy the fine evening. Conti, the Emperor's *chef du cabinet,* and Octave Feuillet, the librarian of Fontainebleau, remained talking in the drawing-room. Sitting in the alcove of a window they presently heard in the next room a piercing laugh, coming in short bursts and going on and on interminably.

"It's the Empress," murmured Conti.

She had just had an attack of nerves. Her laugh filled the rooms and spilled out into the Court of the Fountain. Under the windows, which had not been shut in time, people began to cluster. Corvisart had Eugénie carried to her room, but for several hours the sedatives he administered seemed to have no effect. Pepa was holding her up, and she was crying out indistinct phrases, then going back to her laughing. Only somewhere round two o'clock did she fall asleep. Next day, completely exhausted, she could not appear till evening.

Certain persons thought that, in order to disarm the opposition, the Empress ought to have effaced herself, and to have given up taking part in public affairs. But no one ventured to put this advice before her; it was quite certain to be badly received and to incur her displeasure. Eugénie was not a woman to weaken before the storm. Whether it was clever of her or the reverse, she went on struggling quite openly for her son and for her policy, which she believed the one most capable of consolidating the Empire. Hostile to the ideas of the liberals, in which she saw nothing but anarchy, she tried to lead Napoleon away from that gradual return to constitutional practices to which he had been tending ever since 1863, a return in which Morny, near his death, with a voice already stricken with the chill of the grave, showed that salvation lay.

Persigny, whom the Empress had caused to be removed from active affairs, Persigny, that mastiff growling in his gilded niche of Chamarande, alone tried, with a brutal baying, to open the Emperor's eyes. Napoleon was lying ill in body and in mind. Often now he spent days in his bed. Eugénie was reading him the important passages from the newspapers, which she had run through, as she did every morning, and marked round with blue pencil. Felix, the usher to the cabinet, brought in a heavy letter sealed with wax with the direction "For the Emperor alone, from the Duc de Persigny."

Napoleon looked at it, hesitating to open it.

"Come," he said, "I am sure that's yet another of Persigny's recriminations. How tiresome he is! Here, you read this letter to me, I don't feel strong enough to-day."

The Empress broke the seals, and took out a round dozen of sheets covered with Persigny's neat handwriting.

A recrimination? It was in quite courteous terms a long and severe indictment of Eugénie. Recalling the mistakes of the imperial policy, retreat in Poland, incoherence in Italy, imprudence in Mexico, humiliation after Sadowa, Persigny imputed them all to the influence of the Empress. Her presence at the Council of Ministers, her interference, now still more pronounced, in home affairs, the party she had allowed to form around her, had all by degrees weakened Napoleon's authority. The State now had two masters. A duality that facilitated intrigues, destroyed control and by encouraging the opposition, was leading the Empire to the abyss of destruction. For a situation so critical the Duke saw one remedy only: to restore authority its unity. Napoleon must take France back into his own hands, whilst the Empress should content herself with shining in splendour in the Court fêtes.

As she read Eugénie trembled with fury. She made mistakes, the words were running too quickly before her eyes. Her hand was crumpling the insolent paper. She threw it on the floor when she came to the last lines. Napoleon seemed quite impassive. She burst out:

"Never again will I set foot in the Council, no, never! I will never expose myself again to such affronts. It is too unfair, too humiliating!"

Waves of anger came over her, submerged every thought in her mind; she strode up and down. Persigny! A nobody, an adventurer whom neither power nor riches had availed to change. He had always pursued her with his hatred. She had done everything to make friends with him, for she recognised that he was resolute and devoted. But clumsy, insolent, hide-bound, now that difficulties were piling up around them, he was crushing her. He was throwing on her the whole weight of all the mistakes of the reign. Oh, she would defend herself! Presently she would write to the duke, and tell him what she thought of so treacherous an attack!

The Emperor, annoyed and perturbed, argued with her.

"Calm yourself. This fresh idiocy of Persigny's is of no importance. I consider that your place is in the Council and you shall not cease to sit in it. I am the master . . ."

He tried to excuse Persigny, recalled his past services. She became angry again. He replied without losing his patience. In the end she was pacified; besides, she had well and duly won the game. But as she had vowed, that same day she sent to Chamarande eight pages so hard and bitter that Persigny thenceforth avoided appearing at Court. At long intervals and in private he still saw the Emperor, who kept it secret.

A truce from anxieties, domestic or of the State. The Exposition Universelle of 1867 was opened. Now it was nothing but one long round of fêtes, and over the Empire whose foundations were cracking there was an apparent renewing of splendour, a recrudescence of brilliance that reassured superficial minds.

The Palais de l'Industrie was streaming with flags one morning

Les Archives Photographiques d'Art et d'Histoire

THE SOVEREIGNS GOING TO THE EXPOSITION OF 1867
From the Painting by Porion at Malmaison

in April. The Emperor, in a black morning coat with the broad red ribbon across his breast, appeared in better health. The Empress, in *gorge-de-pigeon* silk, with a lace cloak and a light purple hat, in which a tall aigrette nodded, smiled and looked very beautiful, restored to hope by the acclamations showered on Napoleon as they passed. The newly opened Exposition was still half empty. The din of the hammers came at the tail of the Emperor's speech. Round the sovereigns were still only their intimates and a little handful of princes, the Duke of Leuchtenberg, the Count de Flandre, the Princess of Wales. But when a month had gone by the whole of Europe flocked along, gay and envying in the City enlarged, rebuilt, adorned with the brightness of Spring. The King of the Belgians came, the Queen of Portugal, the heir apparent of Sweden, the Czar with his son, the King of Prussia with Bismarck.

Neither Napoleon nor Eugénie wished to have the last pair of visitors. They were afraid how Paris might receive them, with Sadowa still in mind, and irritated against Prussia by the recent check in the negotiations with reference to Luxemburg. Paris had no cheers for Bismarck, dressed as a white cuirassier, but did not hoot him. Curious and flattered it gazed at this string of kings all athirst for pleasure, coming away from a reception at the Hôtel de Ville or a gala performance at the Opéra to hurry off to visit Cora Pearl or Hortense Schneider.

The Court was in one continual nervous commotion. Every day a great dinner, a concert, or a ball. The embassies rivalled the Tuileries. The Prussian embassy was thrown open one fine June evening for an all-night fête. Eugénie, seated on a throne, watched the dances, with Napoleon on her right and King William on her left. The King, limited, narrow, yet a gentleman, won her liking by his attentions to the Prince Imperial, whom he often took in his arms. Caught in his illusions once more, Napoleon talked with Bismarck. In the garden a Bierhalle had been set up where the officers drank and smoked till morning.

There was a great review at Longchamp. A march past of magnificent men, veterans of Malakoff, of Solferino, of Puebla, torn flags loaded down with glory. France behind them drew herself up proudly under the eyes of the masters of Europe.

Bismarck, however, in a corner of the grandstand, was reckoning up the regiments, scrutinising the arms. He found out about everything. "Wretched guns, bad rifles," he whispers to his king.

On the way back from the review, a workman fires at the Czar and misses. In the carriage Napoleon rises and says to Alexander:

"Sire, we have been under fire together. That makes us brothers in arms!"

"Our days are in the hands of Providence," says the Czar, coldly.

A moment after, he adds:

"That was a Pole."

He was full of resentment. His ear had already been struck at his visit to the Sainte-Chapelle by the stupid cry of Floquet, "Vive la Pologne, Monsieur!" Opinion in France blamed him, well he knew it, for the long drawn-out, the hideous martyrdom of Warsaw. Directly she knew of the attempted assassination, Eugénie hastened to the Elysée where Alexander was staying, embraced him and wept on his breast. In vain. The man may have been touched, the autocrat became stiff and cold. This France was insolent and dangerous. He rejected the alliance that Napoleon and Eugénie desired, that Morny believed he had paved the way for, and he turned towards closer relations with Prussia. Not long before his departure, in any case, a conversation was just getting under way between him and Napoleon. Eugénie came into the room in a whirl, and interrupted maladroitly with frivolous small talk.

Intoxicated by the splendour of the fêtes, the flatteries of crowned heads, she forgot the barely hidden dangers, the régime storm-tossed this way and that, France all alone in the midst of carnivorous States, and over yonder, behind the curtain of the waves, the weak Maximilian awaiting at Queretaro the sentence of Juarez. Till the very last moment, Eugénie had hoped that at least Maximilian's life would be spared. But the Indian, the conqueror of the descendant of Charles V, that butcher of the Aztec race, triumphed after the manner of a savage, who curbs neither joy nor hatred. Maximilian captured was infallibly dead. His trial would inevitably be mere jugglery, the accusations brought against him nothing but pretexts. The United States, the King of Prussia, Garibaldi, appealed to his clemency in vain; Juarez, with his eyes gleaming, and his teeth clenched, commanded the squad that was to lay the Archduke low among the aloes of Queretaro.

The news reached Paris on the morning of the distribution of the awards for the Exhibition. Eugénie read it in a Belgian paper. She hurried to the Emperor's room. Should the ceremony be postponed or should they pretend ignorance a few hours longer?

"Let us not know," replied Napoleon. "Perhaps the telegram is false."

But he knew well that it was true.

She dressed, shaken with sobs the while. They started, shuddering within, huddled against each other in the carriage that the crowd saluted so gaily. On the platform hung with flags, surrounded as they were with the glorification of France, they knew how to restrain themselves. The Emperor delivered his harangue with no weakening in his voice. Eugénie distributed medals and diplomas, ever gracious. But when she had got back to the Tuileries she collapsed and had to be put to bed. For several days she remained hidden. No one but Napoleon, her son, a few close friends, saw her. She dragged herself from one chair to another in the half dark, utterly prostrate. The idea that she had sent Maximilian to his death, Charlotte to madness, never left her. She rejected consolations, refused to listen to any suggested excuses. Loudly she confessed her mistake, her imprudence, the blindness that had led her to disregard so many wise counsels.

"But for me," she said, "they would be happy together at Miramar. . . . People will hate me, and they will be right! . . ."

She turned for succour only to God, prayed in solitude for hours, on her knees in her little oratory. She was seen prostrating herself in the Spanish fashion with her forehead on the floor, and remaining there as motionless as a murdered corpse.

When she appeared again in public she had assumed the deepest mourning. She had grown thin and pale. At certain moments, on a casual word, she bowed her head, her eyes suddenly drowned with tears that fell in big drops.

All the same she recovered from this stupor more speedily than Napoleon, who had been less immoderate. To be reconciled with Austria, whose reproaches she exaggerated in her own mind, after consulting with the Metternichs she persuaded the

Emperor to pay a visit to Francis-Joseph at Salzburg. The journey across Germany revived the fumes of pride within her. Kings thronged the stations to greet her. At Salzburg, in radiant sunshine, most simply clad, she tried to efface herself before the Empress Elizabeth, so young and lovely. The first contacts between the two Emperors were hesitating. They talked of Maximilian mournfully, then of other matters, of Germany, of the East. Their views began to draw together. The Chancellor, Beust, was urging wholeheartedly towards an alliance with France. It was at that moment that Eugénie, becoming mistrustful, found Beust too eager, imprudent. She damped his ardour, and also curbed Napoleon, who in any case always found it hard to come to a decision. They separated, having laid down the lines of an agreement, but without having concluded it.

The Emperor was better, he regained a little vigour during a few weeks, a semblance of health that deceived his entourage, and even the Empress, as to the real seriousness of his disease.

"You are too anxious about yourself," she used to tell him.

And she reproached Conneau for making him "soft." Herself of exceptional vitality, always ready to jump, to run, she could not believe in the exhausted condition of Napoleon, twenty years her senior. While he, dragging himself about the little superheated gilt rooms on the ground floor of the Tuileries, was recovering after an acute attack, she would be redoubling her activities, reading, writing, going out, giving audiences, seeing ministers, taking the Emperor's place in all the duties of his rank that he was unable to fulfil. In spite of fatigues and griefs, she had never been better in health. Her forties were touching her temples with white, but there were easy remedies for that. But in mind, in body, she remained alert, overflowing with energy, eager for movement and action.

At the beginning of 1869, the Emperor, once again tormented by the stone, sent her to take his place in Corsica, where the centenary of Napoleon was being celebrated. She went, full of uneasiness, but hoping for a lustre from the voyage that would war against her unpopularity. At Toulon, underneath the cheering to order she heard whistling, and in the island, the cradle of the dynasty, where the Emperor was worshipped, a frosty chill went with her everywhere. She had expected to walk on flowers, and she had none but the round formal bouquets of the mayors. Biting her lips she weighed the extent of her disfavour, which was emphasised by the hostile Paris newspapers.

A vast disaffection was undermining the Empire. A house without foundations, it was slowly sinking down into a kind of fermenting bog that burst its poisonous bubbles against its walls. Sadowa and Mexico had killed all confidence. As Octave Feuillet, loyal though he was, said, the régime was barely conceded a tomorrow. Those who thought of the future omitted it from their calculations. But the majority lived from day to day, in a kind of timid surliness. All classes complained. A bad harvest had sent up the price of bread. The great public works were suspended for want of money. Trade, which had still been flourishing on the eve of the Exhibition, was languishing.

War was felt to be approaching. Every Spring the country expected it. Napoleon and Eugénie had been warned by their friend the Countess de Pourtalès that in Berlin the conflict was hoped for, was being prepared for. The Minister Schleinitz had said to her at a dinner, alluding to her Alsatian estate of Robertsau:

"Fair Countess, you will soon be one of us. Alsace is coming back to the German fatherland."

Madame de Pourtalès told them of all the work going on in Prussia to unite and fuse the armies of the newly annexed States, the bonds being drawn daily tighter between Berlin and Munich and Dresden and Karlsruhe, bonds that were now turning the Confederation into an organised and very powerful body.

"Yes," replied Napoleon. "Bismarck is thinking of war, I know it perfectly well. But I do not want a war. And it takes two to fight."

Nothing but a close alliance with Austria and Italy could have made Prussia fall back. But the plans of Salzburg had still never been ratified, and in return for joining France Victor-Emmanuel was demanding Rome. Rome! Eugénie could not consent to despoil the Pope of his last rag of temporal power. Rouher, to please her, had uttered his famous cry in the Corps Législatif:

"Never shall Italy enter Rome. Never!"

To which Victor-Emmanuel had replied with a gross laugh:

"We will show him his 'never'!"

Fully conscious of the danger, Napoleon and Eugénie tried to avert it. Five months after Sadowa, the Emperor asked the Corps Législatif to raise the war effectives to 1,200,000 men, the same number as in Prussia. The opposition, moderates as well as republicans, ardently fought the proposal. Jules Favre said:

"Instead of a workshop France will be nothing but a barracks."

Garnier-Pagès exclaimed:

"The true frontier is patriotism!"

And M. Thiers, the prudent, sagacious M. Thiers:

"Our army will be sufficient to stop an invasion. Behind it the country will have time to breathe and to organise its reserves. Volunteers will flock to the colours. You show a great distrust of your own country."

The minister, in the name of the Emperor, insisted in vain. He was obliged to withdraw the bill. Now that he was shaping as a parliamentary sovereign, Napoleon could not seem to coerce the will of his Parliament.

In 1868, with Niel, he returned to the charge. He no longer asked for 1,200,000 men, but 750,000. The opposition was equally violent. And the country, too, was behind them, and even the army. Niel and the Emperor were accused of "wanting to militarise the nation." From the tribune Jules Simon sententiously declared:

"What matters it not the number of the soldiers, but the cause they have to defend. If the Austrians were beaten at Sadowa, it was because they were not anxious to win a victory for the house of Hapsburg against the German fatherland. There is only one cause that makes an army invincible, and that is liberty."

With one concession after another the outcome was a bastard statute. Drawing by lot and the right to send a substitute were retained. The "universal service" adopted in principle was only to be applied to the Garde Mobile, which had no existence except on paper.

Devotee of a complete reform of the military system, Eugénie disapproved the Emperor's conciliatory spirit. "He ought to impose his will," she used to repeat. But Napoleon no longer believed in the continuance of the autocratic régime. He desired to rejuvenate the Empire, to "crown the building" with a liberal pediment. The representatives of the country would find their voices once more, in face of the sovereign appointed by plebiscite. His son would, he believed, reign more easily in consequence. With all her might Eugénie endeavoured to hold him back on this slippery slope. She feared the surprises of popular suffrage. He replied:

"I shall go down into this ocean to baptise myself, not to drown myself in it."

He meant that he would try to surmount its waves. But would he always be able to, and would not a ground-swell come to carry him suddenly off his feet?

He did not listen to her. He now hardly ever listened to her. He followed his own ideas. He saw Emile Ollivier, eloquence itself incarnate, who drew him on after the lovely mirages of liberty. In vain Eugénie struggled against his hold on Napoleon. She had known Ollivier ever since 1865, the time of her second period of regency. She was then bent on turning the prisons for young offenders into penitentiary farm colonies. Emile Ollivier had interested himself in this matter. The Empress brought him to the Tuileries to ask his advice. She liked him pretty well. He liked her exceedingly. He was very nearly won over. But at this moment their two influences were directly opposed to one another. Backed by a mysterious charm, Ollivier was the stronger. On January 2, 1870, Napoleon called him into the government.

The Liberal Empire, in which she saw an anomaly, but which she was unable to withstand, almost immediately ousted Eugénie from power. At the request of Ollivier, she ceased to appear at the Council. She experienced a profound irritation at this, a deep resentment. To have done so much, to have lavished herself merely to disappear in this way from the political stage at the request of a republican of yesterday! She affected to have nothing to do with any business thenceforth, had only relations of formal courtesy with the ambassadors. When she was asked for a recommendation she replied with some tartness:

"Apply to the ministers, I have no credit now."

She said too:

"The President of the Council is everything now. The Emperor counts for nothing. He is simply a signing-machine."

At the same time, in a spirit of proud loyalty, she avoids any semblance of intrigue. The Emperor is trying an experiment.

She gives him a clear field, certain in any case that he will not succeed, that sooner or later he will have to return to authority. She awaits that day. Perhaps she will not have to wait for it so very long. External events may, sooner than any one believes, force Napoleon once more to become the absolute guide he had been in a bygone period, with the whole country solidly massed behind him.

Sometimes, however, for her anxiety compels her, she cannot refrain from questioning the Emperor. She makes as it were an irruption into his thought. He replies evasively. She feels him so distant and aloof, with his taciturn gentleness, his colourless smile, his eyes lowered like the eyes of the dead . . . She shrugs her shoulders and goes away.

"This will never last," she repeats to herself, to keep her patience.

Indeed, it seemed impossible that it would last for long. The return to the constitutional system had weakened the government without bringing about the lessening of tension that Napoleon hoped for. The killing of Victor Noir, and his obsequies, unchained the anger of Paris. Strikes broke out. The ministry were in a bog, stumbling and fumbling. The advanced parties became doubly bold. The liberalism of Napoleon III appeared to them to be a sign of decrepitude. The unmuzzled press began to bark: Rochefort heaped insults on "Badinguet, la Badinguette," and "le petit Badinguet." Gambetta predicted their fall in open session of the Corps Législatif.

Eugénie, less powerful now, was less courted. Her ante-chambers were no longer besieged. She lived more alone, remained more in her own rooms. Her love of going about and of change seemed dulled. She read a great deal, wrote, meditated. Her mouth took on lines of gravity. In front of her closest friends she would sometimes let slip a bitter phrase:

"A coup d'état is a cannon-ball that you drag about after you and which ends by paralysing your limb."

Or else:

"In France at the outset you can do anything; after a certain time you can't even blow your nose."

Clearsighted, she watched Napoleon borne along like a swimmer in a swift stream, with at moments an effort that re-established him as the head. Then he abandoned himself again to the current. She anticipated the worst: the death of the Emperor, revolution, the fearful and ignominious end of everything. She assigned to herself only one part in this tragedy: that of the doomed hero who resists without flinching, who fights with all his muscles, never averts his eyes from the massacre, and closes them only after he has received the death blow. The hyena of the people might devour her, but should never make her flee. Eugénie would fall with her throne. She would die covering the body of her son. . . .

Appearances still call for fêtes. But mostly they have a tang of anguish about them. After the elections of 1869, during the riots of the *blouses blanches,* there was a gala performance for Queen Sophia of Holland and the Grand Duchess Marie of Russia. During the play telegrams came to the Emperor without ceasing. He did not open them, but put them down beside him, applauded the actors. Every one was looking at him stealthily, anxious about what was happening. At the ball that followed, the low roaring sound of an irritated populace floated up through the windows looking on the Place Carrousel. The orchestra played the waltzes of Strauss and Waldteufel for one or two couples only. Every one was listening, waiting. When the violins stopped, the cries of the crowd came through, as the police endeavoured to disperse it. Eugénie was very pale under her jewelleries. She went to a window, then away from it, thinking that the sight of her might fan the clamours to a fiercer height. At supper many of the tables remained empty. Napoleon and Eugénie were almost alone with their royal guests and the members of their household. . . .

"Everybody is afraid without very clearly knowing why," wrote Mérimée. "It is the same sort of feeling that you get from Mozart's music when the Commander is about to appear."

In these days of gloom one last respite presented itself to Eugénie, allowing her to smile once more, to display her graces and glories—the opening of the Suez Canal. For ten years, never holding back, she had energetically supported her cousin Ferdinand de Lesseps. Many regarded him as a visionary. Eugénie kept her absolute faith in him. At her request the French government had subscribed for an enormous quantity of shares. Thus to some extent the Canal was her work. She was proud to become its god-mother. When the Khedive came to Paris to invite her she accepted with delight. Returning to her love of wandering, she gladly absented herself for six weeks from her Court that had become dull and gloomy, and also from the Emperor with whom she had had a last contention, over Madame de Mercy-Argenteau. Surrounded by a suite of her intimates, Prince Joachim Murat, Count Cléry, Count de Cessé-Brissac, her constant friends Madame de Nadaillac and Madame de la Poëze, her nephew and nieces, the Duke of Huescar and the Alba girls, her *demoiselles d'honneur,* Mademoiselle Marion and Mademoiselle de Larminat, she embarked at Venice, where Victor-Emmanuel paid her his somewhat chilly respects. On the imperial yacht, the *Aigle,* she reached Constantinople, having called at Athens on the way. The Sultan staged a magnificent reception for her at Yildiz-Kiosk. She received the religious orders placed under French protection, and when pressed to make a speech, being taken by surprise and deeply moved, she could barely utter a few not very clear sentences, which were immediately covered up with enthusiastic applause.

At Cairo the Empress rested for some days in a palace that the courtly Khedive had built expressly for her on the banks of the Nile. Mariette-Pasha, talking to her of Ancient Egypt while she was in this palace, called up before her the golden ghosts of the Valley of the Kings.

She was then installed on a large dahabieh, drawn by a tug, and went up the Nile. Other boats followed in the wake of the new Cleopatra. A slow journey along the vast roadway of ooze, flanked by two deserts. They stopped at Luxor, at Thebes, at Edfu, at Assouan, to visit temples and excavations. The heat overpowered everybody; Eugénie stood out against it best of all. She complained neither of the mosquitoes nor of the *Khamsin.* Mounted on a donkey or a camel she admired Karnak and Denderah, and saw the almahs dance at Siut. Nevertheless, her thoughts turned back towards France. Almost every day she wrote to the Emperor. From far away the Emperor's conjugal misdemeanours wore a less heinous aspect to her. She knew he was embarked upon a voyage more perilous in another way than that of the *Aigle,* and hoped that in her absence he would not have to face any too violent tempest. It was the moment when Napoleon III was taking the preliminary steps towards his parliamentary conversion. She appeared less hostile to it then than she was to become in the sequel; she did not as yet see all its consequences, and in especial that she would be obliged so speedily to relinquish power.

Sitting in her stifling cabin, after nibbling at her quill for a moment, she wrote long letters, with never a pause for reconsideration, in which her sincere, sensitive spirit, exalted by separation, unbosomed itself:

MY VERY DEAR LOUIS,

I am writing to you as we make our way along the Nile. I have news of you and Louis every day by telegraph. That is marvellous and very pleasant for me, for I am linked to the friendly bank by this wire that keeps me in touch with everything I love. I was greatly worried over yesterday, and to know that you were in Paris without me, but I see from your telegram that everything went off well. I think you must not be discouraged, but continue in the path you have entered upon. I hope your speech will be in this sense.

I am at a great distance and very ignorant of matters to be talking like this, but I am most profoundly convinced that consistency and logic in ideas is the true strength. I have no liking for sudden, spasmodic actions, and I am persuaded that it is not possible to have a coup d'état twice in the same reign. I am writing in rather rambling fashion, for I am "preaching to a converted" who knows more of these things than I do, but I must say something, if only to prove what you know, that my heart is with you both, and if in days of peace my vagrant spirit loves to wander in space, in days of stress and anxiety the place I long to be is with both of you. . . . Far from men and things, one breathes in an atmosphere of healing calm, and I figure to myself that all is well, because I know nothing.

After visiting the Pyramids and the Sphinx in the company of the Khedive, returning to Port Said where Francis-Joseph, Prince Frederick of Prussia, the Prince of the Low Countries, and the Emir Abd-el-Kader swelled her train, followed by a fleet all flags and bunting, Eugénie triumphantly opened the Canal amid the din of salvoes and trumpets, the cheers of the many-coloured crowd, the dazzling lustre of the skies.

"November 16, 1869 . . . my most splendid memory" . . . was what she called it later.

PART III
DOWNFALL

CHAPTER I
War

ON July 28, 1870, at nine o'clock in the morning, at St. Cloud, Napoleon, with Eugénie on his right and the Prince Imperial on his left, walks into the great drawing-room where a silent concourse is awaiting his coming. All the ministers are there, with Emile Ollivier at their head, the members of the two imperial households, a number of the habitués of the palace, of personal friends. The Emperor moves from one to another, shakes hands with a word to each, a mark of affection. His voice seems lower than usual. Some one says to him:

"In a fortnight's time Your Majesty will be in Berlin."

He answers gravely:

"No, do not look for that, even if we are fortunate."

The Empress, wearing a simple grey silk dress, follows him, clasping the little prince by the hand, very smart in his new sous-lieutenant's uniform, with top-boots, and the badge of the Grand Croix of the Légion d'honneur on his breast. He looks very slight, but his colour is good and his eyes are shining. He talks and jokes and laughs, as though ever so little intoxicated. The Emperor, in general's undress uniform, képi in hand, goes from group to group, walking heavily. At moments he twists nervously at his big dyed moustache. He is so pale that he has had to put a little life into his cheeks with rouge.

For the last month he has been suffering again, and more terribly than ever, from his bladder. He has had several attacks of hæmaturia, which Dr. Conneau has concealed at his orders. On July 1, without Eugénie's knowledge, the specialists of highest repute were brought together in consultation at St. Cloud, Nélaton, Ricord, Germain Sée, and Fauvel. The report, drawn up by Doctor Sée, expressed the conclusion that there was a "purulent cystitis necessitating a surgical operation to relieve the bladder of the stone that has formed inside it and is causing the patient extreme pain." But Napoleon did not allow Conneau to submit this report for signature to the other physicians. He had always dreaded an operation, the very same operation that had killed

Maréchal Niel a year earlier. He wished to wait still longer, at least until the moment when the conflict between France and Prussia provoked by the candidature of Leopold of Hohenzollern for the Spanish throne should have found a solution; as he hoped, a peaceful one. The Empress knew that he was ill, that he ought to undergo an examination. But she had never taken this trouble very seriously. So often already Napoleon had gone through crises that passed over quickly enough! She was aware of his physical decline, but this did not alarm her, rather it irritated her, because she attributed it mainly to amorous excesses. Besides, living so close to the Emperor, she did not see him too clearly, she was accustomed to this enfeebled condition, did not observe the sinking in of the face, the tonelessness of the eye, the extreme lassitude of his carriage.

By way of precaution, however, she has had remedies packed for him, all the sedatives and paraphernalia capable of alleviating his malady. Doctor Conneau, a faithful friend and a good practitioner, will in any case be with him all the time. He has promised Eugénie to send her a daily account of Napoleon's health.

The Emperor has ended his farewells. He takes out his watch.

"Come," he said, "it is time."

With his wife and his son, and followed by everybody present, he goes out to the court of the palace. After Eugénie, not without effort, he climbs into the Empress's little carriage drawn by two ponies. Eugénie picks up the reins; she means to drive herself. Behind them the Prince Imperial takes his seat in a victoria, with his governor, General Frossard. A number of ladies, the ministers, the dignitaries, the Emperor's officers, find room in landaus.

Eugénie raises her whip. Napoleon, bareheaded, bows to the people who remain behind in the court of the palace. Then having donned his képi, he gives them a military salute as well. And when the light little carriage has started off at the trot, he looks straight in front of him, without saying a word, like a wax figure.

War was declared on Prussia on July 15. For three years past every one had felt it was coming. Tired of Bismarck's affronts, the whole nation waited for it, hoping to find in it some revenge for Sadowa. That a Prussian should dare to seat himself on the throne of Spain seemed to all a thing not to be borne. France would have been between two fires, as she was in the time of Charles the Fifth. The Emperor alone wished to maintain peace. The report he had from Colonel Stoffel, the military attaché at Berlin, on the efficiency of the new Prussian armament, made him apprehensive of a clash. But when he spoke to the Minister for War, Lebœuf burst out laughing. Stoffel was a pessimist, an *esprit faux,* falling down in admiration before the Germans. This war the old soldier wished for with all his heart and soul, so much that he swore that if it was not plunged into he would give up the ministry and return his marshal's baton. Like him all the generals pressed for it with ardour, with arrogance, and the ministers as well (except Ollivier at the outset), and the Corps Législatif, and the newspapers whether imperialist or republican, and the whole body of public opinion on its hind legs against this fresh attack on the national prestige.

The Empress also wished for war. For reasons of honour and policy, which became more weighty when joined and mingled together.

She did not believe that the Empire could have allowed itself to resist the manifest will of the country. Since 1867 she had felt a disaffection growing up around the régime, which with her uncurbed imagination she exaggerated in her own mind. The plebiscite of May 1870, which had given 7,300,000 "ayes" for the Liberal Empire, had appeared satisfactory to Napoleon III. Eugénie for her part had been scared by the 1,570,000 "noes." The figure in fact stood out as enormous, considering that it had been subject to the pressure of the prefects, the clergy, the magistracy and the army. In reality, she thought, they were supported only by the vested interests. The enthusiasm, the faith of France, had abandoned them. After Mexico and Sadowa, to bow before the intrigues of Prussia was to hasten towards disturbances, perhaps towards downfall. On the other hand, a successful war ought to consolidate the dynasty, to allow the Emperor to seize once more the absolute authority he had lost through weakness, that authority without which she could not conceive the idea of government. Above everything it would secure her son's throne. That he should reign was her one idea, her anxiety, the obsession that now never left her mind for a moment. She had never ceased to regret the retreat of 1866. And yet there were reasons then, she told herself, that the difficulties of that time had disappeared. She judged that the army was strengthened by the late reforms. The old troops of Mexico were now a backbone and stiffening for the conscripts. From the Minister for War to the youngest sous-lieutenant, all the officers predicted a lightning campaign, which, anticipating the Prussian mobilisation by a fortnight, would cut Germany in two and throw the Southern States into our arms. Never, they reiterated, would such an opportunity come again.

Besides, Eugénie counted on an alliance with Austria and Italy. She was persuaded that France's taking the field would oblige them to range themselves by her side. A strange error of judgment, since Francis-Joseph had no intention of acting unless he was certain of Italian co-operation, and since that co-operation depended upon our troops leaving Rome—Rome, which the Empress was unwilling to give up at any price.

Whether wittingly or not, Metternich and Nigra, by their pressing attentions, their flattering courtesies, led her more deeply into her mistake. Thus when in the afternoon of July 12, at St. Cloud, she saw Napoleon coming from the Council of Ministers full of delight at Prince Leopold's renunciation, and calling out in a voice of relief, "It's peace!", she was deeply disappointed. The hoped-for revenge, the needed victory, was receding. France was receiving but a precarious satisfaction. To-morrow Bismarck could begin his threats anew. So that odious Thiers would have been right when he said, "You will put up with everything in Italy, put up with everything in Germany, and on those conditions you will have peace!" Who knew whether Prince Hohenzollern might not go back on his forced declaration, as his brother had done already in Rumania, slip off in a few days' time to Madrid, and, pretending to give in to Prim's importunity, accept the crown of Spain? Then once again Napoleon would appear as a dupe. Irresistible anger would swell up in the hearts of all the French people. And the Empire would go down in shame.

She sees only one way of averting this catastrophe. And this is to adopt a suggestion thrown out by frivolous Clément Duvernois, to demand from Prussia a *guarantee* that she will never allow her vassal to reign at Madrid. If King William gives way, our face is saved; instead of a military triumph, France is at least assured of a brilliant diplomatic success. It will be peace, yes, but peace in honour. If he refuses, well then it will be war.

War Eugénie is not afraid of. Or rather she fears it not so much as revolution.

That same day a long conference took place at St. Cloud with Napoleon and Gramont, the Minister for Foreign Affairs. With her customary passion and eloquence Eugénie extorted the Emperor's consent. Gramont seconded her out of a spirit of chivalry, of gallantry. The demand for a guarantee was despatched. (Ollivier, the responsible minister, was not informed till later.) The ambassador Benedetti carried it to the King of Prussia, insisted clumsily, was dismissed, but with courtesy. At Ems, Bismarck, whom the idea of peace threw into despair, and who when his plans were spoiled was thinking of resigning, suddenly snatched at the pretext, and devised the trick that he knew would "have the effect of a red rag on the French bull." By moral rather than a literal falsification, the interpretation of the King's attitude in an insulting sense, he informed every Chancery in Europe that his sovereign had refused to receive the French ambassador.

This time it was war indeed. Smarting from the slap in the face, Paris rose, went in procession along the boulevards, carrying flags, shouted *"à Berlin."* The corner boys of the barriers and the gentlemen of the Jockey Club sang the Marseillaise. A universal and irresistible enthusiasm. If Ollivier, if the Emperor, had wished to keep patience, to accept the mediation of England, to appeal to a Congress, they would have been swept away like windlestraws.

But they did not resist. The national ferment sent up about them vapours so hot and heady that they themselves for a moment forgot their fears. Napoleon was the first to find them again. He had lived these last two weeks at St. Cloud in an ague of the spirit. As always he kept his anguish to himself. But Eugénie, now that her fever had subsided, could hardly sleep at all. . . .

"A war," she said one evening to her nieces the d'Albas, "is always a leap into the unknown."

Still, at other moments, when from the terrace of St. Cloud her eyes falling on Paris encountered the Arc de Triomphe, she seemed to see, amid the plaudits of the people, Napoleon and his son passing through it as conquerors.

And now, with forehead knit, she sends her ponies on. Their bells ring gaily out in the cool morning air. Under the gold-crowned verdure of the park the landaus tool along behind them to the little station, covered with a mushroom of thatch, from which Napoleon is about to start for Metz, where his headquarters are. The imperial train is drawn up along the platform. A few friends, Edouard Delessert, Henri Chevreau, old Colonel Thirion, receive the Emperor. He wishes to cut his adieux short to avoid emotion. He whispers into Emile Ollivier's ear, "I count on you." He holds Eugénie in a long embrace; she kisses her son. The boy, so proud a moment ago, now weeps in dismay. She chokes back her tears. Napoleon takes the boy by the hand, makes him climb up into the carriage.

"Adieu, Louis," says the mother, "do your duty."

"We will all do our duty," replies the Emperor, from the footboard.

A moment later Eugénie calls out hoarsely:

"Let me kiss Louis again."

The prince comes down from the carriage. His mother embraces him wildly. She blesses him, makes the sign of the cross on his forehead.

"I will be brave, *maman,* you will see," says the child.

She does indeed believe that he will be brave. In these moments she feels herself more a mother than she has ever been. Last night with her own hands she had packed the kit of her little officer. Would she ever see him again? Would she see the Emperor again? He was looking at them in silence. Setting forth to meet the enemy, he was no doubt thinking that all the duty and danger did not devolve on him, that he was leaving a heavy share of it to this woman whom he had loved so much, and who would be the prey of so much hatred in tempestuous Paris in case of any defeat.

He tightened his lips, lowered his lids again over his lacklustre eyes. The hour was now come when they two were paying for their happiness, their marvellous, triumphant fortune. Perhaps this bitter moment might suffice? Perhaps victory, the friend of the Bonapartes, awaited him on the Rhine, victory that would cover with its gold the mistakes of the reign. But he had within him, in his head, in his bones as it were, a wretched dread that froze him.

At a sign from his mother, the child had climbed up again to his side. Blinded by tears, Eugénie hid them with her hands. A whistle. The train moved smoothly along the rails. A great cry went up, "Vive l'Empereur!" At the door of the carriage Napoleon and the little prince, trying to smile, were saluting, waving their képis.

Going back to the palace with the Princess Clotilde, Eugénie went and kneeled in the chapel where, two hours before, the Archbishop of Paris, Monseigneur Darboy, had administered communion to her and the Emperor and their son. There she prayed long for a happy return. Then having bathed her eyes, she went to her cabinet where Emile Ollivier was waiting for her.

Once again she was Regent.

Since the evening of the 14th of July she had once more been present at the meetings of the Council. In so critical a period it was a mistake to devolve the Imperial powers upon her, and this Napoleon had felt. In spite of so much true, or ostensible, charity, in spite of all her advances to the press, Eugénie was more unpopular than ever. A woman, certainly superior to many, at any rate in courage, could never give so highly strung a people the impression of security that a man such as Prince Napoleon would have been able to impart. But the Emperor distrusted his cousin, fearing his nature, at the same time both violent and demagogic. And besides, the Empress would not have endured his appointing to a place she regarded as falling by natural right to her, the man she had always found against her as her enemy.

The powers of the Regent were limited. A constitutional sovereign since the last plebiscite, Napoleon III had only been able to leave her the presidency of the State. The letters patent of July 22 still further curbed her initiative.

"It is not our intention that the Empress-Regent shall have power to authorise by her signature the promulgation of any law other than those which are now pending before the Senate, the Corps Législatif and the Conseil d'Etat."

Emile Ollivier, the chief person concerned, counted on keeping these bands tightly drawn. An absolutist by nature as well as by conviction, Eugénie was to slacken them little by little and seize the effective power once more.

The President of the Council worked in Paris, away from her, and in the first days confined himself to informing her of the decisions taken by the cabinet. Since she was not left any part to play, she carved one out for herself. By various means, letters from herself, moves of Augustin Filon, who had become her secretary, she tried to soften the over-crabbed tone of the press and disarm the Opposition. She also took an active interest in foreign policy. She wrote to General Fleury, whom she had caused to be relegated to the embassy at Petersburg, as his influence over the Emperor had offended her. She had little liking for him. But she could have no doubts as to his complete devotion to Napoleon, or his patriotism. She appealed to his tact, to his clear-sightedness, to procure for France, if need were, at least the moral support of the Czar. At the same time she conjured Metternich to do everything possible to obtain the co-operation of the Austrian army. The ambassador avowed to her, in honeyed sentences, that Vienna had not yet considered the eventuality of taking the field. She protested, in alarm, and said she would go to Metz herself to inform the Emperor.

She never went. While the newspapers were celebrating some slight successes of advance posts, she received from Metz on July 30, a letter from the Emperor which she told her intimates absolutely plunged her into the depths—*"lui cassa bras et jambes."* She made the mistake of showing it to the Metternichs, in an excess of confidingness.

On arriving at headquarters the Emperor had found nothing but jealous rivalry among the chiefs, lack of discipline among the troops, deficiency in the armament. A tremendous confusion hamstrung all efforts. Half the effectives were missing. The eight army corps assembled counted less than two hundred thousand men. The immediate offensive upon which Eugénie and the advocates of war had based all their plans to take Prussia by surprise, rally Bavaria, Württemberg and Baden to the side of France, and make up Austria's mind for her, was becoming impossible. It was necessary to wait, to organise transport and supplies, at the risk of seeing the enemy, ready before we were, across the Rhine.

"Mon Dieu," murmured the Empress, "what are we coming to?"

She convoked the Council, read them the heartrending letter of Napoleon. Since the strategic situation was altogether reversed, and the whole of Germany, it could no longer be doubted, was about to make common cause with Prussia, France could not do without alliances. The Regent declared that in order to obtain the assistance of Austria and Italy, she was of the opinion that they should go to the extreme limit of possible concessions. Was she about to recant on the question of Rome? The ministers looked at her anxiously.

She resumed:

"The war is clearly to be very violent, very dangerous. To-morrow our national independence may be menaced. The co-operation of Austria and Italy would guarantee our victory. But Austria will not move if Italy refused to move. What then is the maximum of honourable concessions we could make to Italy? In my view, that maximum is that we should withdraw our troops from Civita Vecchia. I do not even speak of giving up Rome to the Italians. It would be a felony, an apostasy!"

The ministers all agreed to this proposal. It was useless. Victor-Emmanuel wanted Rome, and even if he had now been allowed to take it, he would not have entered the war. He saw the French defeat coming, and was not the man to ally himself to disaster.

Napoleon had divined as much. At that same moment, at Metz, he was bidding good-bye to Vimercati, the confidant of the King of Italy, who had come to tempt him one last time.

After an hour's consideration, he told him:

"No, it's impossible, I cannot give way about Rome."

It was too late, he thought. He would have dishonoured himself for nothing. When the Empress learned of his answer, she exclaimed:

"The Piedmontese in Rome! I would as soon see the Prussians in Paris!"

Her mind unquestionably did not endorse her words. But these verbal extravagances helped in a way to solace her anxiety.

On August 2 she had a moment of joy, the despatch from Sarrebrück.

"Louis has just had his baptism of fire," telegraphed the Emperor. "He was admirably cool. He was not the least bit rattled and might have been taking a stroll in the Bois de Boulogne.

"We were in the first line; bullets and cannon-balls were dropping at our feet. Louis kept a bullet that had fallen at his feet. Some of the men shed tears to see him so calm."

She forgot her distresses. The gallant boy, how proud of him she was! At that moment Ollivier was announced.

Eugénie handed him the telegram.

"I brought him up to despise danger," she said, "but only actual trial shows the bedrock of human nature. How would he behave under fire? That was what filled my mind. To-day I know. I am content and glad, because I am sure that he is naturally brave."

"We must publish this," exclaimed Ollivier; "it will have a tremendous effect on public opinion!"

The Empress hesitated. The telegram was addressed to the mother rather than to the Regent. The minister insisted, so eloquently and so persuasively that she consented.

Next day as she read the unfriendly newspapers she clenched her fists. The Sarrebrück incident aroused a great outburst of laughter. They christened the little prince *"l'enfant de la balle."*

"How disgraceful!" muttered Eugénie, walking up and down St. Cloud like a lioness in her cage. "What kind of heart must they have to jeer at the courage of a little boy of fourteen, a French boy!"

CHAPTER II

Disasters

EUGENIE was in the big drawing-room at St. Cloud on the first floor, surrounded by the Princesse d'Essling, the Princesse de la Moskowa, Countess Clary, her two Alba nieces, Marie and Louise, Prince Metternich, Count de Cossé-Brissac, Admiral Jurien de la Gravière. Dinner was just over; it was half-past nine. There entered the Marquis de Piennes and Augustin Filon who had gone to Paris in the afternoon to distribute various messages from the Regent to the ministers. They came back with news of a very great ferment and disquiet. The city, cast into consternation the previous day by the defeat of Wissembourg, had hung out its flags to greet the announcement of a great victory by Mac-Mahon. But at the official denial the crowd, suddenly swollen and enraged, tore down the flags and sacked the offices of certain exchange brokers with German names. The Stock Exchange was all demoralised by the wildest speculation. Journalists were besieging the Ministry for the Interior. Filon had gone there, and to Emile Ollivier in the Place Vendôme. The politicians of the highest place seemed altogether dismayed. Piétri, the prefect of police, had said to him: "There will be hot work to-night."

Eugénie listened calmly to this report. Not long after, General Lepic appeared, bringing a letter from the President of the Council who begged the Empress to authorise him to place the capital in a state of siege, and asked her to come back without delay "with the troops at her disposal."

The Regent shrugged her shoulders; there were a hundred and sixty men at St. Cloud. She signed the decree, told the general that she would come back to the Tuileries next day. Then utterly broken with fatigue, she bowed to every one present and retired.

The drawing-room remained dimly lighted. The great windows were open; it was exceedingly hot. A few women were moving about, unable to get to sleep, whispering here and there. Suddenly they saw in the library next door Monsieur de Piennes,

Monsieur de Cossé-Brissac, and Augustin Filon kneeling on chairs and looking at a great map with an air of despair. Princesse d'Essling joined them. Pale and perspiring, the three men were deciphering two despatches just come from the *quartier général* a few minutes away, which announced the defeat of Frossard at Forbach, and of Mac-Mahon at Froeschwiller. A serious twofold disaster: the French troops in full retreat, Alsace invaded, Lorraine laid open, the road to Paris threatened.

The men looked at one another in terror.

"Who is going to take this to the Empress!" asked Monsieur de Piennes.

Monsieur de Cossé-Brissac and Augustin Filon hung their heads. Monsieur de Piennes, more of a gentleman farmer than a chamberlain, but a man of action, said:

"Very well, I will go."

Eugénie was undressed and on the point of getting into bed. Pépa announced Monsieur de Piennes, who insisted on handing her an important telegram.

She dressed again, as she always knew how to, in a moment. When Monsieur de Piennes was ushered in he had not a word to say; she snatched the paper out of his hands. She read, "saw the abyss," tottered as though about to faint. But almost at once, stiffening up, she looked the chamberlain full in the eyes.

"The dynasty is doomed, monsieur," she said, "we must now think of nothing but France."

With precision, even harshness, she gave her orders all cut and dried. All the ministers and the members of the Privy Council were summoned to the Tuileries for two in the morning. The St. Cloud household were to prepare for her immediate departure. At the same time she sent Prince Poniatowski to find the Austrian ambassador at La Jonchère where he was installed for the summer.

Then she reappeared in the drawing-room. The women fell silent at sight of her. Princesse d'Essling went up to her weeping:

"Ah, Madame . . ."

"Please don't say a word," said Eugénie, "I need all the courage I have got."

Fearing that they might go to fetch her nieces, she forbade them to be wakened. Crumpling up her handkerchief in her hands, she went and sat down by a window looking out on the park. No one about her dared to move. Nothing was heard but the rustling of the foliage in the silver night.

Haunted as she had been throughout so many years by the memory of Marie-Antoinette, was Eugénie thinking that this night of August 6, which forced her to go back to Paris, was strangely like the Sixth of October on which the Queen left Versailles for ever? Was not the same fate waiting for her? Would she ever come back to St. Cloud?

The Spanish woman, like the Austrian before her, was about to return to those indefensible Tuileries, where she would be at the mercy of the same disappointed populace, ready for bloodthirsty deeds of madness. Death—especially now that misfortune was surging up to her—did not make her afraid. Death with dignity, on the scaffold, as a sovereign, no, she had no fear of it. She feared only the baseness of revolutions and their outrages. . . . She looked at the alleys of the park, bathed in cold light. She had never much liked St. Cloud. But she had come there as a young wife, glowing and triumphant, her son had tried his first baby steps there; a few weeks ago he was still playing there with his little comrades. Then she felt rising within her a regret for that inconvenient but splendid abode. Sadly, from the bottom of her heart, she bade it farewell.

This waiting seemed interminable to everybody. At last the sound of wheels on the gravel was heard. The Empress rose at once and left the drawing-room. On the staircase she met Richard Metternich.

"I am going," she said, "come with me."

She threw herself into the same carriage that had taken the prince away. Metternich got up beside her.

"To the Tuileries," she said to the coachman.

At three in the morning, the Regent opened the session of the Council with an air of authority that no one had ever observed in her before. The Presidents of the two Chambers, Rouher and Schneider, were there, also General Trochu, summoned by Ollivier. He was very popular for having opposed the Emperor's views on the re-organisation of the army. Ollivier thought it an astute move to annex him to the government.

The general placed himself at the disposal of the Empress "as a Breton, a Catholic and a soldier." Eugénie interrupted this flourish and thanked him in a somewhat curt sentence.

She proposed to convoke the Chambers. The national danger, she said, bade her lean upon the nation.

Emile Ollivier, extremely agitated, his eyes moist behind his spectacles, protested. The powers of the Regent did not give her the right to assemble the parliament. She was about to encroach upon the essential prerogative of the Emperor. Eugénie made an impatient gesture. Why be trammelled with formalities? Had they not been infringed already by the decreeing of the state of siege?

Ollivier then said—and his view was prophetic—that it would be useless, dangerous, even absurd, to give free play to the haranguers of the Opposition in so difficult a moment. He recalled the part played by the Chambers in the Hundred Days. The government had one duty and only one: to reassure France and to rally it around them entire.

The Empress, unjustly, thought that the President of the Council feared above all to find himself before an Assembly whose first vote would overthrow him. But Ollivier was full of illusions as to his own parliamentary position and the confidence with which he inspired the country. Eugénie insisted, saying that the Emperor having promised before his departure to summon the Chambers in case of necessity, the moment had come to keep that promise. Ollivier asked that the Emperor should at least be consulted. The Regent replied that the Emperor had not all the necessary knowledge to appreciate the position and that he would assuredly approve the decision when taken. Then the Prime Minister proposed to invite the Emperor to return to Paris and take the power into his own hands.

"We are competent here," replied the Regent. "The Emperor's place at this moment is with the army. He must not appear again in Paris except as a conqueror." The Council, wavering at first, fell in with her opinion. It was decided that the Chambers should meet the day after the next.

When the Council rose, the Empress went to her own rooms. The vast palace was empty, without servants or sentries. The furniture was still shrouded in its grey dust-covers. Eugénie would not allow them to be taken away.

"What is the use?" she said.

She went to bed and slept for some hours.

In the morning, as she was walking about in her cabinet, absorbed in her own thoughts, waiting for the ministers again, she heard noises below her windows. She looked, and saw a turbulent crowd thickening up against the railings. On waking, Paris had just learned of the twin defeat. Above the gilt spikes a burst of hooting rose when they caught sight of the silhouette of the Empress. Fists were shaken in the air. They cried, *"Déchéance!* Down with the Spanish woman!" She bowed her shoulders and went to kneel in her dim oratory, where for a few minutes she knew she would find peace.

She came back, resolute. To those who, knowing of her return, came to offer their services, to the seekers for news, still more numerous these, who flocked to the Tuileries without ceremony, she repeated:

"Everything can be saved yet if Frenchmen all join hands."

And she added, when they spoke of her own safety:

"I do not need troops to defend me. Let us send our last battalions to the war."

"She is as firm as a rock," wrote Mérimée to Panizzi.

And Trochu said:

"The woman is an ancient Roman."

By her pride, her bravery, her ambition to serve, but in the foremost place, she had climbed from her decorative position to the effective power that orders and controls; she had become the pivot and the soul of the government.

She telegraphed to the Emperor at Metz:

"I am profoundly satisfied with the resolutions taken at the Council of Ministers. . . . I am persuaded that we shall drive the Prussians helter-skelter to the frontier. Courage then; with energy we shall dominate the position. I will answer for Paris, and I kiss you both with all my heart."

At noon she had posted on every wall a proclamation she had dictated to Monsieur de Lezay-Marnesia, her first chamberlain.

> Frenchmen, the opening of the war has not been favourable to us, we have met with a check. Let us be firm in this reverse and make haste to repair it. Let there be but one party among you, the party of France, one single flag, the flag of the national honour.

I am coming into your midst. Faithful to my mission and to my duty, you will see me the foremost in danger to defend the banner of France.

I adjure all good citizens to maintain order; to disturb it would be to conspire with our enemies.

In the evening, she received Piétri, the Prefect of Police, who told her that Ollivier was proposing, in order to avoid possible trouble, to arrest the republican chiefs, Gambetta, Jules Favre, Jules Ferry, and Arago, and send them to Belle-Ile.

"He is mad!" exclaimed the Regent. "Does he imagine that the Opposition will submit, that the faubourgs will not rise, that Lyons, Marseilles, Bordeaux, Saint-Etienne, Limoges will remain quiet? He does not see that he is about to loose a civil war under the enemy's fire! As long as I am Regent that shall never be. Let him know at once."

She was right a thousand times over. Ollivier saw it and abandoned the idea which in any case did not originate with him but with Chevandier de Valdrôme.

The Cabinet was condemned by public opinion. All day long the Empress had this repeated to her by the old adherents of the autocratic Empire, who had been removed from power by the arrival of Ollivier, and who grouped themselves about Eugénie: Baroche, Persigny, Vaillant, Rouher. She thought the same. And so when the three dynastic groups of the Corps Législatif, as soon as it met, sent delegates to her requesting her to form a new ministry, more capable of dealing with the events of the moment, she did not defend the old one.

"I have no right," replied the Regent, "to dismiss the ministry, but in view of the urgency of affairs, I think it will be my duty to replace it if you overthrow it."

The Corps Législatif overthrew it the very first day.

Already the Empress had appealed to General Cousin-Montauban, Count de Palikao, and had persuaded him to be President du Conseil. Augustin Filon, always candid, in vain warned her against this new overstepping of her powers, this usurping of a right that belonged to Napoleon alone. As she was proceeding to sign the decrees appointing the ministers:

"Your Majesty," he told her, "is acting in a revolutionary fashion."

She replied:

"It is absolutely necessary. My conscience bids me sign, and I sign. I shall explain everything to the Emperor later on."

She was altogether sincere. If she accepted responsibility, she claimed the initiative. As Regent, she wished to concentrate in her hands all the civil powers of the sovereign, so long as she gave an account of them when the day came. Did a definite text set limits to her authority? It did not foresee the course of events. And it was by that course of events she must be guided, not by a *senatus-consultas*. She signed the decrees. Made in haste and in a dearth of material, the choice of new ministers was a poor one. Who knew them? What weight did they carry? Palikao, the victor of Pekin, was intelligent in war, but was in the grip of old age. Henri Chevreau, Brame, Grandperret were obscure persons. Clément Duvernois was a braggart. Magne seemed to be in his proper place at the Ministry for Finance, but at the Ministry for Foreign Affairs the Prince de la Tour d'Auvergne was too inexperienced and lacked authority. Only she was on the spot, she herself, and she imagined herself capable of directing everything, of taking everything upon herself. Great ministers would perhaps embarrass her. She would be better able to breathe her own will, her ardour, into new-comers, even if they were mere clerks, provided they had hearts.

On the ninth Mérimée came to the Tuileries. Leaning heavily on his cane, he passed through the deserted ante-chambers and was announced to Eugénie. However absorbed she may have been, she was alarmed at his appearance. She had in front of her a fleshless ghost, yet still straight-backed, faithful to his faded elegance, who only spoke now with an effort. At moments, shaken by a deep-seated cough, he put his hand to his mouth and that grey hand trembled. She made haste to have him sit down.

"Ah, Monsieur Mérimée," she said, "what are you doing here? You ought to have been on your way to Cannes!"

He tried to smile.

"My health is of no consequence now. I have been ill for so many years. I am quite used to it. I shall stay here as long as I think I can serve you."

She turned her eyes away, and spoke with a somewhat factitious confidence. If Paris remained sensible and prudent, the position would speedily improve. What made her most uneasy were the resentments and the ambitions of the Republican deputies. She had approached them, asking for a sort of truce, that together they might think only of the country's peril. She had found Gambetta and Ferry unwilling to listen. But Jules Grévy had accepted her overtures; he would recommend union to his friends. On the other hand, the Regent, whose hopes Metternich had not brought himself to kill, still thought that Austria might come into the war. From St. Petersburg Fleury wrote to her that the Czar seemed disposed to work on Prussia to obtain a peace that would leave French territory intact, and maintain the dynasty.

He listened to her, hands leaning on his cane clasped between his thin knees. He looked at her humbly, sadly. She was beautiful no longer. In a few days she had aged by many years. Her hair, that was not now retouched to gold, was turning to silver. Her complexion was gone. Two great wrinkles hardened her mouth. Her eyelids were reddened and dark rings stood round her eyes, for want of sleep. She had grown thin, seemed floating inside her little beige woollen frock. No doubt she was cold in those high sombre rooms, in spite of the oppressive summer, for she was wearing a black cloth cape with frogs.

She told him of all the efforts that her own energy had multiplied and intensified. A loan of five hundred millions and the compulsory making of bank-notes into legal tender had made good the empty Treasury. Two newly constituted army corps were about to start for the East, with Trochu and Vinoy at their head. The Garde Mobile and the National Guard, reinforced and equipped with arms, and numbering in all two hundred and seventy thousand men, would defend Paris if it was invested. The forts and the walls had been furnished with eighteen hundred guns borrowed from the navy. In the suburban area bridges, sluices, tunnels were blown up to hamper the eventual closing in of the enemy. Three thousand five hundred oxen and two hundred and eighty thousand sheep penned in the Luxembourg and the Bois de Boulogne would ensure the victualling of the city.

She left her armchair. Burning with the fever within her, she could not stay quiet. Her hands behind her back, stooped forward slightly, she spoke on and on without any sign of coming to an end. She said that in case of a siege she would shut herself up in Paris, but that a duplicate government, including five or six ministers, would be installed at Tours to organise the defence of the country south of the Loire.

"We shall fight every foot of ground. The Prussians do not know what they are undertaking. Rather than accept humiliating conditions we shall make war for ten years!"

She added, in a less exalted tone, returning to her fear:

"Unless we are shot at from behind!"

Mérimée asked her if she had thought of seeking the advice, perhaps even the support, of Thiers. His opposition to the declaration of war had brought him an increasing popularity. At the Palais-Bourbon, where he gave unending dissertations on the military operations, for he imagined himself a born strategist, he was listened to like an oracle. This influence he wielded, his unquestionable political experience, his tenacious desire for power might no doubt be used to advantage. Failing his patriotism, what if they tempted his ambition?

She paused in her walking up and down, gathering her brows in reflection.

"Yes, Monsieur Thiers, if he was willing . . . But you know that in July the Emperor did not accept his offer of his services. He did not trust him. Neither did I, for that matter. He does not mean to forgive us. He has intelligence, but no generosity."

Mérimée insisted. He had kept up friendly relations with Thiers. If the Empress authorised him to do so, he could sound him as to his intentions.

"He won't hear anything. He is not a man to go on board a ship in sight of the rocks. But after all, do, dear Monsieur Mérimée. I cannot reject his help. If he gave it to me I should be very glad indeed. Do the best you can. But don't mention my name."

He left her, somewhat revived by the hope of being useful to her.

At the request of Eugénie and the Ministry, the Emperor had been obliged to deprive Maréchal Lebœuf of the duties of Major-general, for public opinion held him largely responsible for the neglect of the army. Almost immediately after, realising that he no longer inspired confidence as commander-in-chief, Napoleon himself resigned in favour of Bazaine.

"I hand over to you," he said, "France's last army. Think of the Prince Imperial."

The change was well received in the Corps Législatif. Jules Ferry declared that the appointment of Bazaine would be approved by the whole country. Gambetta called him "our glorious Bazaine." Paris applauded. The Regent, in spite of the blunders made in Mexico, which she, more than any one else, must needs bear in mind, shared the infatuation.

From Metz Napoleon III and his son had made their way to Châlons where a new army was being formed under the command of Mac-Mahon. Ill as the Emperor was, and his will-power clouded by the pains in his loins, he had not seen without annoyance the progressive usurpation of powers by the Regency. Prince Napoleon, who had not left his side, exasperated by the continually increasing part played by Eugénie (while he played none at all), was full of very bitter speeches. He went so far as to say to the Emperor in a council held at Châlons:

"You no longer command the army, you no longer govern. Then what are you doing here? Are you nothing now but the correspondent of the *Times?*"

He urged the Emperor to return immediately to Paris. Mac-Mahon's army would re-form under the walls of the city. Not merely would this strengthen its power of defence, but any insurrection would be made impossible. On August 14, there had been a kind of skirmish instigated by Eudes and Blanqui. The incident ought to serve as a warning.

Trochu arrived at Châlons and supported the prince's opinion. Mac-Mahon acquiesced. The Emperor realised that from the double point of view of strategy and politics this plan was the best he could adopt. Rouher, coming from Eugénie to oppose the idea of the return, did not dissuade him. On the contrary, he himself was won over. He went back to the Tuileries with the news that Trochu had been appointed Governor of Paris at the instance of Prince Napoleon, and that the Emperor would speedily follow him to take the power into his own hands again.

Eugénie received it angrily.

"The Emperor in Paris! But his carriage will never get as far as the Louvre! He will never get back alive!"

She would contrive to prevent his return.

What would he be in Paris? An embarrassment to the government, the visible symbol of defeat. He had delegated the power to her. She judged herself better fitted to exercise it than he was. Worn out, ill, without prestige, he would be less capable than she of making decisions and taking action. She imagined that she held the nation's interest more than he, because she was a woman, a mother, and because she still believed, even while she forbade herself to believe, in the generosity of the people. So she sacrificed him. She, who had received from him everything she had! Was not this a terrible betrayal? And yet she loved him with a real friendship, grieved for him, wept over his disaster. But she looked upon his part in politics as played out. In her eyes, as in the eyes of the country, the Emperor counted no longer. The *Imperator* can only be conceived as victorious. Vanquished, he must vanish. . . . She abandoned him to his fate, in order to maintain the Empire, to preserve the crown for her son. The dynasty was lost, so she had believed, so she had cried aloud at the news of Forbach. And nevertheless, since then, by a very human revulsion of feeling, she was doing the impossible to save it. Within her dwelt an obstinate hope for some miraculous turn of fortune. God, whom she invoked with so much fervour, could not abandon her wholly! A light would break through all those clouds, a success would re-establish our arms. Bazaine or MacMahon, luckier at last, would halt the enemy, make it possible to treat without too great loss. Then if she too must needs—as was possible—efface herself, she would joyfully sacrifice herself in her turn, if the throne were preserved to her son. . . .

She received General Trochu when he came from Châlons. Old Palikao, Henri Chevreau, the Minister for the Interior, Piétri, the Prefect of Police, Admiral Jurien de la Gravière, and Augustin Filon were present at the conference. It was long and stormy and at times incoherent. The Empress hated Trochu. She disliked his tendency to flourish, his machinations, his ambition, which she believed to be at the service of the Orléans princes, and which unquestionably aimed only at making a great name for himself. Trochu was under no misapprehension as to her feelings. Already the Regent had wounded him by her sharp sallies on two occasions. Admiral Jurien, an old comrade of the General's, clumsily sought to reconcile them. When Trochu came in, he exclaimed:

"Trust the General, Madame! He deserves it. You are made to be good friends. Embrace him, he is an excellent fellow!"

Trochu, all embarrassed, was fumbling with his képi. The Regent pretended not to have heard. She was nervous, her eyes burning, her cheeks feverishly red.

"Sit down, gentlemen," she said. "We have decisions of the utmost importance to make."

At the same time she added some courteous phrases for the new Governor of Paris.

Immediately she spoke of the Emperor's return, and flatly opposed it. It would provoke absolute catastrophes. The new army ought to move to the assistance of Bazaine, who had just had a sanguinary check at Gravelotte, and who was threatened by superior forces. Otherwise the people would accuse Napoleon of thinking only of himself, and betraying the country. As Trochu was protesting:

"General," she said, "do you know that fifty armed men could without any trouble penetrate to this very room and murder me? I am not attacked—why? Precisely because I do not defend myself, because everybody knows perfectly that if I were gone the Empire would still remain untouched. But suppose the Emperor in this palace, which is a trap for sovereigns. What would happen? Imagine the shock and attack of all the hatreds banded together against him. One of two things would happen: either the army would take his side, and then you would have civil war between it and the Parisians in arms, or it would abandon him, and you would have riot and massacre. In either case who would stand to gain? The Prussians."

With the new levies of men, she explained, Paris, all active and feverish and full of enthusiasm, would be able to defend itself. It would not take the view that it must be the only thing thought of. It was demanding, on the contrary, and with the loudest of voices, that Mac-Mahon should go up to the North to find Bazaine and disengage him by a great battle in which the two marshals, having a huge mass of troops at their disposal would no doubt jointly deal more successful blows than they had hitherto done separately. Besides, Palikao, the Minister for War, saw in this the only means of salvation.

Trochu, tightly bundled up in his uniform, with every nerve vibrating, turned towards the Empress his bird-like head with an agitated eye. After an hour's discussion he ended by giving way on the question of Napoleon's return. But he still held out for the return of the army. Profiting by this first advantage, and without waiting, as she ought to have done, for the next day's Council, Eugénie dictated a telegram to Filon. Almost bluntly she invited the Emperor to remain at Châlons. If he came back to Paris he would let loose the Revolution.

When Trochu and the others had left her, Eugénie rapidly wrote, in Filon's presence, a letter to the Emperor to explain her reasons. Filon asked her to soften its expressions. Still carried away by the course of the recent conversation, the Empress had not sufficiently digested her opinions. She ran the risk of seriously wounding the Emperor's feelings, Filon told her. He would have liked her to confine herself to setting forth the material and the moral situation of Paris, with her considered opinion and her grounds for it, but leaving it to Napoleon to take his own decision. Otherwise the Emperor's position would become too humiliating. He had left Metz so that he should not embarrass Bazaine's movements; Mac-Mahon was sending him off to Paris and now Paris was tossing him back to Mac-Mahon again. And this was the man who, as absolute sovereign of France, had vanquished Russia and Austria, and freed Italy! . . .

"Do you believe," said the Empress with emotion, "that I am not the first to feel the horrible nature of the position? But the message you are suggesting to me would not stop him, and he is lost if he is not stopped!"

He drafted a text, the outward form of which at least was moderate; she signed it.

Never in the course of an already long life, and a life full of extraordinary adventure, had Napoleon received so excruciating a blow. Tormented physically, he took into his soul an unexpected stab that nothing could heal. Persist in his plan despite the Empress? He could not do it. He was without authority and without power. He was no longer good for anything but to suffer, and to die. There was no prop or stay beside him. Mac-Mahon, a good second in war, had a subaltern mind. Prince Napoleon had gone to Florence to try to obtain, for want of anything better, the mediation of his father-in-law, Victor-Emmanuel. In solitude, after some hours of agony, like a man drawing his last breath, Napoleon resigned himself. Mac-Mahon, on a formal order from Palikao, moved towards the Meuse. Towards Sedan. The Emperor went in his suite, in a barouche, mixed up with the baggage. Broken by the jolting, sometimes losing his breath amid his horrible sufferings, he had been forced to unbutton his tunic. When his pain was too intense, he would clasp the hand of his son, seated beside him, who gazed at him with unhappy eyes, saying nothing.

Trochu, whose waverings and whose verbosity Paris knew nothing of, enjoyed the very heartiest popularity there. He was the man of the day, the man who would save the city, whose mere name would drive the Prussians back. The Regent should have, and no doubt could have, frankly leaned on him for support. At the first contact he had allowed himself to be captivated. A mystic, he admired Eugénie's faith, a soldier, he honoured her valiancy. But she could never accustom herself to his appearance, to his manners. She had conceived an aversion for him and did little to hide it. In vain did the Governor redouble his assurances of devotion, repeat that "he would die on the steps of the throne," the Empress's distrust broke out in spite of her. She knew from Piétri that the General had meetings with the Republican leaders. Ernest Picard used to go to the Invalides. Jules Favre had an interview with him. Trochu always regretted that Mac-Mahon's army had not been concentrated under the walls of Paris, in accordance with his advice. He declared that the Regent was responsible. He blamed her still more for not allowing him to play the eminent part he had assigned to himself. The coolness of her reception, certain untoward happenings irritated him. His loyalty well on the run, this honest but visionary and vain soldier allowed himself to slip towards the men of the Left, who flattered him to his heart's content, and made him hope that in case of the overthrow of the régime they would make him dictator.

Without troubling about the enemy advancing by long marches, the Opposition was attacking the Emperor and the cabinet by turns. Its audacity increased with each reverse in the field. Jules Favre had demanded the establishment of a Committee of Public Safety. The Empress said:

"We have three Prussian armies against us, but there is a fourth one, the army Monsieur de Bismarck has in Paris, and that is the most formidable of all."

Thiers spoke like a master to the Committee for the Defence of Paris, into which he had come after much entreating. The ministers, too weak for their burdens, and divided among themselves, wavered directly they were no longer under the eye of the Regent.

And she, crammed and heavy laden with regrets, with remorse, continued at her task with intelligence. She had the treasures of the art galleries and museums evacuated to Brest. She received the deputies, the journalists, all who asked for an audience with her. She saw the ambassadors. The idea of Russian mediation followed in her head after the mirage of Austrian intervention. Prince Metternich had at last informed her that she must give up any hope of this.

"Even with the support of Austria, France would be beaten. Prussia is too strong."

"And didn't you know that before?" said the Empress reproachfully. "You might have told me sooner. Many things would have been different."

Every day she visited the hospitals. She had organised one on the terrace of the Tuileries, and a second one in the palace itself, in the hall where the Convention had sat in the old days. She used to go from bed to bed, with an escort of white-capped nursing sisters. Young soldiers shed tears to see her. She soothed the last moments of several of them.

Placed in a situation too much for ordinary humanity, with no way out that was not terrible, she felt all the exaltation and dizzy intoxication of it. Misfortunes and dangers stimulated her, as once good fortune and prosperity used to intoxicate her. The tremendous part she had taken upon herself, to direct the defence of a nation when all about her wavered and tottered, the Emperor, the generals, the armies, when devotion turned tail and gratitude grew faint, that part did not overwhelm her, on the contrary, it elevated her, lent her a new form of greatness. She loved it, threw herself entirely into it, filled it eagerly in every detail. A heroine lay sleeping within her, a Chimène of Castille, a Jeanne of Lorraine who with God in her heart wakes up to "throw the enemy out" of France. She had a mind to ride on horseback through the streets of Paris. She believed the crowd would acclaim her. She was persuaded not to do it. But she only gave up the idea because she had not got a black riding-habit at the Tuileries.

She has very few illusions left now. At any rate her illusions are very rapidly falling to earth, like birds that go on flying after they are shot and presently drop on the ground with a thud. Everything announces the probable fall of the régime, the confusion among intimate friends, the dropping off of officials, the slackness and neglect of the servants. A smell of panic floats in the dark corridors, the drawing-rooms bare of carpets and curtains. The last of the faithful ones speak only with bated breath as though around a wounded man. Every concourse, every murmur of the populace makes them turn to look. Souls appear bare and unveiled. Some of them are calmer and more noble as the peril draws nearer; but in others egoisms and jealousies and intrigues are narrower and meaner than ever, unfolding in the hour of fear. Many are thinking of their safety, anxious not to be buried under this great imperial tent that flaps and groans in the winds, and that a more violent gust may carry away at any moment.

Eugénie hardly eats at all, only sleeps for a few hours with the help of strong doses of chloral. Wearing the same black cashmere dress, with lingerie collar and cuffs, she receives all day long in the gay drawing-room decorated with the floral fancies of Chaplin. She never admits her fatigue, perhaps she is unconscious of it. She keeps a clear mind, a precise clear-cut will, and that vehemence of speech which astonishes her ministers and provokes the gibes of her enemies. The consciousness of her duty sustains her like a skeleton of iron inside her, and no doubt her religion also. She has had Cardinal Bonaparte ask for the prayers and the benediction of Pius IX for her husband and son, for the army, and for France. Every night, opposite Pépa, she kneels devoutly at the foot of her bed.

Much good advice has already been given her, urging her to place her personal belongings and objects of value in safety. She had at first rejected the advice hotly.

"Never will I consent to sequester the smallest iota of the national fortune or my own."

The days go by, pride droops a little, she reconsiders. The papers that Eugénie has amassed during the last eighteen years, and classified minutely in two enormous cupboards, are hastily sifted out by herself, Filon and Conti, and the most important entrusted to the Austrian embassy; the others—since it would have attracted too much attention to burn them—are torn up, soaked in baths filled with hot water and thrown by armfuls down the closets. Then giving way to the importunities of Pépa and the Duchesse de Malakoff, she allows them to take her jewels. The two women carry them to Princess Metternich's at Jonchère, in a portmanteau without their cases, roughly wrapped up in newspapers. The Princess is very reluctant to take charge of them. Pépa kisses her hands, implores her in her frightened jargon. She consents at last. She arranges in proper order those marvellous jewels, the admiration of all the queens in Europe, makes out an inventory, and hands them to the Count de Montgelas, who a short time later deposits them with the Bank of England in London.

Blotting-pad on knee, as often, Eugénie wrote to her mother. A few days earlier she had telegraphed to her, as the Countess de Montijo announced her approaching arrival in Paris.

"Do not come. You would only complicate matters."

Now, fearing some impulsive move on the part of the Countess, she explained the situation to her. Everything was compromised, nothing was lost, they must wait. Four large pages, without hesitation, without a single erasure. She sealed her letter.

Casting her eyes on the clock, she saw that she still had an hour before presiding over the Council, which she was now assembling daily. She took another sheet and wrote to Commandant Duperré, the first aide-de-camp to the Prince Imperial. Ever since the Emperor had, on entering the Ardennes, separated himself from his son, as a measure of prudence, the little prince had been wandering with a weak escort from town to town in the north of France.

The Empress had learned that he was to be taken still farther from the battle-fields and brought to Amiens. Nothing, she thought, could be more awkward for the future. The future sovereign's reputation would be sullied. She meant her son to remain in the theatre of war, even if he must run risks. Already she had vehemently refused to bring him back to her side.

On him too, although he was only fourteen, his name, his rank, his future, imposed the duty of danger.

"You have something still more urgent to think of," she wrote to Duperré, "than safety, and that is honour, and I find this retreat to Amiens unworthy of the Prince and of us. Each of us must to the very utmost of our strength fulfil the arduous duties encumbent on us.

"My heart is torn, but determined. I have no news from my husband nor from you since yesterday. My anguish is extreme, but before everything it is my wish that each of you shall do his duty. Think of one thing: I can weep for my son dead or wounded,—but in flight! I would never forgive you that. And so I am addressing myself to your honour as a soldier. Act for the best, but act as a soldier. I warrant you, and take all responsibility. We shall hold out in Paris, if we are besieged, and outside Paris, still and always. No peace is possible!"

She was laying down her pen when Madame Lebreton came in:

"Here is Monsieur Mérimée," she said in a low voice. "He is hardly able to walk."

Eugénie hurried to meet her old friend.

There was death in his face, death in his whole wilting body. He was panting from having come up the stairs, although so slowly. The Empress made him lie on a sofa by her, and took his hands in her own.

He murmured:

"I have seen Thiers. Your Majesty was right. He is standing aside."

Every word was a pang to him. Yet he mastered himself, and embarked upon his story.

"I said to Thiers: 'You can do us a great service. There is nothing left but France, an Empress, a child. Here is a noble opportunity to set up representative government. . . .'

"Usually so quick and so alert, Thiers had turned to ice.

" 'I cannot do you any service, and after the reverses we have sustained, there is nothing now to be done, absolutely nothing.'

"I begged him at least not to refuse you his advice.

" 'Advice?' he replied. 'It would not be believed sincere. I would not give it with an easy mind myself.' "

Finally, softened by Mérimée's silent reproach, he had added that he could neither support nor replace the ministry. If he was in the place of those who were directing military affairs he would try to get into touch with Maréchal Bazaine and would follow his advice.

"He is waiting for the Republic," said the Empress. "He won't refuse power then."

Bitterly she thought how in an almost similar situation Marie-Antoinette had asked Mirabeau for help, and how Mirabeau had replied: "Madame, now the monarchy is saved." But Mirabeau, for all his faults, was magnanimous. Thiers was nothing but a greedy, verbose old man.

However, she controlled herself, repressed her contempt.

"Monsieur Mérimée, I give you my thanks. Even if it is useless, write to him that I understand his reluctance, but that I would still be glad of his advice."

By a sign he told her such a letter would be unavailing.

She insisted.

"Write to him, please. I am not in a position to leave anything untried. . . ."

"I shall write," said Mérimée. . . .

She leaned towards him:

"I hear that Madame Delessert went to England yesterday?"

His head drooped. Madame Delessert had been merely a friend for him for many years, but a very dear friend. Her departure had distressed him.

"Yes, I said good-bye to her. I shall never see her again. . . ."

"Why? You must go and join her."

He made no reply. They looked at one another, their eyes full of tears. Seeing him so old, so broken, so near the end, Eugénie's courage, great as it was, sank for a minute. Over her there passed a loathing for power, the vast weariness that comes from striving. Disgusted suddenly with all the meannesses and insincerities that were attacking her, her who in all these terrible days had thought only of preserving the throne for her child, she murmured:

"I hope my son will have no ambition and will only think of living happy in obscurity . . ."

Mérimée got up with great difficulty. The Empress held out her hand, saying nothing more, for she would have burst into sobs. This old man who was going away was bearing with him her youth, the fairest and sweetest pictures of her life. He had shown himself so faithful even to the end . . . He bowed over that hand, which had been the hand of his little friend, but as he was about to kiss it, Eugénie drew him to her and embraced him.

He went away, one hand pressed on his frock-coat to overcome the palpitation of his heart. On his way he drew himself erect to salute various persons. His eyes were dry. For the benefit of the curious a thin courteous smile hovered upon his colourless lips. He felt everything within him and about him plunging into the abyss. He could do no more now for his Eugénie. There was nothing left for him but to sit in the Senate and try to die there.

On Saturday, September 3, at three o'clock, the Empress presided over the Council in the Emperor's cabinet. There was a total lack of news. Since the previous day communications with Sedan had been cut off. Palikao feared that Mac-Mahon's army might have allowed itself to be blockaded in it. The rumour of a great disaster was finding its way about Paris. They talked about it in the Chamber, the Stock Exchange, in the cafés, on the boulevards.

Her face drained of blood, her eyelids drooping, the Empress listened, and said little. She seemed far away. For several days she had not slept.

When the meeting was over, she remained perhaps half-an-hour sitting in front of the Emperor's table, her head in her hands, harassed, in dazed somnolence, without any precise thought in her mind. There was a knock at the door. Before she had answered she saw the Minister for the Interior, Henri Chevreau, coming towards her. He did not utter a word; he was trembling in every limb. He held out a telegram to the Empress . . .

The telegram of Sedan!

The army is defeated and captured; having been unable to die in the midst of my soldiers I have been obliged to become a prisoner in order to save the army. Napoleon.

The Empress sprang to her feet, then fell back on her chair, thunder-struck. She swept away the telegram held out to her, threw it on the ground, made a sort of gesture of dismissal in Chevreau's direction. In utter confusion he picked up the paper and hastened away to inform his colleagues and Trochu. Behind him Eugénie rose and walked slowly towards the little stair that joined the Emperor's apartments with hers. She climbed the steps, clinging to the balustrade like a drunken woman. She spoke disjointed phrases. When she was at the top she saw Conti and Filon coming towards her completely crushed. Already they knew. They saw the Empress disfigured, very red, with the eyes of a mad woman, piercing and sparkling. In a dreadful voice deep down in her throat she cried:

"You know what they are pretending? That the Emperor has surrendered, that he has capitulated? You don't believe this infamy?"

The two men were silent. She walked up to them, threateningly.

"You don't believe it?"

Conti stammered:

"Madame, there are circumstances . . ."

She interrupted him, her face terrible to see, vociferating:

"No, the Emperor has not capitulated! A Napoleon does not capitulate. He is dead. . . . You hear me. I tell you he is dead and they are trying to hide it from me!"

Her clenched fists were above her head, blinded by her straggling hair, she was choking.

"Why did he not get himself killed? Why did he not bury himself under the walls of Sedan? Did he not feel that he was dishonouring himself? What a name he will leave to his son!"

But suddenly her fury died out. Tears filled her eyes, slid down her cheeks, fell on her dress. Heavy sobs relieved her nerves. She threw herself on her knees, entreating Napoleon as if he had been close beside her:

"Forgive me, forgive me!"

At last she fell back, unconscious, in a swoon.

CHAPTER III

Flight

BARELY recovered, the Empress summoned the ministers. The subject of discussion was the measures to be taken to stop the Prussians' march on Paris. When they came to the defence of the public services by the troops, in case of the insurrection all saw to be imminent, she came out of her dejection to refuse to have the Tuileries placed under military protection.

"Whatever happens," she said, "the soldiers must not fire on the people."

She had sent a summons to General Trochu by Admiral Jurien de la Gravière. The governor excused himself, saying that he was just back from a visit to the forts, that he was tired, and that he would come and see the Empress after he had dined.

"He hasn't dined," exclaimed Eugénie, "neither have I! At a moment like this, does anybody think about his dinner?"

Trochu did not come. In spirit he had already deserted. The Empress began to open the despatches piled up on her table. They gave poignant details on the military situation, on the hostile manifestations taking place in Paris and in the provinces. She found this letter from the Emperor:

Imperial Quarters,
Sept. 2, 1870.

MY DEAR EUGENIE,

It is impossible to tell you what I have suffered and what I am suffering. We carried out a march contrary to all principles and to common sense; the result was bound to be a catastrophe. And it is complete. I would have preferred death to witnessing so disastrous a capitulation, and yet, in the present circumstances, it was the only way of preventing the slaughter of sixty thousand men.

And again—if all my torments were concentrated here! I think of you, of our son, of our unhappy country. May God protect it! What will happen in Paris?

I have just seen the King. He had tears in his eyes as he spoke of the distress I must be feeling. He is placing at my disposal one of his castles near Hesse-Cassel. But what does it matter to me where I go! I am in despair! Adieu, I kiss you tenderly.

NAPOLEON.

"Le malheureux!" she murmurs.

At midnight the Corps Législatif met, in spite of the promise of its president, Schneider. The Empress was requested to appear. She refused, suspecting a trap. She felt herself surrounded by snares. She did right. Jules Favre put forward a proposal for deposition, against which Pinard fought bravely.

She burned certain papers that she had preserved till then. Throughout this dreadful night she remained without a supporter, without a friend. From her dark windows she saw flowing through the Rue de Rivoli and the Place de la Concorde an enormous multitude carrying torches and flags swathed in crape, cheering for the Republic. It left her utterly unmoved. A strange strength dwelt within her. Amid the echo of this tumult she concocted a telegram to inform her mother of the latest disaster:

> General Wimpffen, who had taken command after Mac-Mahon was wounded, capitulated, and the Emperor was made prisoner. Alone, without a command, he endured what he could not prevent. All day he was under fire. Courage, dear mother; if France has the will to defend herself, she can. I shall do my duty. Your unhappy daughter, Eugénie.

To do her duty, now that she sees that everything is lost, there is her one idea. She will do it entirely, without regard for her own family, even if it kills her.

At half-past seven she hears Mass in her private chapel. Beside her kneel Madame Aguado, Madame Lebreton, Admiral Jurien, Filon, the *femmes de chambre.* After the service she prays before two little images of Notre Dame d'Atocha and Notre Dame del Pilar, and kisses them. Then she visits the Tuileries hospital full of wounded brought back from the front. On the way, Filon, who accompanies her, says:

"Madame, there is nothing more to be done in Paris. You must get away from this hell, carry your government to one of the towns on the Loire and summon the Corps Législatif around you. I take it upon myself to go and find the Prince in the North and bring him to Your Majesty."

She replied:

"That would mean a civil war. Our powers of resistance to the Prussians would be broken in two. And to what avail? Not to have Paris is to have nothing. I shall not budge from here."

"Then Your Majesty will fight?"

"I shall not budge, but not a shot shall be fired."

A note is brought her from Lesseps. He has hurried from London to help, in her hour of danger, the woman who helped him so powerfully in his career. He has just seen his friend Emile de Girardin, the "gravedigger of dynasties," as the Empress, who has already sent him away, calls him. Girardin and Lesseps propose to Eugénie to abdicate in favour of the Corps Législatif. A council of regency will be formed, which will proclaim the Prince Imperial as Emperor.

"That is impossible," says Eugénie. "The sovereignty does not belong to me. I will not abdicate."

She comes back to her cabinet for the Council. They wait a long time for General Trochu. In the end he appears. By way of excuse, he says to the Empress:

"Madame, this is the hour of great dangers, we shall all do our duty."

The meeting begins. Old Palikao has just learned of the death of his son, killed in action. He seems stunned. Clément Duvernois proposes to make use of the state of siege to quell the Revolution that is putting up its head and growling. His idea is rejected. With seven or eight companies of soldiers of all arms, and of doubtful fidelity, the government cannot hope to master the three hundred thousand National Guards and *gardes mobiles* armed by Trochu. Transfer the executive to the provinces? There is no time now. Paris would revolt at once.

"We must fall," says the Empress, "without hampering the defence."

It is decided to present to the Corps Législatif a plan for a Council of five members appointed by the deputies to assist the Regent. It is an attempt to create a government of National Defence. But under the direct threat of insurrection will the Chamber have time or energy to rally to it?

The Rue de Rivoli fills up once more with a noisy crowd. The Place de la Concorde is covered with National Guards, their bayonets fixed. Eugénie every now and then observes them through little opera-glasses. Round her men are saying that they are unquestionably going to attack the palace.

She sends for General Mellinet, the commandant of the Tuileries.

"General, can the palace be defended?"

"I am afraid not, Madame."

"Above everything, there is to be no shooting! On no pretext. I do not wish a drop of blood to be shed for me or mine."

The drawing-rooms fill up with people. The officers and the ladies of the Imperial household present in Paris have all come, and many personal friends. At this supreme moment, when no one has any further doubt as to the imminence of her fall, almost all those who for so many years have formed the intimate Court of the Empress make it a point of honour to close up their ranks around her. The Archbishop of Paris and the Princesse d'Essling, whose carriages were stopped by the crowd, have not been able to reach the Tuileries.

Towards noon a delegation from the Corps Législatif arrived, composed of MM. Daru, Buffet, Dupuy de Lôme, d'Ayguevives, de Pierres, Gaulon, and de Kolb-Bernard. Its mission was to inform the Empress that the proposal for the Council would not be accepted by the Chamber and that if she wished to avoid deposition she must without delay hand over the power to the Assembly, which would exercise it through a Committee of Government.

In the blue drawing-room beside the cabinet, the Regent, with Admiral Jurien de la Gravière and the Countess de la Poëze at her side, listened to the deputies with dignified calm. M. Buffet spoke first and at length, in a tone of veiled compassion. M. Daru insisted on the necessity for abdication.

When they had finished, Eugénie, displaying no other sign of emotion than a short pause after certain of her sentences, replied:

"What you are proposing to me, gentlemen, according to you reserves the future, but on condition that I abandon the present and, in the hour of utmost peril, the post that has been entrusted to me. I cannot, I must not, consent. The future is what I am least concerned with to-day, not, assuredly the future of France, but the future of the dynasty. Believe me, gentlemen, the trials I have just endured have been so agonising, so horrible, that at this juncture the thought of preserving this crown for the Emperor and for my son touches me very little. My one anxiety, my sole ambition is to fulfil wholly and completely the duties laid upon me. If you believe, if the Corps Législatif believes that I am an obstacle, that the name of the Emperor is an obstacle and not a source of strength—to dominate the situation and organise resistance, let the deposition be pronounced, I shall not complain. I shall be able to leave my post with honour: I shall not have deserted it. But I am convinced that the only sensible and patriotic conduct for the representatives of the country would be to close up their ranks around me, around my government, to lay on one side, for the present, all internal questions and to join up all our efforts in order to repel the invasion."

She speaks from the bottom of her heart. She sees unerringly. The deputies feel this to be true. But they are being swept on by so strong and so high a billow that they are no longer exercising their own judgment. Alone, M. Buffet exclaims, with deep emotion:

"For my part I should be ready to do it, if it was still possible. . . ."

She makes a brief reference to the Cortès of Cadiz, who by remaining faithful to their King, although he was a prisoner, had saved the liberty of Spain, then she concludes:

"As for myself, I am ready to confront every danger and to follow the Corps Législatif wherever it will organise resistance. If such resistance were recognised to be impossible, I believe I should still be of use to obtain less unfavourable peace conditions. Yesterday the representative of a great power [she referred to Metternich] offered to propose a mediation by the neutral States on these two bases: the integrity of French territory and maintenance of the Imperial dynasty. I answered that I was disposed to accept mediation on the first point, but I strongly rejected it on the second. The maintaining of the dynasty is a question that concerns this country alone, and I shall never permit foreign powers to intervene in our internal arrangements."

Even as she uttered these wise and manful words she had no idea that they would avail to shake men who were set against her by ambition or by the course of events or by fear. She spoke them without hope, with a shrinking of the spirit, expecting nothing.

The delegates hesitated for a minute, then some of them harked back to the urgent need for a decision.

Then Daru said:

"You are afraid, Madame, that you may be accused of having deserted your post. But you will have given a far greater proof of courage by sacrificing yourself for the public welfare and sparing France a revolution under the eyes of the enemy."

This potent argument shook Eugénie's resolution. It was no longer an appeal to her interests, but to her patriotism. Nervously she clasped and unclasped her hands on her breast and, with trembling limbs, but a firm mouth and steady eyes, she said:

"Do you think it pleasant for me to hold on tooth and nail to power? If I relinquish it, I shall only ask one thing, gentlemen: that I may be assigned some place of residence, any place whatever, that I may be allowed to share to the last moment the perils and the sufferings of the besieged capital!"

They were silent, overwhelmed by her simple greatness. She added, but this time with a breaking voice:

"Yes, you have seen me as the crowned sovereign in days of festival. Henceforth nothing will soften the heartrending memories of this hour. All the woes of France, I shall bear them eternally in my heart."

Messages were coming every moment from the Prefecture of Police, keeping the Empress informed of the course of the disturbances. She handed them to Daru, who read them aloud. A young man, a complete stranger, came into the drawing-room and cried:

"They are in the Place de la Concorde!"

Eugénie remained impassive. But the deputies appeared very nervous.

Strongly pressed anew, she then declared that she was ready to resign the power:

"It is your wish, gentlemen, it was not my feeling in the matter, but I put aside everything personal to myself; only I wish to act in a constitutional manner, I wish my Cabinet to be consulted. If my ministers are in agreement with you upon the steps you propose that I should take, there will be no obstacle on my part. Speak to the Count de Palikao; if he assents, I shall assent."

She rose up, still a sovereign. Each of the deputies, before leaving, bowed before her, filled with respect. The grave Buffet wept. By the door she held out her hand to all of them, friends or foes, for them to kiss.

For two hours Eugénie remained without news from the Corps Législatif, from Palikao, from the ministers. Lesseps, who had gone to the Palais-Bourbon, had not come back. But the cries of the populace massed all along the railings of the Tuileries rose louder and more threateningly. The eagles on the gates had been torn away. Already the insurgents were trying to get into the gardens. Madame de la Poëze advised the Empress to leave the palace so as to avoid falling into their hands.

"I am not afraid," she said; "how could I go away?"

Brought up in the atmosphere of guerilla wars, married by an incredible *coup de théâtre* to a sovereign who had attained his throne by conspiracy, and who only wielded power as a conspirator, she saw without surprise, with a kind of fatalism, the whole artificial and brilliant setting of the Second Empire crumble away without a struggle. She suffered, she was indignant, she wept, cried out, but deep down within herself no doubt she was not *surprised*. For many years, she had said it herself, she was prepared for anything. And that was perhaps why she would know how to confront the most varied forms of misfortune.

At length three ministers appeared: Jérôme David, Busson-Billault and Henri Chevreau. They came from the Corps Législatif. The crowd had broken in. The soldiers were grounding their rifles. Trochu, it could no longer be doubted, was making terms with the insurrection. The Tuileries would be invaded at any moment. They conjured the Empress to leave.

"No, no," she said, stamping her foot. "Here is where I was placed by the Emperor, here is where I shall stay. If there were no longer any recognised authority, disorganisation would be complete and France would lie at the mercy of Monsieur de Bismarck."

At half-past three the Prefect of Police arrived. He announced that the railings were on the point of being forced. The Austrian and Italian ambassadors then came into the blue drawing-rooms. Metternich told the Empress that she could not remain a moment longer in the palace. Nigra, Admiral Jurien de la Gravière, and Conti, all implored her.

She still held out. Standing against a window, her eyes far away, they heard her murmur twice over:

"Empty dreams!"

At last Conti said to her:

"You will not abdicate, Madame? Well then, in an hour you will be in the hands of those who will make you abdicate by force, and you will have sacrificed the rights entrusted to your keeping. If you make your escape, wherever you go you carry those rights with you."

She still rejoined:

"The motto of my family was 'My king before my blood.' For my part I say, 'France before the dynasty!' That is the same thing, do you know that?"

All the same she was struck with Conti's idea. She bade Filon telegraph to Duperré and tell him to take the Prince Imperial over into Belgium without delay.

A huge outcry went up suddenly. The railings along the Place de la Concorde had given way, and the people, with whom the National Guards were now fraternising, poured in towards the private garden. At that moment possibly Eugénie saw herself with her skirts pulled over her head, flogged by termagants, given over to the vilest outrages. That was the one thing she dreaded.

"Madame," said Nigra once more, "do not delay any longer. You will destroy your friends."

Then she decided. She said a few words of thanks, unhurried, to the three ministers, and gave General Mellinet the order to withdraw the troops on guard directly the servants had left the palace. She embraced Maréchal Canrobert, the Duchesse de Malakoff, Vicomtesse Aguado, Madame de La Bédoyère, Madame de la Poëze, Madame de Saulcy, Madame de Bourgoing. They wept and pressed her hands. The Empress said:

"I shall never forget what you have all been to me. I thank you. Adieu, adieu."

Feverishly the Chevalier Nigra urged her:

"Madame, Prince Metternich and I are waiting for you. You must make haste. Otherwise flight will be impossible."

She donned hat and veil, drew a light cloak around her. From her table she took the miniature of her father, from which she had never been parted, and slipped it into her pocket. She forgot a little black leather bag that had been got ready for her, and which contained a few eatables, a nightgown, two pairs of stockings. Followed by Madame Lebreton, Metternich, Nigra, Admiral Jurien, Conti, Lieutenant Conneau (a cousin of the doctor) and a few ladies, she left her room by "the dark corridor" and descended the stair to the courtyard of the Palace. There she meant to take her coupé, which was standing as usual, awaiting orders. But Metternich observed the coachman's livery and the arms painted on the door, and said it would be dangerous to allow the Empress to use it. He suggested his own carriage, which was waiting on the quay. Lieutenant Conneau went to find it. He came back the next moment. Impossible to get through now. The Place du Carrousel was overflowing with a crowd shouting death cries.

Eugénie did not lose her head. She went back up the great staircase, returned to her own rooms, passed through the Galerie de Diane, which only the other day was the resplendent scene of so many entertainments, then turning to the left made her way into the new Salle des Etats where only three months before the results of the plebiscite had been proclaimed with such fervent joy. . . . But when she came to the door that gave access to the Grande Galerie of the Louvre, she found it locked. No one in her train had the key. The yells of the insurgents came through the thick walls. Had the palace been invaded already? That was a terrible minute. Suddenly Thelin, the Emperor's private treasurer, appeared, hurrying after the Empress to offer his services. He had a master-key in his pocket, and opened the door. Eugénie and her friends passed through into the gallery, and crossing the Salon Carré and the Galerie d'Apollon, came out into the Salle des Sept Cheminées.

"I do not wish any one to accompany me farther," said the Empress. "It is too much already. Now you are all to place yourselves in safety."

Before Géricault's picture *le Radeau de la Méduse*—"How strange!" she said as she saw it—she gave the men her hand to kiss, embraced the women once more. She embraced Conti too. She took thought to order Lieutenant Conneau to change his clothes before leaving the palace.

"Your uniform is too conspicuous; it's dangerous."

With Madame Lebreton, and followed by Metternich and Nigra, who as diplomats had nothing to fear, she went through the Greek rooms, descended the stair leading to the Egyptian antiquities, and found herself in the vaulted room opening on the Place Saint-Germain-l'Auxerrois.

Eugénie stumbled; after so many fatigues this journey had exhausted her. She accepted Nigra's arm. Bands of rioters at this moment passed before her in the square, crying:

"Down with Badinguet! Death to the Spanish woman! *Vive la République!*" The fugitives stopped for a moment.

"Don't be afraid, Madame," said Nigra. The Empress drew herself up.

"What do you mean? My arm is resting on yours. Do you feel it tremble?"

She added:

"Let us go now."

"I think we would do well to wait a little longer . . ."

"No, no, we must be bold."

And she was the first to go out. There were few people on the sidewalk in front of the colonnade. But over the way, in the square, two streams of the crowd crossed each other, with songs and wild shoutings.

Metternich left them to look for his carriage on the quay. As time was passing, as waiting might become dangerous if prolonged, as the Empress might in spite of her veil be recognised at any moment, Nigra called a fiacre that was jogging along down the side of the roadway. Eugénie and Madame Lebreton tucked themselves away in it. Then an urchin shouted at the top of his voice:

"There's the Empress!"

Fortunately in the uproar no one heard him. Nigra caught hold of his arm:

"What are you saying?" and kept him in talk.

Meanwhile the cab was moving away at a leisurely trot towards the Rue de Rivoli.

Madame Lebreton had given the address of a friend of hers, M. Besson, a *conseiller d'état,* who lived on the Boulevard Haussmann, and in whose house she hoped to find assistance. The Rue de Rivoli was nothing but a river of humanity, full of eddies. Soldiers of the Imperial Guard, in the windows of the Louvre barracks, were looking on, pipe in mouth, at the swarming riot. Some of them even cried "Depose them!" The Empress murmured:

"They too!"

The crowd as it swirled by was surprised at this vehicle tossed to and fro and these two women in mourning. A workman put his head in through the window and shouted in Eugénie's face:

"Vive la nation!"

As they came up the Rue du 29 Juillet, Madame Lebreton bade the driver go down it:

"We are rather in a hurry, you might take a less crowded way."

He obeyed, whipped up his horses.

At the corner of the Boulevard des Capucines, the cab was held up by a crowd. A group of young people had torn an Imperial scutcheon from a shop front and were kicking it to pieces.

"Already!" said Eugénie.

In front of M. Besson's house the fugitives paid off the coachman and sent him away. They climbed up to the third floor and rang. No answer. They waited patiently for a quarter of an hour sitting on the stairs. Then when Madame Lebreton had rung again, the Empress rose:

"I cannot stay here any longer. Let us go."

In the streets they walked on at first without a definite goal. The quarter was deserted. An open carriage passed, they stopped it and drove to M. de Piennes's house in the Avenue de Wagram. The devoted chamberlain was out. There was a servant in the flat, but he could not open—his master had inadvertently locked him in.

On the stairs Madame Lebreton suggested to go to the American Legation, to Mr. Washburne.

"The Revolutionaries will respect the United States flag. Monsieur Washburne will protect us."

"The American Legation . . . Monsieur Washburne . . ." repeated the Empress. "But we don't know his address."

Suddenly she said:

"I have thought of something: let us go to my dentist, Doctor Evans. He is an American too, with no political functions. He is a friend, he will give us a refuge."

The cabman was given orders to bring them to Evans' house at the corner of the Avenue de l'Impératrice and the Avenue Malakoff.

They got down and rang. A servant took them into the house. The doctor was not in, but was expected to return soon. Left in the library, they fell into armchairs. A clock struck five. It was still no more than five!

"I wonder what General Trochu can be doing," murmured Eugénie.

Trochu? At that moment he was in civilian costume at the Hôtel de Ville, and saying to Jules Favre and his friends:

"I am with you, provided you make me your President."

They acquiesced, enchanted with this windfall. A moment to scrawl a few lines on a scrap of paper, and the Imperial governor of Paris became head of the insurgent government.

Arriving in Paris in 1847, Doctor Evans had since the accession of Napoleon III been dentist to the Imperial household. Extremely skilful, this fat man with greying whiskers had come into Eugénie's friendship. Under this patronage he had made a fortune, had become the best known practitioner in Europe, the dentist of princes and crowned heads. Remaining at bottom American in ideas and tastes, he had nevertheless attached himself to France. Immediately upon the declaration of war, with Doctor E. A. Crane, he had set up a hospital. In her appeal to his sense of gratitude the Empress would not be disappointed.

When the doctor came into the library about six o'clock, a good deal puzzled at what his servant had told him, and saw Eugénie sitting by the window, with the faint light intensifying the pallor of her hollow cheeks, he was stupefied.

"You know what has happened to-day," said the Empress. "The government is in the hands of the Revolutionaries. I have been obliged to leave the Tuileries without any preparations. I have now come to call on you for help. I know I can count on you. The service I am asking from you for myself and for Madame Lebreton will put your friendship to a severe test."

Without a moment's hesitation Evans assured her that he was entirely at the disposal of the Empress and that he would do everything in his power to aid her.

"You see," said Eugénie, in melancholy tones, "I am no longer fortunate. The evil days have come and I am deserted."

Her eyes filled with tears. But she pulled herself together. The doctor, moved in spite of his matter-of-fact mind, asked her if she had any plan.

A plan? No, she had made none. However, in that hour of waiting she had thought that the best thing for her would be to seek a refuge in England. Her son could join her there and she would once more be completely free to communicate with the Emperor. What she desired above all was to leave Paris without delay. Since the Emperor had fallen, since she no longer had a crown to defend, she wished to flee from this city that had acclaimed her in her triumph and that now insulted her. They must be hunting for her. She must not fall into the power of the insurrection. She was ready to take the road that very night, if she was helped to the means of doing so.

Evans discerned extreme fatigue under her nervous impatience. The Empress had reached the very end of her strength. She needed a little rest. And food as well; since yesterday she had taken nothing but some coffee! She had a very heavy cold and was blowing her nose incessantly.

The American had a light meal served in the library for her and Madame Lebreton. Then he went to find his friend Doctor Crane, who was waiting for him before his house, and knowing that he could confide in him, explained briefly what was happening. That very evening Evans was giving a men's dinner-party. Crane would make his apologies to his guests, who were almost all compatriots, and would do the honours in his place, while he would go back to the Empress.

Eugénie, having eaten heartily, seemed less weary. With Madame Lebreton, Evans, and presently Doctor Crane, who, when the diners had gone, had been presented to her, she deliberated. First of all she proposed to go in Evans' carriage to Poissy. There she would take a night train, which would land her at Le Hâvre where she would embark for Southampton. Evans thought this plan dangerous. It would be better, he said, to avoid public means of transport, where the Empress ran the risk of being recognised. After consultation with Crane, a cool man and sound in advice, he evolved another plan. They would leave Paris next morning in Evans' carriage, and with the help of relays would get to the coast of Normandy. Mrs. Evans was at Deauville, and she would be able to help them to hire a yacht to take them across the Channel. Eugénie accepted this; the adventurous side of the affair pleased her. She showed passports that Pietri had brought her, and which Madame Lebreton had taken with her at the last moment. One was viséd by the Austrian Embassy, the other by the English. The latter was made out for an English doctor taking a woman patient, also English, to London, accompanied by two other persons. They would make use of this one. Crane was to take the part of the doctor, the Empress that of the patient. Evans would be her brother, and Madame Lebreton the nurse.

At the moment it was essential that the two women should get some sleep, if possible. The doctor took them to Mrs. Evans' room. Then he went off with Crane to look for news. Crane went down into the heart of the town. He found Paris quiet. Sentries were guarding the Tuileries gates. On the walls chalked up in great letters he read *"Propriété Nationale"*—Property of the Nation. Few people about in the streets, except on the terraces of the cafés. This night of revolution was strangely calm. Evans went himself as far as the Porte Maillot. He saw that carriages entering and going out were not searched. He came back, and sat talking with Crane in the library while they waited for daybreak.

Lying down fully dressed Eugénie did not fall asleep for a single moment. How could she, with her nerves in such a state of tension? She thought of the Emperor, of her son, of the last scenes of her Regency. In everything concerning it she judged herself blameless. She had done everything that depended on her. The tempest was too strong, it had swept her away. Yet the pictures of the past, even so recent a past, held her less than those of the future. She did not linger over regrets. Flung to earth so brutally, she was already rising up and hoping. She saw herself reunited to Napoleon and Louis. She would make a new home for them, while they waited for fortune to turn. For to her the fall of the Empire could not be final. In her eyes the Republic was merely anarchy; it could not endure. In any case the deposition had not been pronounced. Even in flight Eugénie remained Regent. She held and preserved the lawful power. It was with her Prussia would desire to treat rather than with the insurgents.

Bazaine retained an army intact at Metz, composed of old troops. She believed him loyal and devoted. The provinces, less hasty and unreflecting, would not follow the example of Paris so easily. The Empire and the Emperor were beloved there . . . Even if they must needs wait for peace, in any event as soon as it was signed a restoration would become possible, if not for Napoleon III at least for Napoleon IV.

Through that long September night such were the dreams of this woman whom no misfortune could bend for long, and whose imagination, like her courage, always rebounded.

At five in the morning Evans knocked at her door. She was up already, and was brushing with her own hands her black cashmere dress, set off with a little white collar. Madame Lebreton had suggested that she should make herself look older by a change of costume. She refused, made herself up as usual with rouge and powder and that double black pencil line with which she always outlined her eyelids and emphasized her eyebrows. Madame Lebreton, who was frank of speech, murmured:

"The Empress's coquetry will ruin us!"

"But I mean to be recognised if we are taken," replied Eugénie. "Make myself ridiculous—ah, never! By remaining myself I can impose respect on those who arrest me. Don't let us lose that chance."

All the same she accepted a round hat and a veil belonging to Mrs. Evans. Then she buttoned up her gloves, took her reticule, which contained nothing but two handkerchiefs, not a single piece of jewellery. Madame Lebreton kept on her person the change for a five hundred franc note procured on the morning of the fourth.

The two women took their places in the dentist's brown landau, Madame Lebreton sitting on the right, the Empress on the left. Crane and Evans sat on the front seat.

The air turned grey, and day was dawning.

"To Saint-Germain," said Evans to his coachman, whom he knew to be discreet.

In the short run from the Avenue de l'Impératrice to the Porte Maillot, Eugénie observed that the city was waking up with the utmost calm. Nothing showed signs of a crisis. The sweepers were cleaning the gutters, the shopkeepers opening their shops, the milkmen's carts were going along with their bells jingling.

At the gate Celestin pulled up his horses. The chief of the post came up to the carriage door. Evans, hiding the Empress with an open newspaper, said that he was going into the country with his friends, that he was an American. . . . The officer did not even ask his name. He drew back and said to the coachman:

"Go on!"

The carriage swung along the high road through Bougival, Marly, Le Pecq, all still asleep. Eugénie talked without feverishness but with the eager animation that action always excited in her. She went back to the events of yesterday, and explained to the two Americans why she had refused to abdicate.

"I was fully disposed to place in the hands of the people's representatives all my powers as Regent; but it seemed to me necessary, in the interests of France, that the Regency should be nominally continued, so that it would be possible to meet the needs of the moment. And I told those who endeavoured to make me abdicate that the only thing that ought to occupy our minds was the military situation, and our armies, and that for the defence of the country I was ready to assist and support any persons whosoever, provided they possessed the confidence of the nation!"

It was clear that what she regretted most was not to have been able to show the country the full measure of her courage. She would fain have been allowed to suffer and to fight with Paris.

"I could have been of use in many ways. I might have set an example of devotion to the country. I could have visited the hospitals. I could have gone to the outposts. I could have encouraged the troops by my presence at every point of danger, and so stimulated the defence."

And becoming excited, she exclaimed:

"Oh, why did they not allow me to die before the walls of Paris!"

She was silent for a moment, looked dimly at the road, the trees, then went on:

"The French have great and brilliant qualities, but have few convictions and they lack constancy. Their minds are supple, but their characters are fickle. They love glory and everything that is brilliant or showy, but they do not know how to endure the strokes of misfortune. For them right is confused with success. In France you are honoured to-day and banished to-morrow. I have sometimes told myself that the French put their heroes on pedestals of salt, so that at the first storm that beats upon them they fall down, to remain for ever lying in the mud. There is no country in the world where there is so little distance between the sublime and the ridiculous. And how history repeats itself! For a hundred years every government in France has ended in revolution and flight. Only the other day when some persons expressed the fear that a fresh defeat might bring about the fall of the Imperial government, I declared to them that I would never leave the Tuileries in a cab like Louis-Philippe. And that's exactly what I have done!"

She smiled ruefully. The first houses of Saint-Germain appeared. They got through the *octroi* without difficulty. The landau moved on into the forest, passed through Poissy, Triel, Meulan. The sun was dazzling, the heat overwhelming. About eight miles out of Mantes the horses appeared to be worn out. At sight of a cabaret, Evans asked that they might be allowed to rest a little. He and Crane got out and had lunch; the Empress from motives of prudence would not leave the carriage. The two men returned with bread and a piece of Bologna sausage. Sad and dejected, Madame Lebreton refused them, while on the contrary Eugénie ate heartily.

At Mantes Evans hired a carriage and horses to take the place of his own, which he sent back to Paris. He handed the Empress the *Journal Officiel,* which he had found at a bookseller's—the Republic proclaimed at the Hôtel de Ville, . . . Trochu President of the Government of National Defence. . . .

"No, no, that's impossible," Eugénie said at first.

Then as she read she was convinced. She threw the paper away and exclaimed:

"How could he have betrayed us like that? After so many oaths of fidelity! Who could I have trusted, if not him, a soldier singled out by the Emperor himself as especially worthy of confidence, who had accepted the duty of defending me, and who to the very last moment swore to be faithful to me?"

Her voice trembled. She wept and fell silent.

A little later she took the paper again and read the names of the ministers in the government. She repeated aloud with contempt:

"Minister for Foreign Affairs, Jules Favre; Minister of the Interior, Gambetta!"

She shrugged her shoulders.

"I shall presently be in England," she said, "and then I shall know what is to be done."

At Pacy-sur-Eure they changed carriages again. This time it was a wretched affair upholstered in a very dirty blue stuff, perched on miserable wheels, drawn by a big grey mare and a little bay horse, and the harness held together with bits of string. The four travellers could not find room inside it, and Evans sat with the driver.

Evreux was very noisy, with *gardes mobiles* marching through singing the Marseillaise. In the great square the Empress saw the new prefect, just arrived from Paris, proclaiming the Republic. Night was approaching. Somehow or other, after several halts to repair the old shandrydan, they reached La Rivière-Thebouville, an out-of-the-way little village where Evans with great trouble found two rooms for the night in an inn. Doctor Crane helped the Empress, who limped and played the invalid. She went into the bar-rooms where several drinkers were at tables, climbed a twisty staircase that brought her to a room so bare and so poverty-stricken that she broke into laughter as she dropped on a chair.

"It's really too comical!" she exclaimed.

"Ah, mon Dieu, Madame," whispered Madame Lebreton, terrified, "how can you laugh at this wretched situation we are in? When everybody is watching us and people next door can hear you!"

The Empress shook her head without answering, took off her gloves and her hat. She dined in her room with her friend. The night was disturbed by a great clatter of horsemen, blows and knocks on the door of the inn. A troop of gendarmes no doubt on a round. . . . Eugénie slept profoundly and never woke. In the morning, having washed her two handkerchiefs and dried them against the window-pane, she took counsel with her companions. Evans wanted to continue their journey by carriage. But they would have to send to Bernay for one. The landlady when they consulted her was all astonished. Why not take the train? The station was less than a mile away.

"Let us take the train," said Eugénie. "We shall gain time."

They went on foot to the station, the Empress continuing to limp. Waiting for the time of departure the Empress pretended to read, with her veil lowered. She got into an empty compartment with her friend. At Serquigny they changed and took the Paris express which arrived at the same instant. Nothing untoward happened. But there were alarming moments when a railway employé or a traveller stared at them, though quite innocently. At Lisieux they left the train, went down into the streets. Evans went to find a carriage to take them to Deauville. It was raining. Eugénie and Madame Lebreton took refuge under the *porte cochère* of a factory. A young man offered the Empress a chair. She thanked him, refusing. She preferred to remain standing in the entrance. That rain falling on her clothes unheeded solaced and appeased her.

Evans arrived with a landau. The fugitives went on their way. The clouds had dispersed and the sun was shining once more. Eugénie was gay. She displayed her handkerchiefs. Weren't they nice and white?

"When we are not driven by hard necessity," she said, "we never suspect our capacity for doing certain things."

About three o'clock they at last came to Deauville and the Hôtel du Casino, where Mrs. Evans received them. The Empress threw herself into an armchair, saying:

"Oh, mon Dieu, I am saved!"

Not yet. While she rested, Evans and Crane went to Trouville where they saw in the dock a little fifty-foot yacht, the *Gazelle,* very light, but capable of crossing the Channel. It belonged to an English officer, Sir John Burgoyne, who was on board with his wife. Evans introduced himself. Sir John in the friendliest fashion took him over the yacht and said he intended to start with the tide next morning for England. The dentist then took him aside and confiding in his honour, asked him to receive the Empress and to take her over to England.

To begin with, Sir John refused.

"With the kind of weather we are certainly going to have, this little schooner might founder."

Crane persisted. Lady Burgoyne was consulted and did not hesitate.

"I shall be happy," she said fervently, "if I can render a service to the Empress. Let her come to-night or directly she can do so without danger."

A few hours later, in a deluge of rain, Eugénie and her companions, stumbling and wading in the night, reached the quay. Lady Burgoyne was most attentive, brought the Empress and Madame Lebreton to the single tiny cabin, gave them warm clothes and hot punch. Eugénie asked if the English papers contained any information about the Emperor and the Prince Imperial. Nothing was known of them. The ladies retired. The night went by calm and peaceful. At daybreak Sir John gave orders to weigh anchor. Doctor Crane took his leave of Eugénie, who gave him a list of persons he was to see in Paris to tell them what had happened. At seven the *Gazelle* left harbour.

The sea was running high. The weather, unfavourable at first, soon became threatening. The Normandy shore had barely fallen out of sight when the storm swooped down. The yacht laboured, pitched, rolled, shipped sea on sea. She was making for Southampton, but could not keep her course any longer. Sir John Burgoyne debated with himself whether it might not be better to put back and take shelter in a French harbour. That was Eugénie's one dread. The turmoil did not frighten her in the least. Sails furled, the schooner lay in the deep trough of the sea, her deck swept by a boil of water and a terrific din. Several times the Empress thought the little vessel was about to go down. If it was her fate, she was resigned to it.

"If I were to disappear now," she thought, "death could never come at a better moment, nor give me a grave more to be desired."

Madame Lebreton at her side was praying and weeping. Hearing a sailor call out, "We are ashore!" "What are they saying?" she asked in terror.

Eugénie, not to send her still more distracted, replied:

"They are saying that we are at the land!"

There was a certain humour in that. Through the twilight they were beginning to descry the Isle of Wight. But it was still a matter of hours to reach it. Towards midnight the wind dropped a little. The yacht was able to run up some sail. At daybreak she at last got into the roadstead at Ryde.

At the Pier Hotel the Empress and her companions were turned away because of their wretched appearance—clothes wet and bedraggled, no luggage. They found little rooms under the rafters of the York Hotel. Evans went out and saw in a morning paper that the Prince Imperial had arrived in Hastings. He did not tell Eugénie, fearing to agitate her too much. But he proposed to her to go to Brighton. She seemed delighted. By the steamboat *Princess Alice,* then by tram to Portsmouth, then by train, they reached Brighton. There Evans told the Empress that her son was close at hand. At once she demanded that he should take her to Hastings. They got there by night. The American left the two women and went to find the Marine Hotel where, he was told, the Prince was staying with Commandant Duperré and Count Clary. The boy overwhelmed the American, as soon as he saw him, with questions.

"Have you news of my mother?" he cried. "Where is she? No one can tell me if she is still in Paris or if she has left France! It's four days now since anybody knows what has become of her. And I am so anxious! Please tell me if you have any news of her!"

To spare the lad's extremely sensitive temperament, Evans merely answered that the Empress was safe and sound, and that she had just arrived in England. He promised to get further information.

Then going back to Eugénie at the Havelock Hotel, he found her in hat and cloak, sitting on a chair with her little bag in her hand, quite ready to start again.

She sprang up.

"Tell me, have you seen my son? Is he well? How does he look?"

As soon as he had reassured her she took hold of his hand and drew him towards the door.

"Where is he? Let us go and find him at once!"

Evans demurred. He thought it was for the Prince to come to his mother. But Eugénie, especially at such a moment, cared nothing for formalities! She ran down the stairs followed by the doctor and Madame Lebreton.

In the office of the Marine Hotel, the proprietor, taking her for a Sister of Charity because she had thrown the hood of her cloak over her head, told her it was too late to disturb the Prince.

"You must come back another day."

Another day! Pushing past, she went upstairs. Evans went into the Prince's room. Questioned by the boy's eyes, he pointed to the door. The Prince opened it and fell into his mother's arms.

CHAPTER IV

Eddies

DURING the days that followed Eugénie found herself confined to her room at the Marine Hotel. That dreadful night at sea, the cold, the excitement that ever since the morning of September 4 had been stretching her nerves to snapping point, had exhausted her strength. Long spasms of coughing shook her, she could hardly speak, and shivered with fever under her shawls. Nevertheless, lying on an uncomfortable sofa chair, she received the friends who hurried down to Hastings on learning of her arrival: the Duc and the Duchesse de Mouchy, Princess Metternich, Princesse Murat, Countess Clary, La Valette, Filon, and Lieutenant Conneau (whom she sent off immediately to fight), her nieces Louise and Marie, and the Prince Imperial's faithful nurse, Miss Shaw, "Nana" as he called her, who had stayed on at the Tuileries for a few days after the Revolution.

Princess Metternich, stricken at the sight of the poor room, threw herself into the Empress's arms and wept. Before anything else, she gave her Marie-Antoinette's book of hours, which Metternich had taken from Eugénie's table at the moment of her flight.

"She was worse off than I am; I have still got my husband and my son," murmured the Empress as she took in her hands that relic, given her long ago by Viel-Castel. She was exceedingly attached to it.

Finding her so bare of necessities, the Princess and Madame de Mouchy on returning to London, where they were staying, sent her a trunk full of linen and toilet articles.

With La Valette and Rouher, who had escaped from the not very energetic searches of the police, and who had reachel Calais among Princess Metternich's retinue, Eugénie discusses plans. In the opinion of both men, as the deposition had not been formally pronounced the only regular and legitimate government of France remained that of the Empress-Regent. The King of Prussia and Bismarck would, they said, prefer to treat with her rather than with a government sprung up out of insurrection, which a fresh national convulsion might overthrow to-morrow. Eugénie believed this too. But she did not wish in any way to embarrass the efforts of the chiefs of the National Defence to reach a speedy peace. To help them, on September 13, she even wrote of her own initiative, from motives of generosity, from motives of patriotism, to the Czar, begging him to intervene with Prussia on behalf of France, without allowing himself to be influenced by the change of régime.

> Away from my own country, I write to-day to Your Majesty. Only a few days ago, when the destinies of France were still in the hands of the power constituted by the Emperor, if I had taken this step, I should perhaps, in your eyes and in the eyes of France, have seemed to doubt the vital forces of my country. The latest events set me free, and I can address myself to Your Majesty's heart.
>
> Sire, fate has been against us. The Emperor is a prisoner and the prey of evil tongues. Another government has usurped the task that we looked upon as our duty to carry out.
>
> I entreat Your Majesty to exert your influence to bring about the conclusion of an honourable and durable peace. . . . May France *whatever be her government,* find in Your Majesty the same sentiments you displayed towards us in these bitter trials. . . .

She wrote also to Francis-Joseph, who answered with a *non-possumus* elaborately wrapped up in honey. She made no movement in the direction of Victor-Emmanuel. She knew what to expect from the chivalry of the *Re galant-uomo.* The Italian troops were bombarding down the Porta Pia, stripped of its French defenders. Pius IX had taken refuge in the Vatican.

"The cowards!" complained Eugénie. "They were waiting our misfortunes!"

The Czar was touched. He made strong representations at Berlin to get Bismarck to listen to Jules Favre and conclude an armistice. Thus was brought about the Ferrières interview, which was nevertheless in vain.

From the first arrival of the Empress at Hastings there prowled about her a cynical and self-important adventurer, who had dabbled in law and in medicine, who had married a rich Englishwoman and lived now in Paris, now in London. It has been said that Régnier was in German pay; he must have been far more of an intriguer than a spy. On September 12 he submitted to

Eugénie a plan for the restoration of the Empire under cover of the army of Metz, offering himself as an intermediary to negotiate with Prussia. The Empress, mistrustful with good reason, replied that she could do nothing and that the one thing at stake was the interest of France. Having pressed unsuccessfully for an audience, he lay in wait for the Prince Imperial and Filon and accosted them in the middle of a walk. He said he was starting for Wilhelmshöhe and asked the boy to write his name and a few lines on three photographs of Hastings, which he would take to the Emperor on his behalf. Filon allowed himself to be hoodwinked, and in spite of the Empress's explicit prohibitions, gave these signed photographs to Régnier, who made use of them as credentials to Bismarck, to whom he betook himself forthwith. The Chancellor sent him to Bazaine, in order to discover his plans and to get him to surrender Metz. Already Filon was regretting his imprudence. He confessed what he had done to the Empress, who took him most severely to task.

"You behaved extraordinarily badly. This man is a spy of Bismarck's or an agent of the Paris government, which is trying to dishonour us in the eyes of the nation by making it appear that we are intriguing with Prussia."

She forgave him in the sequel. But she waited in great uneasiness for what might be the outcome of these sinister doings.

She could not continue to stay at the Hastings hotel, surrounded by inquisitive persons and evil tongues. Evans and Madame Lebreton set to work to find her a more suitable abode. They found at Chislehurst, twenty minutes by rail from Charing Cross, a great red-brick pile dating from the beginning of the century, and belonging to a Mr. Nathaniel Strode, who had known the Emperor in the old days. Camden Place was surrounded by a beautiful park. Black cedars on the lawn set off the house admirably. Eugénie rented it for six thousand francs, a singularly moderate figure, for it was sumptuously and even beautifully furnished. On September 24 she installed herself in it with her son and the persons belonging to her suite.

When she arrived she saw on the front of the house a clock with this inscription

"Malo mori quam fœdari."

"That motto was made for me," she said.

The next day, a Sunday, she went to Mass in the little Catholic church of St. Mary. She failed to find a place for herself and remained down by the door mingling with the poor people of the parish. That did not displease her. Proud in the face of men, she gladly made herself little before God.

The same day as she read the *Times* after dinner, in the big drawing-room, she came upon this curt line.

Monsieur P. Mérimée, the celebrated French novelist, died yesterday at Cannes.

So he was dead. . . . Don Prospero, the mentor of her youth, friend of her golden hours, the confidant of her evil days. This trusty, subtle-minded man knew her without a doubt better than any being in the world. With him there crumbled away a huge slice of the past. Forty years! He had not been able to survive the disaster of his "poor Biarritz friends." He had left Paris directly he knew Eugénie was in safety, and had gone to die without fuss on that Provençal coast where for these many winters past he had nursed his asthma between his two old Englishwomen.

"Monsieur Mérimée!" sighed Eugénie. She had no tears for him. She had shed too many already. Indeed this death brought her a kind of relief. She had seen him so broken, so wasted. . . . He was doomed. It was better for him not to see the hideous development of the war, the invasion of the France he continually mocked at, but which in the depths of his heart he had dearly loved. Now he was at peace in the fragrance of the pine trees, under the sun. . . .

She crossed herself and prayed fervently for the disciple of Voltaire who held none of her beliefs, but who under his mocking shell hid, as well she knew, a warm and tender heart.

On Wednesday morning she was in her room on the first floor, when Madame Lebreton came in to her in a whirl, crying:

"Madame, my brother is here!"

Her brother? But she must be mad, thought Eugénie.

"Come, my dear friend, calm yourself. General Bourbaki is in Metz with his soldiers."

"Look, Madame, here he is . . ."

Bundled up in civilian clothes that hung loose about him (Bazaine had lent them to him) the general appeared before Eugénie, petrified with astonishment.

"What are you doing here? Has Metz fallen then?"

The general, who thought he was expected, stammered a reply.

"No, Madame, here is a letter from Maréchal Bazaine, who directed me to come to Your Majesty to receive your commands."

"My commands? But what commands? I have none to give you. I am in the dark. What have you brought me? What does the Maréchal want, what is he asking for?"

"I know nothing, Madame," said Bourbaki, "here is the letter."

Out of his depth in this imbroglio, a brave man, but not overburdened with brains, he began to weep.

"All I know is that I am dishonoured in the eyes of the army, for I have left my soldiers in front of the enemy!"

The Empress consoled him as well as she could and took him into her cabinet.

"This is the work of that fellow Régnier," she thought.

She was not mistaken. Régnier had persuaded Bazaine that in conjunction with the Empress he could make peace and reestablish the former government. The Maréchal sent Bourbaki to Camden Place to come to an understanding with Eugénie in order to negotiate with Prussia.

Bourbaki explained the business in a confused fashion. Eugénie in vain plied him with questions. His only concern was with himself, imagining himself the plaything of a conspiracy that was destroying his honour as a soldier. To pacify him, through Lord Granville she informed Count Bernstorff, the Prussian Minister in London, that she had given Régnier no authority of any kind, and asked permission for Bourbaki to return to Metz through the Prussian lines. The general at once set out for Brussels, and not having received the authorisation sought for, went as Princess Metternich had advised and offered his sword to the Tours Delegation, with Eugénie's approval.

In the midst of these happenings Régnier crossed the Channel again and dared to come and ask the Empress for an audience. This time she did receive him. She saw a kind of old non-commissioned officer of vulgar but alert appearance, and a penetrating eye, who talked copiously and with an air of authority. She reproached him for having abused Filon's confidence and for having gone to Bismarck when he ought to have gone to the Emperor, and finally for deceiving Bazaine by boasting of an imaginary and pretended mission.

He excused himself with complete coolness, said that she must make up her mind to treat with Prussia if she wished to avoid too severe an amputation of French territory. Bismarck, he avouched, would only demand money from her, a great deal of money, the disarming of the frontier, and some districts of Alsace. If she refused, the peace would be signed by the Republic. And that peace—a peace of annihilation—would take the whole of Alsace, perhaps even Lorraine. He ended by exclaiming in dramatic tones:

"There is still time, but make haste! Every day that goes by is costing France millions, is tearing away a piece of her flesh. Madame, save the army of Metz and save France!"

Eugénie was impressed. But her mistrust continued. She answered the adventurer.

"Monsieur, I find fault with your behaviour, but I do justice to your intentions. There is much truth in what you have said, unhappily you do not seem to know your fellow-countrymen. They will never forgive whoever gives up a piece of France; they will always say—and their sons after them will say—that if the struggle had been carried on to the end, the victory would have been won. And there is something else: the peace would not be recognised or accepted, and after the foreign war there would be civil war."

Régnier withdrew and never appeared again.

Eugénie sent Clary first, and then Evans, to Wilhelmshöhe to establish contact with the Emperor better than by letters and telegrams. She had wanted to share his captivity. Napoleon refused, saying that Eugénie's place was with her son. Besides, as she had remained the sovereign power *de jure,* the nominal mistress of the army of Metz, she could not come among the enemy. She obeyed, champing at the bit . . . Visits from numbers of friends who had found refuge in London or its neighbourhood, and who composed a little buzzing court for her, helped her to pass the hours. She adopted their illusions. She saw France collecting all her strength to drive out the invader. She might detest Gambetta; she thrilled with enthusiasm to read his bulletins, his bombastic proclamations. The smallest success made her pant with hope. She believed that the army of the Loire was going to thrust back the Prussians, that a massed sortie of the *gardes mobiles* of Paris would throw the besiegers into confusion, while by a supreme effort the army of Metz would at last succeed in breaking through the vice that gripped it. She imagined the League of Neutrals bearing hard on Prussia to force her to a generous peace.

In the negotiation of that peace she was more and more reckoning that a decisive part would fall to her. All her entourage had for days been repeating to her, after Régnier—and in fact it was true—that Prussia now asked only to treat, and that the conditions she would lay down for Eugénie would be infinitely milder than those she would impose upon Favre, Gambetta, or Thiers, who inspired nothing but distrust or contempt in Berlin. Flattered in the high idea she entertained of herself, happy to come back upon the stage and again take hold of the action that had escaped from her, without forgetting the notion (a mad one, but always there) that she might put together once more the timbers of her son's throne, she hoped by a spectacular and brilliant service to force the esteem and the gratitude of France.

She was watching for an opportunity for such a service.

General Boyer, despatched by Bazaine, who was troubled at Bourbaki's silence, then arrived at Chislehurst. He was a completely honest man, modest and serious. When he came before Eugénie she fancied she saw in him the spectre of the army of Metz, so pale and emaciated was he. He was the bearer of two letters, one from the Maréchal, the other from General Frossard. The Prince Imperial's former governor implored Eugénie to negotiate, claiming her quality and status as Regent. He answered for the besieged troops that they would re-establish the Imperial government and impose order on the country.

"I do not know," he wrote, "what the full conditions of peace may be, but if they are not wholly unacceptable, I think, with all the chiefs of our army, that Your Majesty will do well to accept them, in order to save the country, which is being crushed and killed by the prolonging of the present state of things."

She consulted at length with Boyer, who, having had an interview with Bismarck at Versailles, informed her of his conditions, to which Bazaine was subscribing.

The army of Metz would declare itself in favour of the Napoleonic dynasty. It would surrender the town to the Prussians, and with arms and baggage would make its way to a port, Le Havre or Calais, and place itself under the authority of the Regent. The latter, returning immediately to France, would without discussion and with closed eyes sign preliminaries of peace, and would then bring the Chambers together to make them ratify these preliminaries.

At Eugénie's request Boyer wired to Bismarck. Before taking any decision the Empress demanded that Metz should be revictualled for a fortnight.

She assembled a council at Camden Place at which Rouher, Persigny, Chevreau, La Valette, Prince Napoleon, were informed of the proposed pronunciamento. They were of the opinion that it should be furthered. Boyer repeated that, failing a speedy solution, Metz must very soon capitulate. As Rouher, with his lawyer's eloquence, was resuming the theme of the less drastic demands which the Empress would have to face, she interrupted him:

"These demands I must know in detail before I accept them!"

So far Bismarck had refused to indicate clearly the indemnities and cessions of territory he had in view.

"If we want to save the army," said Boyer, *"however exorbitant the demands appear,* they will have to be accepted."

Eugénie exclaimed with indignation:

"What they want to extort from me is a blank cheque. How could the generals at Metz have imagined that I would give it?"

Her eyes darted lightnings at Boyer, who did not utter another word.

She dismissed the council, saying that she would do nothing unless she knew what it was she was being pledged to. Then she asked for an interview with Count Bernstorff. She received him at Lady Cowley's house in Albemarle Street. He did not wish to tell her his sovereign's intentions with regard to the bases of the peace without the Chancellor's authorisation to do so. He promised his good offices, did his best to hearten and reassure

Eugénie, even assured her, lying boldly, that it was a question merely of a negligible cession of territory.

"That is an impossibility," said the Empress. "A cession of territory I shall never consent to!"

She had put on rouge so as not to appear too broken, but she could not hide her tears. She declared that she envisaged a treaty that would make Strasbourg a free town, and give Germany an indemnity and a colony, such as Cochin China. Bernstorff allowed her to understand that these sacrifices would not be enough . . .

She returned in despair to Camden Place. After long hesitation, taking, as she said, her courage in both hands, she decided to write direct to King William to conjure him not to demand the dismembering of France. Inflexible behind the formalities of courtesy the King replied that he was obliged to insist upon an annexation, *by way of guarantee* against the spirit of revenge of France. Bismarck wished to have a glacis . . .

On the 27th, Metz capitulated. General Boyer informed Eugénie. She was expecting it, but the fact dazed and overwhelmed her. The pivot of her last illusions was torn away. She shut herself up, refused to receive any one, even M. Tissot, the London Chargé d'Affaires of the Government of National Defence, who came to thank her for her good offices with the Czar.

When she appeared once more among her intimates, she announced her departure for Wilhelmshöhe. She wished to see the Emperor without delay. Her anterior defences, she said, had fallen with Metz. She must now decide with Napoleon what course was to be taken in face of a new situation. Bazaine's surrender removed all authority, every guarantee, from the Imperial régime. Not another moment was to be lost in negotiating with Prussia, if there still remained any chances of doing so.

She told Clary that he was to go with her.

For several weeks, as she confessed to her closest friends, she had been uneasy about Napoleon's state of mind. She found reticences, a coldness in his letters. She knew he was surrounded in his princely prison by men who were not at all friendly to her. She must have been blamed for many mistakes, the responsibility for Sedan and the fall of the régime must have been thrown on her on account of her forbidding the Emperor to reappear in Paris unless victorious. But she had not only to explain her attitude, to justify her past intentions, it was still more important to see eye to eye with regard to the present. Away from her influence the Emperor had not yet been able to come to any resolve. She wished to regain his confidence, and, united with him in public harmony, bring together the scattered forces of the Imperialist Party.

She crossed the sea and reached Cassel on the afternoon of October 30. Clary went on before and went to announce her to Napoleon. Wrapped in a waterproof, her head covered by a veil, she appeared at the foot of the steps. She sprang to the Emperor, and would have thrown her arms about him. He restrained himself, held her hands, while she sobbed, then giving her his arm took her to his cabinet. On the way the French officers of the suite saluted her, and she gave them her hand to kiss. Napoleon presented the Governor of Cassel, General von Monts, to her. When they were alone, she wept a long time on his shoulder. Most poignant minutes these. To find each other again like this, after barely three months, during which the abyss had opened and engulfed their fortune and the fortune of France! . . . Napoleon did not keep her at arm's length now. He was touched by an emotion he saw to be so sincere, in which he thought he could discern regrets. She questioned him about his health. He was better. Rest and attention had alleviated his sufferings. He spoke to her of their son. Had he not been too much affected by events? Had he resumed his studies with Filon? He had written charming letters to his father.

"How he loves him!" she said to herself. "He thinks of nothing else!"

Half envious and half pleased, she answered him. Now they were no longer dethroned sovereigns facing their disaster, but a father and a mother smiling as they leaned over their child. Every now and then they looked at each other, without either of them daring to prolong the look. How old he had grown! His eyes were dimmed, his cheeks flabby and fallen, a dreadful weight bowed his shoulders down. And she, in her black clothes, such simple modest clothes, her eyelids reddened, her complexion patchy, she had nothing of her beauty left. Thus despoiled, more human, both of them felt nearer one another. And each of them pitied the other.

Eugénie was the first to emerge from this soft, melancholy mood. It seemed to her that she had an account to give, that she must lay down her burden. And yet she avoided speaking of what still lay too much between them, the acts of the Regency which had dispossessed, which had cast aside the Emperor. She harked back to the events of September 4. He listened without interrupting her, twisting his moustache. He had heard a great many things through Evans, but she alone knew all the details of that terrible day. When after perhaps a couple of hours she had ceased, harassed and distressed, he spoke in his turn, in a dead, monotonous voice. He made no reproaches against her. His kind nature made him incapable of long-continued resentment or rather kept him from giving expression to it. She had sacrificed him after his reverses, and by so doing had precipitated the catastrophe. He would never cease to hold this view. But she had been thinking of her son; as for her mistakes, she had committed them only for her son's sake, and that son he loved far too much not to incline to forgiveness.

And so on this first day he too refrained from touching upon politics. He talked of the war, of the privations of his soldiers, of their bravery. . . . He did not venture to utter the name *Sedan*. . . .

In spite of Napoleon's physical decline, Eugénie felt diminished in his presence. Perhaps some vague remorse stirred within her? Hitherto she had acted alone, and with a high hand, like a true member of the dynasty. Now she found herself on a secondary plane. The mild authority that emanated from the Emperor was at work upon her once more, was dominating her as in the old days at the beginning of their married life. And at the same time, to see him so melancholy, so quiet, an unwonted tenderness took possession of her. She forgot, once and for all, her jealousies, her disappointments as a wife. She loved her husband with a warmer heart than she had ever loved him before.

Next morning she had a long conversation with him. She broached the plan for the pronunciamento of Bazaine, agreed to by Bismarck. Napoleon saw nothing in it but a trap. Bismarck wanted to make sure of Metz. Then Eugénie revealed to him the negotiations carried on in the last few days, the council held at Camden Place, the interview with Bernstorff; she showed him William's letter. Napoleon expressed astonishment that she should have gone so far without consulting him. True, she had remained Regent, but although a prisoner, he had not ceased to be the Emperor. Had she forgotten that?

She drooped her head.

"Anyhow," went on Napoleon, "now that Metz has surrendered, it is no longer with us that Prussia will want to treat."

Eugénie was of the contrary opinion. She remained persuaded that Bismarck, who feared the establishment of a Republic in France, would prefer to negotiate with the Imperial régime.

"I should have to consent to too great sacrifices. I have enlarged France; how could I sign her mutilation?"

The Empress insisted, carried away, eloquent. Nothing but the interests of France, she said, was in her mind. Yes, it was true, peace concluded now, and by them, would undoubtedly cost Alsace. But concluded later, and by the insurgent government, it would cost Lorraine too. With men like Jules Favre and Gambetta, Prussia would be ruthless. With themselves, who had made the Tuileries a hostelry for kings, William would be obliged to certain observances. There was a solidarity among sovereigns. . . . She too, and before Napoleon, had rebelled. She had declared to Régnier, to Boyer, to Bernstorff, that she would refuse any cession of territory. But she had reflected during her journey. . . . However bitter might be the cup, she was resigned to the draught, if the Emperor would authorise her to drink it.

Napoleon made a sign with his head that he would not.

And yet she was right. To negotiate now, after a brief war, and before Paris had fallen, would lighten the sacrifices. Napoleon was treading on his own toes in his regard for honour. The Republicans had stabbed him in the back. But he would do nothing to paralyse their efforts at defence, and above all he would not run any risk of provoking a civil war. France might have shown herself to be ungrateful and unfaithful, he would not take possession of her again with the help of the foreigner. If peace must needs be purchased by the giving up of a province, he would leave the responsibility to the men of the Fourth of September.

Later on they would see. He believed in the future. . . . She answered, argued, obstinate and desperate. The Emperor's stubbornness, she thought, would doom their son. He would never reign! That idea tormented her, sent her beside herself. Forgetting herself she gave vent to unjust and bitter words. The Emperor let them pass. She got nothing by it. The *"doux entêté"* remained inflexible. The old influence no longer worked upon him. He did not even allow her to remain, as she had hoped, at Wilhelmshöhe. She must go back immediately, to watch over Louis. She made little resistance. What would have been the use? She felt herself disarmed. She was nothing now. Only the Emperor counted. She measured the distance between them and went back to her own place. . . .

Once more in Camden Place, henceforward she kept aloof from all negotiations. She even, when she came to know of them, disapproved of the clumsy attempts that Napoleon, when his eyes were at length opened, made to deal with Bismarck, judging that they were too late, that they had no longer any chance of success. She thought only of the war, of Paris in the death throes, prayed untiringly for a miraculous change of fortune.

"If God will give a victory to the army of the Vosges, I shall be consoled for all our misfortunes."

But there was no victory. Everywhere defeat. And weariness. . . . And in the end, the dreadful peace, roughly patched up by Thiers, which once more provoked her to despair and contempt. Then the Commune, which horrified her and for which she yet found an excuse:

"Those poor people! They could not endure all that shame!"

Then the fresh siege, the week of blood and fire, the savage repression by the light of the braziers in which the whole of Imperial France was consumed. . . .

Napoleon III, set free by the signing of the peace preliminaries, had been at Chislehurst from the 20th of March.

PART IV
EXILE

CHAPTER I

Chislehurst

At Camden Place were installed Madame Lebreton, Madame de Saulcy, Mademoiselle de Larminat, the Conneaus, Corvisart, Franceschini Pietri, Augustin Filon. In the village of Chislehurst the Bassanos, the Aguados, the Clarys, the Davilliers had found quarters in modest houses. The Duchesse de Mouchy, the Murats, the Jérôme Davids, the Duchesse de Talleyrand, the Duchesse de Tarente, the Clement-Duvernois, were in London; the Chevreaus and the Rouhers at Richmond. Nearly all of them came every day to Camden Place. They formed an honorary service, a court in miniature, barriers against the foreigner, which allowed Napoleon and Eugénie to live in that atmosphere of respect which saddens and solaces the vanquished at the same time.

English visitors were numerous—Lord Malmesbury, a tried friend of old, Lord Sydney, lieutenant of Kent, Lord Buckhurst, the two Cavendishes, Lord Henry Lennox, a dandy out of his time, Lord Russell, the Primate Archbishop Tait, Lord Glenesk, the manager of the *Morning Post,* Blanchard Jerrold, the Marquis of Ely, Madame d'Arcos and her sister Miss Vaughan, old friends of the Empress. And lastly, Queen Victoria, although Gladstone sought to dissuade her, made it a point of honour to pay several visits to her allies of the Crimean War in order to display a friendship that the political differences of the last few years might have weakened but which misfortune confirmed and strengthened. Since her widowhood the Queen was even more puritanical and straitlaced than before. She could not understand Napoleon's utopias or Eugénie's enthusiasms. But she continued to feel sincere sympathy with them and considered it her duty to let Europe see that even fallen sovereigns remain sovereigns still.

These demonstrations of fidelity fortified the deposed pair, helped them to endure the accusations and calumnies that circulated here and there, as soon as the braziers of the Commune had died down, launched by the whole of France against them, calumnies the echo of which, but little lessened by distance, buffeted them in Camden Place. Never were such shameful and cruel insults heaped upon an abolished régime. No doubt France had suffered too much to be fair. But the insults were often too foul and degrading, and the Emperor, patient as he was, could not refrain from clenching his fists when he read that he had run away at Sedan, after sending waggons full of gold into Germany.

The Paris newspapers gravely computed the huge fortune amassed over many years by Napoleon and Eugénie, and deposited in safety in English banks. In reality the early days of their residence at Camden Place knew real straits for lack of money. When at Wilhelmshöhe the Emperor had sold the Cesarini palace which he owned in Rome, and at the Empress's request had the price, six hundred thousand francs, sent to her. On reaching Chislehurst, being harassed by urgent askers for help—for the Empire, whose prosperity had founded few fortunes, had by its fall cast many into distress—he asked Eugénie to return him this amount. She replied that she had nothing left, that it had all been spent. He was silent in astonishment, not being a person to ask for any accounts. Later on she was of her own accord to confess that she had kept this money in order to establish with the sum recovered at Baring's Bank a fund capable of maintaining their rank and their hopes. She knew the Emperor's lavish bounty. So she made herself his treasurer and kept a tight hand on the purse-strings. Through Count Clary she had sold the greater part of the jewels saved by the Metternichs; they went to adorn various Indian princes. Substantial loans had also been placed at their disposal until the sequestration on their property in France should be removed.

If the Emperor appeared resigned, Eugénie did not hide her resentment. She could allow the loss of the throne, but could not endure ingratitude and meanness. Her anger was not so much directed against the Republicans as against those who, having been laden by the Empire with titles and favours, were openly rallying to Thiers. Trochu above all the others aroused her hatred. He had betrayed her, she repeated, he had trampled upon his "honour as a Breton, a Catholic, and a soldier." He was a vile creature, an Iscariot. . . . But in this general smash how many others sang their palinode, repudiated their homage of yesterday. Drouyn de Lhuys, Viollet-le-Duc, Edmond About, even Galliffet

Galliffet, who had been at every fête, whom she had treated as a real friend! His wife, for her own part, remained faithful and devoted. But he was only a harum-scarum fellow, a *reître,* capable of anything, a hero at Puebla, a butcher in the Commune! And that other one, still more honoured by the Emperor, made a duke, made a Marshal, Mac-Mahon, that ambitious booby who let himself be pushed up into the dictatorship, wearing his defeats like a decoration! How easily men turn their backs on misfortune! Caro, that court philosopher, who at Compiègne used to lift sheeps' eyes to her, was already turning them towards more useful beauties; Zorn de Bulach, yesterday a chamberlain at the Tuileries, was offering his services to the Emperor William; Nieuwerkerke, a cynical pleasure-hunter, had sped off to Italy at the very beginning of the catastrophe, and had installed himself there with his pile, without a letter or a word of farewell to the Princesse Mathilde, from whom he had had everything down to his very shirts, and whom he was casting aside like a prostitute, after an association of twenty years. With these vilenesses she compared the attitude of Abd-El-Kader. The Emir had addressed to her a noble epistle from Damascus, couched in flowery language: "Only the sun and the moon know eclipse!" he said.

"It is an Arab, an ancient foe, who writes that to me! What a lesson for the French!"

Boxes of papers that had escaped from pillage had arrived at Camden Place, thanks to Metternich. The Empress, Clary and Filon unpacked them, arranging what was of use, throwing away everything that seemed worthless. The Emperor was there, every now and then running through a letter, and tossing it away. Suddenly Eugénie straightened up and held out a sheet to him, exclaiming:

"At last! I have been looking for it such a long time! Read that, just read!"

It was a letter of Guizot's. During the Empire, although he had remained hostile to the régime, he had come to the Tuileries to ask help from Napoleon. A son's debts had brought him into a dreadful impasse. After he had said his say, the Emperor had opened in front of him a drawer full of banknotes, and walking to the window with his back to Guizot, had said:

"Take whatever you need. . . ."

After September 4, Guizot, a drab and icy-hearted creature, writing against the Empire had shown himself full of gall and wormwood.

Napoleon took his letter, which thanked the Emperor in these words: "Sire, you have saved more than my life, you have saved my honour."

He murmured.

"I had forgotten that."

He made to crumple the paper up and throw it into the fire. The Empress snatched it away from him.

"Leave me that: it is my revenge!"

Napoleon looked reproachfully at her and said, in a tone of authority which he seldom assumed:

"No, Eugénie, I will not allow it. That is not the way one avenges oneself."

And he left the drawing-room.

In September 1871, Eugénie went to Spain. The Emperor and the Prince Imperial accompanied her to Waterloo Station. At Southampton she went on board the steamer *Oneida* which took her to Lisbon. The Duke of Alba, her brother-in-law, was waiting for her there. She barely paused in Madrid, wishing to go at once to Carabanchel. Her mother and she embraced each other with no excessive display of emotion. The Countess was all but blind, but was unwilling to acknowledge it. She would go knocking herself against the furniture, feeling with hands stretched out in front of her, and no one said anything, to avoid making her angry. Her face, rouged at haphazard, still retained traces of beauty. She talked with all her old fluency, her head still full of plans and projects. She gave *tertulias* and continued to be an indefatigable matchmaker. Miss Flower, who had never left her, an old poodle under her frizzy fair wig, helped her to do the honours of her house. The meals, just as in the old days, were very mediocre, and the whole housekeeping very casual. Eugénie, at every step coming upon reminders of her youth, did not find it depressing. On the contrary, her vigour was renewed on this arid soil, with its hidden virtues, to which she was attached by so many ties. In November she passed through Madrid again, then crossing the sea once more, she joined the Emperor at Torquay where he had spent some weeks. When they were back at Chislehurst, it was decided that the Prince Imperial should go every morning to London and take the lectures at King's College, Strand. Napoleon felt that an ordinary course of education was becoming essential for him. He knew that he was spoiling his son too much, his heart had the upper hand. The Empress still blamed him, but less harshly than of old.

The good understanding between them had been restored. The Emperor, enfeebled, aged, and ill, no longer thought of the *distractions* that had raised so many domestic storms. And Eugénie showed him more affection than she used to do . . . in compassion for his misfortunes, in respect for his courage, his melancholy serenity, in regret for having thought for a moment of sacrificing him to save the dynasty, in remorse for having vented those hideous cries of rage against him on the morrow of Sedan, cries that he would never know of, but which she could never forget. She surrounded him with attentions, sometimes excessive, so much that he seemed embarrassed by them. On his side he did everything he could think of to alleviate the exile that must needs weigh so heavily on a proud and vibrant nature. While she was in Spain he had prepared a surprise for her. She had always regretted her little library in the Tuileries. He had it duplicated, complete and identical, in cases elbow-high set against the walls of the big drawing-room; he had arranged with his own hands the volumes stamped with the crowned E which he had secretly ordered from his old bookbinder in Paris.

Often rising before daybreak, he would work in the narrow cabinet he had kept for himself beside his bedroom. There was only room in it for his desk, two armchairs, the big cupboard that held his papers, his letters, various souvenirs, the volume bound in red leather that contained the memoirs of Queen Hortense.

There, smoking interminably, he revised his old essays on artillery, put together materials for a work on the military operations of 1870. For his copying and his correspondence Franceschini Pietri used to help him, or Doctor Conneau, or Count Clary, sometimes even Augustin Filon.

Alongside, the Emperor had arranged for Eugénie what she called her "corner"—a big bedroom and an octagonal cabinet, which she furnished with odd pieces in a way that reminded her of the Tuileries. In a cupboard with glass doors, and shelves covered with blue velvet there rested the relics that friends had been able to rescue from the former Imperial homes, and to send her. On the table a great many photographs of her family looked on as she wrote. A gilt trellis-screen entwined with a trailing ivy plant had been presented to her by the members of her household.

Through the great bay window she saw a misty landscape sprinkled with clumps of trees, a less fat Normandy, and dotted over with sheep and cows. There she used to spend nearly the whole of the morning. As soon as she was dressed and her hair done, always a rapid business, she received her maître d'hôtel, arranged her household affairs like the expert she was, looked over her accounts, then read her large correspondence, the French or English papers, marked the principal articles in them with blue pencil for the Emperor's benefit, wrote numerous letters, long ones, in her swift, well-shaped, almost masculine handwriting, an echo of her quick speech that was vividly full of images. She came down for luncheon. Almost always along with the usual table companions there sat down a number of guests who had come from London or from the Continent. The Emperor as a rule did not talk much. But the Empress kept things going, discussing the news, asking sudden questions. Napoleon would interrupt her by a slight sign when politics were taking up too much space or when he sensed some imprudence on its way. After luncheon he would go into the gallery where he talked with his visitors as he walked up and down, smoking incessant cigarettes. The Prince Imperial often went out riding from two to four, as he had done in France, with Louis Conneau and his Alba cousins. Bachon the groom accompanied them. Sometimes he made an excursion here or there, to the Tower of London, to the Crystal Palace, or Hampton Court, or the farming colony at Farningham. The Empress, with Countess Clary or Madame Lebreton, would take the train and go to London, where she did her shopping, went to call on her bankers, visited her friends, especially the Duchesse de Mouchy, with whom she could talk her fill, and who without having the wisdom of the smart world had the wisdom of the heart. She would go to the Jesuit chapel in Farm Street to say a prayer. One day when she was there with Augustin Filon, while she was kneeling in the confessional an unknown artist improvised a sad and noble air on the organ. Later Eugénie learned the name of the musician, Gounod, only the other day a guest at Compiègne and in the Tuileries, who was making a stay in London. He had recognised the Empress by her walk, and had meant that discreet homage for her.

She would get back to Camden Place about five, and have tea served in the hall. More conversation. "You have no idea how much exile makes you talk," said Madame Lebreton. Some one would point out that it was about to strike seven. Then she would rush away, and all the rest after her, to dress.

After dinner the men spent a little time in the smoking-room or in the billiard-room, the women sat in the big drawing-room. Madame Clary and Madame Lebreton, and Mademoiselle de Larminat would do fancy work. The Empress would start a game of patience, with the Duc de Bassano and Doctor Conneau standing beside her. The Emperor, buried in a great plush armchair by the fireplace, smoked, with eyes closed upon who knew what dream. From the hall would be heard the laughter of the Prince Imperial, his girl cousins, Madeleine Davillier, Louis Conneau, the mediocre sounds from the old grand piano on which Jacqueline de Saulcy would strum out some air of Strauss or Offenbach.

At half-past nine the Prince Imperial went up to his room after kissing his parents good night. The Emperor retired soon after. At eleven Eugénie in her turn got up and before the court of exile, all bowing, made her long, her marvellous curtsy of the Tuileries, an evocation so poignant that Filon, being young and emotional, felt a catch at his heart.

On Sundays the Imperial couple went on foot across the common to hear Mass said by Father Goddard at the little church of St. Mary. Numbers of friends from London or from the neighbourhood always appeared at lunch. The three o'clock train brought a stream of visitors. On certain days Madame Conneau, who had a voice of exquisite purity and considerable power, would sing. Sullivan improvised melodies at the piano. In summer tea was on the lawn. The women chatted gaily; the men made a circle round the Emperor or talked in low voices in little groups. The English sun shone on the leafy greenness, on the bright-coloured dresses. They were sad no longer, they had hopes.

In the summer of 1872, the Emperor, who was again troubled with the stone, had gone to Cowes at the advice of his physicians. Eugénie wanted to show Scotland to her son. It was one of the countries she liked best. She loved its transparent, washed sky, its green moors, its lakes scattered everywhere like sprinkled drops of purest water. The Duke of Tamamès, who was to marry Maria d'Alba, went with them. "A regular steeplechase," said Mademoiselle de Larminat, recalling the expedition afterwards. The Empress, whom nothing could tire, ran her companions off their legs. The young prince quickly had enough. He regretted Camden Place and his friend Louis Conneau. The journey seemed too rapid for him. Neither Edinburgh, nor Abbotsford, nor Dalkeith, where they enjoyed the magnificent hospitality of the Duke of Buccleuch, took hold of his imagination.

"All that," he said, "is good enough for the albums of old Englishwomen. I always have the feeling that I have seen it already. . . ."

But, as he was always very deferential to his mother, admiring her without sharing her tastes, in order to shorten his travels he expressed a desire to go and join the Emperor, who had been left alone, and whom he thought very tired. She gave her consent, and he went off to Cowes, while Eugénie continued her round by the Caledonian Canal and Inverness. Ever since her childhood, passed as it was among open trunks, travel remained her greatest pleasure. Nothing disgusted her: bad meals, hard beds, dirty hotels.

"I have seen plenty in Spain," she used to say.

She kept a good appetite and slept well; the various incidents of the road made her gay. But to follow her called for endurance and good humour. She would start out unexpectedly, without deigning to ask for directions beforehand, trusting to chance, to her instinct, desirous of getting to know the country and its people through her own eyes, especially all the things that others never saw. In hotel-registers she wrote the name she had already used in the days of the Empire, which then seemed only a coquetry and now was heavy with memories, with griefs: *Countess de Pierrefonds.*

Louis was sixteen, and attended King's College. The Empress proposed to enter him at Woolwich Academy, from which he might emerge as an artillery officer. She said that would be keeping to the Bonaparte tradition. Queen Victoria had promised to facilitate his admission, as well as Louis Conneau's. Augustin Filon, installed in a little house close by, would look after them. Once again the Emperor resigned himself. Impatiently he waited for the Saturdays that brought back to Camden Place the cadet in his red tunic with white facings. And on the Monday mornings, when he had to go back, the young man often had tears in his eyes. The years brought father and son more and more together. They had always loved each other tenderly. But now they adored one another. To please the Emperor Louis worked with a zeal he had never shown before. He was at the bottom when he entered the Academy, but soon went up. While the French press was declaring him the *"fruit sec"*—the dunce—of his year, he was to come out of Woolwich seventh on the list.

Meanwhile political activities once more absorbed the inmates of Camden Place. They thought less of the events of yesterday than of to-morrow's, which they imagined their long debates, their letters, their moves, were shaping and preparing. All felt certain that the state of affairs was temporary only. They saw themselves back in France and invested with power before a very few months had gone by. The Imperialists who had remained on the Continent were all united in foreseeing a Napoleonic restoration centring either on the Emperor or on his son. Eugénie inclined to the latter solution. Napoleon would abdicate, and during the minority of Louis she would take the Regency again. These notions flattered her ambitious imagination. The Emperor did not lend himself to them. Upon him, since it had fallen by his fault, it was incumbent to raise the Empire again. That was his task, and he would not yield it to any one else. Later on, when the Prince could reign alone, without a mortgage, with no diminution of prestige, Napoleon would efface himself, and would present his son's youth to a reconciled France.

In reality, in France it seemed impossible for any stable régime to be established. The Royalists were drawn their way, but were in any case divided, and ill-served by a claimant who disdained the throne. The Republicans fought against them, with a vehemence of doctrine and voice that displeased the masses in the provinces. The Bonapartists, who had lain very low at first, were little by little raising their heads. In the elections of February 1872, in spite of all the pressure brought to bear by Thiers' agents, Rouher had been elected deputy for Corsica. Rouher, with the legend that clung to his name, Rouher, the vice-Emperor, in the National Assembly! Napoleon and Eugenie had seen a kind of presage in it. The Empire had left behind it in the administration, the magistracy, the army, the clergy, *cadres* almost intact and unimpaired, all ready to second a Restoration. Business men, bankers, industrialists, severed from the enormous prosperity that accompanied the reign, wished for its return. A constant to and fro of friends ensured communication between France and Chislehurst and marked the way.

Napoleon's plan was ripe. Defeated like his uncle, exiled like his uncle, he would reappear like his uncle. The return from England would be a pendant to the return from Elba. He had settled all the details with Rouher and Chevreau (Persigny was dead). He meant to enter France through Belgium and appear at Châlons where the great majority of the generals, veterans of the Crimea and of Italy, would declare for him. If at the last moment difficulties arose he would cross over into Switzerland, and picking up Prince Napoleon at Prangins he would go to Bourbaki, the commandant of Lyons, who remained devoted to him. The powers would look on with a favourable eye. Napoleon even flattered himself that by the intervention of Austria and possibly of the Czar he would obtain from Germany a serious lightening of the Treaty of Frankfort. The future rôles were all assigned, Rouher was to be Président du Conseil, Kératry Minister of the Interior. Fleury was to have the Ministry of War or the military governorship of Paris. There would be no resistance, no fighting. The Empire would rise up again as though of itself, without costing martyred France a drop of blood. From Châlons or from Lyons to Paris, riding at the head of the army, Napoleon III would find the same welcome at every point as Napoleon in 1815 in his march to Notre-Dame.

Eugénie was aware of the plan, and knew the posture of the negotiations. But the Emperor had concealed from her a great many of the details of its proposed execution. He distrusted her enthusiasms, feared over-audacious advice from her; he pushed aside, gently and without seeming to, the tutelage she had exercised in the last period of the reign, which had, he thought, borne ill results.

Eugénie felt his reticence, but did not venture to complain. She had summoned up the hope that was never far from her, and already, certain that she would once more find herself mistress in Paris, was confiding to her intimates the ideas that were to dominate the new Empire. The sovereigns would install themselves in the Louvre. There would be no more "Compiègnes." The summer would be spent at Trianon. The Court would be small, serious, sparing of fêtes. The era of frivolities was ended. The Empress wished to gather about the throne, in view of the no doubt soon-to-be reign of her son, all the sound and honest elements of the country, to concentrate and bring together the goodwill of all parties to heal the wounds of France. She thought that the miseries of the invasion, the madnesses of the Commune, were to be succeeded by an era of patriotic quiet and recuperation that would impress Europe.

Everything in these plans pivoted upon the Emperor. Yet she could see him becoming increasingly weak and ill. In November 1872 he had gone riding in the park at Camden Place, and attempted a railway journey with his cousin Charles Bonaparte. Each time he had not stood the test too well. His bladder trouble, which had given him some respite, now caused him excruciating pain. So that he might reappear in France with a good face at the head of his troops, he decided, after consulting English specialists, to undergo an operation which by successive crushings would rid him of his stone. The surgeons answered to the Empress for the success of the operation. On January 3, and again on January 6, he placed himself in their hands. But his physical condition was too much exhausted to endure such a severe ordeal. Uræmia set in. He drifted from slumber to death in the morning of January 9, 1873. Eugénie, Conneau, Corvisart, tried in vain to resuscitate him. Clary had hurried to Woolwich to fetch the Prince Imperial. When pale and bewildered he came to the door of the room, the Empress fell on his neck and said, weeping:

"I have only you now, Louis."

In the hall draped with black, between the torches, lying at full length in the lead shell lined with white silk, Napoleon III, embalmed, with waxed moustache and imperial, clad in general's uniform, received the homage of the thousands of Frenchmen who had crossed the sea to salute him once more. He had been greatly loved. His kindness, his generosity, even his weakness, had attached innumerable hearts to him. Poor folk, working men, had come; many wept. . . .

The coffin was soldered up, and Eugénie, surrounded as in her days of good fortune by the Duchesse de Mouchy, Countess Clary, Vicomtesse Aguado, Madame de Saulcy and Madame Lebreton, all came to keep the last vigil for the dead man.

She kneeled. It was twenty years since Napoleon had brought her to Notre-Dame, fourteen since they had both escaped the bombs of Orsini. Beside the dead man she prayed with all the faith that was in her. Then when she had sat down, during the silence of the chilly night, eyes closed, tearless, immobile, she immersed herself in thought.

She was sad, but she did not find that she was discouraged. Gratitude, so many years of splendour and power, and above all, misfortune, had bound her to Napoleon. And yet she never felt for him more than a routine and customary affection, and her heart had not broken when his had ceased to beat. She was still young and vigorous, and within her there abode a tough will. Once its due tribute had been paid to sorrow, she could not prevent her mind from turning back to politics. Still more than widow she felt herself regent. And this preoccupation was by no means born of egoism or vanity; it was noble, she saw in it her first duty towards the Emperor. He was bequeathing to her the task he had been unable to finish. It was she, with her son and for her son, who would bring about and ensure the restoration of the Empire. In this way she would pay her debt to the man who, because he loved her, had throned her on the highest peak in Europe. She would lead their son to his destiny. That destiny would be the compensation for theirs. Valiant as she was, a heavy duty did not alarm her. In that long-drawn-out night, in which she heard nothing but the soft crackling of the wax tapers, the low murmur of the nuns, she thought that nothing was lost, that she would be able to mould and shape the future, and avenge him whom for many years she would now always speak of as "the poor Emperor" for all that excessive injustice he had borne.

Bowing to etiquette, she did not attend the funeral. Standing behind the shutters of her bedroom, she saw her son come back, slender and strong, in the black coat crossed by the grand cordon of the Legion d'honneur. He was surrounded by princes and by his father's old servants. A crowd followed him with heads uncovered. When he passed through the gate they came to a stand and shouted "Vive l'Empereur! Vive Napoleon IV!"

The young man turned round, and with a gesture of his hand imposed silence upon them. His voice, which was not enfeebled by emotion, but seemed on the contrary louder and more penetrating, rang out through the misty rain:

"Do not shout 'Vive l'Empereur!' Shout 'Vive la France!' "

Every one obeyed. Then, as though carried away by their hopes, with an enthusiasm in which their strained nerves found relief, when he reached the threshold with one single voice they shouted once more.

"Vive Napoleon IV!"

The Empress, folding her hands on her breast, trembled with joy.

The Prince saluted and went into the house.

Next day Eugénie made a point of giving audience to those who had come from France for the obsequies, and who were on the point of returning home again. Leaning on her son's arm she slowly passed in front of the women, lined up in the dining-room. Then she went into the gallery where the men were. To all of them she gave her hand, which they knelt to kiss. Not a sound was heard but the slow rustle of her dress, half-uttered phrases, sobs. She went from one to another weeping behind her veil, broken, but glad and satisfied to fill her rôle as chief among these loyal ones who had come in disinterested haste, and who thrilled with ardent faith.

Prince Napoleon had been one of the first to arrive at Chislehurst after the Emperor's death. Eugénie received him, exchanged a few words with him and asked him, in his quality as next of kin, to go into his cousin's cabinet and proceed with Pietri to take an inventory of his papers. He refused at first, then as the Empress insisted he gave way to her wish. The seals had been placed on the desks and boxes. The Prince observed with some sharpness that the wax only bore the imprint of a ring of Pietri's. Questioned, the latter replied that he had acted in this way at the Emperor's express command, before the first operation, to prevent his papers "being handed over to all comers." When the seals were broken, Prince Napoleon examined with the Emperor's secretary the contents of the drawers of the bureau and of the great cupboard. He saw a mass of documents of varying importance, requests for help, plans for propaganda articles and pamphlets, a copious correspondence, and quantities of diplomatic papers. He turned them over at great length, anxious to place in security the drafts of the projected alliances with Italy and Austria drawn up on the eve of the war, which Napoleon III had given him to read the last time he had come to Camden Place. He found only the Italian protocols. He looked again. The sketch of the treaty with Vienna, which bore the manuscript corrections of Francis-Joseph, and which was accompanied by a letter from Beust, promising the help of the Austrian army in case of war with Prussia, had disappeared. The Prince expressed his astonishment in no friendly terms.

"These drawers have already been ransacked. The disorder of the papers show that they have been picked over. I am well aware by whose orders. . . ."

In point of fact, Pietri might have told him, a footman had recently been dismissed, having been found out to be a spy for Thiers. He might have stolen documents. And perhaps too Princess Metternich's visit to Chislehurst the other day had only been to get back the draft alliance the possession of which by Napoleon III embarrassed her sovereign. In any case it was not a document to let out of one's own hands. . . .

Prince Napoleon then asked for the Emperor's will. Pietri gave it to him. It had been opened the day before by the Empress. Written in the Tuileries, it was dated April 24, 1865. Although so old, and in spite of the change in fortune that had come to pass, it bore no codicil. In it the Emperor recommended his wife and his son to the great bodies of the State, to the people and to the army, appointed the Empress to the Regency and bequeathed her the whole of his private property. His face contracted with anger, the Prince said sharply to Pietri, who was all abashed:

"It is useless to go any further. I see how things stand. There is nothing for me to do here."

And he left Camden Place on the spot, returning only on the day of the funeral.

He thought, and did not hesitate to say publicly, that the Emperor had made another will since the war (and doubtless in the weeks preceding his death), and that the Empress, with the connivance of Pietri and Rouher, had destroyed it in order to keep complete and absolute charge over her son, along with the fortune of Napoleon III.

At first sight it did in fact appear very strange that the Emperor, on the point of undergoing a severe operation, should not have made arrangements for the future of the son he loved so dearly. This will of 1865, drawn up at the acme of power, corresponded so little and so badly to the situation of the exiles! However the Empress was not a woman to do away with her husband's last wishes. She had her faults, her misdeeds, but her character prevented her from mean or base behaviour, and for that matter Pietri would never have become the accomplice of such a crime. To his latest day Napoleon had retained illusions with regard to his return to the throne. He had felt weak, but had by no means looked on himself as dying. Furthermore he had never brought his affairs into order. And material interests never counted for him. He might have disliked writing a new will for which he had seen no necessity. Or else, having made one, which on reflection he found unsatisfactory, had he in his last days given orders from his sick bed to Pietri to do away with it? Eugénie always disdained to defend herself. But the ever green hatred of Prince Napoleon never ceased to accuse her.

Still, she realised that a split in the Bonapartist party on the morrow of the Emperor's death must needs entail grave consequences and weigh heavily upon her son's destiny. Meeting Prince Napoleon at the Murats' house in London a few months later she tried to disarm his hostility. She held out her hands to him saying:

"Come, you know that I am not a woman to bear malice. Let

us forget all our disagreements, put your hand in mine and let there be no more question of the past between us."

A frank appeal that could never have come from a heart at fault. The Prince answered rudely:

"Madame, I shall presently let you know what I have decided."

In point of fact he sent Colonel Stoffel to her, who told the Empress that a reconciliation was possible, but on two conditions with regard to which the Prince would not budge. First of all, he was to be recognised as chief of the Imperialist party. A bitter abdication for Eugénie, to which she would nevertheless have resigned herself, she said, for her son's good. But the Prince notified her of another demand! The Prince Imperial was to be handed over to him and entrusted solely to his care. The insult was premeditated, flagrant, odious. The Empress drew herself up:

"And does the Prince wish me to acknowledge that I am incapable and unworthy of bringing up my son? What have I done to deserve such an insult?"

From that moment the rupture between them was complete.

With the Emperor gone, and the Prince Imperial returned with Louis Conneau to Woolwich, life at Chislehurst dragged itself along more dull and gloomy than ever. Napoleon's authority, his kindness, had restrained the tempers around him; after him friction and rivalries and quarrellings marked time in that cramped house where each one lived engrossed in his own fears or his own troubles.

The English mist and the spleen sank into the brain. One day Ernest Lavisse was walking in the long gallery at Camden Place, beside the Empress, who often strolled up and down it after lunch just as Napoleon had done. Leaning her forehead against a window-pane, she suddenly said to him:

"Do you not find that we look like fishes swimming about an aquarium?"

These obligatory assemblings at fixed hours, of the same persons, all broken to the same gestures, the same smile, this life remote from the world, in which the present did not count, in which all minds constantly turned towards the past or towards the future, sometimes crushed her with their atrocious boredom.

"We are here," she used to say, "on the raft of the *Méduse*.

There are moments when we would simply like to eat one another."

She suffered—for pride can make one deny pain, but does not soothe it—to find herself judged without mercy not only by Frenchmen hostile to the Empire, but also by a great number of Bonapartists who had taken the rancours of Prince Napoleon for their flag. Importunate beggars who had been unsuccessful and inveighed against her avarice, ambitious persons who had been disappointed, jealous women, anti-clericals who depicted her at the feet of the priests, united in making up an abominable legend about her from which an occasional shameful echo reached her. It was she who had driven the Empire to disaster. She had set on foot the expedition to Mexico, and, working ruthlessly on Napoleon's sick will, had flung him into the war against Prussia, at the same time by her bigoted zeal for the Church, depriving him of the alliance with Italy and Austria that might well have saved him. She had led to the Fourth of September by opposing, from motives of ambition and pride, the return of the Emperor to Paris. Finally, she was responsible for Napoleon's death, having wished him to undergo the operation so that she might return to France and satisfy her passion for reigning.

In very deed Eugénie did not deserve all that opprobrium. She might be blamed for Mexico, but her responsibility in connection with the Franco-German war was immeasurably exaggerated. The whole country had demanded it as much as she had, and before she did. Only the Emperor did not want it. And they forgot her gallant attitude during her regency, her heroism on the morning of the Fourth of September, the noble disinterestedness that had made her intervene at Petersburg and at Vienna on behalf of the Government of National Defence, at the moment of the first negotiations.

The passions at work against her were still too hot and fierce. And she herself, stiff and uncompromising in her own defence, showed herself in her turn just towards the nation over which she had reigned. She would not admit that the catastrophe had been brought about by the mistakes of the Empire. Yes, errors had been committed, every government commits them, but they were no excuse for treachery in the face of the enemy, the repudiation on the part of a people who eight months before—only eight months!—had once more entrusted the guardianship of its destinies to the Emperor.

Self-willed though she was, she nevertheless had had the wisdom, knowing herself too unpopular, to let the guidance of the Imperialist party pass into the hands of Rouher. Regent *de jure,* she had effaced herself before this burly experienced man who alone could curb the vagaries of Prince Napoleon. For that matter, Rouher's activities were reduced to the sending out of thousands of circulars and newspapers which answered the republican attacks and pleaded on behalf of the abolished régime. He led with much suppleness a group of thirty deputies in the Assembly, who most frequently skirmished like a forlorn hope. All the same they had the pleasure of giving a hand to bring about the downfall of Thiers.

From the discomfort of Camden Place, from her political anxieties, Eugénie as always found distraction in travel. In her son's holidays she went with him to Arenenberg. Hortense's home had not changed at all; the boyhood of Napoleon III still smiled in it from a great picture in which his brother and he in black coat and white tie climbed the slopes of the Bernese Oberland. An old backwater of a house, calm and charming. There the Empress received great numbers of visitors: the Prince of Orange, Count Primoli and his mother, the Countess Tascher, the Rouhers, the Bartholonis, Maxime du Camp, Ernest Lavisse (who gave the Prince Imperial some history lessons), Madame Octave Feuillet, the Duchess of Osuña, M. de Beauverger. . . .

On March 16, 1874, the Prince Imperial was eighteen. To celebrate his majority all that was left of the Empire appeared at Chislehurst: twelve former ministers of Napoleon III, the Bonapartist deputies, the Prefects who had been displaced on the Fourth of September, followed by eight thousand members of the party. The Empress at first was opposed to this show, and the Prince too. They feared lest Woolwich might shut its doors against him at the instance of the French government. But Rouher had insisted. He pointed out that since Prince Napoleon put himself forward, with absolutely no right, as chief of the party, it behooved Eugénie's son to knit up the Imperialist tradition and

Les Archives Photographiques d'Art et d'Histoire

THE PRINCE IMPERIAL
LOUIS-EUGÈNE-NAPOLEON

From the Portrait by R. Lefebvre in the Museum of Versailles

to establish himself as the claimant, before the deputations that had flocked to celebrate his entry into political life. The young man did so in bold phrases that aroused high enthusiasm. People wiped their eyes, saying, "Did you hear? How well he speaks, the little prince!" He made an affectionate reference to his mother, and the Empress was saluted with a prolonged ovation. Then the Prince, accompanied by Rouher and the Duke of Padua, reviewed all the assembly, grouped along the alleys in the park. The cry of "Vive Napoleon IV" echoed as far as Paris, where it alarmed the Legitimists and the Orléanists, busy about the fusion that was to bring back the Bourbons.

The Prince returned to the Academy to finish his studies. The *Times* had announced that after that day he would go back to France, entry to which was in any case not prohibited to him. The Empress vehemently denied this:

"He will not do such a stupid thing," she said. "Prestige is ruined at home; it shall be exile or the throne."

She was right.

He came out of Woolwich a year later, and as Louis Conneau had left to enter Saint-Cyr, in order not to be separated from his comrades Woodhouse, Slade and Bigge, he got himself attached as Lieutenant to a battery at Aldershot. He liked camp life. He slept in a tent, ate in mess, scrupulously careful to avoid any extra privilege. It sometimes fell to him to make the soup for his gunners. This regular and wholesome existence finished making a man of him. Delicate for so long, he had filled out well and seemed robust; somewhat short in the leg like his father, he carried his head high with the elegant and supple air of a real soldier. He resembled his mother chiefly by his eyes, which grew paler immediately he felt any annoyance or distress. His features were clear-cut, and mobile, his complexion *mat*. He had a great deal of gaiety in him; he laughed like a child, loved jokes and games. Nevertheless he retained a kind of foundation of mysticism, surprising in so young a man. His religious faith was lively and profound, stricter even than that of the Empress. He surrounded Eugénie with a charming affection, in spite of often finding himself in disagreement with her, for he had inherited her strong will. A chivalrous spirit and a warm heart, although not worn on his sleeve; if the Emperor had lived he would have been proud of him.

The Empress showed her pride in him. But he often left her. And in dull Camden Place, alone and chewing the cud of thought, she wore through the days as best she could.

Sometimes she was depressed, so much as to write to Marie de Larminat, then in France:

> My day is over, it is the turn of the others now. People who fall from a ground floor seldom hurt themselves in the fall; I have fallen from so high that everything has been broken inside me and now I can hardly perceive if my life is monotonous. . . .

A little later she wrote again:

> There are days when I long to escape and go on walking straight ahead, or else I dream like Ophelia of lying down in the water and following a wake of light, but as long as it seems to be worth while I shall be patient. The day I believe my task finished I shall follow the instinct of the moment, and then it shall be as God wills, for I must confess it, everything is worn to nothing, faith, courage, everything. I am above all weary like one who has travelled a long long road, and I fear everything that hurts me. . . .

Thus she would pull against her chain, and then grow calm after long solitary tramps in the park, in which she tired her muscles, straightened out her nerves.

CHAPTER II

Mother and Son

THE Prince Imperial, who had been spending the afternoon in London, came back to Camden Place in a gay mood. These last few days he had seemed preoccupied, and his usual cheerfulness damped down. To-night on leaving the dining-room he went to and fro in the drawing-room, teased Madame Lebreton, played a military march on the piano, hummed a tune, imitating the fifes of Aldershot.

"What is the matter with you to-night?" asked the Empress, astonished.

"If I told you," he answered, laughing, "you wouldn't sleep to-night."

A little later, as he was bidding his mother good night:

"Do you suppose," she said, "I am going to sleep after what you've been saying to me? I shall be conjuring up dreadful things, for example, that you have asked to be allowed to go and serve in Africa against the Zulus."

Stupefied at such perspicacity, he hesitated for a moment, then his natural frankness carried the day. He told his mother that she had guessed right.

An English column had just been surprised and wiped out at Isandhlwana by Cetewayo's Zulus. The Prince's comrades had at once asked to be included in the avenging expedition. Slade and Bigge had gone on board already. When Woodhouse came to say good-bye to him, Eugénie's son told him that he "would leave no stone unturned to join him." And the same day he had written to the Duke of Cambridge, the Commander-in-Chief of the British army, to ask the favour of being allowed to make the campaign. He hoped to see his request granted. That was why he was cheerful.

The Empress cried out against it, overwhelmed with dismay. So intense was her emotion that her voice was a mere quaver. Louis cut short her reproaches and said firmly:

"Wait until to-morrow, my dear mother, I do beg of you, then I shall tell you my arguments and listen to yours, which will have all the more weight since you will have had a longer time for reflection."

They parted on that truce. Before clashing they both needed to think matters over. Soon after, Eugénie lying in her bed with her hands clasped behind her head, entered on a meditation—which lasted all night through.

Her son had acted without consulting her: she knew why. The previous year he had wished to take service in the Austrian army mobilised for the annexation of Bosnia. The Empress had opposed this. What would the son of the victor of Solferino do in an Austrian uniform? Look just a little more like the Duc de Reichstadt?

He had answered:

"Anyhow, I do not want to pine away and die of boredom like him!"

He did not want to die of boredom. . . . His mother could not but know it—he was bored. His youth too often beat its wings against the walls of the house. That restricted atmosphere depressed him. One day when he was making a pen-drawing of the grenadiers of the Guard in front of Lavisse, the historian had asked him:

"Monseigneur, what are you thinking of?"

"I was thinking that I should give a great deal to see the Grenelle-Porte Saint-Martin bus coming out of the Rue du Bac. . . ."

He dreamed of emerging from this cocoon in which he was being stifled. He aspired to liberty, to action, to danger. He was three-and-twenty! The Aldershot manœuvres were nothing but a distraction. He needed a profession. And there was only one trade for a Napoleon, as long as he was not reigning, the trade of a soldier. With all his heart he envied Louis Conneau, now an officer in the French army. What was he to do? Go to banquets, go shooting, go to parties, to balls? He had many invitations. He was much liked in England, looked on almost as a member of the royal family. But man does not live by fêtes alone. Travel? Every year he went with his mother to Arenenberg. In 1876 he had spent the autumn in Florence, going on as far as Rome where his godfather, Pope Pius IX, had received him, though without encouraging him. He had told the Pontiff, in his boyish confidence, that if he came to the throne he would be the most zealous defender of the faith. Pius IX had smiled without replying. The following summer Louis had wandered through the Scandinavian countries with Count Murat and Franceschini Pietri. Like his mother he loved changing horizons, the sea, the diversity of manners and languages. But it is impossible to be travelling always. He must needs come back home, to that foggy Camden Place haunted by old men and by women, go riding, take tea with the neighbours, receive French adherents, listen to their advice, even their reproaches, draw up manifestoes that would be corrected by Rouher and then filled with erasures by his mother. . . .

Now that Louis had fully come to man's estate, Eugénie had honestly and sincerely tried to withdraw into the background. She wanted the homage of visitors to be paid to him in the first place. But she had for so many years been accustomed to act that at every moment, despite her own intention, she intervened with regard to the party. To be treated as dowager sovereign in this England, always generous to the banished, was not enough for her, nor to watch over her enormous and complicated private interests. She must needs meddle once more with politics which were her dearest, profoundest passion that nothing had subdued, she must see with her own eyes, make inquiries, discuss. Hence there arose occasional conflicts. She feared her son's disposition, too disinterested, too chivalrous, which might easily be abused by adventurers such as always prowl about claimants to a throne. Again on Rouher's advice, by a prudence that some thought excessive, she had for a long time supplied him very sparingly with money. Generous like his father, Louis had often found himself greatly embarrassed by this. But she wanted to make him thrifty. She was piling up for him a veritable war-chest, which he would need to reconquer his throne, to win accomplices, to pay for services rendered. He must not fritter it away with boon companions and grisettes. So young a man with a name like his and too much gold in his pockets, what a prey he would be!

She knew he had a liaison, very natural at his age, to which he did not himself attach very much importance. But she trembled at the thought that there might be a child. Louis was too noble in sentiment to refuse to recognise it, and perhaps even to marry the mother. That would spell complete ruin for his future. She did not wish to broach the subject, which was hateful to her, and about which they would certainly have found it impossible to agree. They loved each other dearly, but proud both, and autocratic, their very likeness to one another was a peril to their harmony. She would have liked to make a marriage for him. Princess Beatrice, Queen Victoria's daughter, seemed to like him, and Eugénie did not think she would meet with opposition from the royal house. He replied that he did not mean to let his wings be clipped by a marriage.

"Possibly I shall not wait until the years have left me bald like Corvisart or paunchy like Rouher before contracting matrimony, but for the moment I have no fixed intention in the matter. No doubt I cannot look forward to the happiness of marrying in accordance with my affections, but I know enough of life never to consent to marry against the grain. . . ."

She did not insist. Already she had departed to some extent from her stringency, fearing lest he might think he was being kept too dependent on her. During his Scandinavian travels she opened an unlimited credit for him, on which he drew largely. She did more. Since in certain imperialist circles she was reproached for taking advantage of the only will of Napoleon III that had been found, in order to dispose of his entire fortune as sole mistress, she summoned to Chislehurst three trusty counsellors, famous lawyers, Pinard, Grandperret and Busson-Billault, and by their advice decided to place in her son's hands one-half of the paternal inheritance. He would further receive the income of the property of Princess Baciocchi-Camerata, who had bequeathed him her Italian estates. That irritating question of money, which is so painful between near relatives, was thus settled. If he found Camden Place too restricted Louis could now, as he had desired to do, take a house in London and receive his friends.

And so, the Empress thought, there was no longer any reason for disagreement henceforth. Yet he wanted to go. . . . She would prevent him. Up till now she had succeeded, either by arguments, for he was fair-minded, or by appealing to his heart, for he was affectionate, in swaying him towards what she had believed to be the better course. He was so young. . . . Ah, impetuous youth, the terrible youth that intoxicates our children! Would Eugénie always be able to defend hers? She was alone. . . . If the poor Emperor had been there, Louis would not have wanted to go. . . .

In the morning they were face to face again. After breakfast, left alone together, they walked for a long time in the gallery on the ground floor, between the ebony and tortoiseshell cabinets, under the ceaseless ticking of the gilt clock.

"As long as a single one of the officers of my battery remained in England," said the young man, "I could stay myself without dishonour. But when they are all over there in the field, how could I show my face again at Aldershot?"

Usually so mild and quiet, he spoke with a firmness that hurt her. She did not know how to entreat, she became angry.

"But that is thinking like an English officer! And what about France?"

"France, I am not forgetting France. It is above all for her sake that I want to go, to let her know at last who I am. Except for a small number of friends who come in contact with me, nobody knows me, and I can say that in France, while my name is a symbol, my person and my personal worth, whatever they may be, are utterly unknown. They see me always just as they saw me over there. Even in the eyes of my followers I am still nothing but a child. They do not heed me; they often do the opposite of what I have advised. Some have even gone so far as to say that I was a coward. Do you remember how they jeered at the 'Saarebrück bullet.' I am supposed to have a hereditary disease. . . . Do you want me to be always the *little prince* to everybody? They must see at length that I am a man, of clean blood, and that I am fearless."

She said that he would betray his party, his faithful adherents, by going so far to run so many risks.

"I shall run less than you imagine. Before my father attained the Empire, had he run no risks? A man must not take too much care for his mere existence. I have no other way to raise myself in public opinion. You know my motto: *'Passe avant le meilleur.'* A country like France will never entrust herself to any but a man whose energy has been tried and proved.

She answered, full of bitterness:

"If you come to grief, my poor boy, not merely will your followers not pity you, but they will owe you a grudge for it!"

"That may be. . . . But why should I come to grief? To stay on here, to be nothing but a claimant, that cannot suffice for me. To write letters of condolence, to receive politicians, be hail-fellow-well-met with journalists, make myself their familiar friend and work with them at canvassing social problems, that is what our wiseacres call 'bringing myself into view.' That is not enough for a Napoleon. When you belong to a race of soldiers, you make a name only sword in hand. The Zululand disaster gives me the opportunity I sought. I shall not let it escape me. . . ."

To the joy of the Empress, the old Duke of Cambridge, alarmed at the responsibility involved, replied by a refusal. The Prince insisted, got his former chief at Woolwich, General Simmons, and the Prince of Wales, to bring pressure to bear on him. And the Duke acquiesced. At once Eugénie summoned to Chislehurst Rouher, General d'Espeuilles, Tristan Lambert, those who had, she thought, most influence over the Prince. A whole long evening they maintained the attack in the working-room in Camden Place, but failed before his smiling, serene, invincible resolution. What could Eugénie do now? Forbid Louis to go? Set up her maternal authority against that youthful will which aspired to space, to adventure, to glory? Indeed she too would be bound to fail. She would arrive at nothing but a break between them. If her son went disobeying her, he would leave her without an adieu, without a farewell embrace. Whatever may be said, she loved him too much to bring about such a painful ordeal. She had wanted to make a man of him, and he had become a man. At heart she could not disapprove of him. Taking into consideration his free, his vagabond youth, she kept telling herself that in his place she would have done the same. It was he who was in the right, not she in her self-centred fear. And in any case, would this expedition be so dangerous? A little war in a healthy country, against savages armed with assegais. . . . The officers among whom the Prince would have his place would take care of him. . . .

She gave way.

On February 27, in the snowy morning, he heard Mass with Tristan Lambert and communicated in the little chapel of St. Mary at Chislehurst. Unknown to his mother, he entrusted his will, drawn up during the previous night, to Pietri. In it he disinherited Prince Napoleon, who had never ceased to show hostility to him, even to the point of finally going over to the Republic, and transferred his eventual rights to the Prince's eldest son Prince Victor. Then he left Camden Place, accompanied as far as Southampton by his mother. Eugénie saw her son on board the *Danube*.

On the deck, level with the quay, for a moment longer he looked at her sadly. These late years had left unkind marks upon her. Her hair would have been almost white if it had not been dyed. Her delicate nose was conspicuous against the coarsened oval of her face. He felt a great compassion for her, all in black, shrunken, as she leaned her elbows on a wooden barrier. But he knew her to be so courageous . . . She could endure his absence. And he could not endure the life of the idle prince any longer. He was sorry to grieve her, but his prevailing feeling was joy. She smiled at him once more, sedulous to hide her tears from him.

Back at Camden Place, she was tormented by anxiety. An incomprehensible anxiety, which she had not felt until the anchors were weighed, but which now darkened her mind, haunted her continually. Certain newspapers had published a false report that the Prince was ill at Madeira. She was not at all reassured by the denial. She had occupied a few days in arranging with her own hands her son's books and papers and belongings, even his French uniforms, which he had ordered with an eye to his return to Paris and his future reign. Alas, would he ever reign? May 16 had brought Eugénie a painful surprise. She was struck by the fact that Mac-Mahon's fall had brought about no disturbance, that Grévy was succeeding him without difficulty. Was then the Republic going to endure? What would fate have in store for her son in that case? She found in his prayer-book a prayer in his own handwriting, two lines of which frightened her:

"My God, grant that there may be no more happiness for me! I flee from it. Remove it from my path."

How mystical he was! Though she was so devout a believer she had never known such spiritual transports. Under the gaiety of Louis there beat a heart athirst for sacrifice. He was her son, she loved him, and she did not know him.

She knew a return of hope, hearing a French missionary priest preach in the chapel one Sunday on this text from Ezekiel.

"Ecce ego aperiam tumulos vestros et educam vos de sepulcris vestris, populus meus, et inducam vos in terram Israël." "Behold, O my people, I will open your graves, and cause you to come up out of your graves, and bring you into the land of Israel."

Always on the lookout for omens, she was struck by this sermon which seemed to her a voice from heaven, a promise from God. She had been cast down from on high, her pride had been chastened. But through her son she would receive the compensation for her griefs, after so many mournful, heavy years, she would enter into the happy land.

Then anxiety laid hold of her again. Her son's letters, full of enthusiasm, copiously illustrated with sketches, failed to reassure her.

She now reproached herself for not having prevented his departure. She thought of going to join him in Africa, or at any rate to watch over him from nearer at hand. The Duke of Cambridge had written to Lord Chelmsford, the head of the English army in Natal, commending the Prince to him: "My only anxiety on his account would be that he is too plucky and go-ahead." That was Eugénie's fear too, as she thought of the little officer of the Royal Horse Artillery, who, all smart and well set up in his blue tunic, was roaming the veldt, where sometimes as night was falling, there glided black shadowy figures in the long grass. Too courageous indeed he was, among those who were not courageous enough. For if there was talk of treachery, of a plot, that was a mere fable. He was laid low by the assegais of the Zulus, on June 1, during a reconnaissance in which his leader, Captain Carey, unskilful, imprudent, faint-hearted, abandoned him. He had fought like a lion, the natives said. His body, gashed and stripped, lay for a whole night at the bottom of the rocky donga. One of his eyes had been torn away, the other, wide open, stared at the sky.

That first of June, a Sunday, was marked at Camden Place by a hurricane. The owner of the house, Mr. Strode, had brought from St. Helena a cutting of the willow that shaded the Emperor's tomb. That cutting had become a vigorous tree. Now, on the day that Napoleon III died, half of the tree had broken. On the first of June the storm carried away the remainder.

The Empress was overwhelmed when she was told of this.

It took eighteen days for the news to reach the British cabinet. Queen Victoria immediately sent her Lord Chamberlain, Lord Sydney, to Chislehurst to break the news to the Empress, and forestall the shock of finding it in the newspapers that were already selling in the London streets. The Duc de Bassano received him. He was stricken with dismay. The thought of telling his sovereign made his knees give way under him. But this cruel honour necessarily fell to his years and his faithful friendship. Totteringly he went up the stairs, knocked at the Empress's door. She had risen and was walking up and down her room, her chest out, her hands behind her back, as she often used to do when intent on some thought.

She sees Bassano livid, his mouth quivering. At once she goes up to him, searching him with an all too penetrating eye.

"My son is ill?"

He keeps silence.

"He is wounded? Do speak! I am going to Africa. I am going this moment!"

He keeps silence. The old man shuts his eyes under the gaze of those terrible orbs. She understands, and with a cry she falls into the arms of Bassano, who need hold back his tears no longer.

For a long time she remained unconscious. Doctor Corvisart tried to bring her out of that abyss where at any rate she was spared the agony of thought. She came to herself, emerged from forgetfulness, fell into another swoon. All that day and the following night, she was like a corpse. Her servants believed—almost hoped—that her reason had left her. But consciousness revived. For many days, neither weeping, nor moving, nor complaining, with only now and then a few words in a low voice, she remained in her little drawing-room, shutters closed, curtains drawn, . . .

vacancy wherein she strove to find her son again. She saw him once more, an infant in his little grenadier uniform, then starting for the War of 1870, slender and boyish and jaunty, then making his horse jump and rear on the lawn at Camden Place. She heard his laugh, his step, an air he had a frequent trick of humming. He was still a little with her. . . . Why had she let him go, so young, so far away? He was returning, dead, on a slow boat. Now Eugénie had lost throne, husband, child. She had nothing left, was nothing but martyred flesh in which only the power to suffer remained awake. . . .

She received no one. For Mademoiselle de Larminat, who had brought her a letter, she scrawled a few pencilled words: "I cannot speak to you. I have not the courage; I am reserving my scrap of strength for his return. Pray for him, for his father, and pray too that God may give me strength and resignation."

All the faithful ones came to Chislehurst, the Duchesse de Mouchy, the Murats, Prince Charles Bonaparte and his family, the Aguados. Pietri came back from Corsica with Rouher. He opened the Prince's will. The Empress heard it read with perfect calmness, gave Rouher full powers to arrange the funeral ceremonies, then plunged again into her night of gloom. On July 10, the coffin, which had arrived at Plymouth on the *Orontes,* was taken by a small boat in which there was only a monk kneeling in prayer, to the *Enchantress,* which brought it to Woolwich. Next day he returned to Camden Place. From her room the Empress heard the shrill fifes of the English band playing a funeral air. She came down the stairs like an old woman and in the draped and lighted hall fell on the bier, which she enfolded in her arms. In this posture she remained for several hours, her forehead resting on the black cloth. She never moved. Around her stood the boyhood friends of the Prince, and his relatives, waiting, frozen in spite of the warm night.

When day came again the Duchesse de Mouchy went to the Empress and raised her gently. She stood up, swathed in crêpe, and consented to leave the hall. In her room Aline Pelletier undressed her and put her to bed. She allowed her to do as she wished, her own will completely annihilated. Docilely she swallowed a few mouthfuls of soup in which a narcotic had been mixed. She stared about her as though astonished to find herself alive. She uttered a moan when the guns proclaimed her son's last departure. Then the opium acted, her eyes grew heavy.

A hundred thousand bared heads bowed round Camden Place as the corpse, placed upon a gun-carriage drawn by eight horses, was making its slow way towards the little chapel, surrounded by the Woolwich cadets. Queen Victoria had come in person, an unexampled honour, to lay a laurel wreath upon the coffin wrapped in French and English flags. The ambassador of the Republic had, however, asked that the homage accorded to the dead youth should be limited. More generous than a Gladstone, Disraëli dismissed him stiffly. Princess Beatrice was there, weeping with her mother. They went to embrace the lifeless Empress, while the "little prince" of the Tuileries, of St. Cloud, was moving to his rest.

She emerged from her silence to think of Carey, who, back again in Europe after he had been cashiered by the court-martial in Durban, appealed against his sentence. She had read the degrading letters he had written to his wife, the official reports communicated to her by the War Office. For the sake of her son, who had been a part of the English army, she asked that this uniform, even though worn by an unworthy officer, should not be sullied. She wrote a somewhat disjointed note, which, brought before the Duke of Cambridge, saved him from punishment, not from contempt:

> My one source of earthly consolation, I find in the idea that my beloved child fell like a soldier, obeying *orders,* in a service *commanded,* and that those who gave him those orders did so because they looked upon him as capable and useful. Enough of recriminations. Let the memory of his death unite in one common sorrow all those who loved him, and let no one be a sufferer either in reputation or interests. I, who can now desire nothing more upon this earth, I ask this as a last request.
>
> EUGÉNIE.

This request was granted. Carey was reprieved and went into the Indian army. There he died some years later, surrounded by a disgust that not even a coward could endure.

After this effort, which must have cost her terribly, the Empress fell back into apathy. Her nerves seemed broken. Nothing interested her any more. She ceased to go out, lived withdrawn upon herself. She talked of nothing but her son, but above all of her son when he was a child. She would say, *"Mon pauvre petit garçon, mon petit."* Often in the evening she would remain standing at the window from which in the old days she used to see him coming. She gave her thanks for attentions, but seemed indifferent to them. When the Duchesse de Mouchy left again, she gave her one of the few pieces of jewellery she had retained: the emerald trefoil the Emperor had presented to her at Compiègne shortly before their betrothal. She had prized it highly. Since 1873 she was in the habit of wearing no jewels. But when Louis had gone to Zululand she had pinned this on her bodice every day, as though to conjure away ill-fortune. When she learned of his death, she tore it off.

"Take it," she said to the duchess. "It is not for me any longer. Let it be a token of happiness and friendship for you."

Despair flooded over and around her, stopping every pore of her being. She moved feebly in that acrid tide. She no longer read the newspapers, at most a few letters and hardly that, but she could not but know that in France animosities and injustices and hates unbridled were piling up against her. She was accused of having made life unbearable to her son by her avarice, by her harsh discipline. He had gone, disheartened, to find death in Africa. She could not protest. Any word would have been unworthy of herself and of her misfortune. She had perhaps been wrong at times, made mistakes. Who has not? Slight mistakes, mistakes of parents who love without always understanding. But she had done everything possible to bring her boy up worthily, to enable him one day to reconquer the crown, in any case to deserve it. She had striven very hard to prevent his departure. He had gone, not because she had tyrannised over him, but because she had respected his will as a man and a chief. He had gone because he wished to join his comrades, because at twenty-three he was eager to taste a new air, to find a gilded scrap of glory. It was his youth that had carried him away to Africa. Youth that can never be chained down. . . .

In this period of utter desolation, she would perhaps have

killed herself if she had not had her God. In those dreadful weeks prayer alone gave her respite. She had God. Less perhaps than was imagined. Speaking of her dead, she declared:

"I do not possess that faith which causes everything here below to disappear leaving only heaven in sight. I see nothing but them on the yonder side of life, to join them where they are is all my hope. The convent is too crowded, only the desert is fit for those whom fate has made acquainted with every sorrow."

Those who lived about her had never thought that she loved her son with such deep ardour. No doubt she did not know it herself. When the Emperor died she knew hours of distress. But she still had a stay, a presence, an affection capable of filling all her dreams. Now her life was widowed and bereaved, she no longer looked forward to anything but old age and death.

Thus broken, she seemed more of a mother, more of a woman; she lost something of her mannishness, her virility. Her grief swallowed up her pride. When Maréchal Canrobert's wife spoke to her of the hopes swept out of existence by the Prince's death:

"Hopes?" she said, astonished. "That is true, the hope of reigning. Oh, no, I never think of that. It is my child I weep for."

Many members of the Imperialist party, and at the outset Prince Napoleon, reproached her for living in England, when her son had lost his life from being deserted by English soldiers. Even her own entourage, who avoided the sight of the *redcoats,* and who after such a disaster were wretched at having recourse to British hospitality, did not understand her at all. At one moment she herself thought she might retire to Arenenberg. But she would have had to transport with her her two coffins, from which she meant never to part. So long a journey would have seemed like sacrilege to her. Then that country, despite what in the end it had cost her, had been a friend to her and hers. There they had been surrounded with sympathy and respect. After his fall the Emperor had not ceased to be treated there as a sovereign. There the Prince had grown up, there he had become a man. They had all loved it. Against her relatives, against her friends and her enemies, she was without a doubt right in wishing to remain there.

Queen Victoria, gone back to Balmoral, offered her a very simple house belonging to her, two miles from the castle. It was a gloomy, ascetic retreat, on a high rock plateau. The Empress was tempted by the solitude of Abergeldie Castle. She went there with Mademoiselle de Larminat. Autumn was drawing on. The wind sweeping in from the sea sprinkled its salt on the heather of the Grampians. Every day the Empress, accompanied by the girl, went walking over those bleak expanses where nothing was heard save the curlews crying from amid the rushes or the call of the far-wandering gulls. Through the rain, through the wild gusty weather, they would go on and on, heavy footed, dumb, their faces buffeted, while the great clouds drove in overhead pursuit. And they would not return to shelter till it was night. These unlimited tramps relieved the Empress, restored to her a little of her lost physical equilibrium.

Sometimes the Queen came to visit her. She talked with the Empress, alone together. She never attempted to console her, but with the utmost delicacy, talked to her of things unconnected with her life at the moment, of history, of politics, of travel. By degrees the absent mind came back, the machine came into gear again. She still, especially at night, had hours of utter desolation, but her strong nature was beginning to react.

In October she returned to Chislehurst. Every day she walked over to St. Mary's Chapel, where the Emperor and her son lay at rest. Over them she arranged the flowers that were sent her from France or those that the Queen had gathered for her in her greenhouses. She went from one tomb to the other. She wept and prayed, and then went back to Camden Place by long roundabout ways, only arriving in the twilight.

Gradually she recovered strength, her blood and her nerves returned to their normal state. She lived, she could live. She began once more to read the newspapers, to write letters. She was annoyed at the palinode of an ungrateful friend, at an open or a covert attack. . . . Besides, a new anxiety was occupying her mind. The Countess de Montijo was summoning her to Madrid. She was eighty-three. The death of her grandson had been a cruel blow. Her astounding vitality was fading out. The Empress went to Spain, but her mother was dead before she arrived. She remained in Madrid for a month to arrange Doña Manuela's complicated affairs with her Alba nephews and nieces. While there, too, she suffered, on her own avowal, from the discrepancy between the state of mind and everybody round her and her own feelings. They wanted to distract her; they only annoyed her. Even Miss Flower, the associate of her own youth, and her mother's companion until the end, irritated her by her talk, the talk of an elderly child. Before she left she made liberal provision for Miss Flower's life, which was prolonged for some years still in Madrid. . . . Camden Place was very dull and sad, but she came back to it with a kind of pleasure. "Here," she said, "there is no false note."

Long ago she had resolved to go on the anniversary of her son's death and pray on the very spot where he fell. Every one tried to dissuade her, representing the fatigues and the risks of a journey in a country where rebellion was barely extinguished. She answered Franceschini Pietri:

"I feel drawn to this place of pilgrimage as strongly as the disciples of Christ must have felt drawn to the holy places. To see, to follow the last stages of my beloved child's life, to find myself at the place that was the last sight his eyes rested upon, at the same time of year, to spend the night of the first of June watching and praying in this memory, is a need of my spirit and a goal in my life. Since the ending of the war has allowed me to envisage this with more chances of success, it has become my dominant thought. . . . This idea sustains me and keeps up my courage, without it I should have no strength to react and I should let myself go, waiting for sorrow to wear me away. . . . I have no illusions, I know the grief and pain that await me out there, but everything vanishes before the thought of Itelezi."

Queen Victoria, acceding to her friend's wish, appointed General Sir Evelyn Wood and two of Louis's old comrades at Woolwich, captains now, Slade and Bigge, to be her guides in Natal. Lady Wood, Napoleon de Bassano, son of the duke, Doctor Scott, who had gone through the campaign of the previous year as a military surgeon and had embalmed the Prince's body, accompanied the Empress.

After twenty days at sea, so hot that she found it impossible to sleep, she reached the Cape, staying at Government House, where her son himself had stayed, and was the centre of the most delicate attentions. The Marquis de Bassano visited Cetewayo in the citadel where he was imprisoned. The King of the Zulus, through an interpreter, answered his questions with a primitive nobility. Of his own accord, in homage to the Prince's bravery, he had restored the sword of which his warriors had despoiled him on the first of June. The Empress took ship again and from Durban went on to Maritzburg, whence she wrote to Pietri:

> The welcome I am everywhere receiving is touching. Not a word or a shout, but a respectful silence, such as people try to maintain in a sick room, but not a head remains covered. Even the Blacks seem to understand that there is nothing left to be wished for by the woman to whom God gave so much and from whom He took away one by one everything He had given, leaving her the bitterness of regret for her sole companion on her way. . . . This morning I saw the sisters who aided my dead darling with their prayers. Everybody talks to me of him in terms that hurt me and yet flatter my maternal pride. . . . Why did he go so soon and why did he leave me behind him? . . . I do not know where you are at this moment, give my news to those who wish for it, if there is any one who does. . . .

She left Maritzburg at the beginning of May for Zululand, travelling with Lady Wood in a carriage driven by the general. The government had furnished an escort of seventy-five mounted men and two hundred horses and mules for baggage and provisions. By the same stages the young lieutenant of the Royal Horse Artillery had followed the column, climbed by degrees the terraced plateaux of Natal, crossed Buffalo River and Blood River. By day it was very hot, the nights were chill. In the evenings the tents were set up. The Empress had had a fever for several days. She hardly ate anything. She was sad, but filled with impatience and as though animated by superhuman energy. For three weeks she went on in this way through those solitudes, by tracks covered with burnt-out grass, her eyes fixed on the pale-hued barren mountains. Under skies in which there shone stars unknown to her, on the evening of May 24, Sir Evelyn Wood informed her that she was now but a few miles from her journey's end. The tents were set up against the kraal where the Prince had made his last halt. Long afterwards, the Empress confided to Madame E. Stern that next morning, waking in the grey dawn, she had dressed without a sound and gone out unobserved from the little camp, which lay asleep.

"I wandered on haphazard, not knowing where I went, a supernatural will seemed to direct my feet. I ask myself how without a guide and alone I was able to walk without stumbling along deep-rutted tracks in which I sank ankle deep. After several hours of walking I came to a place where paths crossed one another. There I paused, undecided. The scene around me was desolate, only a few reeds stood up in a corner. Weariness suddenly overwhelmed me, and in that half-conscious state into which I was plunged I all at once felt a gust of fragrance invade my nostrils, a perfume of verbena that was my poor boy's favourite perfume. And then I thought I heard a voice, the beloved voice, murmur in my ear, 'Mother, it was here.' I understood, and I fell on my knees. . . ."

She came back to the camp, harassed. General Wood, anxious about her disappearance, had sent horsemen to look for her. She said nothing to him. But the next day, she herself took on her to guide the expedition. She walked in front, with brow uplifted, eyes wide open, looking far away. Her train preserved a respectful distance. Her lips were moving; no doubt she was speaking to her son. When she came to the crossways, she turned to the general.

"This is the place, is it not?"

He bowed his head.

She spent the night between the first and the second of June in prayers before the cairn of dry stones raised by the soldiers. With her own hands she had planted on it a willow and an ivy shoot brought from Camden Place. Over it had been heaped wild flowers, heather, geraniums. Stuck into the ground wax candles burned straight up into the windless air. Kneeling on the chapped earth, the mother joined her hands.

"More than once," she told Augustin Filon afterwards, "I saw black heads appear on the top of the slope, they moved into the openings in the long grass so as to watch me. Those eyes were curious, but not in any way hostile, I would rather think that they expressed sympathy and pity. . . . And these without a doubt were the men who had killed my son on that very spot. . . ."

"Towards morning a strange thing happened. Although there was not a breath of wind, the flame of the tapers sank down, as though some one had tried to extinguish them. And I said to *him:* 'Is it you, are you there? Do you wish me to go away?' "

Docile, she went back into her tent.

The Zulus who had taken part in the attack of the first of June had been brought together. General Wood questioned them before M. de Bassano. They all confirmed the Prince's bravery and Carey's flight. They added that if the latter and his men "had only turned back, they would have abandoned the pursuit."

Zulus who had made peace were presented to the Empress in battle array. It was her own wish, born of a kind of sombre pride. She shuddered, but held herself erect before the assegais, the sisters of those that had shed that blood. . . . She too had a soldier's heart.

On her return, after fifty nights spent under canvas, she was exhausted. But her great desire was accomplished, and appeasement grew within her. She could envisage her return to Camden Place without apprehensions. Nevertheless, she wrote to Pietri that she did not as yet wish to see there any one but those who were accustomed to live in it.

"The further I go forward in my sad existence, the more does the need for rest and solitude assert itself. No one can fill the huge void that has been made in my life, and I feel only the weariness of seeing people, without my heart finding any satisfaction."

CHAPTER III

Wanderings

So she will live. It seems impossible that any one could survive these misfortunes piled up by fate as though to rival the great classical tragedies. To lose the Empire, that was merely an adverse stroke of fortune, and was by no means unexpected. To lose the Emperor—he was old and ailing; for years she had been growing accustomed to his decline. But to lose her son, at twenty-three, in the most futile of adventures, her only son, dearly loved, full of hope, and then behind him, with nothing to sustain her (save prayer, and that not always) to go on breathing, moving, speaking, accomplishing those acts that are so empty and ridiculous the moment the individual is no longer moved by the desire to do them. . . . Were her enemies right, then? Was her heart so hard and sapless, was she merely an egoistical woman who could become reconciled to anything provided she kept a title, money, servants, a vague atmosphere of sovereignty? No, it was not so. She would endure and live, and for a very long time yet, because there dwelt within her an almost unsubduable force, a profound power of resistance of body and brain that would take many years to wear out, to lay low. And as is the wont of human nature, as she went on living her pleasure in things, her interest in events, her regard (though more vague) for persons was to revive. In her long old age she would have as it were the shadows of pleasure. The seventeen years of her reign, as they recede in history would gradually come to seem to her no more than a brief and distant dream from which she had awakened to lassitude, but the secret of which is known to her alone. The Emperor she would often speak of, without sadness, with respect, with gratitude, solicitous to defend his memory, to deny his mistakes. Her son she would speak of less. Up to the very end that was still so far away, the memory of the young horseman who fell in the thickets of Zululand remained an open, incurable wound in her mind. And when she uttered his name she never smiled. Her lips, thinned by age, would pucker up and she would droop her eyelids as though the better to endure a shock deep within herself.

The moment she was alive again she must needs be doing. Directly she returned from Natal one great project occupied her, which was to give her two dead a sepulture more dignified and more durable than that of the little chapel at Chislehurst, and to secure a place for herself beside them. It was impossible to extend the church, there was no room for it. And the chapel that had already been built on to receive the tomb of Napoleon III could not be enlarged. The Prince Imperial's coffin rested under a side porch, poorly sheltered from the weather. And the owners of the neighbouring ground refused to sell even at a high price. The Empress then considered the offer of a large estate, Farnborough Hill, situated between Aldershot and Sandhurst, which had belonged to Mr. Longman the publisher. The house was nothing but a great cottage, but the park was a huge expanse in a melancholy verdant landscape. She bought Farnborough, and on a ridge fledged with pine trees she herself marked with her stick the place where there was to rise not only a chapel, inspired by the Abbey of Hautecombe, but buildings to shelter the Premonstratensian monks who would be the guardian of the tombs. The work lasted four years, after which, not without sorrow, the Empress left Camden Place, following her husband and her son who were laid to sleep, right and left of the altar, in the crypt constructed under the nave, in the sarcophagi of Aberdeen granite, Victoria's gift. (Gladstone having refused to allow a statue of the Prince Imperial to be erected at Westminster, the Queen had given him one under her own roof, in Windsor Chapel.) Between the two tombs, behind and beneath the altar, the Empress had reserved a place for herself.

For the years that were left to her before she was to occupy that place, the long tale of which was beyond her imagining, she arranged her earthly home, enlarging it at several different times, for she was given to building, in a style that was half Swiss, half French, turning it into a vast residence where she could receive her nephews and her last remaining friends. She filled those exotic rooms with furniture, with pictures, with the myriad objects associated with her life. As far as she could she had reproduced certain aspects of Camden Place. From her bedroom windows she saw the votive church and the valley dotted with oaks and elms through which the Blackwater slid in its sickle curve. On the other side of the London road running through the estate was a green park to which she gave the name of Compiègne. As she walked in it she sometimes heard the thin far sound of the fifes at Aldershot, which only the other day ordered her son's military existence.

In the marble vestibule she had placed the affected but graceful picture in which Winterhalter had painted her sitting in a nook of the park at St. Cloud in the midst of her ladies, the child's cart given by the Prince-consort to her son, and various pieces of furniture once belonging to Queen Hortense, which had come from Arenenberg. The drawing-rooms on the ground floor, and the long gallery that gave access to them were adorned with Gobelin tapestries, with cabinets full of Sèvres of the First Empire, with portraits of the Bonaparte family. The Empress, all in red velvet, smiled from the wall, holding in her arms her son, a mere babe, decorated with the cordon of the Légion d'honneur. Another portrait, saved by the steward of Fontainebleau, showed her in profile, with her hair in ringlets. And Winterhalter had also painted those heads of the two women she had unquestionably loved most of all, her sister Paca, Duchess of Alba, and Anna Murat, Duchesse de Mouchy.

The dining-room, lighted by two huge windows facing west and north, displayed a painted ceiling. The walls were covered with tapestries, the Don Quixote set that in the old days had served as the background and frame for the homelike evenings at Biarritz. The Empress spent the greater part of her time in her study, furnished just as it had been in Camden Place, with Carpeaux's statue of her son at the far end, gleaming against a curtain of grasses and reeds brought back from Zululand. On the right-hand wall, a poor painting but a good likeness of the Emperor by Cabanel brought them both under her eyes. The next room contained numerous relics of the Prince, his school-books, his last note-books, the portrait Cannon had painted at Vienna, illuminated every evening, and near the fireplace a large photograph adorned every morning with fresh flowers.

A house of remembrance, a collection of the flotsam of a past too rich and too burdensome. Eugénie had become attached to it with the lapse of time, because it was for the most part her own creation. She was always glad to return to it. And yet whenever she had lived in it for some months, she found a sort of oppressiveness emanating from its immobile, almost stagnant, atmosphere, from those encumbered rooms. She had to go away. From her mother, that indefatigable pilgrim, she had inherited the continual need for a change of horizon. She would go back to the Queen's house, to Abergeldie Castle, or would visit her at Osborne, at Windsor. She saw Italy once more. But she refused ever to see King Victor-Emmanuel again, who had been too ungrateful, she said, to the Empire, and who had not shrunk from flaunting before her, when he had received her in Florence after the war, the helmeted, massive, triumphant photographs of the sovereigns of Germany. She made several cruises in the Mediterranean on Gordon Bennett's yacht. Touching at Naples, she received a visit from the Duc d'Aumale. He recalled the far-off time—when Louis-Philippe was on the throne—when in Madrid in the days of the "Spanish marriages" he danced with her at the house of the French ambassador, Bresson, who had since committed suicide.

"What a lovely girl Your Majesty was!"

She did not look at him, she gazed at the sea.

"And you, Monseigneur, what a handsome cavalier you were! . . ."

Later on she returned his visit in Sicily at his estate of Zucco, where she met the Duc d'Orléans. They talked at great length and even gaily. Travelling restored her animation to Eugénie; possibly that was why she was so fond of it. It brought her the old illusions, joined up some threads of her dreams. . . .

She had finally after many hesitations risked going to Paris again. That was an hour she had both dreaded and desired. In May 1882 she stopped there on her way back from Nice. Discreetly, but without concealment. At the Duchesse de Mouchy's house she received many of her friends of former days. She went to see the Emperor's old aide-de-camp Edgar Ney, confined to bed with the illness that was destined to kill him. The following year, on the morrow of Gambetta's unexpected death, Prince Napoleon, thinking that his hour had struck, issued a manifesto calling for a plebiscite. He was arrested and detained for some days in the Conciergerie. This time Eugénie stopped at the Hôtel du Rhin in the Place Vendôme, where Louis-Napoleon had resided once upon a time, where she herself had stayed with her mother, a few yards away from the house where she had received the Emperor's official request for her hand.

The Bonapartist party was in the throes of a serious crisis that threatened its complete dissolution. The greater part of its chiefs, faithful to the terms of the Prince Imperial's will, recognised in Prince Victor, the eldest son of Prince Napoleon, the only claimant to the throne. They had no desire to accept as their eventual master a man against whom they held his anti-clericalism and his unbridled private life. Eugénie sent for them, and forgetting her own wrongs, said to them:

"I have forgiven him, why should not you forgive him too? It is the only way to preserve our party its unity and even its existence."

They refused to listen to her. They moved on a different plane from hers. But Prince Napoleon had been touched by that chivalry, and on the following first of June he crossed the Channel and came to Chislehurst to attend the anniversary service for the Prince Imperial.

She had forgiven him . . . A forgiveness of the brain rather than the forgiveness of the heart. However, in spite of so many years in which they had not been able to encounter one another without hatred, she was capable of understanding that nature of his, too strongly marked not to become rebellious, that character thirsting after a glory that escaped him, that intellect which beyond a doubt would have left its mark on history if fate had been more friendly, for it never gave him anything but the second place when he was made to have the first. Eugénie did him justice. After his death, in 1891, in a house in Rome not far from the palace where his grandmother Laetitia had shut herself away, she said of him:

"I found it possible to detest him. I never despised him, he was open and candid."

Although now she seemed remote and aloof from politics, Prince Victor frequently saw that she was consulted. In any case she used to follow events in France with attention. The struggles in parliament, the Panama affair, Boulangism, had all held her passionate interest in turn. She still remained keen in distributing praise or blame when she was among a circle of trusty friends. She was among the first to believe Dreyfus innocent and to demand the reconsideration of his case. In face of the agitations and uncertainties of French politics, those heavy ground swells that arose to shake the bark of the Republic, she thought of her son. She would say to herself, "He would have reigned." No one among those who have pondered the history of the last half century has any doubt of it. In a day of uncertainty and disgust, France might well have given herself to the Prince Imperial, once the idol of Paris, if he had not fallen under the assegais. But since he was dead, his mother no longer desired the overthrow of the régime with the same ardour. If a new revolution must come about in order that a Bonaparte might attain the throne, she would hesitate before desiring it to happen.

The sequestration had long since been lifted from the Empress's property in France. She had been able to concentrate her scattered fortune, satisfy the debts of the civil list by giving up her farms in the Landes and the Châlet at Vichy. To cope with the costly constructions at Farnborough she sold the villa at Biarritz and the estate of La Jonchère. She gave the Pharo estate to the city of Marseilles. The municipality out of simple demagoguishness had in the deed given the donor's name as *veuve Bonaparte*. When it was put before the Empress, she declared proudly that the deed must be drawn up afresh and that she would not sign it unless every time she was referred to she was described as Her Majesty the Empress Eugénie, widow of His Majesty Napoleon III, Emperor of the French—*S.M. l'Impératrice Eugénie, veuve de S.M. Napoléon III, Empereur des Français.*

Marseilles gave way, in order to have the estate, perhaps also because since men are never altogether without some nobility that lofty protest of an aged and defenceless woman had moved some hearts. She wished to be treated as a sovereign, not for herself, since she had known the emptiness of titles, but out of respect for what she had been, for the memory of her husband and her son. She brought a lawsuit against the French State, which refused to give up to her numerous *objets d'art* belonging to the private domain, and which now figured in the museums without even an indication of their origin. This regrettable litigation lasted a very long time, the stubbornness of both parties exhausting all the successive degrees of jurisdiction. The Empress at last gained the day, with much satisfaction to herself. She liked to give, but she would not allow others to take from her. She made very generous gifts to Malmaison, presenting that Napoleonic abode with pieces of very great historic and intrinsic value. In memory of the generous hospitality once given to Queen Hortense and her son by the Canton of Thurgau, she gave it the little Château d'Arenenberg, stipulating that a school of Arts and Crafts should be set up in it.

Her fortune, thanks to skilful management, to which she gave her close personal attention, had never ceased to grow. She was now drawing the rents of her properties in Paris. The Spanish estates, the usufruct of which she had left to her mother while she lived, had given her a good return since the death of the Countess de Montijo. Very extensive, with vast stretches of uncultivated land, they were uncertain in their yield. But the property left to the Prince Imperial by Princess Baciocchi, which had now come to Eugénie, the lands in Piedmont, the Villa Vicentina near Trieste, the Villa Mezzolava in the Romagna, brought in large revenues. Especially after the Empress, whose age did not hinder her from engaging the income a long way ahead in order to improve the principal, had had the marshes drained and turned into fertile land. In France, her agents handled on her behalf a bourgeois portfolio of investments not much above two million francs. In London she had with Baring's, the Emperor's bank all through his life, a very large deposit the income from which exceeded £75,000 a year.

She made lavish use of it, keeping open house on a costly scale, giving discreetly to charities, pensioning old servants, and old friends too, who had fallen into straits. Even so, she set aside substantial amounts every year. She was not miserly, but orderly. This passion for order grew in her with age. Extravagant in her youth, she had begun to count her money for the Emperor, for her son. She still counted her money, now that they were no longer there, less for the sake of amassing than because she had contracted the habit, the trick of it, the ugly trick, if you like.

On the platform of the Paris-Lyon-Marseille railway station one November morning, a lady well on in years walks along with a still springy step, barely leaning on her black walking-stick. The veil fastened to the crape hat allows a glimpse of white hair and handsome features. Under her somewhat voluminous black garments her figure has elegance. Her blue eyes, close together, are very direct of look. A few persons escort her, with much respect. Travellers meet and pass her without recognising who she is. Railway officials look at her vaguely. No one uncovers. She goes on, talking quickly, rather loud . . .

She gets into her carriage, settles down, asks if the two ladies with her are comfortable. Attentive hands have brought flowers, which are before her on the little movable table in the compartment, covering up reviews and newspapers. She takes her place in front of the open window, says a few words, smiles. She is pleased and content. She has seen her friends again. She is about to see once more the South she loves, whither she now goes every winter to find the sun, a milder, more equable climate than that of her own Spain. The train glides away. A little group bows. Graciously the aged lady salutes with a supple bending of her neck. The Empress Eugénie is on her way to Cap Martin.

Although tardily, she had taken Mérimée's advice, and since 1888 had spent her winters on the Provençal coast where her old friend's last troubles had found soothing. She had come to Cap Martin at the repeated suggestions of the Marquise de Galliffet. The first year she resided in the hotel at which the Empress Elizabeth was staying. These two ladies, who had been so beautiful and so unfortunate, each in mourning for her only son, now in the declining years of life, used to go walking quite plainly dressed, side by side along the high road or in the country, sometimes for long distances. Elizabeth, lofty of mind, a philosopher and poet, spoke of the soul, of destiny. Eugénie, more of a realist, more concerned with facts, talked history and politics. Two monologues, in fact. Their minds did not meet and mingle at all. But they found it pleasant and comforting to walk together, in a noble landscape, to take tea and look out over the sea. The following year Eugénie bought a piece of ground planted with pines and built on it a villa to which she gave the Greek name for Corsica, Cyrnos.

Les Archives Photographiques d'Art et d'Histoire

COUNT PRIMOLI
From the Portrait by Spadini in the Luxembourg

"It will be my Achilleion," she said.

It was very different from the Achilleion, that splendid empty palace made to play the *Oresteia* in. Cyrnos was only a white, cheerful house, fronting the sea, with the rock of Monaco for its background. A big terrace, a ground floor, a single storey above, with a return pavilion from which could be seen a huge expanse of sea to the horizon. There the Empress found herself at ease, and she received a great deal. She made long excursions walking or driving. One day, having gone to Cannes for her shopping, she wished to see Mérimée's tomb. She went to the cemetery on the arm of her nephew, Count Primoli. She crossed herself before the stone on which the replica of Iselin's bust had not yet been set up, and prayed, bent and leaning on her stick, among the rustle of the pine trees mingled with the shrill singing of the grasshoppers. One of the two old Englishwomen who had been Mérimée's friends was at rest beside him, the other close by.

When Eugénie had prayed, she still remained a certain time without moving. He was dead so long now that his memory no longer held any pain. Eugénie saw him with that still air of his, half professor, half dandy, his white trousers, his frockcoat, his high cravat, coming towards her through the alleys of Compiègne, grey silk hat in hand. Would she meet him again one day, this unbeliever who had so enraged her by his ill-will towards the Church and the Pope? Perhaps. God's mercy and compassion know no bounds. But then how changed he would be! Monsieur Mérimée in Paradise . . . Monsieur Mérimée no longer doubtful of anything, believing everything. How she would tease him! For even in Paradise she would still love to tease.

"Dear Monsieur Mérimée," she said as she reached the gate of the cemetery. "He has been there now for thirty years, and here am I still living. Is it not strange? It looks as if God has left me behind for a purpose. He is making ready something he wants me to see. . . ."

On the way back to Cyrnos in her carriage, with her nephew, an attentive listener, she spoke of Mérimée, and then of his friend Stendhal, whom she never called anything but Monsieur Beyle, with a kind of respect. He came to see them often, her and her sister, when they were young, and he used to tell them the story of Napoleon. She still had in her bedroom a picture of the battle of Austerlitz that he had given her. He was very fond of children. He was very kind and gentle. And what lovely flowered waistcoats he wore, with fob-pockets adorned with dangles! They said he had written novels. She had never read them. Were they good at all?

"I doubt whether Your Majesty would like them," answered Primoli.

He smiled in his beard, which was turning grey already, at the simple idea she had built up for herself of the sceptical, egoistical Stendhal. He did not attempt to enlighten her as to his real character. It would have been a wasted effort. When her opinion was formed about a person or a thing she never changed it.

"Old people are obstinate," she said.

But she had always been like that.

So that she could make short cruises, on the coast of Norway, or the coast of Scotland, and what she liked best of all, in the Mediterranean, she had bought a yacht christened the *Thistle,* which in reality was small and far from comfortable, and much dreaded by those members of the Empress's suite who did not possess good sea legs, for it pitched and rolled to the smallest waves. But Eugénie loved it dearly. A born traveller, sea travel was what she liked above any other kind. Far more than on land her vagrant old age enjoyed itself on board a frail hull that only stopped for a moment, then was off again.

"The sea is my element," she said one day to M. Maurice d'Ocagne. "It is the cure *par excellence* for every physical and moral sickness. I should like to live on the sea all the time. I know that people are not far from thinking I am a little mad for this reason. Just think of it—to go so far at my age, at the risk of never coming back! But that is not going to stop me; when it comes to leaving our little terrestrial ball for the last voyage, what does it matter from what point on that little ball we take our departure?"

Every year, and often several times in the same year, she embarked on the *Thistle,* or if the cruise was to be a more extended one, on a steamboat. And then she felt herself relieved, almost happy. She loved to lean over the waves for long spells, or walk on the bridge talking with some companion who had come with her or whom she had fallen in with on board. In this way she rambled about all the Mediterranean coasts, Italy, Greece, Asia Minor, Africa, Spain: she knew inlets and capes like a professional seaman. She needed movement and space. To stay in the same spot was for her to sink in a quickstand. She almost seemed to feel the earth rising about her and choking her.

The Empress is seated in a very commonplace drawing-room, in the middle of a group of visitors, relatives, and friends: the Princesse de Moskowa, the Duchesse de Mouchy, the Duchesse and Mlle de Bassano, Monsieur and Madame de Beauverger, Doctor Hugenschmidt, Count Chevreau, Count Primoli, Monsieur and Madame d'Attainville, Mme and Mlle Conneau, Pietri, Lucien Daudet. Beside her stands a table laden with English and French books, newspapers, photographs. Before those of the Emperor and her son, together in one morocco frame, a bunch of roses. On the side a little travelling clock on which she sometimes turns her eye.

The tall windows open on a noisy street, railings with gilt spikes, a garden . . . the garden of the Tuileries. . . .

She now makes frequent visits to Paris. The Hôtel Continental reserves this suite of rooms on the second floor for her. A bedroom, two drawing-rooms . . . numbers 181, 182, 183. Little space—or else too much—for one who has reigned. She raises the curtain and looks out, blinking her eyelids, her mouth shut tight. She sees the alley-ways in which she once walked with Napoleon, where their son played as a child. Then very softly her hand drops the tulle upon the garden, upon the sky, upon the past.

This setting, which was the culminating setting of her life, this spot exuding history, which knew her so lovely and so powerful, and from which she took flight, driven away, she can find herself back in it without distress. An apparent insensibility that arouses a good deal of astonishment, sometimes insulting. It seems that these ghost-haunted Tuileries have little by little lost their terror for her and that on the contrary she finds a kind of melancholy sweetness there.

"Nothing," she tells Monsieur Maurice Palaeologue, "nothing affects me now, I have suffered too much. As I now live only with shadows, I seem a shadow to myself."

But a shadow so animated, so alive, erect in her armchair, her head high, pulling up her black lace scarf on her shoulders with a graceful gesture. She still retains beauty. Her dazzling complexion has gone, wrinkles have come; the oval of her cheeks has become heavy. Yet the nose, the mobile mouth, the eyebrows remain almost untouched. Her eyes are still bright with a hard gleam, azure or dark blue according to the degree of light. No coquetry now: always the same mourning dresses, full, modest, a skirt on the short side, a straight coat of a cut borrowed from Queen Victoria.

An age in which the body has almost ceased to count, the better perhaps to allow the mind to take the foremost place. The years have not blunted Eugénie's. They seem even to have enriched and fulfilled it. Thanks to her continual reading, her meeting with eminent men, whom she, so to speak, turns over like the leaves of a book with lively curiosity, she has become cultivated, has by degrees filled up the yawning gaps in her education. Her marvellous memory for facts, for dates, for precise details, astounds her hearers. *Ingenio vir:* More and more her brain appears to belong to a man. She still talks a great deal, with the same quick changes as of old.

Old adversaries, surprised and won over by her dignity, her courage, the poignant prestige of an Æschylean misfortune, occasionally asked to be granted an audience. She readily received them. In this way she had conquered Jules Claretie, who swung round completely from his one-time antipathy, and Joseph Reinach, Gambetta's friend, who wanted to write a book about her. Certain manifestations of mere curiosity, however, irritated her. She said one day to Madame Octave Feuillet, now a widow too: "I know; people come to see me like a fifth act." But if she warded off the indiscreet, she looked with pleasure for the faithful, especially those who belonged to the good days. When the Duke of Sesto, who had once been the handsome Marquis of Alcanizes, came to the Hôtel Continental, she welcomed him with a smile in which there flickered the reflection of their youthful years. They spoke Spanish together, thee'd and thou'd each other, called each other Pepe and Eugenia. Round the two ancients every one kept silence.

She often went out and about in Paris with one of her nieces, or with Pietri, or with Count Primoli. Her step was still elastic.

Sometimes disdaining the carriages placed at her disposal she would get into trams or omnibuses; often without the least aloofness, returning to the true Spanish familiarity, just like her mother, she talked to her fellow-passengers. She visited the museums, the exhibitions, lingered in the shops. She went to the Archives to verify certain facts in the life of Marie-Antoinette, who had never ceased to be her heroine, in consequence of a long talk with Monsieur G. Lenôtre at the Duchesse de Mouchy's.

She went to all the places that had seen her in her heyday. She visited St. Cloud, a visit described by Lucien Daudet in an exquisite book. It was a little before the ruins of the château, which had been burned down by the Prussians, had been levelled away. Wandering among the debris, she recognised a slab of marble, the remains of the fireplace of a drawing-room where she had held her circle many an evening. Later, before she went away, seeing a rose tree of the old days now turned into a great straggling bush, she wished to pluck a rose from it. "She found herself, she knew not how, caught on every side by the spiny branches, held and entwined, as though the very plants remembered what men had so soon forgotten."

On another occasion, in the garden of the Tuileries, as she bent down to a bed to take a flower from it, a keeper rushed up to her. He was about to admonish her when Primoli stopped him:

"It is the Empress," he said in the man's ear.

The keeper, an old soldier with the Italy medal, stood to attention and saluted. Eugénie thanked him with a melancholy smile and passed on, the flower tightly clasped in her hand.

She went to Compiègne incognito, accompanied by the Princesse de la Moskowa. They went through the palace with an attendant. Coming to the Prince Imperial's bedroom Eugénie went straight to the inner shutter of one of the windows, on which she used to mark her son's height with a lead pencil. It had not been touched. The lines and the dates were there, a little faded, but still distinct. The Empress could not restrain herself. She sat down, sobbing. The attendant left the room, beside himself, to find the keeper; he had recognised Eugénie. When he came back she had recovered her composure. But she was broken down and went away at once.

Later on she went among the ordinary public to visit Malmaison. She was touched to see many articles displaying the label: "Given by the Empress Eugénie"—*Don de l'Impératrice Eugénie.* (Primoli had warned Monsieur J. Ajalbert that the impertinence shown by certain museums had annoyed her. Thus in the Carnavalet a cradle of the King of Rome, presented by her, was labelled *"Don de M. Pietri."*) Thenceforth Malmaison was the recipient of most of her gifts.

She went to Saint-Gratien to attend the funeral of Princesse Mathilde. Throughout the Empire, under the outward guise of an obligatory courtesy, they had kept their distance. The caprices of the princess, her daring life, her factious entourage displeased Eugénie, and Mathilde had never forgotten that the Spanish woman had ascended the throne that might have been hers. The fall of the Empire had drawn them together, although Eugénie had resented the coolness shown by Mathilde to the Prince Imperial on his departure for Zululand. The years gradually dropped like a curtain over bitter memories. Now every time she passed through Paris the Empress saw her cousin. In summer she would go and lunch at Saint-Gratien. For a long time the princess was going downhill. She had fallen and fractured her thigh. Eugénie was grieved for the death of this ancient rival.

She was becoming accustomed to see all those who had walked alongside her on her way pass out of sight. This one and that, man or woman, were asleep in the grave. She went on all alone, or beside her only the descendants of the friends of old, with whom she had no memories now in common, to whom she could only repeat her own memories. With them she made her escape from too familiar places, even from the *Thistle,* condemned to coasting runs only. Thus she went to North Cape, accompanied by her niece Madame d'Attainville (to-day Countess Baciocchi), Madame de Beauverger, the daughter of Countess Clary, Monsieur Raimbeaux, and Pietri. She had taken the ordinary steamer. No one troubled her; she was surrounded by a discreet respect. With the Princesse de la Moskowa and Mlle de Bassano she visited Egypt, and went up the Nile as far as Wady-Halfa. Incapable of fatigue, at eighty she rode on donkeys to make excursions in the desert under an overpowering sun. She would have liked to go as far as Khartoum. Monsieur and Madame Lebaudy, whom she met on the journey, dissuaded her: the heat there was torrid. Regretfully she turned North again. She enjoyed the climate of Africa beyond any other. One evening she said to Princesse de la Moskowa:

"It is strange that I should be so drawn to this land. Perhaps it is because it has taken my all from me."

After that she undertook her longest journey, which brought her, on the mail boat *Mooltan,* of the Peninsular & Oriental Company, to Ceylon. She had taken with her Madame d'Attainville, Miss Vaughan, Mademoiselle de Castelbajac, Joachim Clary. Passing through the canal that as a sovereign she had inaugurated, leaning over the side, her mind filled with visions, the aged traveller for a long time remained in silent meditation. At Kandy the governor's palace was placed at her disposal, and she resided there for six weeks, which she employed in excursions through the island. She did not go into India at all. The heavy damp heat of Ceylon had tried her severely.

"That will be for another time," she said.

The frail skeleton was giving way by degrees; the spirit never bent.

She came back to spend the spring at Cyrnos, and then home to Farnborough.

She had become much attached to this second home of her exile, which she knew to be the last. She had transformed and beautified it. She now went walking in the shade of the trees sprung from the chestnuts she had picked up on the gravel of the Tuileries and planted. She never desisted from building. The better to entertain her nephews the Moras she added a great wing to the house. In the park, near some old stables she set up within ivy-draped walls a Napoleonic museum. Seconded by Pietri, she had arranged with meticulous detail in the cases famous cloaks, portraits, decorations of historic arms, and the baby clothes of the "little prince," the uniforms ordered for his return to France . . .

Saint-Michael's had become a real abbey. The small buildings originally intended to lodge the four Premonstratensian monks employed in the service of the church and in watching over the tombs, now sheltered forty Benedictines, expelled from Solesmes, who in this corner of Hampshire continued their learned labours. The Empress frequently visited the crypt in which her dead lay at rest. On her son's granite sarcophagus mouldered the bunch of heather once gathered by Princess Beatrice, now the mother of grown-up children. She was the godmother of one of the Princess's daughters, Victoria-Eugenia, Ena, as she was called, who used to spend occasional week-ends at Farnborough Hill. The Empress loved her almost like a grandmother, and planned to marry her. She no longer went to hear Mass at Saint-Michael. A Benedictine came every Sunday and said it in the little bare chapel she had fitted up on the second floor of her house. Age did not render her faith timid or narrow. She had always believed, had never known doubt. That was the one distress from which she had never suffered. Even in her youth she had shown much more tolerance than was publicly known. And now she displayed perhaps even more. She respected the liberty of others. But apostates she despised. For a long time they hid from her that Monseigneur Bauer, who had once been her chaplain and her protégé, and to whose sermons so many fair penitents had flocked, had cast aside the soutane, had married and become a constant figure in the Opera foyer. When she learned this—by chance—she was visibly displeased and sad.

"I shall never admit," she said, "that any one should be such a turncoat."

She seldom spoke of religion, except to tease some very bigoted old friend or other, but sometimes allowed herself to turn the conversation on spiritism, on the unknown world that is all about us, that penetrates into every nook and cranny of our being, incites us to surprising actions, the world in which the dead continually intermix with what we call life.

She confessed to superstitious ideas from which her reason, robust as it was, could not protect her.

"When I came to Chislehurst after the war," she related, "the mirror in my bedroom suddenly broke. I saw a presage of misfortune in it, that the Emperor would die soon and never return to France."

She regarded Sunday as her unlucky day. Yet it was on a Sunday that she married Napoleon. But the Empire had fallen on a Sunday. Her son had perished on a Sunday. "I shall die on a Sunday . . ." she would say sometimes.

She applauded progress of every kind, readily took advantage of modern inventions. She was among the first to have a motor-car, to install the telephone, to use electricity. No novelty was repugnant to her, not even novelties in fashion, though she no longer followed it, but for ten years wore a Worth dress and a hat with black feathers, which she called in a somewhat childish way "my beautiful hat."

Elegance pleased her, if she did not care to show off. When from Cyrnos she used to go to Monaco or Nice, she was greatly interested in the spectacle of the streets. One day in Monte Carlo she observed women dressed with extreme luxury, very loud, with huge diamonds. She murmured:

"Just think that I used to be blamed for my clothes!"

No doubt she saw them again in her mind's eye, those clothes, her dresses of the Tuileries and St. Cloud, her great *cloches* of satin, of faille, of muslin, with their frills, their flounces, their wreaths of artificial flowers, her capes of velvet, of gros de Naples, her *rotondes,* her *visites,* her bright-coloured shawls. All that had excited the pamphleteers, and yet it was all so modest, so simple, so inexpensive by the side of the display of these bourgeoises or these fashionable courtesans who shot by her in their dazzling cars and forced the old Empress, tiny under her black veil, to stand aside.

Among the conquests of time there were yet some against which she rebelled. She approved that women should be better educated and be given more freedom. But she was no feminist. To her it was woman's part to guard the home, not to be her husband's rival at work. In any case her own preference was for masculine activities. She was often heard to say:

"I should have liked to be a man . . . Ah, if I had only been a man!"

Perhaps for her happiness nature had indeed made a mistake.

At Farnborough Hill immediately after lunch was over every one was free to do as he pleased. Some went off to London, others went up to rest or to read in their rooms. Impervious to fatigue, the Empress wrote her letters. With Mlle Gaubert she attended to requests for help, which were always numerous, sometimes touching, and which she usually met with liberality. When she had nothing more urgent to do, driven by her mania for orderliness, she re-arranged her papers or a shelf in a bookcase. At length she would go out with the hardiest of her guests. In every sort of weather, cold or hot, in spite of the fogs lying in yellowy blankets on the ground, even if she was feverish or had a cold, mocking at the entreaties of her people, the prescriptions of the doctors, she would leave the house and go off either in the park or along the road, walking, talking, tiring her companions. She came back for tea, never confessing to the least fatigue. On the contrary, she would declare:

"That air has done me good. I feel much better."

Very refractory to doctors' orders, she would jeer at the Faculty with her old friend and neighbour Doctor Scott, who had long ago gone with her to Natal, and with Doctor Hugenschmidt who often came to Farnborough or to Cyrnos. Every one knows that this delicate-minded kind gentleman, who has recently died, was very near akin to Napoleon III. The Empress had not wished to see him before her son's death. Later she desired to make his acquaintance. When he was brought to her she looked long at him, then murmured:

"How like *him* you are!"

To the doctor, in spite of his origin, or because of it, since all our motives are mixed, she was a good providence. She helped him through his studies, arranged for his becoming Doctor Evans's assistant, and enabled him to take up his practice, which was the most famous in Europe. She gave him many souvenirs of the Emperor and his family. She had complete confidence in him, and almost always followed his advice, but those of the friend rather than those of the physician.

Towards her eightieth year she had a slight stroke. Doctor Hugenschmidt who was at Farnborough at the moment, ordered leeches. She protested. He insisted, she still refused. Then he threatened to go away. She surrendered.

"I submit," she told him, "only to please you."

The doctor at once applied leeches, and she was relieved.

That evening, after a last visit to his patient, he ventured to tell Aline Pelletier that he had never seen in any woman of her age shoulders of such a pure and youthful curve, or so white.

The maid repeated this to her mistress, who when she saw Hugenschmidt next morning asked him knowingly:

"And so, Doctor, you find I still have beautiful shoulders?"

Poor Hugenschmidt could only bow in confusion, but the Empress's eyes shone with pleasure. She had been happy to be beautiful. She did not mourn after her beauty—but that some one should pay homage to it touched her heart.

Although she neglected her health, only had recourse at long intervals, and that by correspondence to Doctor Robin, her official doctor, it remained excellent. Her only troubles were colds, which never kept her from going out, in mid-winter, in an open carriage, and which she treated in the good old fashion with possets and *pâtes de Regnault.* Often when she had one she did not go to bed, but passed the night on her *chaise-longue,* keeping Aline with her and talking to her till two or three in the morning, only stopping when she heard her faithful maid actually snoring. Then resigning herself to silence, she too would close her eyes. . . .

During Eugénie's reign, from her natural regard for order, from a kind of foresight too, she had collected a great mass of papers: correspondence from sovereigns and statesmen, confidential reports addressed to the Emperor, diplomatic documents. She often turned them over like a treasure hoard. However, when old age had come, after long hesitation she decided to destroy many of them, among others everything that when she had gone could no longer serve the Bonapartist cause, but might embarrass it, might annoy persons her resentment against whom she had allowed to soften or vanish. Assisted by Joseph Primoli she burned a great number of them. As she bent over this melancholy task, she found once more those note-books in which during the Empire and even later she had summarised for herself her readings on the most varied subjects: philosophy, history, general knowledge. She wanted to throw them into the fire. Primoli begged permission to preserve them. She consented, on condition that he would not show them to anybody.

"Above all," she said, "don't talk about them, people would think they were my memoirs."

She betrayed in that one of her constant preoccupations. She had no intention of leaving anything from her own hand behind her that might, however little, look like an apologia, the explanation of her acts. The Emperor had said nobly: "One does not make an indictment against one's own people." Like him she desired no justification, or rather that justice she only looked for from the future, from a generation that had suffered less, would be more serene. When a newspaper attacked her with regard to the foreign policy of the Second Empire, she said to Primoli:

"When one has had the misfortune like me to become a historical personage, one must resign oneself to be discussed by political passions in the sharpest and most unjust manner possible while one is still alive. I shall never reply, I shall deny nothing, however painful it may be for me. I cannot bear a war of recrimination. I believe firmly that time will do justice to the Emperor in the first place, and perhaps to me."

Nevertheless, there was one reproach that always remained bitter to her. When she came upon a book or an article that cast doubt on her feeling for France, she recovered the fire and spirit of her youth. Striking the ground hard with her cane, with flashing eyes that suddenly turned almost black, her cheeks coloured with a wave of blood, she would exclaim:

"Not French, I not French! And I would have laid down my life for France. I may have committed mistakes, I *have* made mistakes, yes, I know . . . perhaps I could not have avoided them. But I have always set France before everything, before the Emperor, before my son! . . . And now that everything has been taken from me, now that they are so hard on me, I would still sacrifice what life remains to me in order that France may be great and glorious!

"So they do not know, the people who call me the Spaniard, that a foreigner who sets the crown of France on her brow has a mean and cowardly soul if she becomes French only by halves. I love Spain, I make no secret of it, I shall love her always; I live in England where my own are buried, but I have only one country, France, and I shall die with her name graven on my heart!"

Impelled by this anxiety to avoid everything in the shape of polemics, she disliked the thought that books might be written about her.

"It is not time yet for that," she often said.

The only one that found favour in her eyes was the one Lucien Daudet had asked permission to publish, the book of a poet rather than a biographer, a sensitive and true portrait of an old age that remained vigorous despite so many disasters. In her large handwriting, so clear and so rapid, she thanked him "for having dispelled the often cruel legends that cling to the vanquished."

Age, after misfortune, had refined her, perfected her. Her resentments had died out at last. She too, by this prolonging of her earthly course, felt her spirit become less intense. A living witness of a period as yet lost in darkness, rather than misjudged, she kept it all in mind, but passion was leaving her. She now understood facts, events, men that she had failed to understand before. She still kept her own ideas on the Fourth of September, which remained a betrayal to her, but she made excuses for a proud people stung by defeat. . . . At last attained to serenity after so much grief and distress, she smiled and blinked her failing eyes. More and more she lived by her mind. She followed scientific research closely, aviation, wireless telegraphy, and so forth. She helped the first experiments of the then unknown Marconi by having him on board the *Thistle* between Nice and Corsica. She made Doctor Hugenschmidt and M. Maurice d'Ocagne tell her all about radium and its uses in physics and therapeutics, about liquid air and the application of cold in industry. She still assiduously read newspapers, reviews, works on history or practical science. She no longer made notes—her sight was becoming dim. But her extraordinary memory retained dates and facts and details like a sensitive plate. Questions of foreign policy interested her beyond everything. This was a natural result from her frequent contacts with the royal families of England and Spain (she had married her goddaughter Ena of Battenberg to young Alfonso XIII), of Russia (the dowager Czarina Marie Feodorovna was on terms of close friendship with her and they wrote to each other often), of Austria (she had invited Francis-Joseph to Cap Martin and been his guest at Ischl where he had shown her exceptional attention). She was the recipient of very important confidences from English personages of the highest station, and from many ambassadors, and she knew the secret history of many affairs of diplomacy.

In Paris, in her drawing-room at the Continental, at Cyrnos, she gave M. Maurice Palaeologue, for whom she had conceived a real liking, valuable hints for facilitating the task of M. Delcassé. She informed him of certain intrigues while they were still being hatched. When Pope Leo XIII refused to grant her an audience because she had crossed the threshold of the Quirinal (in 1876!) and paid a visit to Prince Humbert of Italy, she warned M. Palaeologue that on his approaching visit to Rome M. Loubet would not be received at the Vatican either, which foreshadowed a serious crisis in the relations between the Church and France.

As she had said herself, she had not become a Republican, but being above all things alive to facts, she saw this Republic she had loathed now rooted deep and firm in the heart of the country. In certain aspects, especially its anti-clericalism, it still provoked her dislike. Yet Eugénie's mind was much too perspicacious not to see its merits. It had rebuilt France, re-established the army, made the finances secure, created a colonial domain only to be compared with the British Empire. And all that she frankly admired.

"We were the first," she said, "to think of Indo-China. And it was I who wanted to annex Cochin China."

A stable constitutional policy had been set up; the country was prosperous, the life of the people was making unbroken progress. By means of a moderate and conciliatory policy the Republic had created a network of *ententes* and alliances that had by degrees restored to France, if not the eminence the Empire had enjoyed, at any rate a position that was honourable, advantageous, and not lacking in respect.

One day when a guest at Cyrnos was criticising certain Republican ministers unmercifully, she answered him somewhat stiffly:

"You speak of decadence? I do not see any trace of it. France is held in high esteem abroad. I know very eminent statesmen in Paris. *We* have good ambassadors. What force there is in that country! What a great country!"

She was nearly ninety at this time.

CHAPTER IV

The Other War

IN July 1914 the Empress was visiting the Dalmatian coast after spending a few days in Venice and Ravenna. Austria's ultimatum to Serbia put an end to her travelling.

"We must go home," she said to Madame d'Attainville, who was with her. "This time it's war."

By way of Switzerland and Calais she returned to Farnborough as speedily as possible.

She had foreseen war ever since Agadir, even further back, since her meeting with William II in the Bergen fjord in the summer of 1907.

The Kaiser, arrogant and jumpy, had paid her a visit on board the *Thistle*. He talked to her sadly of France, of England with hate.

"I should like to be on terms with France, to be allied with her, to co-operate with her on broad lines of policy. Quite impossible! The French do not understand me; they have taken a dislike to me. Just think, several times I have let them know that I wished to go to Paris. But, oh, no! they do not want to see me . . ."

There was a quite different tone for England.

"For more than twenty minutes," the Empress told M. Palaeologue, "he inveighed against her and especially against King Edward, whom he accused of every kind of wickedness. As he was leaving me he noticed a portrait of Queen Victoria on one of the tables, the photograph you see there, which never leaves me. Then he stopped, his clenched hand on his hip, his chest thrown out, with a whole air of fury. And in this theatrical attitude he exclaimed:

" 'When she died, they gave me nothing of hers, not the least souvenir! They excluded me from the family like a reprobate, like a plague spot!' "

This war, which she expected, filled her with anxiety. She knew, better than she did in 1870, the might of the German army. From her English friends, from the statesmen and ambassadors who used to visit her at Farnborough, she knew the social chaos that reigned in Russia, that land of velleities and treacheries. Would the war then resolve itself into a duel between France and Germany? Would France be able to endure so terrific an assault? How would French opinion behave in case of defeat? The propaganda of Socialism gave her infinite concern.

If England went into the conflict she had no doubt of the issue. She had the admiration of a connoisseur for the inexhaustible British tenacity. But affairs were in the hands of a Liberal Cabinet, little inclined to march against Germany. The invasion of Belgium rescued her from her fears.

"This time," she said, with a tremor that alarmed her intimates, "this time we have them: our time has come!"

Everything that a woman of her great age could still do, she did, with an energy that shook up her whole life. Seeing that the whole weight of Germany was falling upon France, she wrote to her friend the dowager empress Marie Feodorovna to entreat her to use her influence with the Czar to hasten the Russian mobilisation, and to have a first army, to be sacrificed if necessary, invade East Prussia. Writing to King Carol of Rumania she adjured him, although he was a Hohenzollern, not to join the Central Empires. Did he not owe his Kingship to some extent to Napoleon III, to herself?

She wished to establish, and to maintain at her own expense, a hospital in her villa at Cap Martin. She was refused permission, thanks to the meanness of the military or civil authorities. She resigned herself to organise a hospital for English officers at Farnborough Hill, devoting to them the whole of the great wing she had added to her house. And as soon as there were wounded men installed in it she went to visit them every day.

To the British Admiralty she gave her yacht the *Thistle* on which she had travelled so much, and which she loved so well.

When Brussels was threatened she offered hospitality to Prince Victor, Princess Clementine, and their two children. She became attached to the latter, although in the old days she had often declared that she disliked *les marmots*.

Patiently and ardently she followed all the changing fortunes of the war. In spite of the cataract closing down upon her eyes, she endeavoured to work out the operations by means of maps on which she carefully marked the position of the troops with pins.

She seldom gave her opinion, too much of a realist to meddle with strategy. After Charleroi she was terrified. She walked about the gallery and the drawing-rooms, almost unceasingly, without speaking. Sometimes they heard her murmur:

"God will never allow that!"

She was kept very accurately informed by the English court, but she insisted on reading the newspapers herself, fearing lest they might try to conceal a defeat from her. The Marne threw her into a delirium of joy. She seemed to be twenty again. She declared to every one she met:

"Now it's quite safe and certain: the war will go on a long time yet, but we shall not be beaten."

Yet she had to tremble again, this time for Verdun. Certain mistakes of the English and French chiefs exasperated her. She could never understand why the Allies had not already come to adopt the single command. But she was impassioned in extolling the silent, obstinate effort of France, the union of all classes, the truce between all parties, the workman shoulder to shoulder with the bourgeois and the peasant in the deadly trench, out of which victory would slowly arise.

"Ah," she would say, "why was this *union sacrée* not achieved round us in 1870! We too would have conquered in the end! Why were hatreds and appetites and passions all let loose against us after Froeschwiller and Forbach, if they were so self-controlled after Charleroi? Why did no one listen to me on the Fourth of September when I begged every one to drop all internal quarrellings and think only of the country!"

She reduced her household, sent all the Frenchmen in her service to fight. The faithful Pietri died after half a century of close devotion. She scrutinised the accounts herself, examined every evening the roll of visitors, who were very few at the moment. She had a Requiem Mass said every month for those who died at the front. She never missed it. She knelt for a moment beside her two coffins and went home in silence, now bent heavily over her walking-stick and with gradually shortening steps.

She gave largely, especially to the French Red Cross and other French charities, but without allowing her name to be disclosed. On January 26, 1915, she wrote to one of her nieces: "The thought that our poor soldiers have not even a bed torments me. [In the hospitals of the Argonne there had been such an influx of typhus patients that the less seriously affected had to be laid on the ground.] This must positively cease. If you need more money, let me know. So much is spent without our knowing whether it was wisely given that it is a pleasure to be sure that this time it will be profitably employed. I ask only that I am to remain anonymous. I detest the idea that I am trying to put myself forward or seeking after popularity. My rôle in this world ended in 1879, and I am now nothing but a piece of wreckage from a calumniated past. I still feel the wound always; it makes me more pitying to the wounds of others."

When a Zeppelin came up overhead in the district, the policeman stationed in front of the gates warned the house to have all the lights extinguished; the Empress wanted to go out and look. She called her niece, Madame d'Attainville:

"Antonia, come quick, come along!"

And in the cold, or even in the rain, often without a cloak, out she went to gaze up at the sky. When some one ventured a remonstrance:

"Pooh," she said, "it's not at my age one begins to be afraid."

The only thing she feared was that she might die before the end.

"I should not like to die now. There will be great things happening that I would like to see. I feel them on the way. God will grant me a little respite, I am sure."

Nevertheless, she had set her affairs in order, and although her eyesight was worse and worse for writing, she had imposed on herself the task of writing her will entirely with her own hand. She had drawn up other ones in earlier days, but she was not now satisfied with them. By two separate deeds, one in Spanish, the other in French, she left her Spanish properties to her nephew, the Count de Montijo, Duke of Peñaranda, Farnborough Hill with its furniture and its collections to Prince Victor, the Villa Cyrnos to Princesse Laetitia. She made Prince Victor, the Duke of Alba and the Duchess of Tamamès universal legatees in equal shares. She made various donations to her charities, bequeathed 100,000 francs for the re-building of Reims Cathedral, annuities and souvenirs to relatives, friends, and servants. Among other such bequests was a Greuze to Colonel Sir John Burgoyne in grateful remembrance "of his chivalrous attitude to me on September 6, 1870."

Still obsessed by her fear, she declared that she had never written notes or a diary, and asked her two executors Don Luis de Errezu, and the Marquis de Girardin, to prosecute the authors of any pretended memoirs that might be published under her name.

The war was very long, was very bitter. She still kept her certainty as to the outcome.

"There are so many dawns that have not shone, says an Indian sage. I believe in those dawns!"

She seemed never to doubt the ultimate victory. Very well informed as to the diplomatic agreements of the Allies, long before 1918 she was keenly discussing the peace terms. To Princess Bibesco, who went to see her at Farnborough, she explained how, if she still occupied the throne,

"You Rumanians would have Transylvania and the Banat, but we could not give you the Ruthenians."

She always said *we* when she spoke of the French.

In September 1917, in conversation with the Empress, Doctor Hugenschmidt learned that she had in her archives the letter, which every one had forgotten, in which King William of Prussia had replied on October 26, 1870, to Eugénie's request that he should conclude peace without forcing France to give up any of her territory. Deferential in form, brutal in substance, the letter contained the following passage:

> After the immense sacrifices she has made for her own defence, Germany desires to be assured that the next war shall find her in a better position to repel the aggression upon which we can count as soon as France has repaired her strength or procured allies. It is this unhappy consideration alone, and not the desire to extend my country that forces me to insist on cessions of territory, which have no other purpose than to set back the starting point of the French armies in the future.

This was an avowal that in 1870 Germany had not claimed Alsace and a third part of Lorraine as historically or ethnographically German territory, but that she insisted on annexing French provinces for strictly military reasons, in order to furnish herself with a redan against a possible future revenge. When the time came to make peace, such a document, shown to England and America, would lend great authority to our negotiators when they claimed the return of the departments lost under the Treaty of Frankfort. When Clemenceau came to power, Hugenschmidt, who was in touch with him, thought he ought to tell him of the letter. Clemenceau jumped at this windfall.

"I should think so indeed, it is of the greatest value!" and enjoined on the doctor to obtain from the Empress the letter and authority to publish it.

Hugenschmidt went to Farnborough and asked for it "in the name of France."

"You shall have it," exclaimed the Empress.

Fumbling, barely able to see what she was doing, she searched through her files and handed the King of Prussia's declaration over to the doctor. An incautious phrase of Hugenschmidt's came within an ace of spoiling everything. As he read the letter in the Empress's presence, he exclaimed:

"Ah, Madame, what a justification this is for Your Majesty!"

"What?" she said, frowning. "I want no justification. I have no need of such a thing."

She allowed him to take the document away, but did not let him have the correspondence she had received from Francis-Joseph and from the Czar at the same moment on the same subject, which she had originally intended to give him as well.

That document, handed over to Clemenceau, was read in full session at the Sorbonne in the presence of the President of the Republic and of the ambassadors of the Allies. It cannot be doubted that, with President Wilson especially, this revelation had very great weight, and that it was largely due to this that Alsace was restored to us without discussion—and *without a plebiscite.*

"You did good work," said Clemenceau to Hugenschmidt as he gave him the rosette of the Légion d'Honneur.

And the rebel of 1870, President of the Council in the day of retribution, wrote an autograph letter of thanks to the Empress.

Dom Cabrol, the Abbot of Saint-Michael's, who received it from M. Cambon, the French ambassador in London, took the letter to her. She could not decipher it. The abbot read it slowly out to her word by word. The Empress smiled radiantly.

"Clemenceau! He writes to me, to *me!*"

A man who had been so harsh to the Empire! She had no grudge against him now. She admired him, loved him for having stood at the helm of France in her darkest hours. In her eyes he was the incarnate symbol of the country. His signature was that of a people and sacred in her eyes.

When Foch's offensive took shape and the Germans gave way, in October 1918, her imagination carried her to the East where day by day the allied wave leapt in pursuit of the German wave. Again and again she said:

"If Foch could only catch them at Sedan!"

Like the Emperor, whose last word it had been, she thought of Sedan without ceasing, after all those years, like a wound whose pain even the egoism of age had not dulled.

On the eleventh of November, the Prince and Princess Napoleon being away from Farnborough, the Empress was alone with her niece Madame d'Attainville.

During the morning telephone call succeeded telephone call from London announcing the concluding of the Armistice. But the Empress waited for its official confirmation. It came at last, from King George, a little before eleven o'clock. Bristol, the maître d'hôtel, received the message and ran to tell the Empress, who was walking up and down in the gallery to kill time. In a choking voice she called her niece, but could not speak to her. She stood there weeping and motionless. Then she mastered herself and wiped her eyes. The two ladies went to the hospital, and went down between the beds of the English officers who all sat up, pale with emotion, and gave them a military salute. She shook hands with each one in silence . . . every heart was beating too violently for speech. . . . They heard the hundred and one guns proclaiming at Aldershot the end of the war.

Back at home again, the Empress lunched with Madame d'Attainville and Lieutenant Herbert Scott, the son of her old friend and neighbour the doctor, who had been seriously wounded. She installed herself in the drawing-room after lunch, knitting in hand. Telegrams arrived by sheaves, to be read by Madame d'Attainville. Then the newspapers. The Empress herself settled her spectacles and read the last French communiqué.

"If my poor boy was here," she said, "how happy he would be."

Now she could depart. The delivered spirit might bid farewell to the body that had prisoned it so long. Before leaving the world where she had shone in splendour, where she had suffered, where she had gone to and fro for half a century clad in her sombre crape, she knew France avenged, re-established as in the proudest days of her reign. Wissembourg, Forbach, Gravelotte, Sedan and Metz were buried under the ashes. The Marne, the Yser, Verdun, had cancelled and abolished them. When Dom Cabrol and a number of monks came in the afternoon to see her, she almost sprang to her feet.

"I give thanks to God," she said to the abbot, "I thank Him on my knees for letting me see this day! . . . It makes up for everything, it obliterates everything, it repays me for all my grief, it allows me to die with my head held high, in peace with France, which will have nothing to reproach us for . . . I have been perhaps the most unhappy of all women. But such a turn of fortune as this makes it all forgotten . . ."

She coughed, a cough that brought once more a touch of red to the translucent skin of her cheek.

"When I die, for I shall die soon—there is nothing left for me here below—when I die, how *they* will welcome me above, bringing them this news! They had left me behind on earth. For long, long years I have not known why. It was to await this day. I tell you, the day of the armistice will have been my first day in Paradise."

She added, after a moment:

"The lost flags will come back to us, will they not?"

That night, in a neighbouring house, a gramophone played the Marseillaise. The Empress was sitting by the fire. Contrary to her habit while the war lasted, she had dressed for dinner. Hearing the distant thin strains of the hymn penetrating the night, she said:

"The Marseillaise! My son and his friends sang it in the park at St. Cloud the night before the Emperor started for the front. I hated to hear it . . . it frightened me. But to-day . . ."

Her head buried in her hands, she was once more in July 1870.

Six days later, she received at Farnborough Hill Mr. Henry Wickham Steed, the correspondent of the *Times,* just back from France. Making him sit beside her, the Empress asked him at once:

"You were in Paris on the day of the Armistice? That must have been marvellous. Tell me. How I should have loved to be there!"

Mr. Steed described to her, without using any art, in disjointed phrases, the delirious joy of Paris, all the inhabitants streaming out of their open doors at eleven o'clock amid the shrieking of the sirens and the riotous pealing of the bells, the guns dragged along by the crowd, the lorries, filled with allied soldiers waving their flags, clattering along the boulevards amid terrific cheering, men, women, children, all strangers to one another, embracing, talking, weeping, heart to heart together, while mothers swathed in mourning black smiled for the first time on their sacrifice. The outburst of one unanimous spirit such as had never been seen and that will perhaps never be seen again.

The Empress, transported, cried out:

"That Clemenceau . . . I could kiss him for all the good he has done to France!"

"May I give M. Clemenceau that message, Madame?" asked Mr. Steed.

The too direct tone displeased her.

"No," she returned sharply. "No message. I died in 1870."

"But, Madame, 1870 is now dead. Your Majesty can live again."

"No, no! I am quite dead. But Clemenceau blundered. He should have attended the *Te Deum* in Notre-Dame. He would have united France. He would have taught a great lesson of moderation and unity. He might have become Consul."

She uttered the word "Consul" in a tone of rapture, raising her hand until it pointed to the ceiling.

"I fancy," said Mr. Steed, "that M. Clemenceau cherishes no such ambitions."

"No matter. He can make good his mistake. He is going to Strasbourg presently."

"May I give M. Clemenceau this advice from Your Majesty?"

"No! I tell you I died in 1870."

Then she spoke of Spain, criticised the Spanish government, whose slackness and inertia were opposed to the development of great domains like hers. . . . Mr. Steed, who had come to lunch, was kept on by the Empress till five o'clock, in an uninterrupted discussion of international questions. He was exhausted, while the Empress on the contrary seemed untouched by fatigue.

Clemenceau heard through Steed of this Farnborough conversation, and said gruffly:

"What is that old woman meddling about?"

All the same he took from it, as it were, a kind of advice, not personal but historic. On Sunday, December 8, after his entry into Strasbourg, he went to the Cathedral to hear the *Te Deum.* And before the Chamber, speaking of those hours of reparation, he repeated the very words of the "old woman."

"Those days in Strasbourg are graven on my heart. I saw in the heart of the crowd, a nun who, with eyes lowered under her coif, was softly singing the Marseillaise. Ah, messieurs, what a lesson in unity and moderation!"

The Empress was told how her advice had been followed. She was very happy to know it.

In her little private chapel, above her bedroom, where she heard Mass every Sunday, the Empress still kept the talisman of Charlemagne, preserved after so many perils and vicissitudes. On many occasions the Archbishop of Cologne had begged her to restore this jewel to the treasure of Aix-la-Chapelle. She had always refused, saying:

"I will give them the piece of the True Cross if they wish, for other pieces can be found elsewhere. But this talisman is unique and they shall not have it."

When she heard of the bombardment of Reims she decided to present it to the mutilated cathedral.

"That," she exclaimed, "will be the punishment of the Barbarians."

On the advice of the Abbot of Farnborough she surrounded the gift of this illustrious trinket with an elaborate network of precautions to ensure that "in no circumstance the Archbishop of Reims nor even the Holy See" would have power to alter the destination of the talisman.

CHAPTER V

The Palacio de Liria—Sunday, July 11, 1920

ON the deck of the steamer from Marseilles to Gibraltar a very old lady is reclining in a long canvas chair, wrapped about with shawls and rugs. She is talking and smiling with a few people who form a deferentially attentive group around her. But it is the smile of a ghost. A shrunken face in which the bones strain against the skin, the complexion yellowed, the mouth seemingly grown large, and bloodless, withered sockets in which the eyes, clouded by cataract, are of a dulled and poignant blue. Veined and trembling hands, feet so tiny and so slender that they seem too frail to carry a body. And for all that she still walks, and often, with feeble steps, leaning heavily on her black walking-stick. She coughs every now and then, with a heavy hollow cough, and each time she presses her hand on her breast to ease the strain. But she attaches no more importance to her health now than in the old days. Her own will is the only thing that counts. She laughs at doctors.

For the first time in five years she has spent the winter at Cyrnos. With her hospital shut up behind the last wounded patient, before leaving Farnborough Hill, she paid a last visit to her dead in their tomb in the abbey Church of Saint-Michael pausing a moment in front of the tomb of Pietri, who desired only a burial place at the door of the crypt as modest as his life had been, with barely a name to distinguish it.

In Paris she received a few friends in the Hôtel Continental, went to Notre-Dame-des-Victoires to attend a Mass for the victims of the war. She consulted several oculists who one and all refused to operate on her cataract: an operation in itself benign, but entailing a risk to life at her great age.

The Empress displayed great annoyance.

"Come," she said, stamping her stick on the floor, "that is the very point, at my age what have I to lose? I shall take the operation. I want to look to my affairs myself, to be able to read, able to write. If I have got to live in cellar darkness I might as well be dead."

She retained all her interest in everything, her far-reaching memory. Hers was an astounding longevity. Would the prediction of her girlhood be realised in full? *"You will be a queen and you will live a hundred years."* A hundred years—already she was not far off the count, especially if, from a touch of vanity that has been too much whispered about, she was really a year or two older than her papers showed.

She spent two weeks at Seville in the Las Dueñas palace, where her godchild the Queen of Spain came to see her. She had wanted to go to Granada to visit the house where she was born. But already the heat was too great. And the cataract was growing thicker over her eyes, so that she now could only walk by feeling her way, with distressing impatience. She thought more and more of the operation, but said nothing about it. In the early days of May she installed herself in the Palacio de Liria at Madrid, the home of her nephew the Duke of Alba.

The old Montijo house had disappeared. Very dilapidated, it had been sold and pulled down a year before.

The Palacio de Liria is one of the stately homes of Madrid, built somewhat in the style of the Elysée, in the heart of extensive gardens. It contains magnificent collections, priceless carpets and pictures. The suite in which the Empress took up her abode had belonged to her sister Paca. There was first a drawing-room, which was called the *salon des miniatures.* There, above a sofa, might be seen Winterhalter's best portrait of Eugénie, in a great ermine-trimmed cloak, with her head lightly leaning on her hand. Paca loved it best of all for its ethereal and fluent grace, and the Empress, in memory of her, had given it to her brother-in-law that he might hang it in his dead wife's drawing-room.

Next came the bedroom, which was very large, furnished in princely fashion with a huge four-poster bed, and with rugs of great value on the floor. Facing the bed was the portrait of the Duchess of Alba in white, young, very lovely, smiling.

Between the windows the Empress found the great console table of carved wood with purple marble top that had once adorned her mother's drawing-room, and also a little armchair she had sat in as a child, which Paca had always kept.

During the first few weeks all her relatives or her friends in

Spain came to greet her in that *salon des miniatures* where they found her seated under the Winterhalter. Was it a piece of coquetry? Between the sovereign in her dazzling youth and luxury and this tiny black shape there was a contrast so cruel that the visitors were sometimes struck speechless for a moment. M. Ch. Widor and M. Imbart de la Tour saw her at this time. They found her in gay spirits.

"I have come home again," she told them. "How sweet the flowers smell here! And the sun, how good it is! In the old days I used not to like it . . ."

She paid a number of visits, even staying with him for a short time, to her nephew the Duke of Peñaranda, the Duke of Alba's brother, and to her niece the Duchess of Tamamès. Her intimates thought she had given up the idea of the operation. She surprised them by sending for Doctor Barraquer, who showed none of the apprehensions of his French colleagues. He asked the Empress to appoint a day.

"Whatever day you please," she replied, "except a Sunday."

Her unfailing obsession. . . . The operation was carried out with great skill, and succeeded. After a few days in a dark room, the Empress was able to open her eyes again, equipped with powerful black spectacles, to her great joy. Once more she could see! . . . She looked out of the window at the sky, although she had been expressly enjoined not to. She said:

"I see my sister's portrait."

In secret, for it was still too soon for that, she read some letters. She was heard murmuring to herself:

"How curious. It seemed as though I had left the world, and here is the world making its way back to me."

Reassured as to the results of the operation, the Duke of Alba left Madrid and went to London where he was to join his fiancée. Leaving his palace at the disposal of his aunt, he even took pains before his departure to forbid his chef to prepare certain dishes that might not agree with the Empress.

She could not go out yet, but she was already busying herself with her affairs, talking of her speedy return to Farnborough, making appointments for meeting friends in Paris. On her way she wished to settle the too long unsettled question of the Prince Imperial's mausoleum. She wished also to draw up a codicil to her will, appointing that a museum should be established at Farnborough Hill to contain articles that had belonged to Napoleon III and to her son. She meant to give a substantial legacy to Malmaison, and to leave souvenirs to numbers of friends who had not been named in previous documents. She would arrange and dispose of all these matters in Paris. . . . She had a saloon carriage engaged for July 14.

She had caught a cold, was coughing a great deal. But she was subject to these attacks. The week slipped away; she was quite recovered.

On Saturday, July 10, she woke early, in excellent health and spirits, and told her femme de chambre, Aline, that in the afternoon she would go for a motor-drive. That would be her first outing.

At one o'clock she lunched lightly, but with a good appetite, in her drawing-room—for a month she had not been presiding at table—she even wanted to eat asparagus, which she was forbidden. Soon after she felt indisposed. In that extreme heat, she was cold.

"I shall not go out to-day either," she said.

Her ordinary physician was at once sent for, and spoke of a touch of indigestion. But he appeared anxious. The Empress lay for a few minutes on a *chaise-longue,* shivering. Then she complained of acute pains and began to vomit. Her niece, Madame d'Attainville, and Aline put her to bed. Her transparent complexion had suddenly turned red and congested. She closed her eyes, with, perhaps for the first time in her life, a strange expression of lassitude.

In the next room the three most highly reputed doctors in Madrid had a brief consultation over her case. They had no hesitation or doubts. The Empress was suffering from an attack of uræmia. Her age forbade all help, or any hope.

The threat of uræmia, which had killed Napoleon III, had always loomed over her. Strong as she had been, since her pregnancies she had suffered from her kidneys; but thinking it was rheumatism she paid little heed to it.

And now, lying in that great bed which had been her beloved Paca's, she writhed in convulsions that left her breathless. She made no moan. But once, as they sponged the sweat from her forehead, she said:

"Better die at once than suffer like this!"

Death, now so close at hand, had no terrors for her. She looked on him with no shrinking of the flesh.

Night had come. All her own were gathered beside her, her nephews and nieces, the Duke of Peñaranda and his wife, Doña Sol, the Duchess of Tamamès and two of her daughters, Monsieur and Madame d'Attainville, Count Baciocchi. Her face was now blotched; convulsions and frightful attacks of nausea still at intervals racked her slight frame. When the heavy eyelids lifted the reverted eyeballs showed nothing but their whites.

The fever was increasing by degrees. From that moment she seemed to suffer less. Taking advantage of this relief, the Duchess of Tamamès brought in a priest who remained for a moment alone with the Empress.

No doubt it was a confession without words. Contrition of the spirit that now appeals only to the pity of the Deity. What could she have said, that woman so old, so stricken, who had known the heights and the depths of this human world, whose life had been above all other lives laden with marvels and with woes, what could she have confessed in that ultimate distress of her physical body? If God is He had long since judged her and He had been merciful.

The priest opened the door again, and before the Empress's relatives and the servants of the house, all on their knees, he administered extreme unction. He could not give her communion, fearing an attack of vomiting.

Consciousness remained alive in her like a glimmering taper. Sometimes she lifted her white head from her pillows and her eyes found sight again. Her temperature steadily decreased. . . .

The priest began the prayers for the dying.

Well she knew those prayers; in so long a life she had murmured them for many of her friends. Not her near and dear ones: sister, husband, son, mother, all had died suddenly and without her help.

The bedroom was strongly lighted. Only the bed was in shadow. The Empress seemed to be in pain no longer. She was falling into coma, that harbour of refuge whence the soul embarks in peace. Her eyes were closed. Her hands moved no more. A slight shudder ran now and then through her body. So slender, so slight under the coverlet, she seemed to have ceased breathing.

The priest murmured:

"Proficiscere de hoc mundo . . . Depart from this world, Christian soul, in the name of Almighty God Who did create thee, in the name of Jesus Who did suffer for thee, in the name of the Holy Spirit Who hath entered into thee. . . ."

Had she been conscious she might have felt her faith stir within her, and testified to it. She had sacrificed so many human interests to the Church!

"In the name of angels and archangels, in the name of Thrones and Dominations. . . ."

Had she been conscious, she might have seen herself again in her crown and her purples, in the Tuileries ablaze with lights.

"—In the name of the Apostles and the Evangelists, in the name of the monks and the hermits, in the name of the martyrs and the confessors, in the name of all the Saints of God . . ."

Had she been conscious, she might have remembered her sufferings, her griefs, all her woes, all the hates that had risen up against her, her flight on the Fourth of September, the death of the Emperor, her son's cruel end. . . .

"Be now in peace. . . . Go forth from this body, Christian soul, return to thy Creator Who hath fashioned thee of the clay of the earth. May the horror of the darkness, may the burning of the flames be spared thee. May Jesus deliver thee from everlasting death. . . ."

The Duchess of Tamamès and her daughters, very devout, added their low voices to that of the priest. In that sumptuous room there hovered the faith of the early days of the Church.

"Lord, rejoice this soul with Thy presence, forget the old iniquities and the frailties that wrath or the violence of desire have stirred up within it. For if it has sinned, it has not abandoned Thy paths."

At this point she opened her eyelids, and seemed to be soothed and at peace. Then she closed them again to open no more.

Through the shutters had pierced the daylight. In the gardens there were birds cheeping below the windows. From the neighbouring barracks the bugles were heard blowing the reveille.

Round the Empress, now at last seized with the death-rattle, her relations knelt in prayer. They had still to wait. The extraordinary vitality that had animated that poor body was fading out only by slow degrees. It was eight o'clock. The bells were proclaiming the Sabbath.

"Proficiscere de hoc mundo," repeated the priest. . . .

And the soul obeyed, and departed from this world.

PRINCIPAL WORKS CONSULTED

Mme J. Adam	Mes souvenirs et nos idées avant 70.
B-on d'Ambes	Mémoires.
F. Bac	Le Mariage de l'Impératrice Eugénie.
G-l Du Barail	Souvenirs.
Mme Baroche	Souvenirs.
Dr. Barthez	La Famille impériale.
Beaumont-Vassy	Histoire de mon temps.
Jules Bertaut	Les belles nuits de Paris.
Miss A. L. Bicknell	Life in the Tuileries.
Mme de Boigne	Mémoires.
Henry Bordeaux	Vies intimes.
Mme Carette	Souvenirs intimes de la cour des Tuileries.
M-al de Castellane	Journal.
Hippolyte Castille	Portraits politiques et historiques.
J. de Cassagnac	Souvenirs du second Empire.
J. de Chambrier	La cour et la société du second Empire.
Darimon	La maladie de l'Empereur.
Lucien Alphonse Daudet	L'Impératrice Eugénie.
	Le centenaire de l'Impératrice Eugénie.
Etienne Delécluze	Souvenirs de 60 années.
Thomas W. Evans	Mémoires.
Enquêtes parlementaires sur les événements de 1870.	
J. de la Faye	La princesse Mathilde.
Mme Octave Feuillet	Quelques années de ma vie.
Octave Feuillet	Correspondance.
M-ise de la Ferronays	Mémoires.
A. Filon	Souvenirs sur l'Impératrice Eugénie.
	Le Prince Impérial.
	Mérimée et ses amis.
Général Compte Fleury	Souvenirs.
Cte Fleury et Louis Sonolet	La Société du second Empire.
Sir W. Fraser	My recollections.
C-sse des Garrets	Auprès de l'Impératrice Eugénie.
	L'Impératrice Eugénie en exile.
Georges Girard	Vie et souvenirs du Général Castelnau.
E. Giraudeau	Mort et funérailles de Napoléon III.
De La Gorce	Histoire du Second Empire.
P. Guériot	La captivité de Napoléon III.
d'Herisson	Journal d'un Officier d'ordonnance.
	Le Prince impérial.
B-on de Hübner	Neuf années de souvenirs.
Imbert de St. Amand	Louis-Napoléon et Mlle de Montijo.
Roi Jérôme	Mémoires.
Blanchard Jerrold	Life of Napoléon III.
De Lesseps	Souvenirs de quarante ans.
Lacour Gayet	L'Impératrice Eugénie.
Legge	Empress Eugénie.
F. Loliée	Vie d'une Impératrice.
Loudon	Le journal de *Fidus*.

E. Ludwig........................Bismarck.
M-is Ph. de Massa................Souvenirs et impressions.
Lord Malmesbury................Mémoires.
Cte de Maupas...................Mémoires.
Duc de Morny...................Souvenirs sur le coup d'Etat.
Fitzgerald Molloy.................The romance of royalty.
Cte de Maugny..................Souvenirs du second Empire.
Prosper Mérimée.................Lettres d'Espagne.
Correspondance avec La Comtesse de Montijo.
Lettres à une inconnue.
Lettres à M. Panizzi.
Irénée Mauget....................L'Impératrice Eugénie.
Princesse Metternich..............Souvenirs.
Emile Ollivier....................L'Empire libéral.
Maurice Paléologue..............Les entretiens de l'Impératrice Eugénie.
Armand Praviel..................L'Impératrice Charlotte.
La fin tragique du Prince Impérial.
Duc de Persigny..................Mémoires.
Papiers et correspondance de la famille impériale.
Csse de Reinach-Foussemagne....Charlotte de Bélgique, Impératrice de Mexique.
Cte de Reiset....................Mes souvenirs.
Général de Ricard................Autour des Bonaparte.
Alphonse Séché..................Stendhal.
Stoddart ....Life of Empress Eugénie.
H. Wickham Steed...............Mémoires.
Csse Tascher de la Pagerie.....Mon séjour aux Tuileries.
P. Trachard......................La jeunesse de Mérimée.
Colonel Verly....................De Notre Dame au Zoulouland.
Dr. Véron.......................Mémoires d'un bourgeois de Paris.
H. de Viel-Castel................Mémoires.

INDEX

Abatucci, 108
Abergeldie Palace, 304, 312
About, Edmond, 272
Aguado, Vicomtesse, 235, 241, 271, 282
Alba, Duchess of. *See* Paca
Alba, Duke of, 41-42, 63, 78, 274, 334, 343, 344
Alba, Maria d', 278
Albert, Prince, 101, 102, 103, 120, 311
Alcanizes, Marquis of, 46, 81, 106, 133, 144, 320
Aldershot, 289, 291, 295, 310, 337
Alexander, Czar, 120, 125, 156, 190, 210, 220, 257, 264, 280, 332, 336
Alfonso XIII, 329
Algeria, triumphal visit to, 146
Alliance, attempted with Austria, 192
Arago, 218
Arcos, Madame d', 163, 271
Arenenberg, 50, 111, 288, 303, 311, 315
Argonne, 334
Attainville, Madame d', 319, 323, 331, 334, 337, 338, 345, 346
Attainville, Monsieur d', 319, 346
Attempts to assassinate Napoleon III, 104, 118
Augusta, Queen, 153
Aumale, Duc d', 44, 160, 312
Austria, War with, 122-126, 176
Ayguevives, d', 237

Bachon, 276
Baciocchi-Camerata, Princess, 294
Baciocchi, Comte, 54, 56, 62, 65, 140, 346
Baciocchi, Princesse, 115, 150, 315
Badinguet, 243
Baroche, 107, 108, 109, 218
Barraquer, Doctor, 344
Bartholini, Madame, 115
Bassano, Duc de, 82, 271, 277, 299
Bassano, Duchesse de, 98, 271, 319
Bassano, Mlle de, 319, 322
Bassano, Napoleon de, 305, 308
Bauer, Bernard, 58, 168, 324
Bazaine, General, 164, 181, 222, 223, 224, 225, 231, 248, 258, 260, 261, 262, 263, 264, 266
Beatrice, Princess, 294, 301, 324
Beauverger, Madame de, 319, 322
Beauverger, M. de, 288, 319
Bédoyère, Madame de la, 173, 174, 175
Bellanger, Marguerite, 151, 152
Benedetti, 181, 207
Bennett, Gordon, 312
Bernstorff, Count, 260, 263, 264, 267
Besson, 243, 244
Beust, Count, 144, 192, 284
Beyle, Henri, 26-27, 35, 36, 318
Bibesco, Princess, 335
Bigge, 289, 291, 305
Bismarck, Count, 165, 166, 167, 174, 175, 176, 177, 181, 182, 189, 193, 204, 206, 207, 227, 240, 256, 257, 258, 261, 263, 264, 266, 267, 268
Blanqui, 222
Bonaparte, Cardinal, 228
Bonaparte, King Jérôme, 45, 50, 51, 68, 78, 79, 86, 97, 110, 123, 124, 125
Bonaparte, Laetitia, 313
Bonaparte, Louis-Eugène-Napoleon, 108-110, 111, 112, 116, 122, 138, 141, 144, 145, 149, 167, 169, 170, 171, 172, 179, 182, 183, 184, 185, 186, 189, 191, 195, 203, 204, 207, 208, 209, 211-212, 222, 223, 229, 230, 232, 233, 236, 237, 241, 247, 248, 253, 254, 255, 261, 262, 265, 268, 274, 275, 276, 277, 279, 281, 282, 286, 288, 289, 291-301, 303, 304, 305, 307, 309, 310, 311, 313, 314, 319, 321, 322, 323, 338, 345
Bonaparte, Princess Mathilde, 48, 50, 53, 62, 63, 68, 69, 71, 76, 82, 86, 108, 109, 110, 111, 115, 120, 127, 143, 148, 168, 273, 322
Bonaparte, Napoleon, 19, 21, 26, 37-38, 45, 68, 85, 86, 101, 127, 128, 140
Bonaparte, Prince Charles, 115, 281, 300
Bonaparte, Princesse Charles, 115
Bonaparte, Princess Laetitia, 334
Bonaparte, Prince Louis-Napoleon. *See* Napoleon III
Bonaparte, Prince Napoleon, 45-46, 51, 74, 76, 78, 79, 82, 83, 86, 108, 109-110, 114, 115, 118, 120, 122, 140, 143, 149, 155, 178, 182, 209, 222, 226, 280, 283, 284, 285, 287, 288, 297, 303, 312, 313
Bonaparte, Prince Victor, 297, 313, 334
Bonaparte, Queen Hortense, 38, 50, 51, 76, 81, 96, 110, 111, 140, 169, 275, 288, 311, 315
Bosnia, 292
Bourbaki, General, 259-260, 262, 280
Bourgoing, Madame de, 241
Boyer, General, 262, 263, 264, 267
Brame, 219
Bresson, 312

Bruat, Madame, 108, 111, 112, 170
Buckhurst, Lord, 271
Buccleuch, Duke of, 278
Buffet, 237, 238
Burgoyne, Lady, 253
Burgoyne, Sir John, 252, 253, 335
Busson-Billaut, 240, 294

Cambacérès, Duc de, 82
Cambacérès, Duchesse de, 167
Cambon, 337
Cambridge, Duke of, 291, 296, 298, 301
Camden Place, 258, 260, 263, 268, 271, 273, 277, 279, 284, 286, 290, 291, 293, 294, 296, 297, 299, 300, 305, 307, 310, 311
Camp, Maxine du, 288
Canrobert, Maréchal, 241, 303
Cap Martin, 316, 329, 332
Carey, Captain, 298, 301, 308
Carnavalet, 322
Caro, 144, 273
Carol, King, 332
Carpeaux, 138
Castelbajac, Mlle de, 323
Castiglione, Countess de, 115, 123, 135, 150
Caux, Marquis de, 116
Cavaignac, General, 185
Cavour, 115, 119
Cessé-Brissac, Count de, 198
Cetewayo, 291, 305
Ceylon, 323
Châlons, 280
Charlevoi, 333
Charlotte, Archduchess, 161, 164, 182, 191
Chelmsford, Lord, 298
Chevreau, Henri, 208, 219, 223, 232, 233, 240, 263, 271, 280, 319
Chevreul, 138
Chislehurst, 271, 275, 284, 286, 294, 296, 297, 299, 300, 304, 313, 324
Claretie, Jules, 320
Clary, Count, 254, 261, 264, 265, 271, 272, 273, 275, 281
Clary, Countess, 213, 256, 271, 277, 282, 322
Clary, Joachim, 323
Clemenceau, 336, 337, 338, 339
Clementine, Princess, 332
Cléry, Count, 198
Clotilde, Princesse, 120, 122, 143, 209
Committee of Public Safety, 227
Corsica, Eugénie represents Emperor at centenary of Napoleon at, 192-193
Commune, 268, 271, 273, 281
Conneau, Doctor, 108, 119, 139, 148, 192, 193, 203, 204, 271, 275, 277, 281
Conneau, Lieutenant, 242, 256
Conneau, Louis, 171, 172, 185, 276, 277, 278, 286, 289, 292
Conneau, Madame, 277, 319
Conneau, Mlle, 319
Contades, Marquise de, 63, 114
Conti, 179, 186, 229, 233, 241, 242
Corps Législatif, 162, 176, 193, 194, 196, 205, 209, 218, 222, 235, 236, 237, 238, 240
Corvisart, Doctor, 139, 148, 151, 183, 184, 186, 271, 281, 294, 299
Cossé-Brissac, Count de, 213, 214
Cowley, Lady, 263
Cowley, Lord, 115
Crane, E. A., 245, 246, 247, 248, 250, 251, 252, 253
Crimean War, 100, 101, 102, 103, 105, 107, 112, 120, 140, 176, 271, 280
Cousin-Montauban, General, 218
Cyrnos, 316-317, 323, 325, 326, 330, 334, 342
Czartoryski, Prince, 133

Damas-Hinard, 94
Danube, 297
Daru, 237, 239
Daudet, Lucien, 319, 321
David, Jérôme, 240, 271
Davillier, Madeleine, 277
Declaration of marriage, 78-79
Delcassé, 330
Delessert, Cécile, 30, 31, 34, 41, 58, 94
Delessert, Edouard, 34, 44, 115, 208
Delessert, Gabriel, 30
Delessert, Valentine, 30, 31, 32, 33, 41, 99, 231
Disraëli, 301
Dom Cabrol, 337, 338
Doña Manuela. *See* Montijo, Countess of
Doña Sol, 346
Dreyfus, 314
Drouyn de Lhuys, 51, 53, 63, 69, 70, 79-80, 155, 177, 178, 181, 182, 272
Drouyn de Lhuys, Madame, 63, 71
Dubois, Doctor, 107, 108
Dumas, 138
Dupanloup, 155
Duperré, Commandant, 229, 230, 241, 254
Dupuy de Lôme, 237
Duvernois, Clément, 206, 219, 236, 271

Edward, King, 331
Egerton, Lady Catherine, 133
Elizabeth, Empress, 142, 153, 192, 316

Ely, Marchioness of, 52, 102, 103, 108, 133
Ely, Marquis of, 271
Empire, The, recognised by England, 70
Empire, undermining of the, 193
Emperor requested to abdicate in favour of son, 179-180
Emperor taken prisoner, 233, 235
"Empress's little Mondays," 115-116
Enchantress, 300
Espeuilles, General d', 296
Essling, Princesse d', 92, 108, 116, 134, 150, 173, 213, 214, 237
Eudes, 222
Eugénie as Regent, 123-126, 167, 209-268
Eugénie, Letter of, to Duke of Cambridge, 301
Eugénie opposes Emperor's return to Paris, 223-225
Eugénie, *passim.*
Eugénie, public opinion against, 180-181, 185
Eugénie visits Queen Victoria, 100-104
Evans, Doctor, 244, 245, 246, 247, 248, 249, 250, 251, 252, 254, 255, 258, 261, 266, 326
Evans, Mrs., 247, 248, 252
Exposition Universelle, 188-189

Failure of Mexican Plan, 164
Farnborough, 310, 314, 323, 324, 325, 326, 331, 332, 334, 335, 342, 344, 345
Favre, Jules, 194, 218, 226, 227, 235, 245, 251, 257, 262, 267
Felix, 187
Ferry, Jules, 218, 220, 222
Feuillet, Octave, 136, 138, 186, 193
Feuillet, Madame Octave, 288, 320
Filon, Augustin, 184, 185, 210, 213, 214, 218, 223, 225, 233, 235, 241, 256, 258, 265, 271, 273, 275, 276, 277, 279, 307
Flandre, Count de, 189
Fleury, General, 64, 65, 82, 101, 104, 126, 128, 160, 210, 220
Flower, Miss, 32, 33, 35, 36, 39, 42, 274, 306
Foch, General, 337
Forbach, 333, 338
Forey, General, 162
Fortoul, 69
Fortoul, Madame de, 66
Fould, 76, 77, 108, 109, 119, 128, 154
Fourth of September, 287, 288, 329, 333, 347
Francis-Joseph, 98, 99, 126, 161, 192, 199, 206, 257, 284, 329, 336
Franco-German War, 203-287, 300-368
Frankfort, Treaty of, 335, 336
Frederick, Prince, of Prussia, 199
Frederick William, 113
Froeschwiller, 333
Frossard, General, 170-171, 185, 204, 214, 262

Gabrielli, 115
Galliffet, Captain, 162-163, 272-273
Galliffet, Marquise de, 115, 316
Galve, Count de, 63, 81, 133
Gambetta, 196, 218, 220, 222, 251, 262, 267, 312, 320
Garnier-Pagès, 194
Gaubert, Mlle, 325
Gaulon, 237
Gazelle, 253
George, King, 337
Girardin, Emile de, 236, 335
Gladstone, William E., 165, 271, 301, 310
Glenesk, Lord, 271
Goddard, Father, 277
Goltz, von der, 144
Gordon, Madame, 38, 39, 52, 59
Gounod, 139, 277
Gramont, 207
Grandperret, 219, 294
Granville, Lord, 260
Grévy, Jules, 220, 297
Guizot, 119, 273-274

Ham, Fortress of, 39, 104, 131, 160
Hamilton, Duchess of, 59, 62, 72, 76, 115, 139, 150, 153
Haussmann, Baron, 172
Hidalgo, José, 133, 159, 160, 161, 162, 163, 164
Houssaye, Arsène, 138
Hübner, Baron von, 70, 77, 90, 99, 105, 115, 121, 122, 130
Huescar, Duke of, 198
Hugenschmidt, Doctor, 319, 326, 327, 329, 335, 336
Hume, Douglas, 139-141
Hyrvoix, 105, 181

Ignatius, Saint, 175
Imbart de la Tour, 344
Isabella, Queen, 162, 167
Ischl, Eugénie visits Francis-Joseph at, 329
Italo-Prussian Alliance, 176-177

Jerrold, Blanchard, 271
Josephine, 81, 85, 86
Juarez, 160, 161, 163, 164, 190
Jurien de la Gravière, Admiral, 213, 223, 224, 234, 235, 237, 241, 242

Kaledji, Madame, 140
Kandy, 323
Kératry, 280
Khedive of Egypt, 198, 199
King of Rome, 83, 322
Kolb-Bernard, de, 237

Lagrange, Marquis de, 150
Lambert, Tristan, 296, 297
Larminat, Mademoiselle de, 198, 271, 277, 278, 290, 300, 304
Las Marismas, Marquise de, 92, 116
La Valette, 177, 256, 263
Lavisse, Ernest, 286, 288, 292
Lebaudy, Madame, 322
Lebaudy, M., 322
Lebœuf, 205
Lebreton, Madame, 230, 235, 242, 243, 244, 245, 246, 247, 248, 250, 251, 252, 253, 254, 258, 259, 271, 276, 277, 282, 291
Le Hon, Countess, 114, 135
Lennox, Lord Henry, 271
Lenôtre, G., 321
Leo XIII, 329
Leopold of Hohenzollern, candidate for Spanish throne, 204, 206
Lepic, General, 213
Lesseps, Ferdinand de, 45, 48, 70, 71, 159, 197, 235, 240
Letter of King William of Prussia, 335
Leuchtenberg, Duke of, 189
Le Verrier, 138, 169-170
Lezay-Marnesia, de, 217
Lezay-Marnesia, Vicomtesse de, 92
Longman, 310
Loubet, 330
Louis-Philippe, 37, 44, 45, 50, 65, 97, 250, 312
Lourmel, Madame de, 140, 175
Luis de Errezu, 335

Mac-Mahon, General, 213, 214, 222, 223, 224, 225, 226, 232, 235, 273, 297
Madaillac, Count de, 94
Madaillac, Countess de. *See* Delessert, Cécile
Magne, 219
Malakoff, Duchesse de, 114, 115, 229, 241
Malmaison, 321, 322, 345
Malmesbury, Lord, 141, 271
Marconi, 329
Marie-Antoinette, 60, 181, 215, 231, 256, 321
Marie Feodorovna, Czarina, 329, 332
Marie, Grand Duchess, 197
Marie-Louise, 85, 125
Marion, Mademoiselle, 198
Maritzburg, 306
Marne, 333, 338
Marriage of Prince Napoleon to Princesse Clotilde, 120
Massa, Marquis de, 158
Masséna, 92
Mazzini, 121
Maximilian, Archduke, 98, 161, 163, 181-182, 190-191
Méduse, 286
Mellinet, General, 144, 145, 237, 241
Mercy-Argenteau, Madame de, 198
Mérimée, Prosper, 17-33, 35, 36, 37, 40, 41, 42, 47, 48, 51, 52, 53, 54, 62, 65, 66, 70, 71, 80, 81, 90, 91, 94, 98, 100, 115, 119, 123, 124, 135, 136, 138, 150, 165, 166, 167, 174, 197, 217, 219, 221, 230, 231, 232, 259, 316, 317
Metternich, Prince Richard, 130, 131, 138, 142, 144, 148, 155, 163, 206, 210, 213, 215, 220, 227, 238, 240, 241, 242, 243, 256, 272, 273, 284
Metternich, Princess Pauline, 130-131, 133, 134, 135, 137, 138, 146, 148, 149, 155, 157, 161, 162, 163, 173, 229, 256, 260, 272
Metz, 261, 262, 263, 267, 338
Mexico, 159-161, 163, 180-181, 287
Ministry, overthrow of, 218
Mirabeau, 231
Mocquard, 65, 76, 140, 151, 152, 179
Moniteur Officiel, 178
Monnier, Monsieur, 171, 183
Montebello, Comtesse de, 92, 173
Montgelas, Count de, 229
Montijo, Count de, 17, 19, 20, 21, 24, 25, 26, 28, 32, 96
Montijo, Countess de, 17-38, 39, 40, 41, 42, 43, 44, 45, 48, 52, 54, 57, 58, 60, 61, 66, 68, 70, 71, 73, 75, 78, 79, 80, 82, 83, 86, 90, 107, 123, 139, 150, 161, 166, 304, 315
Monts, General von, 265
Mooltan, 323
Morny, 51, 53, 58, 69, 70, 76, 77, 109, 114, 128, 138, 141, 142, 156, 160, 167, 179, 187, 190
Morny, Madame de, 114, 115, 138, 142
Moskowa, Princesse de la, 213, 319, 321, 322, 323
Mouchy, Duc de, 63, 256
Mouchy, Duchesse de, 256, 271, 276, 282, 300, 302, 312, 319, 321
Murat, Count, 293
Murat, Princesse Anna (afterwards Duchesse de Mouchy), 63, 95, 100, 108, 115, 116, 256, 271, 311

Murat, Prince Joachim, 198
Murat, Prince Louis, 63, 108, 109, 271

Nadaillac, Madame de, 198
Napoleon III, 30, 38, 45, 48, 49, 50, 51, 52, 53, 54, 55, 56, 58, 59, 60, 61, 62, 63, 64, 65, 67, 68, 69, 71, 72, 73, 74, 75, 76, 77, 78, 79, 80, 81, 82, 83, 84, 85, 86, 89, 90, 91, 92, 93, 94, 95, 97, 98, 100, 101, 102, 103, 104, 105, 106, 107, 108, 109, 110, 111, 112, 113, 114, 115, 116, 117, 118, 119, 120, 121, 122, 123, 124, 126, 128, 129, 131, 132, 133, 135, 136, 137, 138, 139, 143, 145, 146, 148, 149, 150, 151, 152, 153, 154, 155, 156, 158, 159, 161, 162, 163, 164, 165, 166, 167, 168, 169, 170, 171, 172, 173, 174, 175, 176, 177, 178, 179, 180, 181, 182, 183, 184, 186, 187, 188, 189, 190, 191, 192, 193, 194, 195, 196, 197, 198, 199, 203, 204, 205, 206, 207, 208, 209, 210, 211, 215, 216, 217, 218, 219, 221, 222, 223, 224, 225, 226, 227, 229, 232, 233, 234, 235, 240, 247, 248, 250, 253, 257, 258, 261, 264, 265, 266, 267, 268, 271, 272, 273, 275, 276, 277, 278, 279, 280, 281, 282, 283, 284, 286, 287, 288, 290, 299, 303, 304, 310, 311, 312, 313, 314, 319, 324, 326, 328, 339, 345
Napoleon III, Death of, 284
Napoleon sends troops to Mexico, 160
Napoleon IV. *See* Bonaparte, Louis-Eugène-Napoleon
Natal, 298, 305, 306, 310, 326
Ney, General Edgar, 104, 173, 312
Nigra, Chevalier, 138, 144, 156, 162, 206, 241, 242, 243
Notre-Dame, 84, 85, 125, 280, 282, 339

Ocagne, Maurice d', 318, 329
Ollivier, Emile, 195, 203, 205, 207, 208, 209, 212, 213, 215, 216, 218
Oneida, 274
Opposition to marriage, 68
Orange, Prince of, 288
Orléans, Duc d', 312
Orontes, 300
Orsini, 118, 119, 120, 282
Osuña, Duchess of, 288

Paca (afterwards Duchess of Alba), 17, 19, 21, 22, 26, 27, 28, 29, 30, 31, 32, 34, 35, 37, 38, 39, 41, 42, 54, 70, 86, 95, 146, 147, 148, 311, 343, 345
Padua, Duke of, 289
Palaeologue, Maurice, 319, 330, 331
Palikao, Count de, 218, 219, 223, 225, 226, 232, 236, 239, 240
Palmerston, Lord, 165
Panizzi, 96, 150, 165, 166, 217
Paris, rioting in, 236-249
Pasteur, 138
Peace negotiations, 262-264, 267-268
Pélissier, Maréchal, 114
Pelletier, Aline, 300, 326, 327, 345
Peñaranda, Duke of, 334, 344, 346
Pepa, 58, 94, 106, 108, 186, 214, 228, 229
Persigny, Count de, 51, 58, 63, 76, 101, 114, 128, 131, 141, 148, 154, 160, 187, 188, 218, 263, 280
Persigny, Countess de, 114, 115, 135
Philippe-Egalité, 119
Pianori, 104
Picard, Ernest, 226
Piennes, Marquis de, 213, 214, 244
Pierrefonds, Countess, de. See Eugénie
Pierres, Baronne de, 92, 142, 237
Pietri, Franceschini, 167, 271, 275, 285, 293, 297, 300, 305, 306, 308, 319, 320, 322, 323, 333, 342
Pietri, Prefect of Police, 213, 218, 223, 226, 247, 283, 284
Pinard, 235, 294
Pius VII, Pope, 80
Pius IX, Pope, 70, 80, 92, 112, 113, 121, 127, 155, 168, 193, 228, 257, 292, 293
Plebiscite, the, 62, 205
Poëze, Countess de la, 198, 237, 240, 241
Poniatowski, Prince, 214
Pope. *See* Pius IX. *See also* Pius VII, Leo XIII
Pourtalès, Countess de, 115, 133, 134, 138, 142, 162, 193
Premonstratensian Monks, 310, 323
Primoli, Count, 115, 288, 318, 319, 320, 321, 327, 328
Prince Humbert, 330
Prince Imperial. *See* Bonaparte, Louis-Eugène-Napoleon
Prince-Consort. *See* Prince Albert
Prussia, King of. *See* William, King
Prussia, war threatened with, 177-182, 193

Rachel, Madame, 29, 93-94, 114
Raimbeaux, 322
Randon, Maréchal, 177, 178
Régnier, 257-261, 262, 267
Reichstadt, Duc de, 292
Reims Cathedral, 334, 340, 341
Reinach, Joseph, 320
Return of the Ashes, 37, 45
Reuss, Prince, 115, 138, 144
Robin, Doctor, 327
Roccagiovine, 115
Rochefort, 196

Rouher, 124, 128, 148, 154, 162, 178, 179, 193, 215, 218, 222, 263, 271, 280, 285, 288, 289, 293, 294, 296, 300
Russell, Lord, 271

Sadowa, 177, 178, 180, 189, 193, 194
Saint-Arnaud, Maréchal de, 63, 82
Salzburg, Eugénie visits Francis-Joseph at, 192
Saint-Cyr, 289
Sandhurst, 310
Sarrebrück incident, 211, 212, 295
Saulcy, Jacquetinede, 277
Saulcy, Madame de, 150, 159, 164, 241, 271, 282
Schneider, 215, 235
Scott, Doctor, 305, 326
Scott, Herbert, 337
Sedan, 232, 233, 264, 272, 275, 338
Sesto, Duke of. *See* Alcanizes
Sevastopol, 101, 114
Shaw, Miss, 116, 125, 170, 184, 256
Sibour, Monseigneur, 85
Simon, Jules, 194
Simmons, General, 296
Slade, 289, 291, 305
Solferino, 178, 189, 292
Solms, Countess de, 114
Sophia, Queen, 153, 197
Spain, Queen of. *See* Victoria-Eugenia
Steed, Henry Wickham, 339
Stendhal. *See* Beyle, Henri
Stoffel, Colonel, 205, 286
Strasbourg, coup d'etat at, 30, 38, 50, 110, 115
Strasbourg, 264, 338, 340
Strode, Nathaniel, 258, 299
Suez Canal, opening of, 197-199
Sullivan, 277
Sydney, Lord, 271, 299

Tait, Archbishop, 271
Talleyrand, 128
Talleyrand, Duchesse de, 271
Tamamès, Duchess of, 334, 346, 347
Tamamès, Duke of, 278
Tarente, Duchesse de, 271
Tascher, Countesse, 288
Tascher, Count, de la Pagerie, 92, 94, 116
Teba, Count de. *See* Montijo, Count de
Teba, Countess de. *See* Montijo, Countess de
Thelin, 242
Thèrion, Colonel, 208
Thiers, 45, 53, 77, 176, 194, 206, 221, 227, 230, 231, 262, 268, 272, 280, 284, 288
Thistle, 318, 322, 329, 331, 332
Thouvenel, 155
Tissot, 264
Toulougeon, Colonel de, 66
Tour d'Auvergne, Prince de la, 219
Tour Maubourg, Marquise de la, 92
Trochu, General, 215, 217, 220, 222, 223, 224, 225, 226, 233, 234, 236, 240, 245, 250, 272

"Universal Service," 194

Vaillant, Maréchal, 154, 157, 218
Valdrôme, Chevandier de, 218
Vaughan, Miss, 271, 323
Verdun, 333, 338
Victor-Emmanuel, 120, 127, 156, 176, 193, 198, 211, 226, 257, 312
Victor, Prince, 332
Victoria-Eugenia, 324, 329, 343
Victoria, Queen, 70, 100-104, 108, 120, 121, 122, 127, 148, 150, 156, 271, 279, 294, 299, 301, 303, 304, 305, 310, 312, 320, 331
Vinoy, General, 220
Viollet-le-Duc, 84, 136, 138, 272

Wales, Prince of, 101, 296
Wales, Princess of, 189
Walewska, Countess of, 113, 115, 142, 150
Walewski, Count, 119, 120, 126, 128, 141, 142, 150
Widor, Ch., 344
William II, King, 153, 189, 190, 206, 207, 256, 264, 267, 273, 331, 335, 336
Wilson, President, 336
Wimpffen, General, 235
Wissembourg, 213, 338
Wood, Lady, 306
Wood, Sir Evelyn, 305, 306, 307, 308
Woodhouse, 289, 291
Woolwich Academy, 279, 281, 286, 296, 300, 305
World War, 331-337

Yser, 338

Zulus, 291, 298, 305, 308